Rethinking Social Development

Theory, Research and Practice

Edited by David Booth
Centre of Developing Area Studies, University of Hull

Longman
Scientific &
Technical

Longman Scientific & Technical
Longman Group Limited
Longman House, Burnt Mill, Harlow
Essex CM20 2JE, England
and Associated Companies throughout the world

First published 1994

British Library Cataloguing in Publication Data
A catalogue entry for this title is available from the British Library.

ISBN 0–582–23497–2

Set by 3 in 10/11 pt Palatino

Printed in Malaysia by VVP

Contents

Notes on the Contributors

Alberto Arce is a Lecturer in the Department of Sociology of Rural Development at the Agricultural University, Wageningen, Netherlands. He has done field research in Mexico and Chile, and in Grimsby on Humberside. He is the author of numerous articles on rural development and of *Negotiating Agricultural Development: Entanglements of Bureaucrats and Rural Producers in Western Mexico* (Wageningen University Press, 1993). Among his current interests are globalization issues, local development processes in Latin America, changing patterns of agricultural consumption in the west and the nature of current transformations in the Third World countryside.

Tony Barnett is a Reader in the School of Development Studies at the University of East Anglia. He has researched a wide range of development policy issues, including social and economic aspects of irrigation (*The Gezira Scheme: An Illusion of Development*, Frank Cass, 1975), labour markets in the Sudan and Malaysia, regional planning in Papua New Guinea, cooperatives in Jordan, agricultural development in Zambia and the Gambia, and the social and economic impact of HIV/AIDS in Africa (*AIDS in Africa: Its Present and Future Impact*, with P Blaikie, Belhaven Press, 1992). He is author or editor of several more general books on development, including *Beyond the Sociology of Development* (with I Oxaal and D Booth, Routledge, 1975) and *Sociology and Development* (Hutchinson, 1988). He has recently undertaken a multi-country study of the impact of HIV/AIDS on agriculture for the United Nations.

Anthony Bebbington, a geographer, has conducted research on indigenous resource management systems, rural development programmes and the changing role of NGOs in Latin American development. He is currently Research Fellow at the Overseas Development Institute, London, and was previously a Research Officer at the Centre of Latin American Studies, University of Cambridge. His recent publications include *Reluctant Partners? NGOs, the State and Sustainable Agricultural Development* (with J Farrington, Routledge, 1993), *NGOs and the*

State in Latin America (with G Thiele, Routledge, 1993) and *Tribus, Comunidades y Campesinos en la Modernidad* (with others, Abya-Yala, Quito, 1992). Alongside academic research, he has done consultancy and contract work for the Inter-American Foundation, the Overseas Development Administration, FINNIDA and the FAO, as well as for NGOs based in both North and South America.

Piers Blaikie is a Professor in the School of Development Studies, University of East Anglia. A geographer by training, he has worked extensively in Nepal and India, and also in Morocco and east and central Africa. His main fields of interest are rural development, the political economy of agrarian change and environmental management. He has authored or co-authored nine books, including *Family Planning in India* (Arnold, 1975), *Nepal in Crisis* (OUP, 1980), *Peasants and Workers in Nepal* (Aris and Philips, 1981), *Political Economy of Soil Erosion in Developing Countries* (Longman, 1985), *Land Degradation and Society* (Methuen, 1987), *AIDS in Africa* (Belhaven, 1992) and *At Risk . . .* (Routledge, in press).

David Booth is a Senior Lecturer in the Department of Sociology & Anthropology and Centre of Developing Area Studies at the University of Hull. He has done research in Latin America – on politics and social change in Cuba, and on the military and social reform in Peru – and has also worked on social dimensions of structural adjustment in Africa with particular reference to the experience of Tanzania. He co-edited *Military Reformism and Social Classes: The Peruvian Experience, 1968–80* (with B Sorj, Macmillan, 1983) and has co-authored *Social, Economic and Cultural Change in Contemporary Tanzania: A People-Oriented Focus* (with F Lugangira and others, SIDA, 1993). He has also written about broader issues in development sociology, in *Beyond the Sociology of Development* (with I Oxaal and T Barnett, Routledge, 1975) and 'Marxism and Development Sociology: Interpreting the Impasse' (1985).

Frederick H Buttel is Professor of Rural Sociology at the University of Wisconsin, Madison, and was previously Professor of Rural Sociology and Science and Technology Studies at Cornell University. He is co-author or co-editor of six books, the most recent of which is *Towards a New Political Economy of Agriculture* (with W Friedland and others, Westview Press, 1991). Buttel is a Fellow of the American Association for the Advancement of Science, has served as President of the Rural Sociological Society of the USA and since 1988 has been co-editor of the Cornell University Press series on 'Food Systems and Agrarian Change'.

Stuart Corbridge is a Lecturer in South Asian Geography at Cambridge University and a Fellow of Sidney Sussex College. He has previously taught at London University and Syracuse University, New York, and has been a Visiting Professor at Jawaharlal Nehru University, New Delhi. Among his publications are *Capitalist World Development* (Macmillan, 1986), *Debt and Development*, (Blackwell, 1993) and *Money, Power and Space* (edited with R Martin and N Thrift, Blackwell, 1994). His main research interests thus far have been in the fields of tribal policy and politics in Bihar, India; the geopolitics of debt and finance; and development theory. His current research is on issues relating to migration and forestry in tribal India, and he is preparing a monograph for Cambridge University Press with the title *State, Tribe and Region: Policy and Politics in the Jharkhand, India, 1820–1990*.

Michael Edwards is Head of Information and Research in the Overseas Department of the Save the Children Fund, London. He was trained as a geographer at Cambridge, and was awarded a PhD by the University of London for a study of housing in Latin America. He went on to work for a number of years for OXFAM. Throughout his career he has endeavoured to bring development practice and development research closer together through the medium of NGOs. He is the co-editor (with D Hulme) of *Making a Difference: NGOs and Development in a Changing World* (Earthscan, 1992).

John Harriss is Programme Director of the Development Studies Institute in the Department of Anthropology, London School of Economics. He was previously Reader and Dean of the School of Development Studies at the University of East Anglia. He has held research fellowships in the Research School of Pacific Studies of the Australian National University, and at the Maison des Sciences de l'Homme in Paris. His interest in agrarian institutions and rural poverty has involved him in extended periods of fieldwork in both south and east India, as well as (rather less intensively) in Sri Lanka, Nepal, Indonesia, Mexico and Tanzania. His interests have also extended to studies of industrial labour processes, and he is currently concerned with the implications of 'Japanization' and rapid industrialisation in south and South East Asia.

David Hulme is a Reader in Development Studies at the University of Manchester where he directs the Institute for Development Policy and Management. He studied economic geography at Cambridge University and later completed a PhD at James Cook University in Australia on the economic and social planning of agricultural development schemes. This led to an interest in applied sociology and in 1990 he co-authored the text *Sociology and Development: Theories, Policies and Practices* (with M Turner, Harvester-Wheatsheaf). Much of Hulme's research has been focused on Papua New Guinea, Bangladesh and Sri Lanka, but he has also worked in Malawi, Kenya, Mexico, Malaysia and Indonesia. His most recent research has been concerned with poverty-focused credit schemes and with the changing roles of NGOs in development.

Norman Long is Professor of Sociology in the School of Social Sciences at the University of Bath. He was formerly Professor and Head of the Department of Sociology of Rural Development at the Agricultural University, Wageningen, Netherlands, where he continues to occupy a part-time research chair. He has carried out rural research in both Africa and Latin America, and has published extensively on the sociology of agricultural knowledge and practice, economic anthropology and development planning. His books include *Social Change and the Individual* (Manchester UP, 1968), *An Introduction to the Sociology of Rural Development* (Tavistock, 1977), *Peasant Cooperation and Capitalist Expansion in Central Peru* (edited with B Roberts, Texas UP, 1978), *Miners, Peasants and Entrepreneurs* (with B Roberts, Cambridge UP, 1984), *Encounters at the Interface* (Wageningen UP, 1989) and *Battlefields of Knowledge* (edited with A Long, Routledge, 1992).

Philip McMichael is a Professor of Rural and Development Sociology, and Director of the International Political Economy Program at Cornell University. He is author of *Settlers and the Agrarian Question: Foundations of Capitalism in Colonial Australia* (Cambridge UP, 1984), which received the Social Science History Association's Allen Sharlin Award, and he has edited *Agriculture, Food and Global Restructuring: Toward the Twenty-First Century* (Cornell UP, 1994). His research interests include historical sociology of the world economy, global regulation and current agro-food system restructuring in the Pacific rim.

Nicos Mouzelis is Professor of Sociology at the London School of Economics. He has written widely on sociological theory and the sociology of organizations as well as on comparative historical topics. His books include *Organisation and Bureaucracy: An Analysis of Modern Theories* (Routledge/Aldine, 1967), *Modern Greece: Facets of Underdevelopment* (Macmillan, 1978), *Politics in the Semi-Periphery: Early Parliamentarism and Late Industrialisation in the Balkans and Latin America* (Macmillan, 1986), *Post-Marxist Alternatives* (Macmillan, 1990), *Back to Sociological Theory* (Macmillan, 1992) and *Sociological Theory: What Went Wrong?* (Macmillan, 1994).

Jan Douwe van der Ploeg is Professor of Rural Sociology and Director of the Centre for Rural European Studies (CERES) at Wageningen Agricultural University. Having previously been engaged mainly in research in Latin America and Africa, he is currently directing comparative research within Europe, focusing especially on heterogeneity in agriculture. His recent publications include *Labor, Markets, and Agricultural Production* (Westview Press, 1990) and 'The Reconstitution of Locality: On Technology and Labour in Modern Agriculture' (1992). He collaborated previously with Normal Long in *The Commoditization Debate: Labour Process, Strategy and Social Network* (Wageningen University, 1986).

Magdalena Villarreal is a Research Fellow at the Instituto Nacional de Historia y Geografía, Guadalajara, Mexico, and a doctoral candidate at the Agricultural University of Wageningen. Prior to this, she was involved in popular education and peasant organization programmes in western Mexico. She is currently interested in countervailing power and the negotiation of identity in the face of state intervention in rural change, with particular reference to gender. Her previous publications include 'The Changing Life-Worlds of Women in a Mexican Ejido' (1989) and 'Exploring Development Interfaces' (1992), both with N Long.

Pieter de Vries was born in Colombia and educated in Peru and the Netherlands. He has done field research on regional systems in Peru, on agricultural marketing and technological innovation in Colombia and on rural colonization in Costa Rica. He is currently engaged in research on state intervention and local organization in western Mexico. His published PhD thesis *Unruly Clients* (University of Wageningen, 1992) is a study of land reform organization in the Atlantic zone of Costa Rica.

Preface

World events during the closing years of the 1980s and early 1990s have done a good deal to turn upside down our basic perceptions of the shape and future of the planet and its people. Though scarcely amounting to the 'end of history' proclaimed in some quarters, the abrupt conclusion of the Cold War and the dissolution of the Soviet state involve a more dramatic transformation of the basic parameters of world power and ideology than anyone expected this side of the millennium. Together with the increasingly awesome signals of the non-sustainability of current patterns of global resource use, these new factors in the international scene have reshaped the context in which we have to confront that other awesome challenge to the future of the Earth: the continuing and in some respects growing problems of human misery and localized environmental catastrophe in what we have been accustomed to call the 'Third World'.

The challenge of world poverty, like that of global environmental change and the construction of a minimally viable order in the international system of states, is both a political challenge and a scientific one. Perhaps even more clearly than the other issues, the problem of development is not one to which there are obvious solutions, there for the taking just so long as we can build up sufficient 'political will' and impose a sufficient level of collective self-denial. To an important extent even now – after witnessing the palpable success of a few poor Asian countries raising themselves most of the way to 'developed' status within the last generation – we do not know how to bring about development and put an end to mass poverty, though we do know it is not just a matter of trying. The challenge to the understanding is every bit as real as the challenge to the will.

The scientific challenge, moreover, is as much a matter for the social sciences as for the natural and engineering disciplines. Less obviously, it is at least as much an issue for the 'soft' social science specialisms – political science, anthropology, sociology, human geography, and so on – as for allegedly 'hard' subjects such as economics. Together with the work of natural scientists, engineers and economists, social research in this latter sense has much to contribute to our understanding of the problems faced by the world's poorest people, and to our ability to respond sensibly to the complex and difficult issues they entail. Indeed, if there is anything that emerges strongly and consistently from the experience of development success and failure over the years since the Second World War, it is that overcoming poverty is not just a matter of setting the economic parameters correctly (either 'getting the prices right' or fixing an appropriate style and pace of accumulation and technological mastery). Social research has a useful, and even critical, part to play, not only as a specialist field concerned with measuring improvements or declines in 'social' indicators, but also in understanding the process of change and development as a whole.

The importance of development studies, and the importance of making it a genuinely inter-disciplinary undertaking in which political, social and spatial/environmental dimensions figure prominently, has never been greater than in the 1990s. Thus far it does not seem that the gloomier predictions of a few years ago have been realized concerning the likely redirection of international interest from the Third to the former Second World. Aid donors in general also seem to have been persuaded that their projects have lesser chances of failure if some element of social (that is, not just economic) research goes into the planning. At least among the European donor agencies, the trend is to employ more anthropologists, 'socio-economists' and the like, and to pay (somewhat) more attention to what they say. But to what extent are specialists in these areas in a position to make the sort of contribution that is required? How well placed are *social* development researchers to rise to the challenges of the rest of the 1990s and beyond?

Until recently, the answers to these questions were less clear than they might have been. Important and useful work was being done on various social (including, from here on, spatial and political) aspects of development, but to many people it seemed that the field as a whole was suffering an acute sense of lost direction. Theoretical analysis was widely considered to be at a standstill. Research efforts were producing results, but these often lacked cumulative impact, and crucial real-world issues were being ignored. A fair number of social researchers, both within and outside academic institutions, had been involved in development consultancy and other more or less 'applied' work. However, in general these activities neither influenced nor were much affected by what was widely taken (and taught to students) as the mainstream of social development thinking. Among development practitioners of various kinds, there was growing concern at the gulf between academic research and the worlds of policy and action. And when some radical voices went so far as to question the 'relevance' of development studies as a whole, few specialists felt confident enough to rebut them.

In the mid-1990s, this book contends, social development researchers can look forward with greater confidence. Though many problems remain, the atmosphere of intellectual stagnation and self-imposed isolation from practical development issues that was so strong in some quarters in the early 1980s has largely cleared away. Not only are there

new issues and new ideas, but also the convergences of style and perspective across a range of research fields are sufficiently strong to justify
the idea of a new overall research agenda.

Cutting across a great variety of substantive issues, we maintain,
there is a fresh approach, best characterized intellectually as a renewed
interest in the diversity of development experience within global,
national and local contexts. This intellectual reorientation has helped to
bring the social study of development into closer touch with the alternatives facing real actors – governments, business enterprises, mass organizations, local communities, official and non-governmental aid donors,
and so on. Deliberately or otherwise, the relationship between theory,
research and practice has been redefined.

The new tendencies in social development research are of course far
from uniform. They reflect not only a rich patchwork of substantive
interests, and differing attitudes towards the integration of theory and
practice, but also a number of, at best, loosely related theoretical or
methodological trends, 'post-Marxist', 'post-modernist', actor-oriented,
neo-structuralist and so forth. At one level, this intellectual ferment is a
cause for celebration. At another, the contributors to this book believe, it
raises issues that warrant systematic consideration with a view to con-
serving and consolidating the sense of renewed collective direction that
has been achieved.

The revival of interest in the diversity of development which we see as
the core or main outcome of the current rethinking is bound up with a
cluster of related intellectual tendencies all of which came to the fore
during the 1980s, but whose perspectives and priorities differ significantly. On the one hand, expressing itself most often in a 'post-Marxist'
or neo-Weberian language, interest in diversity stems directly from a
critique of the highly generalized and economistic theoretical frameworks of Marxist or neo-Marxist origin that tended to dominate the field
in the 1970s. Here, what is significant is the new attention being given to
the independent variability and causal significance of previously under-
estimated 'partial structures' or contextual factors, such as modes of
political domination, patterns of gender, ethnic and cultural differences,
and society's relations with its natural environment. The approach is
conceptually innovative, but comparative and structural.

On the other hand, taking some of their cues from post-structuralist
and post-modernist critiques of the dominant orthodoxies of our day,
social researchers have turned their attention to deconstructing the institutional forms and clusters of social meaning that constitute development situations. Interest here is in the diversity of outcomes from the
active and interactive, creative and communicative, dimensions of social
processes, and hence in the varieties of knowledge and the malleability
of power. Probing the limits of human creativity and resistance (the
'room-for-manoeuvre', the scope for indigenous alternatives, for 'development from below'), research in this vein displays, in certain hands, a
markedly individualizing and anti-theoretical bent.

In view of these and other differences in approach, it is appropriate to
ask how much the new lines of research owe to antagonistic and poss-

ibly ephemeral influences such as post-Marxism and post-modernism, and how much to deeper and more durable shifts in thinking. How valid, to begin with, is our contention that the new research directions are best distinguished by a focus on diversity as against, for instance, the renewed interest in agency, or deconstruction? What is it about the political and moral climate of the times that has encouraged this convergence of perspective? And, to the extent that there is a broadly shared analytical agenda, how close is the consensus on the desirability and attainability of 'relevance': what is, or ought to be, the relation between research and practice in development studies?

Given the tendency for opinions to divide between those emphasizing structural diversity and those defending 'actor-oriented' perspectives, there are, in addition, a number of more difficult methodological issues that are worth exploring (or re-exploring, since in a more general form, they are all perennial questions in social research). Can we reconcile the culturally embedded and 'constructive' features of social processes with the analytical requirements of comparison and theory-building? What is the scope for interactionist micro-investigations designed not so much to probe the limits of structural constraint as to uncover the processes that produce and reproduce macro-structures? And are there practical ways of integrating insights about indigenous alternatives and room-for-manoeuvre in local settings with the kinds of understandings of larger structures without which they will lack realism and, hence, effective purchase on decisions about policy or action? These are a few of the more challenging questions that are addressed in the pages which follow.

Rethinking Social Development provides the first comprehensive report on the reorientation of social development thinking and the issues it poses. The book contributes to a much-needed sharpening of reflection and discussion among those presently engaged in, or about to embark upon, social development research. It seeks to explore a range of possible solutions to difficult issues such as those identified above, while also surveying and exemplifying some of the best current work in the social development field in a form that will be accessible to the more advanced students in a range of social science subjects as well as to development researchers, teachers and practitioners.

The eleven chapters have been commissioned and written so as to reflect as far as possible both the variety of substantive topics addressed by social development studies, and the range of theoretical perspectives that have contributed to the current rethinking. Among the contributors – sociologists, social geographers, anthropologists and both teachers and practitioners of development management – are some of the leading exponents of social development research in Britain, the Netherlands and the USA.

Nine of the chapters were presented in an earlier form to a conference on 'Relevance, Realism and Choice in Social Development Research' organized by the Centre of Developing Area Studies at the University of Hull in January 1991. All were rewritten, and some completely recast, in the light of the rich discussion that took place there and also in subsequent meetings at the London School of Economics and the Catholic University of Nijmegen, Netherlands. Two of the chapters were invited from conference participants who had not presented papers, in order to improve the coverage and balance of the volume. The conference was assisted by grant from the Nuffield Foundation, whose support is gratefully acknowledged.

In order to guide the reader through the cross-cutting and potentially confusing themes of the book, the contributions have been presented in three parts, each of which has an editorial introduction providing some guidance as to the context, content and mutual relations of the different chapters. The main body of the volume is introduced by a wide-ranging overview by the editor, beginning with a re-evaluation of his own 1985 analysis of the 'impasse' in social development theory. The Afterword contains two contributions that sum up and assess the implications of the preceding discussion.

Introduction

CHAPTER 1

Rethinking social development:
an overview

David Booth

In the early 1980s there was a widely shared sense that social research and theorizing about development had reached some kind of impasse. Interesting and valuable work was still being done but in many areas of inquiry there had been disappointingly little cumulative advance along the lines mapped out during the 1970s. Initially stimulating theoretical debates, most of them originating within or on the fringes of the Marxist tradition, had run into the sand, bequeathing few if any guidelines for a continuing research programme. Crucial real-world questions were not being addressed and the gulf between academic inquiry and the various spheres of development policy and practice had widened to the point where practitioners were raising fundamental doubts about the 'relevance' of academic development studies.

In the mid-1990s the state of the social development field by no means justifies complacency; yet the heavy atmosphere of intellectual stagnation and self-imposed insulation from practical issues that was so prevalent in the early 1980s (at least among those influenced to some degree by the theoretical leitmotivs of the 1970s) does seem to have cleared. Not only is fresh and exciting work being carried out at a variety of levels on a host of new substantive topics, but also the convergences of style and perspective are sufficiently striking to justify the notion of a new overall research agenda.

Identifying what it is that effectively distinguishes that agenda is no easy matter given the variety of substantive concerns and cross-cutting intellectual influences that have played a role in its emergence. One thing, however, is obviously and importantly new: the interest shown at all levels and in relation to the whole gamut of substantive problems, in the investigation of diversity in development. Whereas formerly influential theories ignored in more or less deliberate ways the complex heterogeneity of the real world of development, the styles of research that have come into prominence since the early 1980s take as their central task explaining significant variations in patterns of development in different local, national and regional settings. Since diversity implies choice, and some sort of choice is the key to effective action, the new

3

trends are significantly more attuned than the old to the urgent needs of development policy and practice.

The range and substance of what we might now dare call 'post-impasse'[1] research on social (and political and spatial) aspects of development is a cause for celebration. However, both the variety of the contributing perspectives and the ad-hoc manner in which the rethinking of the social development agenda has taken place, raise issues which merit systematic consideration. It is time to take stock; time to consider not only whether it is true that some progress has been made along the lines suggested, but also where precisely it gets us and what if any steps need to be taken to guarantee the renewed sense of collective direction that has been achieved.

This chapter hâs two purposes: to set out some of the evidence in support of the idea of a new social research agenda for development; and to provide an initial critical overview of its problems and possibilities. The chapter begins by characterizing briefly the sense of impasse that may be seen as the starting-point for the rethinking that has been done. The next section reviews the emergence of a new intellectual style among social development researchers, going on to indicate some of the differences in outlook that might seem to cast doubt upon its coherence. The remainder of the chapter provides a provisional conspectus of the conceptual, methodological and practical issues confronting these new tendencies in the social development field.

Out of the impasse?

The malaise of the early 1980s was not universally recognized. It clearly appeared differently to researchers of different persuasions and belonging to different intellectual generations. It is no doubt true that while some people felt they were struggling out of an 'impasse', others were in a position to congratulate themselves on being clever enough to anticipate and avoid those sorts of problems. Certainly, there was no general paralysis; most of those with a scholarly and/or practical interest in social development were getting on with their own work.[2]

Nevertheless, because of the influence of Marxist and *marxisant* ideas on the generation that came to teaching and research in the 1970s, the sense of unease *was* widely felt. Among those who shared this perception and thought seriously about it, there was also a substantial measure of agreement as to at least some of its major features and immediate causes. Many of the most significant gaps and weaknesses in research seemed to be connected with the highly generalized and economistic explanatory frameworks of Marxist and neo-Marxist origin that dominated social development theory in the west during the 1970s.

In many respects, it was emphasized, the 1970s theories embodied important advances relative to what had gone before. But they had aspired to excessive explanatory power. Failing to reflect the diversity and complexity of the real world of development, they were incapable of explaining it. What was more, by refusing to make diversity a focus of

4

particular attention they had contributed little or nothing to illuminating the alternatives facing policy-makers and other responsible actors concerned with less developed countries. Whether as a cause or as a consequence of their generality, they also seemed to neglect or even deny much of what is specifically human about human societies: action and interaction, history, culture and the 'social construction of reality'.

These were the more or less shared and more or less elaborated contentions of what became a longish series of articles and books appearing in print from around the middle of the decade (Long 1984; Booth 1985; Corbridge 1986; A Richards 1986; A M Scott 1986b; Hall and Midgley 1988; Mouzelis 1988a; Vandergeest and Buttel 1988; Hulme and Turner 1990; Arce and Mitra 1991). Disagreement centred on the degree to which these difficulties were intrinsic in and peculiar to the Marxist project (Sklair 1988; Corbridge 1990). The particular issue of the perceived 'irrelevance' of much current development research was addressed most strikingly by Edwards (1989), although it was an underlying theme in much of the other writing.

In an article that was representative of this trend of thinking (Booth 1985), I argued that metatheoretical influences within Marxism had helped to force discussion into restricted channels. The major theories that had been influential in recent development sociology were grand simplifications that were either simply wrong (untenable empirically, conceptually unstable or redundant) or else pitched at a level of generality that made them irrelevant to the most important practical issues facing developing countries. The deeper reasons for this state of affairs needed to be explored.

The article developed this argument in two stages, which are worth reviewing briefly. First, it sought to show that the impasse in Marxist-influenced development sociology was indeed a general one: not the product of the weaknesses of one particular perspective (neo-Marxist dependency theory) or even of a mutually contradictory pair of approaches (dependency theory vs the 'classical' Marxism of Bill Warren) but the result of a generalized theoretical disorientation. There was no viable middle position between the polarized paradigms of the 1970s; basic Marxist concepts such as 'mode of production' had proved incapable of consistent application to the subject matter of development studies, the approach to political analysis was invariably reductionist and the neglect of current policy issues (e.g. 'urban bias' or new fashions in poverty-focused aid) was almost complete.

The second stage of the argument concerned the deeper reasons for the impasse in theory. The article suggested that behind the distinctive preoccupations, blind spots and contradictions of Marxist-influenced development sociology there lay the metatheoretical commitment to demonstrating that the structures and processes of less developed societies are not only explicable but also necessary under capitalism. This general formula was intended to cover two forms of 'necessitist' commitment in Marxism: the notion that the salient features of capitalist national economies and social formations can be derived or 'read off' from the concept of the capitalist mode of production and its 'laws of motion', and the various forms of Marxist system-teleology or functionalism. Along with a revitalized interest in the real-world problems of development policy and practice, an enhanced sensitivity to metatheoretical issues of this type was an essential first step in any attempt to deal with the impasse in social development theory.

The suggestion, also made by Corbridge (1986; 1990), that Marxism is intrinsically inclined towards 'essentialism' and system-teleology proved controversial. A number of commentators on the impasse debate (e.g. Larrain 1989; Peet 1990) argued not merely that not all interpretations of Marxism have suffered from these tendencies – a view I would accept[3] – but also that Corbridge and I were misled into a peculiarly narrow understanding of the core of Marxism by Hindess and Hirst, a point usually made with more innuendo than argument. Taking a subtly different line, Sklair (1988) thought that while my critique of Marxism had some substance, its particular formulation confused theoretical and metatheoretical issues.

Several of the more sympathetic rejoinders to my article were concerned, instead, about the limited scope of the critique. Both Vandergeest and Buttel (1988) and Corbridge (1990) drew attention to my concentration on the functionalism and essentialism of the Marxist tradition to the exclusion of mainstream sociological functionalism, neo-liberal economic theory and other non-Marxist sources of these ills. Mouzelis maintained separately (1988a; 1988b) that Marxism compares favourably with mainstream sociological functionalism in its handling of the structure/agency issue, and would be an entirely suitable basis for a comparative inquiry into development trajectories but for one 'pervasive flaw', that of reductionism in handling politics.

A number of the foregoing points are of continuing interest. But a more widespread and enduring reaction to my article was to accept most of what it said while deploring its largely negative thrust. If these things were true, what was the way forward? Were there not any examples of theoretical ideas and empirical research that pointed the way out of the impasse? All of the more welcoming comments on the impasse article drew attention to these issues, and several (especially Vandergeest and Buttel 1988; Corbridge 1990) went on to provide more or less convincing examples of recent work that was breaking new ground in the required direction both theoretically and, indeed, metatheoretically. Others (e.g. Long 1984; 1988; Mouzelis 1986; 1988a) could claim with some reason that they had been doing such work for some years.

In retrospect, it seems to me that in many respects the lacunae left by the dominant research trends of the 1970s formed patterns sufficiently distinct by themselves to define the outline of an alternative research agenda. At any rate, the way forward seemed clear enough to those working on various kinds of development topics. Without waiting for a definitive resolution of the metatheoretical issues (or in blameless ignorance of that debate) researchers formerly influenced by one or other of the extant grand theories had already started posing new sorts of research questions applicable to their particular corners of the social development field. At the same time, the world itself was changing in ways which virtually imposed fundamental shifts in intellectual and political outlook from whose influence development studies could not remain immune for long.

Rediscovering diversity

Since the late 1970s, I want to argue, social, political and spatial research concerned with development has gained substantially in coherence and bite as various groups of scholars, unannounced but decisively, have assumed the task of exploring variation and, hence, illuminating the scope for choice in development. In obvious ways, changes in global reality have helped to fuel shifts in thinking. The increasingly dramatic divergences in development experience between the different subdivisions of the developing world, socialism's crisis of confidence in the west followed by its collapse in the east, and the steadily growing vitality of single-issue campaigns and grassroots movements around the world, all helped to drive home key messages. But the new research questions also had more purely intellectual sources, affecting sensitivity to difference, particularity and the local dimensions of global processes. Changes of approach reflecting this combination of influences have been apparent within the development literature on at least three different levels.

From macro-diversity to responsible politics

Most obviously, macro-work on the development of national economies and societies has become increasingly concerned with national and regional specificities. Starting at the end of the 1970s, sociologists and political scientists whose previous work had helped to establish generalizing constructs about Third World change began to converge with those emphasizing distinctive national experiences on the need for systematic comparative studies. Across the board, there was a new emphasis on exploring the differences lying beneath or beyond the commonalities derived from structural location or developmental stages.

The lead was taken by students of Latin American politics and development. Having pioneered comparative studies within a dependency framework in the 1960s (Cardoso and Faletto 1979/1967) and essayed a plausible hypothesis about economically rooted developmental tendencies in the 1970s (O'Donnell 1978), Latin Americanists became increasingly disenchanted with the former's class reductionism, and with the latter's over-simple economism (see e.g. Collier 1979; Roxborough 1984; Mouzelis 1986). In the later 1980s writers such as Sheahan – a polymath economist in the tradition of Albert Hirschman – typified the trend by placing the study of Latin American development on the explicit basis of illuminating policy alternatives through systematic work on the diversity of national experiences (see especially Sheahan 1987).

The new interest in diversity and difference was not restricted to Latin America. As the full weight of the East Asian 'miracle economies' began to bear on the consciousness of social scientists in the west around the turn of the 1980s, a cartload of premature generalization about the Third World had to be dumped (cf. Buttel and McMichael, Chapter 2). There followed a flurry of interest in the national or perhaps regional specifi- ties accounting for the remarkable achievements of South Korea, Taiwan and, to a lesser extent, Hong Kong and Singapore (Ruggie 1983; Evans *et al.* 1985; Deyo 1987; White 1988; Amsden 1989; 1990). The spotlight then fell on systematic differences between East Asian NICs (newly industri- alizing countries) and comparable cases in Latin America (Anglade and Fortin 1987; Gereffi and Wyman 1991; Jenkins 1991).

As the growing gulf between Asian development performances and those in Sub-Saharan Africa helped to announce 'the end of the Third World' as a minimally uniform and coherent entity (Harris 1986), studies of the politics of economic decline in Africa moved rapidly from gener- alities about the post-colonial state towards more or less serious efforts to specify characteristics of politics and the state *in Africa* (Bates 1981; Hyden 1983; Chabal 1986; Ergas 1987; Rothchild and Chazan 1988; Bayart 1993/1989), as well as valuable studies of national differences (Bates 1989; Lofchie 1989; Manor 1991). Continuing interest in politics and policy-making for structural adjustment (Nelson 1990; Grindle and Thomas 1991; Gibbon *et al.* 1992a; 1992b; Healey and Robinson 1992) has produced a wealth of controlled comparative analysis across countries, both within and between major world regions.

Investigations such as these have enhanced enormously our sensi- tivity to historically grounded variations in national political economies. In different ways, they help to undermine the once common notion that socio-political development conforms to a pre-written script (though groups of countries may share common 'political trajectories'), adding force to the appeals of James Manor and his contributors for a funda- mental rethinking of Third World politics (Manor 1991). Most of them also illustrate the virtues of a non-reductionist approach, providing ample support for the theses of Skocpol (1979; 1985) and Mouzelis (1984; 1988a; 1990; 1991) on the specificity of the political and the usefulness of 'bringing the state back in' to comparative sociology.

Variations in state structures (Skocpol) or 'modes of domination' (Mouzelis), as distinct from societal structures and modes of production, are now established as worthwhile objects of enquiry a way that they were not in the late 1970s. This is an important point from several points of view. It matters most because evidence continues to accumulate that political variables often exercise a critical influence on development pro- cesses, accounting for significantly different outcomes in broadly similar socio-economic settings. The issue is explored in this book by Mouzelis in Chapter 5 and, with reference to important literature on India and South East Asia by John Harriss in Chapter 7.

The studies referred to in this section do more than illuminate the past. By privileging diversity and at the same time questioning the schematic and reductionist formulas that used to govern socio-political analyses of national development, they help to bring development studies back into contact with the world of development practice. Some are perhaps 'policy relevant' in a quite usual sense. Of the others, it is not too much to hope that they will have a significant practical impact in the longer term, contributing in some way to the demise of political cultures based on appeals to spurious necessity and the denial of choice by leaders and political movements (cf. Unger 1987a; 1987b).

Meso-diversity: gender and class

At an intermediate analytical level, gender relations and class structures are among the issues on which thinking and research have undergone analogous changes. For some, the 'discovery' of gender as a central topic for development research has seemed by itself to provide a pathway out of the impasse in development sociology (e.g. Sklair 1988: 702–4). In my view this is too simple. Gender analysis, and feminist research more generally, are worthy of the attention of non-specialists in those areas, but not because methodologically and theoretically they are on a different plane or untroubled by the dilemmas that are characteristic of more established fields of study. Indeed, the best recent survey of feminist theoretical debates (Barrett and Phillips 1992) throws up a striking number of close parallels with the themes discussed in this book.

In this sense, what is relevant is the way that since the early 1980s the study of gender, within and beyond the development field, has successfully disentangled itself from the universalist and functionalist pretensions with which it was initially encumbered. As compared with earlier attempts to set out a Marxist-feminist approach to the Third World, recent research has uncovered a previously unimagined, or at any rate unanalysed, variety and subtlety of mutual relations between gender and development (for surveys, see Wilson 1985; Townsend and Momsen 1987; Charles 1993). Work in this vein has focused not only on transformations in gender relations through economic change (e.g. A M Scott, 1986a; forthcoming Campbell 1991; Faulkner and Lawson 1991; Mbilinyi 1991), but also on the implications for socio-economic change of differences in patterns of gender (e.g. Swantz 1985; Mackintosh 1989; Sender and Smith 1990; Simo 1991) and problems in the translation of concepts of gender oppression between western and other cultures (e.g. Mohanty 1988; 1992). A more directly action-oriented literature has been able to build on these foundations (Wallace 1991; Østergaard 1992). Meanwhile, our understanding of development issues generally has been deepened by this liberation of the study of gender from the limiting paradigms of the 1970s.

The study of social class in developing countries has also made progress, although much more hesitantly. Students of class formation have begun to abandon their previous preoccupation with the fit or lack of fit between Third World social conditions and essentialist imagery of one kind and another ('is there a genuine national bourgeoisie in Chile, in Kenya?' etc.), moving on to produce studies that have a bearing on choices other than superficially simple dilemmas of the reform-versus-revolution type. In my view, this tendency is in its early infancy. Nevertheless, we are beginning to see case studies in class formation which offer raw material not only for systematic comparisons between different locations and countries (Harriss 1980, 1987; Becker 1983; MacGaffey 1987), but also for analyses that treat class structure and other aspects of group formation and interest-articulation, without reductionism, as variables in relation to critical issues of public policy and institutional reform (Moore 1985; Bates 1989; Lofchie 1989; Boone 1990; Gibbon 1992; Moore and Hamalai 1992).[4]

From meso-diversity to micro-diversity: room-for-manoeuvre in rural development

Marxist rural development studies were, and to some extent still are, defined by a dialogue between 'Leninist' agrarian transition analysis (commoditization leading to depeasantization) and various more or less functionalist accounts of the persistence of peasant economy or simple commodity production. As I argued in 1985, the often excellent research done under the influence of these ideas came quite quickly up against two difficulties: first, the unexpected diversity of empirically documented patterns and trends of Third World agrarian change, and second, the relative poverty of the prescribed explanatory frameworks ('reading off' from a universal transition model, reference to the 'needs of capital', and so on). Despite widespread acceptance of the reality of these difficulties, essentialist, functionalist and economically reductionist formulas do linger on in both militant and shamefaced forms.[5]

At the same time, since the early 1980s there has been a multiplication of efforts to redefine rural development studies in terms of 'taking diversity seriously'. Without losing sight of the constantly growing forces of global integration, rural social studies have been drawn towards systematic comparative studies in different national and local settings.

At the sectoral level of analysis, comparative rural studies have made significant progress with empirical and analytical work spanning the former 'First', 'Second' and 'Third' Worlds (Buttel and Goodman 1989; Marsden et al. 1990; Goodman and Redclift 1991; see also Buttel and McMichael, Chapter 2). As Aidan Foster-Carter has written in a different connection, the best of this work 'avoids any false opposition or one-way determinism between the global and the local – but rather insists on studying both the specificities of particular places and the broader forces which shape and are shaped by particular local circumstances and histories' (1991: 11, original emphasis). Although not entirely immune to premature aggregation and the reification or organicization of socio-economic structures, this work represents a distinct advance on previous approaches to the study of Third World rural formations.

At the sub-sectoral level, one recurrent theme has been the heterogeneity of actually existing agrarian structures and farming systems, and the resulting insufficiency of previously standard analytical categories (Hebinck 1990; Dalling 1991; Long and van der Ploeg, Chapter 3). Another is the investigation of differential responses to, and different outcomes from, the 'central tendencies' of agrarian change (Long 1988). Social scientists whose research entails working 'downwards' from the national level to particular sectoral institutions and programmes (e.g. Grindle 1980; 1986; Clay and Schaffer 1984; Apthorpe 1987) have found common ground with those working 'upwards' from the micro-level of the individual household (e.g. Arce 1987; Long 1989; 1990; Arce, Villarreal and de Vries, Chapter 6), in focusing on the 'space for change' or 'room for manoeuvre' in rural development situations.

Placing emphasis on the actual workings, as distinct from the formal objectives or abstract representation, of key development processes, recent rural development research has done much to demystify not only the excessively aggregative formulas of neo-Marxist development sociology – peripheral capitalism, agrarian transition, etc. – but also the official ideologies and institutions of rural 'planning' and agricultural 'modernization' (Elwert and Bierschenk 1988; Long and van der Ploeg, Chapter 3). Others, probing the limits of human creativity and resistance, have explored the technological resources of rural people and the scope of indigenous alternatives to state-sponsored rural development (Chambers 1983; P Richards 1985; J C Scott 1985).

To a greater or lesser extent 'actor-oriented', these new directions in rural development research have revealed the important extent to which changes in the well-being of rural people are the result of complex interactions between individuals and groups endowed with different and changing amounts of knowledge and power. This being the case, they may seem to represent the intellectual counterpart of the growth since the 1970s of grassroots movements of the poor and self-help activities under the auspices of non-government organizations (NGOs) (Schneider 1988; Clark 1991). On the other hand, they provide one sort of basis for the greater involvement of anthropologists and other grassroots researchers in aid policy and practice, that other important wave of the last decade (Grillo and Rew 1985; Cernea 1991; Pottier 1993). Potentially at least, this is 'relevant research' (Edwards 1989) in the most obvious sense; its findings relate directly to the means of empowering and improving the lives of the wretched and the downtrodden of the world here and now.

The problem of theoretical coherence

In my 1985 article I expressed hope that the excursion into metatheoretical issues that I proposed would only be brief, and I stand by that preference. None the less, the most obvious question begged by the kind of rapid survey I have just conducted is whether there is really much of any great substance that unifies the work alluded to. To what extent does an interest in the variety of things, even when combined with a general aspiration to improve the scope for rational decision-taking by real-world actors, amount to a single 'approach', let alone a coherent theoretical or methodological framework? Are we in a position to answer the charge that what I have called post-impasse research is not only varied in terms of subject matter and the product of people with enormously diverse intellectual biographies, but also quite simply a mish-mash?

The revival of interest in the diversity of development is, certainly, both child and parent of a rather heterogeneous set of related intellectual developments, with different perspectives and priorities. At one level, the new directions in social development research are the expression of more or less explicit and self-conscious 'post-Marxist' critiques or neo-Weberian revivals. In this context, interest in diversity (comparative studies) is bound up with limited theoretical assertions about the independent variability and causal significance of such 'partial structures' or contextual factors as modes of political domination, patterns of gender, ethnic and cultural differences and a society's relations with its natural environment. Such claims are meant to qualify the substance, but in a sense continue to occupy the terrain, of classical social theory. The approach is conceptually innovative but structural, if not perhaps structural-*ist*. Criticisms are made of the epistemological basis of particular sorts of classical claims (e.g. that modes of production have 'laws of motion', that social classes are historical actors) while others (e.g. that there are institutional preconditions for economic development, that social injustices have structural roots) are regarded as unobjectionable.

A second broad tendency takes a 'constructivist' view of the social reality of development, drawing on a long tradition of social phenomenology (Schutz) and interactionist anthropology (Barth) as well as, to a greater or lesser extent, the critical techniques of post-structuralist or 'post-modernist' writers such as Foucault (discourse analysis) and Derrida (deconstruction). One focus of special interest here is the multiple forms of social knowledge and their relations with power. Another is the diversity of outcomes of social processes that becomes visible once the constructedness and interactive character of such processes are given their due. Criticism is directed towards those forms of structural analysis which either by their explanatory procedures (essentialism or teleology) deny the possibility of such differences, or by sheer aggregation and abstraction effectively suppress them as objects of analytical attention (cf. Long 1988: 108–18). In this sense, though not necessarily in any others, the approach is *anti*-structuralist.

It cannot be assumed that those who borrow analytical methods from post-structuralist or post-modernist sources necessarily share any of the wider views about the state of the world and the nature of social science expressed by such theorists of post-modernism as Lyotard (1984). In any case, there seem to be good grounds for doubting whether post-modernism in the social sciences amounts to anything more precise than a 'relatively widespread mood', broadly analogous but no more, with the similarly named movements in the arts (Boyne and Rattansi 1990: 9–13; see also Callinicos 1989; Giddens 1990; Rosenau 1992). The recent interest in diversity and difference, and in the multiplicity of perspectives, in development, is none the less at least broadly consonant with the characterization of 'post-modernity' given by Lyotard and others. To the extent that this is more than a casual connection, it is relevant to note the radicalism of Lyotard's claim, as summarized by Boyne and Rattansi (1990), that 'all of the grand discourses of Western society, which is to say all of the legitimating narratives which purport to provide valid and definitive principles, in any sphere, across all societies, can now be seen to be defunct' (1990: 16). The view of post-modernist radicals is no less than 'that the modernist project in social theory, in all its Marxist and sociological variants, is both historically and conceptually exhausted' (Crook 1990: 47).

The actual or potential divergence of approach between the post-Marxists or neo-Weberians on the one hand and the various constructivist tendencies (with or without post-modernist coda) on the other is certainly the most important problem to be explored here. However, matters are complicated by a third important collection of influences on recent social development research.

In one form this is the sort of 'actor-oriented' work that aspires not so much to explore the limits of structural constraint as to uncover through interactionist investigations the very processes that produce and reproduce particular structural forms; the micro-foundations of the macro-framework (Long 1989; Long and van der Ploeg, Chapter 3). A distinct but allied tendency is the 'new political economy' of the 'collective choice' school of Robert Bates (e.g. Bates 1983; 1988), the thrust of which is 'that "economic reasoning" can be employed to explain the way political processes and political institutions affect how individuals' desires for valued but scarce resources aggregate into outcomes for entire societies' (1988: 3). Though the general idea of seeking to explain institutional outcomes by reference to the choices of individual or collective actors scarcely counts as a new theme in the social sciences, the recent convergence on this point between the anthropological interactionism of the 'Manchester' school (Kapferer, Long) with Bates's notably non-neo-classical application of rational-choice analysis in the field of development studies adds up to a significant trend.

The multiplicity of the theoretical influences that have played a part in (and been advanced by) the rethinking of the basis of social development research is potentially a great source of strength. It is also potentially destructive of the limited sense of renewed direction that those doing research in this area now feel, the head-on challenge of the post-modernists representing perhaps the most disturbing problem. There is therefore much to be gained from a constructive dialogue aimed at mapping out areas of agreement and disagreement on at least a few of the outstanding analytical and methodological issues.

The issues that we may hope to address effectively at this point would seem to belong to three broad categories: first, questions about *theory and method*, especially the desirability and methodological implications of translating the gains from recent research into consolidated theoretical advances; second, new and perennial issues, or perennial issues in new guises, concerning the relationships between *agency, structure and explanation*; and third, the ramifications of the proposal that social development research can and should be assessed in terms of its *'relevance'*.

Theory and method

The problems to be considered under this first heading revolve around the charge, lurking in the background if not explicitly formulated by anyone, that the 'post-impasse' tendency in social development research is simply glorified empiricism. It is a suggestion that gains plausibility from the seeming inconsistency of views about the role and importance of theory between the different strands of post-Marxist and post-modernist critique. Not only are currently influential ideas on this subject varied, but also in certain instances it is not at all clear that they are not contradictory. Contrasting assessments of the role of theory are related closely to divergent understandings of what is entailed by 'the rediscovery of diversity'.

On the one hand, the latter refers above all to an increased sensitivity to systematic variation, that is to say diversity about which it is possible to generalize at a certain level. For those who take this view, the most powerful research methodology is comparative analysis, or perhaps more specifically, what Buttel and McMichael (Chapter 2) call 'incorporated comparison'. The generation of theories – higher-order explanatory propositions employing appropriate abstract concepts – remains the ultimate objective of social science research. Contributions from Mouzelis (1988a), Corbridge (1990) and Buttel and McMichael (Chapter 2) among others contain eloquent statements of the case for reconstituting the sociology of development on such a basis.[6] As a rule, post-Marxist and neo-Weberian critics of older social development perspectives go along with this positive view of theory, insisting that their reservations concern the effects upon theoretical work of particular rationalist epistemologies (Corbridge) or metatheoretical commitments (Booth), not the value of theoretical work as such.

At the other extreme lies the position of all those for whom the rediscovery of diversity refers more to variety rather than variability, more to the *celebration of difference* than to the recognition of patterns of diversity. On this side of the argument, method is all and theory is nothing. According to the explicitly post-modernist variant of the position, all generalities are suspect, linked as they are to one or other of the grand discourses or 'meta-narratives' of modern western thought. These in turn are vitiated by their 'foundationalism': their adherence to theories of knowledge that 'seek to guarantee the validity of substantive enquiries in *a priori* formulae' (Crook 1990: 51). Foundationalist social theories in these terms are those which 'proceed from epistemological or ontological principles to privileged and speculative accounts of the nature of social reality, the direction of social change, and the role of social practice'. Despite the claims of their founders to be transcending metaphysics, both 'historical materialism and sociology are ... the subject of foundationalist guarantees: both establish what social reality is like, and how it is to be known, prior to enquiry itself' (Crook 1990: 51–2). Those who take this view are unclear and thus far divided about where exactly it leads, but it commonly generates ambivalence towards the whole idea of a generalizing social science.

The affinities are real between the 'incredulity towards metanarratives' that typifies the post-modernism of Lyotard and others and the critiques of Marxist and non-Marxist grand theories that were the stuff of the impasse debate. Lyotard's attack on foundationalist social theory is broadly consistent at least in respect of Marxism with the 'post-Marxist' views of Hindess and Hirst, which are cited by Booth and Corbridge. As Corbridge (Chapter 4) has shown, however, post-modernism goes some way beyond post-Marxism in the sweep of its condemnation of the concepts and methods of modern social science. Its careless espousal of relativistic and nihilistic positions, and its illogical extension of the critique of a prioristic notions of progress to cover all general inquiries about process, render it singularly unsuited to the task of reconstituting the basis of social development research.

The challenge to the theoretical ambitions of post-impasse thinking comes, however, not merely in the highly articulated form of post-modernist particularism. It also comes in more mundane guises. Together with pressures that are beyond our control, such as the limited budgets of research funding agencies and the practical difficulties of doing fieldwork in more than one location, the 'innate' intellectual proclivities of those working at the micro, or more actor-oriented, end of the social research spectrum may also weaken the thrust towards systematic comparative work and the development of new strands of substantive theory.

In a number of sub-fields of social development research in the 1990s, synthetic and comparative work is lagging well behind the production of detailed empirical studies. At a large conference held in France on peasantries and agricultural change in Latin America (IPEALT 1990) a major theme of the rapporteurs' remarks was the relative abundance of micro-studies documenting varied and often remarkable local processes of change, together with a great dearth of generalization. In future, it was thought, more effort needed to be given to comparison and synthesis, and to the design of projects with this in mind. Studies should be undertaken to try to identify macro-dynamics beginning from micro-studies (on which more below); and more needed to be done to communicate the understandings derived from this work to farmers' organizations and intermediary agencies.

The state of the art of social development research is similar across a broad front, including non-micro and non-rural fields of study. We face the danger that social researchers, disillusioned with the old theoretical certainties and perhaps also a little intoxicated by their renewed immersion in an ever-surprising empirical reality, will become very good at producing detailed case studies but rather bad at communicating the general implications of their work to a wider academic audience, not to speak of a wider public of development practitioners. Accelerating the rate at which empirical findings are translated into 'theoretical' formulations is important not particularly because doing theory is intellectually more satisfying, but because it is only at the theoretical level that research findings achieve a sufficient level of generality to be of interest and relevance to those wider audiences. If we fail to produce new theories, our claims to relevance and responsibility will begin to appear hollow.

In what form are new theories of development likely to emerge? The question may well be unanswerable at this stage. Even to establish the kinds of answers we might give, however, it is necessary to consider the several issues raised in the next section regarding the different and possibly competing claims of structural, 'constructivist' and actor-oriented research and analysis.

Agency, structure and explanation

Diversity versus agency?

Let us begin with the relation between the systematic investigation of diversity in development, and adopting what Norman Long calls an 'actor-oriented approach' to research and analysis? On the face of it, two opposing views may be taken on this issue, well illustrated by the writings of Long and his collaborators on the one hand and those of Buttel and McMichael (Chapter 2) on the other. Both make particular reference to the field of rural development.

In work stretching back over three decades, Long has built up a strong case for thinking that an actor perspective, and especially a focus on interactive relations at the 'interface' between official agencies of rural development and their clients, is the key to uncovering a diversity of outcomes of rural planning efforts which is or ought to be of interest to anyone with a responsible interest in such matters. In Long's programmatic statements (e.g. 1989; Long and Long 1992) actor-orientation, or interface analysis, is the 'paradigm', while the discovery of variable outcomes, unanticipated consequences, self-fulfilling prophesies and so forth, is the payoff.

Buttel and McMichael advance a closely argued critique of this way of putting the matter. They reject the view that what is new and promising in post-impasse research is to be found on the side of the *explanans*, that is to say, in the form of new explanatory frameworks. They are in any case sceptical of the claims made for 'actor orientation', but their argument is a more general one: what specifies best the advances that have been made in recent development sociology is the discovery of a new problematic or *explanandum*, diversity, and the corresponding flowering of new forms of comparative analysis. The argument is illustrated by reference to ongoing work on agro-food systems and the role of what they call 'incorporated comparison'.

This view is close to one advanced, with reference to different examples, by Mouzelis (1988a; 1990; 1991), and it is not inconsistent with the approach adopted in the earlier sections of this chapter. Certain sorts of interesting diversity clearly belong to the realm of actors and action as opposed to the realm of structures; but structural diversity, differences between relatively permanent institutional arrangements across regions or countries, can also be interesting and may be perfectly adequately explained by reference to other structural differences. Contrary to the suggestions of Long and van der Ploeg (Chapter 3: 80), it is not the case that all invocations of structures as *explanans* have unjustified necessitarian implications, even when the *explanandum* is action. As Mouzelis has shown, being serious about structural diversity does mean getting rid of economic reductionism and functionalism in all their forms (which may mean reminding ourselves regularly of the philosophical point that structures are only nexuses of congealed action, that people make their own history, etc.). However, this does not seem to entail any particular privilege for actions as opposed to structures as foci of empirical research or analysis. Explaining diversity is the general case, and actor-oriented accounts of such diversity are one form among others.

This having been said, it does not follow that proponents of comparative structural analysis can afford to be complacent about the strictures of the constructivist point of view. Buttel and McMichael do seem to be right about the general character of the post-impasse trends, but in my judgement they are in too much of a hurry to dispense with discussion about appropriate explanatory frameworks; this is not entirely an either/or issue. In the next sections, I want to argue that the structure-agency issue remains a central topic for the future of social development research, both because of the importance of structures for actor-oriented studies, and because of what an actor or constructivist perspective can do for structural analysis.

There are three topics to which specific attention can be given here: first, how to reconcile insights about indigenous alternatives and room-for-manoeuvre in local settings with the kinds of understandings of larger structures without which they will lack realism; second, the potential role of 'actor' or collective choice analysis in the reconstitution of structural analysis or 'political economy'; and third, how to reconcile the analytical requirements of comparison and theory-building with the 'constructed' and multidimensional character of social processes, and vice versa.

Action and structural context

As we have seen, post-impasse social research on development topics includes a significant body of work whose distinguishing feature is an analytical emphasis on agency, the social construction of development situations and the sorts of opportunities for alternative approaches to development that remain obscure so long as the variety of development experience is treated in purely structural terms. Interest in such issues need not imply a blanket refusal of conventional methods of structural analysis (e.g. cross-country comparisons). In fact, most practitioners of actor-oriented research acknowledge in principle the interdependence of action and structure. It is, however, one thing to recognize what is the case in principle and another to build it effectively into the design of one's research. A specific problem of this sort arises from the fact that most actor-oriented studies are not only 'micro' in the sense of being concerned with face-to-face processes, but also highly localized spatially. It is not always clear how the findings of such studies can be made to reflect not just local realities and room-for-manoeuvre, but also the kinds of constraints upon action that may emerge only at the regional or national level (or over longer time-periods).[7]

If I am not mistaken, post-impasse research trends have led, not by design but by default, to a re-opening (or at any rate a continued lack of closure) of the gulf between localized micro-studies and the kinds of understandings of larger structures that are needed to place them in their proper context. For those engaged in local studies, disillusionment with neo-Marxist structural theories has tended to lead in *practice* to abandonment of the terrain of 'political economy'. To be sure, those doing participatory research or conducting case studies in particular regions of developing countries invariably concede that to be realistic their interpretations and recommendations need to draw on an under-standing of the wider social, economic and political context. Long and van der Ploeg, for example (Chapter 3: 78–9), vigorously refute the suggestion that their approach implies a neglect of the contexts of action. Nevertheless, today as in the past most local studies remain determinedly micro in both senses, the wider context being allowed to escape from view in a way that is disturbingly reminiscent of the bad old days of functionalist anthropology.

What is worse, we seem to have slipped backward since the 1970s, when Norman Long and Bryan Roberts pioneered the idea that collabor-ative projects with a regional (that is to say relatively inclusive) focus could be an effective vehicle for integrating micro-action studies with the exploration of issues of political economy. The results of their work (1978; 1984) generally vindicated the claim. Yet to my knowledge the experiment has not been repeated, either by Long and Roberts or by anyone else.

Practical difficulties undoubtedly weigh very heavily where such am-bitious collaborations are involved, but the problem also has an intellec-tual dimension. The contribution to this book by Anthony Bebbington (Chapter 8) illustrates one way of bridging the gap between local action studies and macro-structural analysis. Commenting on the strongly polarized debate between students of indigenous technological change (P Richards 1985; Chambers *et al.* 1989) and some of those interested in the political-economic context of such change in West Africa (Watts 1989), Bebbington argues that such a degree of polarization is unnecess-ary and untenable; neither approach is as comprehensive and self-sufficient as its advocates maintain. Moreover, certain topics, such as the role of peasant organizations and the evolution of rural civil society, are equally ignored by both. Using such bridging themes it is possible within the limitations of existing fieldwork methods to do research that both takes peasant agency seriously and gives proper attention to struc-tural constraint.

Reconstituting political economy?

Even if, as this suggests, we are in a position to achieve better linkages upwards from the micro to the meso and the macro, there remains the whole question of the conceptual language and forms of explanation that are appropriate to analysing these latter, wider structures. Addressing this issue, Buttel and McMichael (Chapter 2) wish to reclaim major parts of the classical tradition of social theory, while Corbridge (Chapter 4) insists on the continuing intellectual vitality of important aspects of Marxism. Bebbington (Chapter 8) is not alone in seeing contemporary relevance in such classical concepts as 'civil society' (cf. Booth 1987). But are there not major limitations to detaching concepts from the wider theoretical nexus to which they belong so as to put them to purposes for which they were not intended? Surely there are more radical and satisfying ways of going about reconstructing the political economy of development. Do micro-studies and actor-oriented research perhaps have a role to play in reconstituting the analysis of the structures of development and underdevelopment on non-essentialist, non-functionalist lines?

The answer to the last question seems to be yes, in at least two different senses, to be discussed in this section and the next. To the first I would prefer to say no more than 'maybe', for reasons explained further on.

A persistent suggestion, coming now, as we have seen, from at least two distinct quarters, is that actor studies hold the key to a better understanding of the structures that constrain developmental possibilities, because of the way they may illuminate the micro-foundations of macro-processes. As Norman Long has argued (1989: 226–31), the use of micro-action studies to illuminate structures does not imply radically individualist or reductionist assumptions. The focus of such studies is not so much individual decision-making as interactional processes embedded in systems of belief and in both local and intermediate social relationships or networks. It is on this basis that Long commends Randall Collins's (1981) proposal for a 'reconstitution of macro-sociology on the basis of its necessary micro-foundations', involving a systematic programme for the '"unpacking" of macro-sociological metaphors'. The problem of 'emergent properties' means, moreover, that there can be no question of conceiving macro-structures as mere aggregations of micro-episodes: 'Macro-structures are in part the result of the unintended consequences of numerous social acts and interactions which, as Giddens (1984: 8–14) explains, become the enabling and constraining conditions of social action itself'. The promise of micro-studies to macro-understanding thus lies not in the reduction of the latter to the former, but in the disentangling of the invariably complex web of unintended consequences and feedback effects that form the link between action and structure.

Long and his collaborators are not alone in seeing in all this a fascinating challenge to sociological explanation in the development studies field and beyond. The 'collective choice' approach pioneered in its application to African development issues by Bates (1981; 1989) involves a similar conception. Regrettably, the reception of Bates's most widely read book (1981) has been coloured by the close coincidence of his opening account of the proximate economic causes of the decline of

African agricultures with that of the World Bank's somewhat notorious 'Berg Report' (1981). As Mick Moore (1987; 1990) has shown, however, the originality of Bates lies in his persistence in seeking not economic but political explanations for economic failure. The stuff of his analysis is an unravelling of various macro mysteries by reference to the unanticipated consequences of the interlocking preferences of relevant groups of actors – peasants, bureaucrats and politicians. It is worth emphasizing also that Bates's actors, like Long's, are more often collective than individual, and that their choices are not assumed to be reducible to the neo-classical paradigm of rational decision-making, that is abstracted from their social and cultural context.[8]

Reconstituting political economy on a non-essentialist and non-teleological basis is not going to be the work of a single day. Nor, in spite of Long's claims for interface analysis or those of Bates for collective choice, is it likely to rest on the achievements of a single school of thought. Nevertheless, such issues as the basis on which significant groups are formed and their interests defined, the rationales of institutions and patterns of interaction which structure markets in particular ways, with differents sorts of implications for growth or poverty-alleviation, and the dogged persistence of certain apparently 'irrational' patterns of policy output in some LDCs (less-developed countries), do seem to be central topics in the contemporary political economy of development. They are also problems that seem to be amenable to a style of analysis that moves back and forth between the macro and the micro. Are there indeed any areas in which we can say with confidence that there is no scope for realizing these kinds of analytical poten-tialities?

Deconstruction and concepts of structures

Whatever answer is given to this question, it seems unreasonable to suppose that explaining structures and structural diversity by reference to other structural variables will ever cease to be an important sort of analytical activity for social development researchers. Nor, despite Long and van der Ploeg's (Chapter 3: 80) wish to say a 'definite *adieu* to structure understood as explanans', should we regard this as in any way undesirable – provided appropriate concepts and explanatory procedures can be found. On the other hand, arriving at a suitable body of de-essentialized, non-teleological and non-reductionist concepts for structural analysis may be easier said than done and here lies another important role for the action-oriented strand of recent thinking.

Thinking about structures in a new way requires new structural concepts. As the work of Nicos Mouzelis (1986; 1990) shows, it may be possible to arrive at such concepts by judicious adjustments to classical concepts from Marxism and elsewhere. Mouzelis's elaboration of the concept of 'mode of domination' is a case in point. This is modelled in some but not all respects on Marx's 'mode of production' (in Mouzelis, there are forces and relations but no 'laws of motion' or structures that secure their own conditions of existence), and it serves well enough to direct comparative analytical attention to a range of vital issues that have been neglected by previous work. Parallel use has been made by Skocpol and her collaborators (Evans *et al.* 1985) and by such writers as Grindle (1986) and Migdal (1988) of concepts extracted critically from the tradition of Max Weber.

Such concepts should of course be subject to critical deconstruction, and in particular they need to withstand the test that they have indeed shed their skins of pre-impasse essentialism and functionalism. But this is different from saying that structural concepts are out of order *per se* or need to be replaced wholesale and regardless of the purpose in hand by descriptions of interactional processes and their outcomes. Particular social scientists in particular contexts may be guilty of premature aggre-gation and structuralization of interactional events; but there will also always be occasions when it is legitimate and illuminating to place the 'micro-foundations' on one side or 'between brackets'.

That having been said, there is a level of structural concept formation where in the future it is going to be necessary to promote a more direct dialogue between structural and actor-oriented or constructivist work than has occurred until now. I have in mind the level at which the researcher attempts to characterize the mode of domination or the class structure, or the gender relations, at a specific place and time. At present there is a large gulf between the more structural and the more actor-oriented approaches to these issues.

Currently, actor-oriented rural researchers tend to substitute for the old Marxist and Weberian analytical categories – agrarian capitalism, simple commodity production, rural proletariat, etc. – not alternative analytical categories but actors' self-descriptions: 'entrepreneur', 'small producer', 'campesino', and so on. This stems from a worthwhile effort to incorporate the lived experience of rural development, to penetrate inside the 'life-worlds' of the participants. With good reason it is argued that not only the 'hard' Marxist concepts but even such seemingly inno-cent terms as 'village', 'peasantry' and 'working class' have been ren-dered problematic; that 'our categories have been so essentialized that even using common terms tends to pitch us back into the use of a discourse replete with transcendant entities' (Hobart 1990: 15). But this, it may be argued, deals only with the most obvious and least plausible alternative to actors' categories and falls short of providing a convincing rationale for *exclusive* reliance on life-world descriptions.

The challenge to structural concept formation today is, surely, to arrive at ways of using life-world categories to inform 'objective' state-ments about the structural locations of individuals and groups, *and vice versa*. It is a truism in social anthropology that while accounts of actors' culturally informed definitions of activities and institutions are in-variably an essential ingredient of any explanation, they are often insuf-ficient on their own, if only because what people say they do commonly differs from what they really do. Observers need also to draw on their own observations, which need in turn to be disciplined not only by sensitivity to cultural differences but also by a conscious reflexivity – an awareness that they themselves are part of the process being described.

The mutual indispensability of the 'emic' (description of cultural meanings) and the 'etic' (observation of behaviour) is fairly well-trodden terrain in textbooks of anthropological method (e.g. Pelto and Pelto 1978: 54–66). It seems to me that there are tasks arising from these observations that need to be tackled urgently by sociologists, human geographers and political scientists concerned with the meso and macro as well as the micro structures of Third World societies.

John Harriss (Chapter 7) makes a significant contribution to the elucidation of this thorny problem on the basis of a reanalysis of agrarian change in a district of Tamil Nadu in south India. Harriss presents a mature and sobering account of what he sees as a continuing impasse in Indian rural sociology:

> On the one hand there is a mode of analysis which, in spite of the advances which it has marked in understanding of rural production, is frankly economistic. On the other there is a growing literature which is concerned with politics and culture/ideology but which seems to entail an epistemology which rejects the possibility of 'development'. (Chapter 7: 176)

The succeeding analysis starts with a compelling case for integrating state-level politics into an account of socio-economic change in the district since the 'green revolution', exemplifying, along the lines of our earlier discussion, the gains to be had from comparative inquiry into structures of political domination and their implications for development. More relevantly for the immediate argument, it goes on to provide a richly illustrated discussion of how social class relations can be effectively analysed in ways that recognize their 'constructed' character and the role of cultural definitions of what it is to belong to a particular group, including 'caste' and what is referred to in other contexts as the 'moral economy' of peasant societies. Such a subtle and many-stranded account of class is necessary – Harriss shows – in order to begin to make sense of observed patterns of rural politics and agrarian change in India, and the variability of such patterns between states.

Harriss ends by distinguishing his position from that of Indian postmodernists whose 'deconstruction' of class leads to its dissolution in an uncritical cultural particularism. He also registers his reservations about the more recent writings of James C. Scott (1985; 1990), for their failure to provide means of 'distinguishing between ideas which are effective in transforming people's circumstances and those which are not' (Chapter 7: 192), a criticism that might also perhaps be levelled at the contributions by Arce, Villarreal and de Vries (Chapter 6). The point is to achieve an effective marriage of the emic and the etic, not to correct Marxism's heavy reliance upon the latter style of analysis by dissolving it into the former.[9]

This is ground-breaking work and correspondingly difficult, but it is clearly one of keys to the sort of thoroughgoing critical regeneration of the lower-order concepts of the Marx-Weber tradition that is essential for a proper reconstitution of the political economy of development. Such relatively sophisticated understandings of current changes in

Third World economies and societies are valuable, once again, not just because they satisfy our intellects, but because for many important purposes they are a precondition for rational and effective action.

'Relevance', realism and choice

From the beginning of the discussion about the impasse in development sociology, a major concern of many people was not just that the established theoretical controversies were getting nowhere, but that the subject was failing to respond creatively to the great public issues of the day in the 'real world' of development. Once again it is worth making a couple of concessions. A fair amount of directly 'applied' work obviously was going on, especially in multidisciplinary development centres such as those at Sussex, East Anglia and Swansea in the UK. And not everyone in the social development field was either interested in theory or burdened with the particular forms of theoretical baggage that the impasse discussion was most concerned about. It remains the case even so that in the late 1970s and early 1980s central issues of policy and practice were getting less attention than they deserved from those specializing in the social, spatial and political dimensions of development, and the reasons were at least partly to do with the nature of the theories that were most influential in those specialisms at that time.

In any case, the plea for social research in and about the developing world to become more responsive to the concerns of those who formulate, execute or benefit (or suffer) from, development policies, programmes and projects, has been made in recent years from several different quarters. The gulf between research (especially of the theoretically oriented kind) and practice became more pointed over the decade of the 1980s for a number of different, although perhaps related reasons. One was the belated conversion of a number of large aid donors (e.g. the British Overseas Development Administration – ODA) to the view that anthropology and other 'soft' social sciences had something important to say about the conditions for equitable and sustainable development. Another was the multiplication of the numbers and range of practitioners and intermediary organizations concerned with Third World issues.

The expansion of the roles of non-government organizations (NGOs) throughout much of Africa, South and South East Asia and Latin America in the 1980s (Poulton and Harris 1988; Schneider 1988; Bratton 1990; Lehmann 1990; Clark 1991; Fowler 1991; Edwards and Hulme 1992) was a particularly powerful force bringing with it new sources of dissatisfaction with the orientation of academic development research. To date the most radical and articulate statement of this latter kind of concern is Michael Edwards's angry declamation on 'The irrelevance of development studies' (1989; see also Edwards's Chapter 11 in this volume).

Despite the memorable title, Edwards's argument was directed against 'development studies of a particular form' (1989: 131) rather than against the entire output of the subject. Nevertheless the scope of his critique is quite broad, and it is by no means clear that much of the research that has been characterized here as post-impasse escapes its strictures. To the extent that the article reflects in whole or in part a view that is common among NGO workers and advisers – and possibly among a much wider range of development and aid workers in national and international agencies – it deserves very serious consideration.

Edwards's general concern in looking at the relationship between research and development is about 'the absence of strong links between understanding and action' (1989: 117). His particular *bêtes noires* include the cult of the expert and the devaluation of local knowledge, the tendency for research to be guided by the professional interests of the researcher rather than the needs of those being researched, the concentration of knowledge and hence power by elites, and the lack of an ongoing relationship between research and appropriate forms of involvement in development processes: 'Development has become a spectator sport, with a vast array of experts and others looking into the "fishbowl" of the Third World from the safety and comfort of their armchairs' (Edwards 1989: 124). Since increasingly ' "popular participation" is accepted as the only real basis for successful development', the key to a better model for the future is the spread and consolidation of 'participatory research' or 'action research', understood as research linked to projects which aim at 'facilitating people's own development efforts' (1989: 123, 129). Not all useful research can or should be directly participatory, but 'such higher-level work must grow out of and be based upon participatory research at lower levels' (1989: 130).

Our response to the 'NGO view' (if that is what it is) needs to take the form of a dialogue, a consideration not just of how well current research efforts measure up in terms of practical criteria, but also of what those criteria ought to be. There are also a number of preliminary issues that cannot be skipped over entirely. To what extent is there agreement on the meaning, desirability and attainability of 'relevance'? Are moral concerns the essential driving force, or to the contrary the bane, of development studies? Having settled these points, we can go on to ask: do NGOs know what research they want, and is this what they need? Is relevant research the same as applied research? Is macro-work less relevant than micro-work? And when it comes to applied research and practical intervention, how much and what ways does 'theory' matter?

The meaning and desirability of 'relevance' in social development research turns out, somewhat surprisingly, to be one of the *most* controversial issues among social development researchers. Differences on this issue, moreover, do not correspond at all closely to disagreements on the other dimensions reviewed here. Buttel and McMichael (Chapter 2), writing from the perspective of development sociology conceived as comparative structural inquiry, make a strong appeal for a greater separation than has existed in the past between the mainstream of the discipline and 'applied development studies'. In their view, the search for generalizable recipes for development problems was one of the main sources of the overgeneralized and one-dimensional theorizing of the 1960s and 1970s.

From a position which on the face of it is no less structuralist, Corbridge (Chapter 4) makes the sharply different plea that our relations with 'distant strangers' are an undeniable moral issue, and that the study of development is correspondingly imbued with ethical as well as scientific concern. This view, which by no means implies a reduction of development studies to an 'applied' field (Bebbington, Chapter 8: 202), seems to be widely shared, especially by those such as Barnett and Blaikie (Chapter 9), whose own work has spanned the 'pure' and 'applied'. It is not, however, a universal view, even among researchers whose findings seem to be redolent with practical implications at the grassroots level.

Edwards's appeals are directed at everyone, but they have a special significance for those who have been doing research among poor people and of a kind that is or could in principle be directly participatory. Proponents of actor-oriented 'interface' (Long 1989) and other research on local movements and power structures such as the UNRISD Participation Programme (Pearse and Stiefel 1979; UNRISD 1981; Vandergeest and Buttel 1988) do claim that their work has a payoff in the form of understandings which make possible improvements in rural programmes and/or direct measures to empower the powerless and the poor. This, however, is not the same as offering a recipe for 'getting development right' (Long and van der Ploeg, Chapter 3: 83). It is certainly a different matter from holding that research should be invariably linked to empowerment schemes or participatory projects. Actor-oriented research is not the kind of 'participant observation' in the service of improved top-down planning upon which Edwards heaps scorn, but neither is it to be equated with 'action research'. It should not be 'embraced as a kind of new panacea for ameliorating the poverty, uncertainties and vulnerabilities of disadvantaged groups although it can afford various social actors a useful conceptual framework for analysing their own life circumstances and for assessing possible strategies for action' (Long and van der Ploeg, Chapter 3: 82–3).

One of the implicit concerns here is the issue of 'who decides?' One of the worries that academic social researchers often feel in the face of demands for greater relevance is that the necessary question 'relevant to whom and for what purpose?' has not been properly answered or its implications pursued. It is for this reason rather than for a lack of concern about practical issues that they prefer to let their work 'stand or fall by its analytical results' (ibid.). For related reasons, research on NGOs and NGO projects may be done best if it is the fruit of a collaborative relationship between NGOs and academic researchers, rather than defined and controlled by the former from the outset (for a full exploration of this issue, see David Hulme, Chapter 10).

There is also another set of questions about to what it is that relevant research is supposed to be relevant. Although, as we have seen, Edwards does not restrict the characterization 'relevant' to local participatory projects to the exclusion of all other forms of development research, the criterion that the entire field should 'grow out of and be based upon' such projects is very restrictive indeed, particularly when accompanied by references from which one infers that other criteria of a more political sort may also be involved (Edwards 1989: 130). The underlying proposition that popular participation has been shown to be the only real basis for successful development seems to me to be problematic, not because I doubt the achievements of the better NGO projects and of the new 'grassroots' movements as a whole, but because especially outside Africa there is a good deal of developmental success that has nothing to do with this sort of activity.

Should local studies enjoy a special privilege when we are talking about relevance to practice, or even relevance to people? Given the capacity of an unfavourable macro- or meso-context to dissipate the gains from merely local efforts, is not research on the regional, national and international levels potentially the most 'relevant' of all – provided it is good research (cf. Bebbington, Chapter 8)? As Barnett and Blaikie (Chapter 9) show, even directly applied work which perforce 'ignores the wider picture' may nevertheless need to draw on a good 'toolbox' of theoretical issues and concepts. Perhaps after all this is what it means to say that macro-research should 'grow out of' participatory work, but in that case the formula is ambiguous and we should give our minds to how it might be sharpened up.

Beyond a certain rather general level of discussion, it seems to me undesirable to enter into discussions about which sorts of research are 'relevant' and which not. What does seem clear and worth reaffirming is the general interdependence that seems to have been established between the trio relevance, realism and choice. By adopting a research agenda centred on diversity, social development studies may not have fully attended to the 'irrelevance of development studies' in the eyes of the NGO activists. But because of the association of diversity with choice, an agenda constituted in this way is relevant to the world of practical concerns in a way that previous agendas were not, and this is surely a good thing. True relevance also depends on the realism of the findings of research, which means attempting to resolve the difficult dilemmas outlined in the middle sections of this chapter – between theory and empirical work, between action and its structural contexts, between emic and etic methods – few of which are likely to be satisfied by a single pattern of localized and participatory research. While much remains to be done in these respects, there is much promise in the recent trends to which it has been possible to refer.

Conclusion

The echoes of the 'impasse debate' are still with us and will no doubt continue to be heard for some time yet. But in important ways, I have argued, the field of social development research has already been reconstituted on new, more productive and more challenging, lines. What is common to the new directions in which research is moving is the attention being given – at macro-, meso- and micro-levels – to the investigation and explanation of diversity.

To put the matter in this way, it has been conceded, does give a misleading impression of intellectual coherence, belied by the observation that interest in developmental diversity is the child and parent of three or four distinct strands of theoretical critique. Diversity means different things in different contexts, and different sorts of contributors to 'post-impasse' thinking are not of one mind on such issues as the proper place of theoretical work, the relationship between 'actor-oriented' and structural analysis, and the desirability of judging research by the criterion of relevance.

As this chapter has tried to show, however, the tendency of recent discussions has been to bring forward more evidence of agreement, and fewer signs of fundamental disagreement, than many would have expected. I have no brief to present a consensus and the chapter has not attempted to construct one. Nevertheless, I believe that there is a good measure of agreement behind a number of the propositions advanced here. Diversity can and should be the subject of generalizations and theoretical work. While both action-based and structural explanations are permissible, there are limits to the productive pursuit of either on its own – the gulf between local action studies and 'political economy' must be bridged, and deconstruction and social choice brought to bear on the reconstitution of the latter. Finally, it is both desirable and possible for post-impasse research to achieve a 'relevance' that was denied to or rejected by earlier work on the social, political and spatial dimensions of development.

Notes

1. The expression has the advantage of allowing us to sidestep the issue of whether labels like 'post-Marxist' are applicable or make good sense (cf. Geras 1987; Corbridge 1990; Mouzelis 1988b). Although I have some sympathy for Corbridge's handling of the question, there is no doubt it is a can of worms.
2. To borrow the words of an anonymous reviewer of a draft of this chapter.
3. A few years back, several contributors to the *Socialist Register* (especially Cammack 1990; Geras 1990) expressed reasonable concern about a general trend towards casual misrepresentations of the Marxist tradition, including by authors referred to favourably in this chapter.
4. The earlier stages of this evolution as they relate to Africa are usefully explored by Kennedy (1988). Relevant points about theory and method are made by Corbridge (1982), Kitching (1985), Hindess (1987; 1989) and Moore (1990).
5. For example respectively Brass (1990; 1991) and Bernstein (1990).
6. In Mouzelis (1991: 1–6) this is related to a broader plea for a return to the specific business of *sociological* theorizing following a long period in which it has been fashionable for theoretically inclined sociologists to restrict their interests to what is often referred to as 'social theory', that is ontological/epistemological investigations and/or relatively casual borrowings from recent developments in such adjoining disciplines as philosophy, psycho-analysis and linguistics.
7. As Terry Marsden has pointed out to me, this way of putting it deals only

with a small slice of a large problem, namely giving adequate attention to sets of agency-structure interactions at every level from the strictly micro to the macro, and developing what he calls a 'generative' approach appropriate to each (University of Hull, personal communication). Cf. also Mouzelis's important points about not identifying 'micro' with face-to-face situations so that we are prevented from analysing the very different positions of single actors at the base of the social hierarchy and both collective actors and what he calls 'mega-actors' – 'single individuals whose . . . social power makes the consequences of their decisions widely felt' (Mouzelis 1991: 106–7).

8. Sandiland (1985) provides an excellent demonstration of the superiority in practice of this substantially modified rational choice approach over other applications of the doctrine in the field of Third World politics. A further issue worth considering is whether all or any of these efforts at micro-macro integration are open to the charge laid by Mouzelis (1991: ch. 4) at the doors of Berger and Luckman, Collins and Knorr-Cetina, namely that their formulations do not take seriously into account the hierarchical aspects of social life.

9. Bayart (1991: 63) puts it well in connection with the need for studies of 'cultural configurations of politics' in the developing world instead of purportedly universal approaches based exclusively on western experiences of the state. To go to the other extreme and adopt a strictly emic approach would simply 'replace an imperial scientific provincialism with a series of country-specific scientific provincialisms: the need for common "problematisations" is not in question'.

References

Amsden A H (1989) *Asia's next giant: South Korea and late industrialisation*. New York, Oxford University Press

Amsden A H (1990) Third World industrialization: 'global Fordism' or new model? *New Left Review* 182

Anglade C and **Fortin C** (1987) The role of the state in Latin America's strategic options. *Cepal Review* 31

Apthorpe R (ed) (1987) Institutions and policies. Special issue, *Public Administration and Development* 6(4)

Arce A (1987) Bureaucratic conflict and public policy: rainfed agriculture in Mexico. *Boletín de Estudios Latinoamericanos y del Caribe* 42

Arce A (1989) The social construction of agrarian development: a case study of producer–bureaucrat relations in an irrigation unit in western Mexico. In: Long N (ed)

Arce A and **Long N** (1987) The dynamics of knowledge interfaces between Mexican agricultural bureaucrats and peasants: a case study from Jalisco. *Boletín de Estudios Latinoamericanos y del Caribe* 43

Arce A and **Mitra S** (1991) Making development relevant: beyond the impasse in development studies. Occasional Paper 7, Department of Sociology and Social Anthropology, University of Hull.

Barrett M and **Phillips A** (eds) (1992) *Destabilizing theory: contemporary feminist debates*. Cambridge, Polity Press

Bates R (1978) People in villages: micro-level studies in political economy (review article). *World Politics* 31

Bates R (1981) *Markets and states in tropical Africa: the political basis of agricultural policies*. Berkeley, CA, University of California Press

Bates R (1983) Conclusion. In Bates R *Essays in the political economy of rural Africa*. Cambridge, Cambridge University Press

Bates R (ed) (1988) *Toward a political economy of development: a rational choice perspective*. Berkeley, CA, University of California Press

Bates R (1989) *Beyond the miracle of the market: the political economy of agrarian development in Kenya*. Cambridge, Cambridge University Press.

Bayart J-F (1991) Finishing with the idea of the Third World: the concept of the political trajectory. In: Manor J (ed)

Bayart J-F (1993) (1st French edn 1989) *The state in Africa: the politics of the belly*. London, Longman

Becker D G (1983) *The new bourgeoisie and the limits of dependency: mining, class, and power in 'Revolutionary' Peru*. Princeton, NJ, Princeton University Press

Bernstein H (1990) Agricultural 'modernisation' and the era of structural adjustment: observations on Sub-Saharan Africa. *Journal of Peasant Studies* 18(1)

Boone C (1990) The making of a rentier class: wealth accumulation and political control in Senegal. *Journal of Development Studies* 26(3)

Booth D (1985) Marxism and development sociology: interpreting the impasse. *World Development* 13(7)

Booth D (1987) Alternatives in the restructuring of state–society relations: research issues for tropical Africa. *IDS Bulletin* 18(4)

Boyne R and **Rattansi A** (1990) The theory and politics of postmodernism: by way of an introduction. In: Boyne R and Rattansi A (eds) *Postmodernism and society*. London, Macmillan

Brass T (1990) Peasant essentialism and the agrarian question in the Colombian Andes (review article). *Journal of Peasant Studies* 17(3)

Brass T (1991) Moral economists, subalterns, new social movements, and the (re-)emergence of a (post-)modernised (middle) peasant. *Journal of Peasant Studies* 18(2)

Bratton M (1990) Non-governmental organizations in Africa: can they influence public policy? *Development and Change* 21(1)

Buttel F H and **Goodman D** (eds) (1989) Class, state, technology and international food regimes. Special issue, *Sociologia Ruralis* XXIX(2)

Callinicos A (1989) *Against postmodernism: a Marxist critique*. Cambridge, Polity Press

Cammack P (1990) Statism, new institutionalism, and Marxism. In: Miliband R *et al.* (eds) *Socialist Register 1990*. London, Merlin Press

Campbell J (1991) Household and gender in urban East Africa. Unpublished paper, Department of Sociology and Anthropology, University College of Swansea

Cardoso F H and **Faletto E** (1979) (1st Spanish edn 1967) *Dependency and development in Latin America*. Berkeley, CA, University of California Press

Cernea M (ed) (1991) *Putting people first: sociological variables in rural development*, 2nd edn. New York, Oxford University Press for the World Bank

Chabal P (ed) (1986) *Political domination in Africa*. Cambridge, Cambridge University Press

Chambers R (1983) *Rural development: putting the last first*. Harlow, Longman

Chambers R, Pacey A and **Thrupp L A** (eds) (1989) *Farmer first: farmer innovation and agricultural research*. London, Intermediate Technology Publications

Charles N (1993) Gender divisions and social change. Hemel Hempstead, Harvester-Wheatsheaf

Clark J (1991) *Democratizing development: the role of voluntary organizations*. London, Earthscan.

Clay E and **Schaffer B** (eds) (1984) *Room for manoeuvre: an exploration of public policy in agriculture and rural development*. London, Heinemann

Collier D (ed) (1979) *The new authoritarianism in Latin America*. Princeton, NJ, Princeton University Press

Collins R (1981) Micro-translation as a theory-building strategy. In: Knorr-Cetina K and Cicourel A V (eds) *Advances in social theory and methodology: towards an integration of micro- and macro-sociologies*. Boston, MA, Routledge & Kegan Paul

Corbridge S (1982) Urban bias, rural bias, and industrialization: an appraisal of the work of Michael Lipton and Terry Byres. In: Harriss J (ed) *Rural development: theories of peasant economy and agrarian change*. London, Hutchinson

Corbridge S (1986) *Capitalist world development: a critique of radical development geography*. London, Macmillan

Corbridge S (1990) Post-Marxism and development studies: beyond the impasse. *World Development* 18(5)

Crook S (1990) The end of radical social theory? Notes on radicalism, modernism and postmodernism. In: Boyne R and Rattansi A (eds) *Postmodernism and society*. London, Macmillan

Dalling M (1991) Representations of farming in Britain. Unpublished paper, Department of Sociology and Social Anthropology, University of Hull

Deyo F (ed) (1987) *The political economy of the new Asian industrialism*. Ithaca, NY, Cornell University Press

Edwards M (1989) The irrelevance of development studies. *Third World Quarterly* 11(1)

Edwards M and **Hulme D** (eds) (1992) *Making a difference: NGOs and development in a changing world*. London, Earthscan

Elwert G and **Bierschenk T** (eds) (1988) Development aid as an intervention in dynamic systems. Special issue, *Sociologia Ruralis* XXVIII(2/3)

Ergas Z (ed) (1987) *The African state in transition*. London, Macmillan

Evans B *et al.* (eds) (1985) *Bringing the state back in*. Cambridge, Cambridge University Press

Faulkner A H and **Lawson V A** (1991) Employment versus empowerment: a case study of the nature of women's work in Ecuador. *Journal of Development Studies* 27(4)

Foster-Carter A (1991) Development sociology: wither now? *Sociology Review* 1(2)

Fowler A (1991) The role of NGOs in changing state–society relations: perspectives from Eastern and Southern Africa. *Development Policy Review* 9(1)

Geras N (1987) Post-Marxism? *New Left Review* 163

Geras N (1990) Seven types of obloquy: travesties of Marxism. In: Miliband R *et al.* (eds) *Socialist Register 1990*. London, Merlin Press

Gereffi G and **Wyman D L** (eds) (1991) *Manufacturing miracles: paths of industrialisation in Latin America and East Asia*. Princeton, NJ, Princeton University Press

Gibbon P (1992) Understanding social change in contemporary Africa. Workshop on The State, Structural Adjustment and Changing Social and Political Relations in Africa, Scandinavian Institute of African Studies, Uppsala, May

Gibbon P, Bangura Y and **Ofstad A** (eds) (1992a) *Authoritarianism, democracy and adjustment: the politics of economic reform in Africa*. Uppsala, Scandinavian Institute of African Studies

Gibbon P, Havnevik K and **Hermele K** (1992b) Adjustment and agriculture in six African countries: Ghana, Kenya, Mozambique, Tanzania, Uganda, Zambia. Workshop on The State, Structural Adjustment and Changing Social and Political Relations in Africa, Scandinavian Institute of African Studies, Uppsala, May

Giddens A (1984) *The constitution of society: outline of the theory of structuration.* Cambridge, Polity Press

Giddens A (1990) *The consequences of modernity.* Cambridge, Polity Press

Goodman D and **Redclift M** (1991) *Refashioning nature: food, ecology and culture.* London, Routledge

Grillo R and **Rew A** (eds) (1985) *Social anthropology and development policy.* London, Tavistock

Grindle M S (ed) (1980) *Politics and Policy Implementation in the Third World.* Princeton, NJ, Princeton University Press.

Grindle M S (1986) *State and countryside: development policy and agrarian politics in Latin America.* Baltimore, MD, Johns Hopkins University Press

Grindle M S and **Thomas J W** (1991) *Public choices and policy change: the political economy of reform in developing countries.* Baltimore, MD, Johns Hopkins University Press

Hall A and **Midgley J** (eds) (1988) *Development policies: sociological perspectives.* Manchester, Manchester University Press

Harris N (1986) *The end of the Third World: newly industrializing countries and the decline of an ideology.* London, IB Tauris

Harriss J (1980) Why poor people stay poor in rural South India. *Development and Change* 11(1)

Harriss J (1987) Capitalism and peasant production: the green revolution in India. In: Shanin T (ed) *Peasants and peasant societies* 2nd edn. Oxford, Basil Blackwell

Harriss J and **Moore M** (eds) (1984) *Development and the rural–urban divide.* London, Frank Cass

Healey J and **Robinson M** (1992) *Democracy, political change and economic policy: Sub-Saharan Africa in comparative perspective.* Development Policy Studies Series, London, Overseas Development Institute

Hebinck P (1990) *The agrarian structure in Kenya: state, farmers and commodity relations.* Saarbrucken, Verlag Brietenbach (Nijmegen Studies in Development and Cultural Change)

Hindess B (1987) *Politics and class analysis.* Oxford, Basil Blackwell

Hindess B (1989) *Political choice and social structure: an analysis of actors, interests and rationality.* Aldershot, Edward Elgar

Hobart M (1990) Discerning disorder: is it really there? Paper presented to EIDOS Erasmus Summer School, Free University of Amsterdam, June

Hulme D and **Turner M** (1990) *Sociology and development: theories, policies and practices.* New York, Harvester-Wheatsheaf

Hyden G (1983) *No shortcuts to progress: African development management in perspective.* London, Heinemann

IPEALT (1990) *Agricultures et paysanneries en Amérique Latine: mutations et recompositions.* Proceedings of international colloquium held at Université de Toulouse-Le Mirail, 13–14 December

Jenkins R (1991) The political economy of industrialization: a comparison of Latin American and East Asian newly industrializing countries. *Development and Change* 22(2)

Kennedy P (1988) *African capitalism: the struggle for ascendancy.* Cambridge, Cambridge University Press

Kitching G (1985) Politics, method and evidence in the 'Kenya debate'. In: Bernstein H and Campbell B K (eds) *Contradictions of Accumulation in Africa.* London, Sage

Larrain J (1989) *Theories of development: capitalism, colonialism and dependency.* Cambridge, Polity Press

Lehmann D (1990) *Democracy and development in Latin America.* Cambridge, Polity Press

Lofchie M F (1989) *The policy factor: agricultural performance in Kenya and Tanzania.* Boulder, CO, Lynne Rienner

Long, N (1984) Creating space for change: a perspective on the sociology of development. Inaugural lecture, Agricultural University, Wageningen

Long N (1988) Sociological perspectives on agrarian development and state intervention. In: Hall A and Midgley J (eds)

Long N (ed) (1989) *Encounters at the interface: a perspective on social discontinuities in rural development.* Wageningen, Wageningen University Press

Long N (1990) From paradigm lost to paradigm regained? The case for an actor-oriented sociology of development. *European Review of Latin American and Caribbean Studies* 49

Long N and **Long A** (eds) (1992) *Battlefields of knowledge: the interlocking of theory and practice in social research and development.* London, Routledge

Long N and **Roberts B** (eds) (1978) *Peasant cooperation and capitalist expansion in Central Peru.* Austin TX, University of Texas Press

Long N and **Roberts B** (1984) *Miners, peasants and entrepreneurs: regional development in the Central Highlands of Peru.* Cambridge, Cambridge University Press

Lyotard J-F (1984) (1st French edn 1979) *The postmodern condition.* Manchester, Manchester University Press

MacGaffey J (1987) *Entrepreneurs and parasites: the struggle for indigenous capitalism in Zaire.* Cambridge, Cambridge University Press

Mackintosh M (1989) *Gender, class and rural transition: agribusiness and the food crisis in Senegal.* London, Zed Press

Manor J (ed) (1991) *Rethinking Third World politics.* London, Longman

Marsden T, Lowe P and **Whatmore S** (eds) (1990) *Rural restructuring: global processes and their responses.* London, David Fulton

Mbilinyi M (1991) *Big slavery: agribusiness and the crisis in women's employment in Tanzania.* Dar es Salaam, Dar es Salaam University Press

Midgley J *et al.* (eds) (1986) *Community participation, social development and the state.* London, Methuen

Migdal J (1988) *Strong societies and weak states: state–society relations and state capabilities in the Third World.* Princeton, NJ, Princeton University Press

Mohanty C T (1988) Under western eyes: feminist scholarship and colonial discourses. *Feminist Review* 30

Mohanty C T (1992) Feminist encounters: locating the politics of experience. In: Barrett M and Phillips A (eds)

Moore M (1985) *The state and peasant politics in Sri Lanka.* Cambridge, Cambridge University Press

Moore M (1987) Interpreting Africa's crisis: political science versus political economy. *IDS Bulletin* 18(4)

Moore M (1988) Economic growth and the rise of civil society: agriculture in Taiwan and South Korea. In: White G (ed)

Moore M (1989) What and where is political economy? (review article) *Journal of Development Studies* 25(4)

Moore M (1990) The rational choice paradigm and the allocation of agricultural development resources. *Development and Change* 21(2)

Moore M and **Hamalai L** (1992) Economic liberalisation, political pluralism and business associations in developing countries. Mimeo, April, Institute of Development Studies, University of Sussex

Mouzelis N (1984) On the crisis of Marxist theory (review article) *British Journal of Sociology* 35(1)

Mouzelis N (1986) *Politics on the semi-periphery: early parliamentarism and late industrialisation in the Balkans and Latin America.* London, Macmillan

Mouzelis N (1988a) Sociology of development: reflections on the present crisis. *Sociology* 22(1)

Mouzelis N (1988b) Marxism or post-Marxism? *New Left Review* 167

Mouzelis N (1990) *Post-Marxist alternatives: the construction of social orders.* London, Macmillan

Mouzelis N (1991) *Back to sociological theory: the construction of social orders.* London, Macmillan

Nelson J (ed) (1990) *Economic crisis and policy choice: the politics of adjustment in the Third World.* Princeton, NJ, Princeton University Press

O'Donnell G (1978) Reflections on the patterns of change in the bureaucratic-authoritarian state. *Latin American Research Review* 12(1)

Østergaard L (ed) (1992) *Gender and development: a practical guide.* London, Routledge

Pearse A and **Stiefel M** (1979) Inquiry into participation – a research approach. Popular Participation Programme, Geneva, UNRISD

Peet R (1990) *Global capitalism: theories of societal development.* Boston, MA, Routledge

Pelto P J and **Pelto G H** (1978) *Anthropological research: the structure of inquiry,* 2nd edn. Cambridge, Cambridge University Press

Pottier J (ed) (1993) *Practising development: social science perspectives.* London, Routledge

Poulton R and **Harris M** (eds) (1988) *Putting people first: voluntary organisations and Third World development.* London, Macmillan

Richards A (1986) *Development and modes of production in Marxian economics: a critical evaluation.* Chur, Switzerland, Harwood Academic Publishers

Richards P (1985) *Indigenous agricultural revolution: ecology and food production in West Africa.* London, Hutchinson

Rosenau P M (1992) *Post-modernism and the social sciences: insights, inroads, and intrusions.* Princeton, NJ, Princeton University Press

Rothchild D and **Chazan N** (eds) (1988) *The precarious balance: state and society in Africa.* Boulder, CO, Westview Press

Roxborough J (1984) Unity and Diversity in Latin American history. *Journal of Latin American Studies* 16(1)

Ruggie G (ed) (1983) *The antinomies of interdependence: national welfare and the international division of labor.* New York, Columbia University Press

Sandiland M (1985) *What is political economy? A study of social theory and under-development.* New Haven, CT, Yale University Press

Schneider B (1988) *The barefoot revolution: a report to the club of Rome.* London, Intermediate Technology Publications

Scott A M (1986a) Women and industrialisation: examining the 'female marginalisation' thesis. *Journal of Development Studies* 22(4)

Scott A M (1986b) Towards a rethinking of petty commodity production. *Social Analysis* 20

Scott A M (forthcoming), *Gender and class in the Andes.* London, Routledge

Scott J C (1985) *Weapons of the weak: everyday forms of peasant resistance.* New Haven, CT, Yale University Press

Scott J C (1990) *Domination and the arts of resistance: hidden transcripts.* New Haven, CT, Yale University Press

Sender J and **Smith S** (1990) *Poverty, class and gender in rural Africa: a Tanzanian case study.* London, Routledge

Sheahan J (1987) *Patterns of development in Latin America: poverty, repression, and economic strategy.* Princeton, NJ, Princeton University Press

Simo J A M (1991) Gender, agro-pastoral production and class formation in Bamunka, north-western Cameroon. PhD thesis, University of East Anglia

Sklair L (1988) Transcending the impasse: metatheory, theory, and empirical research in the sociology of development and underdevelopment. *World Development* 16(6)

Skocpol T (1979) *States and social revolutions.* Cambridge, Cambridge University Press

Skocpol T (1985) Bringing the state back in: strategies of analysis in current research. In: Evans P. B *et al.* (eds)

Swantz M-L (1985) *Women in development: a creative role denied? The case of Tanzania.* London, Hurst

Townsend J and **Momsen J H** (1987) Towards a geography of gender in developing market economies. In: Momsen J H and Townsend J (eds) *Geography of Gender in the Third World.* London, Hutchinson

Unger R M (1987a) *Social theory: its situation and tasks.* Cambridge, Cambridge University Press

Unger R M (1987b) *False necessity: anti-necessitarian social theory in the service of radical democracy.* Cambridge, Cambridge University Press

UNRISD (1981) Brief history and structure of the popular participation programme. *Dialogue about Participation* no. 1, Geneva, UNRISD

Vandergeest P and **Buttell F H** (1988) Marx, Weber, and development sociology: beyond the impasse. *World Development* 16(6)

Wallace T (ed) (1991) *Changing perceptions: writings on gender and development.* Oxford, Oxfam

Watts M (1989) The agrarian crisis in Africa: debating the crisis. *Progess in Human Geography* 13(1)

White G (ed) (1988) *Developmental states in East Asia.* London, Macmillan

Wilson F (1985) Women and agricultural change in Latin America: some concepts guiding research. *World Development* 13(9)

World Bank (1981) *Accelerated development in Sub-Saharan Africa: an agenda for action.* Washington, DC, World Bank

Part I
Rebuilding the framework: modes of explanation and strategies of inquiry

What distinguishes the successful trends in social development research in the mid-1990s is the attention given to describing and explaining the diversity of development experience across countries, regions and localities, in different large-scale and face-to-face settings. This proposition, advanced in general terms in Chapter 1, forms a major theme of this book, illustrated, interpreted and debated from a variety of perspectives throughout its pages, most particularly in Parts I and II. Two other themes – the relationship between structural and actor-oriented forms of analysis, and the terms, if any, on which development research should be related to development 'practice' – are other regular points of reference.

In Part I these issues are addressed in broad strategic and methodological terms, with a range of illustrations from recent research and analysis. In the remainder of the volume the contributions offer general reflections on the basis of a particular topic or field of inquiry, the specifics of which are able to be set out by their authors at somewhat greater length. As a whole, the book aims to exemplify the new directions in social development research as well as providing a framework of argument about their potential and future.

The three chapters in Part I have a common thrust but they also offer interesting contrasts in a number of respects. The authors share the conviction that the Marxist and neo-Marxist ideas that were the dominant theoretical influence in social development research at least until the mid-1980s have proven inadequate in important ways. All believe that in recent and some not-so-recent social science scholarship are to be found the bases for reconstituting the sociology (anthropology, geography, politics) of development on intellectually more productive and/or morally more defensible lines. However, their priorities and perspectives in defining the new agenda are different and in some respects sharply contradictory.

Partly, this is a matter of different professional biographies and intellectual reference groups, as the contributors themselves acknowledge. Fred Buttel and Philip McMichael, two leading figures in the field of comparative rural sociology in the USA, write from the conviction that social development studies have much to learn, first, from some of the classics of historical sociology, and second, from work in which they themselves have participated, on changing international 'food regimes'. Like other contributors to this book, they were actively involved in the 1970s in the debates prompted by the ideas of such theorists as Frank, Wallerstein and Warren, and like others – most notably Corbridge in Chapter 4, Mouzelis in Chapter 5 and Harriss in Chapter 7 – they are concerned to resist what they see as over-hasty rejection of certain valuable features of the broad tradition of Marxism.

They see the progress that has been made in thinking through the theoretical 'impasse' in development sociology as threatened from two distinct quarters. Until these issues are addressed properly, they maintain, the foundations will not have been laid 'for an enduring research agenda that is sociologically defensible' (p. 43). In the first place, discussion has focused too much on alternative modes of explanation – negatively, in the emphasis given to the avoidance of functionalist and essentialist theoretical formulas, and positively, in the assertion that 'actor-oriented' reformulations of the agency/structure problem provide the basis of a new agenda. Against this they argue that what development sociology should be distinguished by is its 'problematic': that which it typically seeks to explain, or its *explanandum*.

On the other hand, they argue, there is confusion surrounding the relationship between development theory and development *praxis*. In a powerful challenge to the suggestion throughout much of the rest of the book that increased 'relevance to practice' is an important net gain from recent rethinking of the research agenda, Buttel and McMichael point to some significant ways in which the close links between understanding and interventionist action which have typified the field of development studies since its foundation have placed a strait-jacket on the intellectual growth of the sociological branch of the subject.

Here the two parts of the argument link up, in a telling and provocative fashion. The impulse to produce theories which are 'useful' (either in the sense that they generate replicable formulas for 'policy-makers' or as a guide to radical political action) has given us a definition of the field of development sociology which is too exclusive in its focus on poor countries, too much given to the assumption that such societies are essentially similar (hence amenable to standardized solutions) and bifurcated between a tendency to ignore and a tendency to reify the international context of national development. Such explanatory weaknesses as essentialism and teleology are the result, not the source, of this misconstruction of the problematic of development sociology. The solution to be sought is not a new explanatory framework but a clearer distinction between the objectives of development sociology and those of development practice, a result that may be best achieved by a (formal) separation of these activities.

For Buttel and McMichael, reconstituting sociological development studies involves giving pride of place to accounting for diversity 'in Third World formations *and* in global social structures' (p. 44, emphasis added), without privilege to particular explanatory procedures, arbitrary geographical divisions or units of analysis. Recognizing diversity in these terms involves a strategic commitment not only to comparative analysis, but also to historically grounded comparisons which are successful in avoiding both the abstraction of the units of comparison (e.g. nation-states) from their global context, and the reification of the latter to the point where the purpose of comparison is lost (e.g. Wallerstein's world-system). Although not new, and indeed exemplified by much of the work of Marx himself as well as by Polanyi and others in more recent times, this style of 'incorporated comparison' is now well established in writings on international food regimes. Like the parent concept of 'regimes of accumulation' (Fordism, post-Fordism, etc.) discussed in an earlier article by Corbridge, the concept of food regime offers to the social development field not a ready-made category of general applicability, but a useful pointer to a productive level of abstraction and a potentially generalizable way of doing comparative research.

Readers of Buttel and McMichael's penetrating synthesis of the issues facing development sociology in the mid-1990s may end up feeling that rather too much has been laid at the door of the inter-penetration of the academic and practical worlds of development. It is not really clear that normative questions as such generate universalizing answers. What needs to be put behind us is not perhaps the general notion that academic development studies (including more and less 'applied' branches) can help to inform various kinds of action for development, but rather certain specific, historically important but now to some extent outmoded, approaches to development intervention and the corresponding conceptions of 'useful' research and theorizing. The common currency of these ideas, at the level of theoretical perspectives *and* in terms of prescriptions for action, was overgeneralization, a point taken up by Barnett and Blaikie in Chapter 9.

A different kind of qualification of the contribution of Buttel and McMichael is what they freely describe as their 'preference' for reconstituting development sociology 'as a branch of comparative-historical *macro*sociology' (p. 40, emphasis added). Unlike their parallel dismissal of the pretensions of actor-oriented methodology, this does seem to be a matter of taste rather than intellectual substance. Buttel and McMichael do not exclude the possibility that a variety of styles of research of a more micro or meso kind may have a useful part to play in the revitalization of social research on development; they merely choose to illustrate their arguments primarily with references to the sub-area that they know and like best.

Chapter 3 by Norman Long and Jan Douwe van der Ploeg provides a contrast to this in several respects. Although they too describe themselves as rural sociologists, Long and van der Ploeg represent the other end of the macro–micro spectrum in terms of empirical focus, their main research projects having taken the form of intensive field studies of agricultural enterprises or rural districts in both Europe and less developed regions. Like Buttel and McMichael, they are hostile to 'Third-Worldism', that is to the belief that the study of less developed societies calls for *special* methods and theoretical perspectives, the validity of which is restricted to developing-country contexts. However, much of the rest of their argument runs strongly counter to the theoretical and methodological presumptions of Buttel and McMichael.

Based in the Department of Sociology of Rural Development at the Agricultural University of Wageningen in the Netherlands, Long and van der Ploeg are leading exponents and practitioners of what they call an 'actor-oriented' approach to social development research. In their view the limitations of the approaches that have dominated theory in the sociology of development – Marxist, neo-Marxist, modernizationist – are more deep-rooted than Buttel and McMichael (or indeed Booth, or Corbridge) would have us believe. They are sceptical, also, of attempts such as are made elsewhere in this book, to reconcile structural with actor-oriented analysis of development processes, without reformulating 'the essential concepts of such a proposed marriage' (p. 62). In other words, it is a mistake to attempt to define a research strategy without first grappling seriously with the modes of explanation, the concepts of 'actor' and 'structure', that might underpin such a programme.

The point of departure for Long and van der Ploeg is a critique of the concept of structure that leads to the portrayal of social change as a linear, or single-track, process in which external forces 'encapsulate the lives of people, reducing their autonomy [and] resulting in . . . greater centralized control by powerful economic and political groups, institutions and enterprises' (p. 63), giving rise in turn to the idea that development processes can be studied in a largely 'externalist' fashion. What is needed is a more dynamic approach that stresses the interplay and mutual determination of 'internal' and 'external' factors and relationships, one which recognizes the central role played by human action and consciousness. Distancing themselves from earlier conceptions of actor-oriented research in anthropology as well as from sociologically primitive variants of the 'rational choice' doctrine, Long and van der Ploeg provide a lucid and varied survey of the benefits of an approach that builds up to the analysis of structural phenomena on the basis of studies that take proper account of the properties of human agency.

In the context of agrarian development, investigations beginning with an actor perspective have revealed an unexpected heterogeniety of farming styles within otherwise quite homogeneous regions, confounding established typologies based on external technical, economic or political factors. The study of development planning, too, has been much advanced by 'deconstructing' it, 'so that it is seen for what it is – namely, an ongoing, socially constructed and negotiated process, not simply the execution of an already specified plan of action with expected outcomes' (p. 78). Thus, research on planned intervention in rural and other settings should focus on intervention *practices*, the real processes of social interaction that take place, including the attendant forms of discourse and cultural expression, rather than on ideal-typical *models* that the planners or their clients construct of the process.

For Long and van der Ploeg, what distinguishes the actor-oriented approach to issues such as these is not concentration on the immediate context of action to the exclusion of wider social phenomena, but abandonment of simple causative notions, such as 'the logic of commoditization', the 'subsumption of the peasantry' and 'the market'. Structures should not be conceived, as in these examples, as 'driving forces' that are invariably necessary if not actually sufficient to explain action and its outcomes; this amounts in most cases simply to the reification of what happen to be considered the 'central tendencies' of change at a particular moment, and its true explanatory capability is generally very limited. A structure should be viewed instead as 'an extremely fluid set of emergent properties, which, on the one hand, results from the interlocking and/or distantiation of various actors' projects, while, on the other hand, it functions as an important point of reference for the further elaboration, negotiation and confrontation of actors' projects' (p. 81).

Structures, then, are never more than the emergent properties (not, that is, simple aggregates) of specific interactive processes, and their role is never greater than that of providing relatively stable conditions for further action, limiting or otherwise shaping the choices and possible projects open to actors. This formulation provides for Long and van der Ploeg a decisive refutation of the suggestion that actor-focused studies neglect wider structures. However, the reader may feel that this deals too lightly with the specific, but not uncommon, scenario in which the choices of certain categories of actor are severely limited in certain respects by the properties of interactive systems over which *they* have little or no control. The basic point is well made. Actor-oriented studies can reveal – in ways that structural, especially structurally determinist, analysis cannot – important and highly 'relevant' ways in which the outcomes of development processes are open-ended and actually or potentially diverse. But to be realistic and to reveal their full potential, they need to be attentive to the relationships between actor-structure nexuses at different *levels* (e.g. village, district, country) as well as to the hardly negligible issue of initial inequalities in the distribution of economic and political power.

The contributions by Buttel and McMichael and Long and van der Ploeg provide challenging alternative prospectuses for social development research in the later 1990s. Readers of this book, especially perhaps those less familiar with the rural sociology literature upon which both chapters draw, will find much here to stimulate or provoke further thinking about the priorities and potential difficulties facing those concerned to reconstruct the analytical basis of social development studies. Several of the issues raised are taken up in later contributions, including the reservations expressed by Long and van der Ploeg in their conclusion about the confusion of actor-oriented methodology with participatory action research.

Part I concludes with an incisive intervention by Stuart Corbridge, which is also programmatic but in different sense. A social geographer whose critical book on radical development geography was one of the opening shots in the 'impasse' debate, Corbridge is concerned here to identify some of the ingredients for a post-impasse synthesis which is capable of responding to the wider intellectual and moral challenges of the end of the millennium. Like Buttel and McMichael, he wishes to protect some things that remain valuable in the heritage of Marxism both from a possible anti-Marxist interpretation of the current agenda and from the general intellectual fall-out of the recent changes in eastern Europe. Unlike the other contributors in Part I he also wishes to address in a serious way the challenge of 'post-modernism' (including the particular application of the post-modernist critique to Third World issues which calls itself 'post-colonialism') and the distinct but related issue of the moral basis of development studies. Chapter 4 makes the case for a post-Marxist as distinct from a post-modernist agenda, and for giving development studies an explicit ethical dimension.

Corbridge's chapter crosses with deceptive ease the boundaries of half a dozen academic specialisms in the social sciences, cultural studies and philosophy, and his argument is rich in allusions and subtleties of language which will be unfamiliar to some readers. Those who come to this book from a more specialized background may find the chapter difficult, but they should certainly be encouraged to persist. It contains a rare attempt to deal sympathetically but firmly with the recent vogue in critiques of the enterprise of development, and hence of development studies, which purport to adopt the vantage point of the excluded, the disenfranchised and the non-western *vis-à-vis* the dominant themes and perspectives of global (western) society.

Corbridge understands the wish of contemporary 'populists' such as Robert Chambers and Paul Richards to celebrate the voices of the rural poor, and he is in favour of the deconstruction or insistent questioning of received wisdoms about the meaning of development, especially those which can be shown to be an expression of ethnocentrism or western cultural arrogance. But he warns against the apparent corollary, seized upon most eagerly by those who declare themselves post-modernists, that we have entered an era in which no criteria about knowledge and the possibility of progress retain any general, that is cross-cultural, validity. He shares Anthony Giddens's view that such a position is both philosophically self-defeating and badly wrong in terms of the history of ideas. The modern 'western' tradition is a source not just of tyrannical 'meta-narratives' that prescribe what is to be known and what progress shall consist of, but also of the very notions of critique and rebellion that are held to be distinctive of post-modernity.

Marxism's central place within this tradition of radical critique linked to the possibility of social transformation is one reason for espousing a 'post-Marxist' rather than a post-modernist agenda. Another to which Corbridge redirects our attention is the contemporary relevance of Marx's vision of capitalism as a ceaseless destroyer of pre-existing social forms and as a source of the globalization or 'space-time compression' which is recognized as one of the hallmarks of our time. Also to be commended are the post-Marxists' commitment to the analysis of exploitation (not necessarily or preferably the specific variant based on the labour theory of value); Marxism's, and hence post-Marxism's, 'sensitivity to the multiple sites of oppression and unfairness' in the modern world (gender, ethnicity, age, location, etc. (p. 102); and more broadly, the capacity of this tradition to recognize diversity and difference without slipping, as post-modernists do, into moral *in*difference.

For all its emphasis on the linking of theory and action, Marxism is usually admitted to be a poor source of ideas relating to the field of moral philosophy. In grappling in his final section with the specifically ethical dimensions of the challenge of post-modernism, Corbridge therefore turns first to some contemporary scholars who have, as he puts it, interrogated the boundaries between development studies and moral philosophy, and then to the possibility of a radical reinterpretation of John Rawls's well-known arguments about justice in society. From the former and his own earlier account of the nature of modernity, he extracts a telling critique of the moral particularism that asserts that the needs and rights of 'distant strangers' can be a matter of moral indifference. From Rawls, transferred to the global stage and strengthened with some ideas from John Roemer's reworking of the theory of exploitation, Corbridge draws the conclusion that 'the present distribution of rewards and powers is unjust and can be shown to be unjust in ways that have definite, if not determinate, political implications' (p. 103).

CHAPTER 2

Reconsidering the explanandum and scope of development studies:
toward a comparative sociology of state–economy relations

Frederick H Buttel and Philip McMichael

When we initiated our graduate studies in the 1970s, neo-Marxisms in their several variants had become virtually hegemonic in setting the agenda of development studies and the sociology of development.[1] This was so much the case that, for all practical purposes, the most lively, interesting and provocative debates were those *within* neo-Marxism. Thus for erstwhile students of development whose point of entrée was sociology *tout court*, the choice of theoretical frameworks was, for all practical purposes, a choice of which neo-Marxist (or classical Marxist) perspective one would embrace.

Of course, not all sociologists of development at this time were neo-Marxists. In fact, probably a majority of persons in the field worked from a 'modernizationist', populationist or neo-Malthusian, or other non-Marxist perspective. Our point about the dominance of neo-Marxism is that the issues raised within neo-Marxist theories of development (e.g. whether the operations of transnational corporations (TNCs) and international development assistance institutions tended to reinforce 'underdevelopment' whether core–periphery relations tended to lead to the development of the former and underdevelopment of the latter) were the issues with which sociologists of development, regardless of their particular theoretical and methodological commitments, had to contend.

As much as neo-Marxism overshadowed all other rival theories in the 1970s – and we believe this still is more or less the case in the mid-1990s – there remained one dark-horse contender for dominance in the sociology of development, that of Chambers-style (1983) development practice. This perspective, of course, is not a theory as such, and in fact Chambers (1983) and many like-minded researchers are virtually contemptuous of the theoretical projects of their more scholastically inclined colleagues. None the less, at least on this side of the pond, an interest in development practice has been integrally linked to the sociology of development and to 'development studies'[2] in two ways: first, the lion's share of graduate students recruited into the sociology of development were, and continue to be, those whose original interest was in development practice and who felt they needed further training and graduate degree credentialling to operate effectively in this field; and second, the sociology of development has continued to be constituted in terms of its being simultaneously a scholarly field and an applied field. That is, the sociology of development has traditionally been a subdiscipline in which praxis is implicated intrinsically, on a relatively co-equal basis with scholarship, in the very constitution of this field and in which applied research is given more than lip-service.

We would note, by way of historical reflection, that the equation of scholarship in the sociology of development and development studies with development praxis was the case from the start, and has not been an injunction of neo-Marxism as such. What is now known as the sociology of development, development studies, and development practice emerged at about the time of the Korean War, on the terms of 'modernization theory'.[3] This timing was not accidental. The original forms of development theory were, in fact, intended to be sociologized prescriptions for international and Third World officialdoms for avoiding 'more Koreas' (and later 'more Vietnams') (see especially Phillips 1977). Development theory has always had an intrinsic referent of *praxis*, to be implemented, explicitly or implicitly, through the state (Hoogvelt 1978). Even in the mid-1990s, when the sociology of development exists in an uneasy tension with development practice – and this tension is certainly the greatest in the neo-Marxist tradition – there remains a strong imperative for development theory's litmus test to be whether 'it works in practice', can be useful to 'policy-makers', or can lead to the correct political line. This concern with praxis exists across the theoretical–political spectrum – that is ranging from modernizationist preoccupation with creating knowledge useful for policy-makers and/or with making development agency projects more effective, to debating how to achieve socialism on the periphery.

In this chapter we want to reflect on the 'impasse' of development sociology that was depicted in such an effective and provocative way by Booth (1985a). Booth's article and a number of commentaries on or related to his original contribution (Mouzelis 1988; Sklair 1988; Vandergeest and Buttel 1988; Corbridge 1990) have contributed to ferment in the sociology of development and development studies more generally. This has been a creative process, since development sociology's complacency had increased monotonically with the degree to which its theories had taken on pretensions to 'grandness' (i.e. as 'grand theory') through the 1970s and early 1980s. Booth's intervention has arguably been one of the most important stimuli to innovative efforts to reconstitute the field. Thus far, however, the foundations have not yet been laid for an enduring research agenda that is sociologically defensible.

We argue that there are several interrelated reasons why development sociology still has a crisis of confidence despite several years of introspection prompted by Booth's intervention. We begin with the claim that Booth (1985a) and other critics have tended to confine the diagnosis of the impasse of neo-Marxist development theories mostly to the matter of whether their explanatory frameworks are adequate (i.e. are non-functionalist, non-teleological, and 'non-necessitist'). This reflects the tradition in much of western theoretical discourse to see that the most crucial aspect of a theory is its explanatory framework. This is exemplified, for example, by the notion that the 'big three' classical theorists tended to examine approximately the same problematic: that of the antecedents and implications of capitalism and industrialization (as, for example, Giddens (1971) has noted with no small amount of persuasiveness). The classical tradition *is* extremely relevant to modern development sociology and development studies (Evans and Stephens 1988), but not in our view only, or even mainly, because of the fact that the classical theories developed rival frameworks for explaining what can essentially be taken as a common problematic. Indeed, it is our view that the hallmark of the nineteenth-century classical tradition is that Marx, Weber and Durkheim selected quite different problematics,[4] which in turn required quite disparate explanatory frameworks. The traditional western view of the relatively homologous problematics of the major classical theories, originally codified by Parsons (1937) with his claim of the convergence of Durkheim and Weber on the 'theory of action', has its legacy in contemporary development sociology, as we will stress later. The common problematic has traditionally been to understand the generic parameters of Third World development (in other words, to explain in what ways Third World formations are all fundamentally alike), and for this knowledge to be used (or be made available to those who wish to use it) for development practice.

Put somewhat differently, we believe that recent efforts to scrutinize the explanatory frameworks of contemporary neo-Marxist development sociology have touched on, but have not yet effectively grappled with, what we believe is a crucial matter: development sociology's *explanandum*. We shall suggest that reconsideration of the matter of explanandum, and its relation to development practice, is essential for refocusing development sociology and development studies.

We shall suggest that there should be two corner-stones to this reconsideration. The first is that development sociology should (ultimately) take as its central problematic that of accounting for diversity in Third World formations and in global social structures through comparative analysis. Our own preferred way of doing so would be to reconstitute development sociology as a branch of comparative-historical macro-sociology, with particular emphasis on its classical core: state-economy relations.

The second corner-stone for reconsideration is that development sociology and development practice should be (formally) separated. Sociological analysis of Third World development and social change can obviously have potential implications for development practice, but this is not, nor should it be, its principal *raison d'être*. That is, they should be seen as related but distinct areas of work, mainly on account of their different levels of analysis and different problematics.

In this chapter we shall touch briefly on how the two considerations of explanandum and the privileging of praxis relative to theory relate to other widely acknowledged shortcomings of development theories of the 1970s and early 1980s. These include particularly the tendency to deductivism and teleology (especially the tendency to focus empirical research on 'obstacles' to the realization of deductively generated stages or end-points of social change), the inability to resolve the issue of the primacy of society (or nation-state) versus 'world-economy' and the international state system, and the excessive Third Worldism of development theory.

Booth's critique of neo-Marxist development sociology

Booth's arguments

David Booth's (1985a) *World Development* article, and his parallel contribution in the Shaw volume (1985b), represents one of the major turning-points in scholarship in development sociology. Booth's critique carried particular weight because it came from a person who had for some years been closely identified with the neo-Marxist tradition and because it so succinctly diagnosed some of the major problems with neo-Marxist development sociology at a metatheoretical level. There had been and continue to be a good many critiques of the neo-Marxist tradition in development sociology from conventional ('modernizationist') quarters. But most of these modernizationist critiques have convinced the already-convinced (neo-Marxists) of little more than the fact that these critics are unaware of the nuances of the many variants of neo-Marxism. Booth's command of the literature and his authoritative commentary on its metatheoretical shortcomings made his two articles among the more widely read contributions to the field of the mid- to late 1980s.

We take the main thrust of Booth's arguments to be as follows. Neo-Marxist development sociology in its many variants – dependency, world systems, classical ('Warrenite'; Warren 1973) Marxism, modes of production – shares a common metatheoretical commitment to 'necessity' arguments. There are two major (presumably interrelated) variants of necessitism: that Third World development processes can be understood by deduction from Marx's concepts of the capitalist mode of production and laws of capitalist development (such as the self-expansion of capital as a unitary process), and that of the tendency to functionalism and teleology. We read Booth to stress (as in 1985b: 82) that his 'objection is not to the Marxist tradition as a whole', and that development sociology 'does not need to be purged wholesale of questions and lower-order concepts derived from Marx'.

The reception to Booth's claims

There have been a variety of responses to Booth's challenge to neo-Marxist orthodoxy in development sociology. One, of course, has been to reinforce the view among opponents of neo-Marxism that its failures in development sociology, which is arguably one of the areas of sociology in which neo-Marxism has been most influential, portend its over-all demise as a guide to serious scholarship. Another, related to the first, has joined Booth's critique of neo-Marxist development sociology with the 1980s preoccupation in social theory as a whole with 'agency' (e.g. Giddens 1979), to yield an 'actor-centred' sociology of development (e.g. Long and van der Ploeg 1988) that gives primacy to agency over struc-ture.[5] Both of these types of responses appear to read Booth's claims as evidence for the intrinsic determinism and economism of neo-Marxism (which, incidentally, we believe is a claim that Booth did not make, and one that is not necessarily warranted; Shanin 1983; Sayer 1987).

A third type of response, typified by Corbridge (1986; 1990), has been to take Booth's claims seriously on neo-Marxist grounds. In the conclud-ing passages of both of his articles Booth suggests that resolving the impasse of development sociology does not require abandonment of Marxism, but rather the recovery of Marxist traditions that avoid prob-lems of necessitism (i.e. determinism, functionalism, and so on) in the development sociology tradition. We consider this to be the essence of Booth's challenge, and we also find the latter response to be the most interesting and promising (and thus not only – or, we hope, mainly – out of stubborn commitment to political economy). In this chapter we want to contribute to the programme begun by Corbridge and others (e.g. Evans and Stephens 1988). It is our view, however, that the devel-opment sociology community must do so by examining some of the fundamental epistemological, ontological, and metatheoretical foun-dations of the field, including several dimensions that we feel were neglected by Booth and Corbridge.

Reconsidering the explanandum of development sociology

We feel that Booth's critique of neo-Marxist development sociology must be taken several steps further in order to come to grips with the impasse in development studies. We feel that several interrelated issues have not been sufficiently explored in late 1980s introspection in development sociology. We shall take up a number of these issues briefly.

What is development sociology? What is development?

Most development sociologists would tend to see the answers to these two questions as being self-evident. Others' eyes would glaze over when faced with the threat of another uninteresting discussion of how one should define 'development'. In our view, however, these matters bear serious discussion, but in ways that depart from their resolution in development theory and practice since the early 1970s.

Most development sociologists, regardless of theoretical stripe, would tend to define the field as the study of the processes that shape the course of Third World development, or even in more praxis-oriented terms such as the study of how to enhance Third World development. Accordingly, the field has been demarcated by rival definitions of what Third World development is (or what it should be, or how it should be defined). 'Development' is conventionally defined in some ostensibly objective way that, in actual practice, is explicitly or implicitly based on a normatively ordered conception of praxis. Recall in this regard that at the heart of the early neo-Marxist critique of modernizationism was the notion that modernization theories suggested misguided approaches to development practice (a particularly forceful statement of which was A G Frank's classic article, 'Sociology of development and underdevelopment of sociology', originally published in 1967 in *Catalyst* and reprinted as Chapter 2 of Frank 1969).

Thus, the modernizationist tradition has been to define development in terms of per capita national product or income, of the institutionalization of entrepreneurial capacities to engage in accumulation and reinvestment, and so on. But the modernizationist definition of development, and thus its problematic, is essentially a normative one: income growth in aggregate and in its distributive dimension, and the development of institutional capacity to reproduce the conditions for income growth and improvement in living standards, which are seen to be the self-evident referents for constructive 'developmental change' from a western point of view of the nature of the 'good society'. Neo-Marxist theories of the sort discussed by Booth are also based on a seemingly objective definition of development – normally, the extent or pace of capital accumulation or of the emergence of particular kinds of production relations – but are likewise rooted in normative questions such as the implications of these processes for social justice, particularly for the prospects of achieving socialism.

We would be the first to recognize that any ostensibly objective problematic, even the one we shall suggest later, has normative implications or presuppositions, and that application or praxis is a wholly legitimate focus of sociological work. In fact, we would go so far as to accede to a view that development sociology should properly be seen as historical analysis that is concerned, among other things, with establishing the preconditions for practice by demystifying official theory, official policy, and official 'accounts' or 'representations' of historical change and their implications for future interventions. But this conception of development sociology is distinct from development practice *per se*. The normative dimension of development sociology concerns the struggle over representations of the historical process. The normative dimension of the practice side, by contrast, involves concrete struggles for empowerment, delinking, social justice, and so on.

We would argue that the problematic or explanandum of development sociology has been shaped so centrally by particular praxis-related normative considerations – that is, by an agenda to accomplish certain social goals in the Third World – that its social scientific foundation has been seriously compromised. Among the compromises that concern us are the following.

First, development sociology has tended to be strongly Third Worldist in nature, with several typical consequences. One particularly important example is that the preoccupation with Third World dynamics to the exclusion of state–economy relations in the industrial centres and the world system as a whole leads to short-cuts, e.g. in the instance of dependency theory, an idealized view of ('articulated') post-war accumulation in the North (e.g. de Janvry 1981). This idealized view is clearly difficult to reconcile with cyclical phenomena such as the long economic downturn, the demise of 'Fordism', declining real wages, the 1970s decentralization of capital and industry, and related trends since the mid-1970s in the industrial-core countries. It is also difficult to reconcile with more longstanding dynamics such as the movement of transnational capital, and the associated subdivision and restructuring of both industry and agriculture, often geared to integrating production and circulation across national boundaries.

A second compromise of the privileging of development praxis is the tendency to reinforce an explicit or implicit theoretical agenda of generalizing about or across the Third World. The concomitant search for 'universals' in the 'development process', driven in part by the quest to develop transferable formulas for national development policy or subnational developmental strategy (see below), reinforces a problem – that of ahistorical typologism – alluded to by Booth (1985a; 1985b). As we shall stress later, there has been growing evidence that the empirical realities of state-economy relations are distinct across time and space; developmental theory that collapses these distinctions in striving for universal validity across the Third World is, in our view, inconsistent with these realities.

A third compromise is that of premature closure about the appropriate unit of analysis in the sociology of development. Development-practice inquiry essentially presupposes the national-state as the 'unit of development', and thus as the unit of analysis for inquiry (Phillips 1977). This is obviously the case with national development policy, but even local- and regional-level development practice (e.g. in which one seeks to 'develop' a village, or one assists in the empowerment of a community to take charge of local 'development') ultimately presupposes the national-state unit. Most subnational interventions are in fact modes of integration of regions and communities (via education, extension and other supportive policies; the quest for 'national demonstration effects'; the need to demonstrate viability in the national exchange economy) into the national polity, national discourse and the national 'project'. Arguably, Joel Migdal (1988), in his *Strong Societies and Weak States*, is unwittingly attesting to and prescribing this in his arguments about the limits that local strongmen, as colonial legacies, place on the reach of the state.

It is useful to note Anne Phillips's (1977) under-appreciated paper on the topic of how development theory has fundamentally presumed 'national development' as its problematic. She noted that under the conditions of the gold standard (which were those operating at the time of the 'invention' of post-war development theory), capital accumulation (that is 'development') required a stable national trade account in order to maintain low interest rates and therefore a favourable environment for capital. A stable trade situation in turn depended on national success in the world market. Thus, the ideal conditions for 'development' were those elaborated by the nation-state. Polanyi (1957), of course, has shown how we arrived at this international configuration. And Keynes presumably offered a theory of national regulation for managing this problem. In other words, viable capitalist development (and socialist development under the historical circumstances) depended ultimately on the nation-state. Post-war extension of the state system, via decolonization and within a US hegemonic field, was the context within which the real, and ideal, prescription for national development proliferated (Friedmann and McMichael 1989).

As we shall discuss at greater length later, the one comprehensive effort to transcend the national problematic in development theory has been that of Wallerstein. In one of his earliest articles on the topic, entitled 'A world-system perspective on the social sciences', originally published in 1976 in the *British Journal of Sociology* (and reprinted as Chapter 9 of Wallerstein 1979), Wallerstein dismembered post-war 'developmentalism' and its nationally ordered project. Unfortunately, Wallerstein went so far as to throw the state out with the bathwater. None the less, Wallerstein's critique of nationally ordered developmentalism is a potentially useful point of departure when shorn of its essentialism and reductionism *vis-à-vis* the national project and nation-state.

What is the explanandum of development sociology?

We have just commented on the fact that to the degree the field of development sociology is driven by some normative definition of development, there will be scholarly compromises. We have suggested that the two matters of the 'definition of development' and the explanandum of development sociology are by no means the same thing – and that, in fact, they should be seen as being separable. Normative judgements about what is or should be the desired course of development in the Third World tend to lead to several of the problems identified by Booth (necessitist, functionalist and teleological reasoning). Further, the explanatory deficiencies identified by Booth have an integral relationship to the false dualism of the national problematic and the primacy of the 'world-system'. Here we want to share some of our own ideas about how reconsidering the explanandum of development sociology may be important in revitalizing the field, particularly in transcending the national problematic without reifying the world-system and ignoring the role of states.

It is useful to begin this reconsideration by noting several tendencies in development sociology, among both neo-Marxists and non-Marxists. As noted earlier, the field is strongly Third Worldist in nature, which we believe derives from the field being constituted in terms of normatively driven definitions of Third World development and from its implication with international development practice. Second, there has been a strong tendency for rival versions of development theory to be focused on alternative conceptions of homology in Third World development experiences, that is to theorize why Third World formations are essentially similar. This tendency was initiated by 1950s modernization theory, based as it was on the premise of replicating the successful development experiences of the west, but was continued in neo-Marxist theories, which were mirror-imaged responses to the original modernizationist problematic.[6] Third, the common parameters of Third World social structure tend to be defined in implicit (though seldom in explicit) comparison with the advanced industrial countries. The overall tendency is thus a typological one, and moreover an ahistorical typologism. Finally, inquiry tends to be based on one or another essentialist account of developmental laws or tendencies, and accounts for deviations from these tendencies by way of identifying 'obstacles' that militate against their being realized in full-blown form.

By contrast, we believe that a late-twentieth-century development analyst cannot help but be impressed with the observation that 'the Third World' is undergoing a profound process of differentiation (though we do not wish to imply that there was some [idealized] 'starting-point' at which the Third World was 'undifferentiated'). That is, for example, the contemporary dynamics of the bulk of Sub-Saharan Africa vary enormously from those found in the Asian newly industrializing countries (NICs), or the bulk of Latin America for that matter (e.g. Portes and Kincaid 1989). Third World diversity and differentiation have been recognized for many years, and development theories have been taken to task for their inability to grapple with it (e.g. Hoogvelt 1982: 213–14). None the less, the theories surveyed by Booth, all of which are explicitly or implicitly based on theorizing the common properties of peripheral development, cannot help but fail to account for the unevenness of these processes and the variability in their outcomes.

It is thus our claim that the sociology of development must respond to this reality. This claim is, in and of itself, certainly not novel, as it has been stated and restated ritualistically by a wide range of scholars since the early 1980s, (and, as Corbridge (1990: 626) notes, having been recognized by none other than Margaret Thatcher in her reaction to the 'Brandt Report'). Whether it is a 'new reality' is a matter of debate and empirical inquiry.[7] None the less, we believe the more recent manifestations of Third World differentiation are sufficiently clear to dictate that a mature sociology of development must be focused on accounting for diversity of peripheral formations. Development sociology must therefore be comparative.[8] Accordingly, it must be historical – in a double sense: first, of recognizing the realities behind the typologies (that will need to be constructed to capture the diversity of historical trajectories), and second, attaining the kind of sociology of knowledge perspective needed to become more self-conscious about the 'production' of development theory.

We cannot think of a better way to begin this reorientation of development theory than to return to the classical tradition, with its emphasis on comparative analysis of large-scale social change and its focus on state, economy, class and cultural symbols. Our own preference is for the sociology of development to be construed as a branch of comparative-historical macro-sociology focused on comparative state–economy relations (including other factors, such as ideology and culture, that shape these relations), along the lines set forth in related literatures on large-scale social change (Polanyi 1957; Moore 1966; Skocpol 1979; Tilly 1984; Hall 1986; Mann 1986). As we shall suggest later, we believe that the changing relations between global and national state–economy relations, focused on their historically recursive interactions, have particular promise as development sociology's underlying problematic.

The national-state and world-system: a comparative strategy for synthesis

The comparative procedure we advocate, however, is by no means self-evident, though we believe it has significant primogenitors in the development sociology literature (broadly construed as suggested above). We note, with appreciation, some attempts to push forward the comparative sociology of development, particularly Evans and Stephens (1988) and Portes and Kincaid (1989). The Evans-Stephens paper is particularly noteworthy in its self-conscious attempt to go beyond development sociology's long tradition of Third Worldism. We suggest, however, that both of these efforts are focused on what can be called 'comparative *national* development', which involves a form of comparative inquiry – formal comparative analysis – that we believe is limited in transcending the dualism of nationally ordered and world-system-based inquiry.

Formal comparative inquiry is constructed in quasi-experimental terms, in which it is assumed that the units compared are both separate and replicate some universal process – for example, the process of 'national development'. The latter becomes, then, the subject of general, deductive theories, and the basis of stage-like typologies of social change. Cases are normally selected in order to mirror some form of non-recursive causal analysis (such as path analysis), and occasionally the number of cases can be sufficient to conduct formal quantitative analysis (see Booth's (1985b: 86, fn. 27) comments on this tradition of scholarship in development sociology). The procedure essentially is to juxtapose national societies assumed to be unrelated in time and space. This assumption emerged with evolutionary theories, 'in which national societies are self-contained systems with common ontogenic patterns . . . each replicating a common systemic process' (McMichael 1990: 389).

Alternatively, if we believe that social change at the national level has diverse and non-replicable forms, if only because nation-states emerged historically and relationally, then we need a different order of comparative analysis. Thus, where our units of comparison are neither separate nor uniform, our comparative strategy must address the historical context and character of the nation-state. That is, comparison must be fashioned to illuminate historical processes that both generate, and account for, diversity.

One theory that does attempt to posit a relation between theoretically general processes and historically particular outcomes is world system theory (see Hopkins and Wallerstein 1981). In this theory the modern world system pivots on the antinomy between a single world economy and a multiplicity of states, structured according to their position in the global hierarchy of commodity-producing labour. Here, individual states are products of the expansive and competitive dynamic of the world economy (for example, various colonial and post-colonial formations obtained their specificity through metropolitan competition over markets and resources). The competitive logic of the hierarchical division of labour by definition rules out replication across individual states of a common process of development. That is, they are not comparable units as such. They are, however, comparable as systemic units, since they embody the systemic dynamic of hierarchical competition. That is, they can be compared as members of systemic zones (core, periphery, semi-periphery), and as manifestations of systemic processes.

This comparative strategy is unsatisfactory, however, because it accounts for diversity among nation-states only in functional terms. That is the behaviour of the individual units essentially demonstrates, and cannot do more than demonstrate, the existence of 'the system' (Bonnell 1980: 165). Tilly has termed this strategy 'encompassing comparison', involving comparisons that 'select locations within [a large] structure or process and explain similarities or differences among those locations as consequences of their relationships to the whole' (1984: 123). To adopt this strategy is to proceed with the 'world system' as an uncontested unit of analysis, whose origins remain entirely ambiguous (cf. Brenner 1976). On the one hand, the concept of the 'capitalist world-economy' is an ideal-type constructed to distinguish the modern world system from prior world empires (Wallerstein 1974a). On the other hand, the capitalist world-economy is understood as a historical system (Wallerstein 1974b) 'whose future is inscribed in its conception' (Howe and Sica 1980: 255). In other words, the unit of analysis is simultaneously taken as a historical given, at least for the era giving rise to social theory. The theory thus repeats the determinism of liberal, modernization theory, albeit at an elevated plane. Analogously, the comparative strategy remains one-sided, this time geared to generalization about systemic, rather than national, processes of development.

We would resolve this problem by suggesting an alternative form of comparison that avoids reifying either national or international units. Just as world-system theory works with a preconceived whole, so formal comparative-analytic procedures presuppose 'cases as wholes, and they compare whole cases with each other' (Ragin 1987: 3). The key to an alternative method, then, is that comparison would become the substance of the inquiry instead of its framework. It has two requirements: first, ensuring that the units of analysis are historical, and therefore fluid, concepts; and, relatedly, second, addressing the question of historical context by employing the idea of an emergent whole. Here, the units are not subordinated (and compared) as parts to a concrete whole; rather, they are understood as world-historical and active entities in their own right. Totality is in this sense a conceptual procedure, rather than a conceptual premise. It is a conception of an immanent totality, where the whole emerges in and through the parts, without privileging either.

This procedure distinguishes between a historical science and an experimental science (cf. Arrighi and Hopkins 1987: 32). It recovers Marx's historical method from the intervening positivist interpretations of Marx, which misconstrue his use of abstraction, and reduce the theory to natural-science-like models (cf. Sayer 1987). Marx's historical method involved the process of conceptualizing social categories as 'a rich totality of many determinations and relations' (Marx 1973: 100). For example, the concept of 'wage labour' (as a relation of 'capital') was not simply an empirical concept. Its emergence was conditioned principally by peasant dispossession and the formation of states and a world market integrating (and increasingly governing) a variety of forms of labour. That is, these various dimensions rendered 'wage-labour' a historically concrete social category. It could not be conceptualized adequately *in situ* simply as an empirical, passive social aggregate. And despite the fact that wage labour was neither the majority, nor a homogeneous, form of labour, Marx developed its concept not just to record and predict proletarianization as a trend in itself, but to organize analysis of the regime of capital, to put it briefly. That is, the theory of capital includes tendential arguments tempered by the contradictory dynamic of agency and structure inherent in the emerging labour–capital relation. An exemplary presentation of this dialectic is Arrighi's (1990) study of the contradictory world-historical process of proletarianization, governed by the fiction of labour as simply a commodity, as maintained by Marx.

This historical method of conceiving categories relationally incorporates comparison substantively in the differentiation of parts and of part/ whole relations. Here, parts express, constitute and modify the whole. For example, comparative analysis of the NICs from this perspective would relate the NIC phenomenon to the realignment of North–South relations and the fragmentation of the South itself (cf. Harris 1986).[9] Conception of the whole is necessarily comparative in the sense that its components or units, such as national formations, are understood as varied conditions and outcomes of a self-forming whole (Kosik 1976). Whereas conventional comparison treats these units as parallel cases, 'incorporated comparison' understands them as components of a broader, integrated process. We maintain that incorporated comparison provides a potentially more satisfactory approach to the comparative analysis of development among nation-states, as members of a dynamic system of states within a shifting world-economic context.

We hasten to add that our adopted term, 'incorporated comparison', is not a new approach, since it implicitly informs historical inquiry from Marx through Polanyi to various modern exponents of the historical method (see McMichael 1990). As a research strategy it can compare units diachronically and/or synchronically. That is states could be compared as members of a continuously evolving configuration of the state system in and across time, or they could be compared as differentiated units within a competitive global conjuncture, where variation is in and across space. Combining both dimensions in varying proportions (depending upon the type of inquiry) is the most fruitful procedure. Contemporary processes of international integration reorganizing space and time dimensions of social change (Harvey 1989) virtually demand comparative analysis in these terms.

We shall attempt to illustrate the application of this approach, particularly in its combination of synchronic and diachronic research, in the case of ongoing work on agro-food systems. Agro-food systems have been selected for inquiry for several reasons. Agriculture has been central to the national problematic, by way of the long tradition of an idealized view of complementary intersectoral linkages between agriculture and industry that can be achieved by, and make possible, 'articulated' accumulation.[10] Agriculture is obviously of central importance to peripheral countries, and much of development practice consists of attempts to construct 'national agricultures' in Third World countries.[11] In addition, agriculture remains salient politically in the advanced countries and in geopolitical fora, and in world market terms, as the recent problems in GATT negotiations over the EC's recalcitrance in phasing-out agricultural subsidies attests to. Finally, there has been insufficient attention to the important role played by agro-food systems in the transition from the colonial to the 'national movement' in the world economy and state system in the late nineteenth century, and in the current crises of national economy in both core and periphery in the late twentieth century. Here we can give only the most sketchy account of this work, though we hope it helps to illustrate the possibilities of combining synchronic and diachronic strategies of analysis.

In a summary of the trajectory of world agriculture, Friedmann and McMichael (1989) relate the uneven development of the state system since 1870 to capital accumulation and concentration in the agro-food sector, leading to its progressive industrialization. Location of this latter process in the settler states has a double significance. The resulting agro-industrial complex presented a new competitive model of national economy in a world economy traditionally organized around colonial divisions of labour, hence reinforcing the development of the nation-state system as a diachronic process. In a synchronic process, the post-war rise of US hegemony internationalized the US agro-food complex (via state policy, corporate strategy and technological transfer), subdividing and restructuring agriculture across the world, resulting in highly uneven forms of state protection and increasing incoherence in national agricultures.

This research has been focused around the concept of 'food regime', which links international relations of food production and consumption to forms of accumulation (Friedmann 1987). The first food regime was centred on European imports of wheat and meat from the settler states, between 1870 and 1914, during which the colonial movement was culminating in European rivalry over empire and a division of industrial and agricultural labour between metropolitan states and colonies. At the same time, the settler states were undergoing rapid expansion, propelled in part by investments from and agricultural exports to the European powers. Settler agricultural exports underwrote European accumulation and the developing wage-relation, and simultaneously provided the impetus for the rise of the nation-state system, in which the relation between agriculture and industry became one of sectors internal to each national economy (rather than agriculture being a largely residual precapitalist, or a colonial export, sector).

The second food regime has been an intensive one of industrialization of agriculture and food (through use of industrially produced inputs by farmers, and industrial processing of agricultural raw materials). Like the earlier food regime characterized by tension between colonialism and the rise of the nation-state system, the second food regime has been implicated in two opposing movements of the state system and global economy. The first was decolonization, which broke up the colonial trading blocs (and their politically constructed division between metropolitan/industrial and colonial/agricultural labour), and completed the international state system. Decolonization was contradictory *vis-à-vis* Third World countries' agro-food systems, in that it was typically accompanied by imports of cheap grains from the west (to maintain cheap food prices and subsidize industrialization), while at the same time striving to develop national agriculture (e.g. through the green revolution) and an articulated economy (through import-substitution industrialization as a means of escaping their position as primary commodity exporters) in the image of the west. In tension with extension of the state system, and the model of articulated national economy, to the former colonies, was the state-assisted movement of transnational restructuring of agricultural sectors by agro-food capitals, a movement initiated by US support of agribusiness extension into Europe via the Marshall Plan (Cleaver 1977). This was accompanied by *intra*sectoral integration through global sourcing across international borders, particularly in durable foods and intensive meat production (Friedman 1991). Transnational restructuring of the agro-food system proved to be contradictory to the extension of the interstate system in the ex-colonies because of its progressive undermining of the possibilities of articulation or complementarity between agriculture and industry there.

Following this line of argument, further comparative analysis of national development styles/options would elaborate the political and economic forces internationalizing agricultural and food systems in the late twentieth century. For example, transnational corporate strategies of 'substitutionism' (cf. Goodman *et al.* 1987) displace tropical products, and create new possibilities for non-traditional, low-value export crops (as industrial inputs) among Third World states (Friedmann 1991). Whereas the first movement against tropical products deepened the post-war international division of labour in food production (where the First World specialized in capital-intensive production of grain and oilseed crops, and the Third World specialized in a labour-intensive horticultural crops and land-extensive commodities such as cattle), the second movement appears to reinforce the possibility of a reversal of this division of labour, prefigured by the current crisis in First World (especially US) agriculture (Buttel 1989). From another angle, under the direction of agencies such as the International Monetary Fund (IMF) and World Bank, transnational finance capital is restructuring some Third World states in such a way as to institutionalize world, rather than domestic, market-oriented agricultural strategies and to reinforce configurations in the international division of agricultural labour that undermine the viability of Third World national agricultural and food sectors (McMichael and Myhre 1991). These various processes illustrate some of the mutually conditioning national and international forces that (comparatively) implicate a variety of development patterns and possibilities at the national level.

In summary, the goal of 'incorporated comparison' is to blend theory and history in such a way as to avoid abstract individuality (e.g. perceiving national formations or forms of labour in isolation), and abstract generality (e.g. perceiving the state system essentially as a set of states differentiated according to their position in a global labour hierarchy). World-historical comparative analysis of national formations would understand the unity in diversity, and the relation between each, without reifying either the global, or the national level of social change. In so far as it operates with units of analysis specified in time and place, incorporated comparison can provide the basis for a sociology of development that transcends the limits of linear and deductive approaches.

Beyond Third Worldism

Finally, we wish to make a few brief points about the implications of our preceding arguments for 'Third Worldism' in development sociology. We have contended there is ample evidence that the divergent paths taken by various Third World formations have their origins in recursive interactions of both national phenomena and dynamics (class and state structures, resource endowments, and so on) and global dynamics (world economy, geopolitics, international regimes), in which 'national responses' are shaped by, and reshape, the global whole.

The tradition in most quarters of development studies has been to conceptualize these relationships in relatively reductionist terms, for example the expanding 'reach' of TNCs, extraction of surplus from core to periphery (dependency), propulsion of the self-expansionism of capital (Warren), diffusion of technology and social values that undergird income growth (modernization), and so on. We believe these relations are both undertheorized and underresearched. Corbridge (1990), among a few others, has placed particular stress on innovative neo-Marxist[12] strategies for theorizing national-state/global relations (regulation, neo-imperialism) which have significant implications for development sociology's Third Worldist character. Thus, not only must there be greater attention paid to conceptualizing how one does comparative research – on national formations in a global context, without succumbing to reification of the national formation or global formation – the sociology of development cannot be divorced from observation on the 'core' formations and their dominant institutions. Knowledge about core formations can be pursued not only through comparative analysis (e.g. Evans and Stephens 1988), but also by researching the global interrelationships referred to earlier (some notable, but diverse examples of which are Edwards 1985; Krasner 1985; Jenkins 1987; Goodman and Redclift 1989).

Conclusion

We have attempted to demonstrate that development sociology, while it has profited from the ferment generated by Booth's (1985a; 1985b) interventions, has yet to come to grips with several interrelated issues: its problematic or explanandum, and its connections with development practice. Our suggestions in this regard – to see development sociology and development practice as distinct areas of inquiry, and to focus development sociology on explaining Third World diversity through comparative analysis – may also help to resolve some other weaknesses of the field (its deductivism, excessive Third Worldism, and tendency to reify either the national state or world-system).

We hope that our arguments will be construed at two levels. On the one hand, we have presented a diagnosis of some theoretical problems in the sociology of development that may resonate with the concerns and insights of other scholars. On the other, we have presented a particular way of resolving some of these problems about which we have no illusions of persuasiveness. Our efforts on this second score, for example, will no doubt fail to find a receptive audience among those who insist on the primacy of an actor-centred point of view, or among those who want to reconcile academic rigour and relevance to development praxis, especially among those who thought that Booth had buried Marx and political economy once and for all. None the less, we believe that the two central focuses of this chapter cannot be ignored in development sociology, and hope that our observations may be useful in this regard.

Notes

1. While we shall often use the expressions 'sociology of development' (or 'development sociology') and 'development studies' synonymously – in part, because in the current state of affairs they are seen as being actually, or at least potentially, synonymous, and following Booth's (1985a) usage – they should be seen as being overlapping but distinct. That is, the sociology of development is a branch of the larger sociological field of social change in which specific (though not exclusive) attention is given to social change in peripheral areas, while development studies is the field in which sociological, anthropological, etc., approaches to social change focused on peripheral areas are treated in a more or less interdisciplinary manner. We shall also suggest later that development sociology and development studies should be seen as distinct from development practice, which is an applied, eclectic (mostly) social science field that is empirically driven (i.e.

in terms of 'what works'). It should be noted that one of the reasons that the sociology of development and development studies have the coherence they do is because of the predominance of neo-Marxisms within development studies' constituent disciplines.

2. See note 1 about how we define development studies in relation to the sociology of development. Note, however, that in the US context development studies as such tends to be subordinate to the sociology of (and other disciplinary approaches to) development, to area studies (e.g. Latin American studies, South East Asian studies), and to development practice. This contrasts with the situation in much of Europe, particularly the UK, where development studies is a recognized 'interdiscipline' with its own departments and PhD training programmes, and thus its own career tracks.

3. We recognize, following Harrison (1988), that there have been several distinct varieties of modernizationist thought in development studies. None the less, we shall treat modernization theories as a single category, given the fact that they exhibit metatheoretical commonalities, much like Booth has depicted with respect to neo-Marxist theories.

4. In very brief form, these were, respectively: how can we account for the transition from one mode of production to another? How can we account for the fact that capitalism developed initially in the Occident? How is it possible to achieve social solidarity as the division of labour advances? Note that one might identify several other problematics in Weberian sociology such as the origins and consequences of western rationalism, or even more basic ones such as why do people do what they do (they act out of material and ideal interests) and why do people obey (they tend to see domination as legitimate authority). None the less, the point remains that the problematics of the classical theorists, while implicated in parallel transitions in nineteenth-century Europe, were quite different.

5. While beyond the scope of this chapter, we are not sanguine about the durability of actor-centred alternatives to structural theories in the sociology of development. Actor-centredness can be a useful methodological tool if employed in a manner similar to Weber's approach in constructing historically framed ideal-types that combine structural properties with a conceptualization of orientations to action within that structure (e.g. Weber's ideal-types of domination). But as the skeleton of development theory, an actor-centred perspective cannot transcend the teleology of 'adaptive strategies', i.e. the procedure of identifying individual and household practices, which because they exist are held to be 'adaptive'.

6. For example, the dependency critique of modernizationism's optimism about replicating in the ex-colonies an idealized version of the western path of development was the mirror image of modernizational theory: positing a comparable universal tendency to stagnation, and thus of the generalized barriers or obstacles to replicating the western development experience in the Third World. The modes of production perspective and Warrenite classical Marxism (and associated lines of thought such as Brenner 1976) were further mirror images (of dependency and world-systems), as each generated an essentialist conception of whether the character of peripheral capitalism was conducive to vibrant capital accumulation by way of critique of another essentialist viewpoint. Corbridge (1986; 1990) refers to mirror-imaging as 'oppositionism'.

7. Our own view is that peripheral differentiation has been in evidence for many decades. The problem is not so much 'new realities' of peripheral development experiences as the fact that theory has lagged, particularly

following the rupture (from the 1970s) of the belief in the certainty of capitalist advance of the kind apparent in the long post-war boom.

8. The necessary comparative dimension of the sociology of development is among the reasons why it is in some respects orthogonal to development practice, which by necessity is normally predicated on national-level analysis.

9. The key point to make about diversity is that, understood as the increasing heterogeneity of the Third World, it is a property that derives from the intensification of global capital circuits (from the 1970s) within a pre-existing geopolitical structure that privileged certain regions and states via the creation of a sub-imperial network. See, for example, A G Frank's (1979) useful comparative analysis of South Africa, Brazil, Mexico, Argentina, India, Iran, Israel, and other countries, which in some cases (e.g. Korea) discontinued the colonial legacy, and in others simply offset 'development' costs with food, military or economic aid.

10. Much development theory, in fact, sees the very distinction between advanced or core economies and underdeveloped or peripheral ones as being based on an assumption that the former exhibit 'articulation' (that is, the principal motor of growth derives from intersectoral exchanges, for example between farm and non-farm industry, producer and consumer goods industries, rural and urban sectors) while the latter do not (Amin 1974; de Janvry 1981).

11. One outcome of our analysis of the transition of the late-twentieth-century food regime which space prevents us from summarizing here is the fact that national construction of agriculture in the Third World within the frame of articulated development or accumulation is generally precluded, especially under conditions of 'debt stress'. The illusion of being able to do so, however, is nurtured within contemporary development practice due to its (intrinsic) commitment to the national problematic.

12. Also, Corbridge (1990), among others, has helped to establish some of the parameters by which neo-Marxism can be blended with other traditions, such as substantivist economic sociology (Polanyi 1957; Block 1990) and neo-Weberianism (e.g. Becker 1987), and Shanin's (1983) provocative interpretation of the 'late Marx', to yield a 'post-Marxism'. Corbridge (1990: 625–7) has also provided the rudiments of a sociology of knowledge on the 'production' of development theory that we believe are extremely useful in taking stock of the field and pointing the way to promising future directions. Though fans of Corbridge's approach, we remain sceptical whether his advocacy of the category of 'post-modern' is useful in capturing the current anarchy of the world economy.

References

Amin S (1974) *Accumulation on a world scale*. New York, Monthly Review Press.

Arrighi G (1990) Marxist century, American century: the making and remaking of the world labour movement. *New Left Review* 179.

Arrighi G and **Hopkins T K** (1987) Theoretical space and space for theory in world-historical social science. In Wiley N (ed) *The Marx–Weber debate*. Newbury Park, CA: Sage.

Becker D G *et al.* (1987) *Postimperialism*. Boulder, CO, Lynne Rienner

Block F (1990) *Postindustrial possibilities*. Berkeley, CA, University of California Press

Bonnell V E (1980) The uses of theory, concepts, and comparison in historical sociology. *Comparative Studies in Society and History* 22

Booth D (1985a) Marxism and development sociology: interpreting the impasse. *World Development* 13

Booth D (1985b) Marxism and development sociology: interpreting the impasse. In: Shaw M (ed) *Marxist sociology revisited*. London, Macmillan

Brenner R (1976) The origins of capitalist development: a critique of neo-Smithian Marxism. *New Left Review* 104

Buttel F H (1989) The US farm crisis and the restructuring of American agriculture: domestic and international dimensions. In: Goodman D and Redclift M (eds)

Chambers R (1983) *Rural development*. Harlow, Longman

Cleaver H (1977) Food, famine and the international crisis. *Zerowork* 2

Corbridge S (1986) *Capitalist World Development*. Totowa, NJ, Rowman & Littlefield

Corbridge S (1990) 'Marxism and development studies: beyond the impasse. *World Development* 18

Edwards C (1985) *The fragmented world*. London, Methuen

Evans P B and **Stephens J D** (1988) Development and the world economy. In Smelser N J. (ed) *Handbook of sociology*. Beverly Hills, CA, Sage

Frank A G (1969) *Latin America: underdevelopment or revolution?* New York, Monthly Review Press

Frank A G (1979) Unequal accumulation: intermediate, semiperipheral, and sub-imperialist economies. *Review* 2(3)

Friedmann H (1987) Family farms and international food regimes. In: Shanin T (ed) *Peasants and peasant societies*. Oxford, Basil Blackwell

Friedmann H (1991) Agro-industry and export agriculture. In: Friedland W H *et al.* (eds) *Toward a new political economy of agriculture*. Boulder, CO, Westview Press

Friedmann H and **McMichael P** (1989) Agriculture and the state system: the rise and decline of national agricultures, 1870 to the present. *Sociologia Ruralis* XXIX(2)

Giddens A (1971) *Capitalism and modern social theory*. Cambridge, Cambridge University Press

Giddens A (1979) *A contemporary critique of historical materialism*. Berkeley, CA, University of California Press

Goodman D and **Redclift M** (eds) (1989) *The international farm crisis*. New York; St Martin's Press

Goodman D, Sorj B and **Wilkinson J** (1987) *From farming to biotechnology*. Oxford, Basil Blackwell

Hall A (ed) (1986) *States in history*. Oxford, Basil Blackwell

Harris N (1986) *The end of the Third World*. London, I B Tauris

Harrison D (1988) *The sociology of modernization and development*. London, Unwin Hyman

Harvey D (1989) *The condition of postmodernity*. Oxford, Basil Blackwell

Hoogvelt A M M (1978) *The sociology of developing societies*. London, Macmillan

Hoogvelt A M M (1982) *The Third World in global development*. London, Macmillan

Hopkins T K and **Wallerstein I** (1981) Structural transformations of the world-economy. In: Rubinson R (ed) *Dynamics of world development*. Beverly Hills, CA, Sage

Howe G N and **Sica A M** (1980) Political economy, imperialism, and the problem of world system theory. In: McNall S G (ed) *Current perspectives in social theory*. Westport, CT, JAI Press

de Janvry A (1981) *The agrarian question and reformism in Latin America*. Baltimore, MD, Johns Hopkins University Press

Jenkins R (1987) *Transnational corporations and uneven development*. London, Methuen

Kosik K (1976) *Dialectics of the concrete: a study on problems of man and world*. Dordrecht, Holland, D Reidel Publishing

Krasner D (1985) *Structural conflict*. Berkeley, CA, University of California Press

Long N and **van der Ploeg, J D** (1988) New challenges in the sociology of rural development. *Sociologia Ruralis* XXVIII(1)

McMichael P (1990) Incorporating comparison within a world-historical perspective: an alternative comparative method. *American Sociological Review* 55

McMichael P and **Myhre D** (1991) Global regulation vs the nation-state: agro-food systems and the new politics of capital. *Capital and Class* 43

Mann M (1986) *States, war and capitalism*. Oxford, Basil Blackwell

Marx K (1939/1973) *Grundrisse*. New York, Vintage.

Migdal J S (1988) *Strong societies and weak states*. Princeton, NJ, Princeton University Press

Moore B (1966) *Social origins of dictatorship and democracy*. Boston, MA, Beacon

Mouzelis N (1988) Marxism or post-Marxism? *New Left Review* 167

Parsons T (1937) *The structure of social action*. Glencoe, IL, Free Press

Phillips A (1977) The concept of 'Development'. *Review of African Political Economy* 8

Polanyi K (1957) *The great transformation*. Boston, MA, Beacon

Portes A and **Kincaid D** (eds) (1989) Comparative national development. Special issue, *Sociological Forum* 4(4)

Ragin C (1987) *The comparative method: moving beyond qualitative and quantitative methods*. Berkeley, CA, University of California Press

Sayer D (1987) *The violence of abstraction: the analytic foundations of historical materialism*. Oxford, Basil Blackwell

Shanin T (1983) *Late Marx and the Russian road*. New York, Monthly Review Press

Sklair L (1988) Transcending the impasse: metatheory, theory, and empirical research in the sociology of development and underdevelopment. *World Development* 16

Skocpol T (1979) *States and social revolutions*. New York, Cambridge University Press

Tilly C (1984) *Big structures, large processes, huge comparisons*. New York, Russell Sage

Vandergeest P and **Buttel F H** (1988) Marx, Weber, and development sociology: beyond the impasse. *World Development* 16

Wallerstein I (1974a) The rise and future demise of the world capitalist system: concepts for comparative analysis. *Comparative Studies in Society and History* 16

Wallerstein I (1974b) *The modern world-system, I*. New York, Academic Press

Wallerstein I (1979) *The capitalist world-economy*. New York, Cambridge University Press

Warren B (1973) Imperialism and capitalist industrialisation. *New Left Review* 81

CHAPTER 3

Heterogeneity, actor and structure:
towards a reconstitution of the concept of structure

Norman Long and Jan Douwe van der Ploeg

In recent years a great deal of effort has been expended attempting to reconcile structural with actor-oriented analysis of development processes. Much of this work, however, has been vitiated by the failure to reformulate the essential concepts of such a proposed marriage. One central debilitating feature of this unconsummated union has been the naïve assumption that one can simply integrate concepts of 'actor' and 'structure' drawn from earlier theoretical texts into some new framework or synthesis without reconstituting them in any significant way. This applies especially to ideas of structure and structural determinants or constraints, but also pertains to the use of notions of actor and agency.[1]

This chapter opens up this issue again and argues the case for the injection of a more thorough-going and better theorized actor-oriented approach which, by offering a new conceptualization of structure, can help to surmount this theoretical impasse. Although we illustrate our arguments by reference to agrarian phenomena, we believe that what we have to say has important implications for the development of more adequate sociological theorization of development and social change.[2] The chapter concludes by distancing actor-oriented concepts and research from neo-populism as reflected in the now fashionable work on participatory research methods and farmer-first strategies.

Structural models of development

Before explicating the meta-theoretical foundations of an actor-oriented analysis, it is necessary to provide a brief schematic overview of structural models of development. Despite obvious differences in ideology and theoretical trappings, the two dominant structural models, modernization and neo-Marxist theory, contain paradigmatic similarities. These provide the clue to certain common analytical weaknesses.

Modernization theory visualizes development in terms of a progressive movement towards technologically and institutionally more complex and integrated forms of 'modern society'. This process is set in motion and maintained through increasing involvement in commodity markets and through a series of interventions involving the transfer of technology, knowledge, resources and organizational forms from the more developed world or sector of a country to the less developed parts. In this way, traditional society is propelled into the modern world and gradually, though not without some institutional hiccups (i.e. what are often designated social and cultural obstacles to change), its economy and social patterns acquire the accoutrements of modernity.

On the other hand, neo-Marxist theories stress the exploitative nature of these processes, attributing them to the inherent expansionist tendency of world capitalism and to its constant need to open up new markets, increase the level of surplus extraction and accumulate capital. Here the image is that of capitalist interests, foreign and national, subordinating (and probably in the long run destroying) non-capitalist modes or relations of production and tying countries into a web of economic and political dependency. Although the timing and degree of integration of countries into the world political economy have varied, the outcome is structurally similar: they are forced to join the brotherhood of nations on terms determined not by themselves but by their more wealthy, and politically more powerful, industrial partners. Although this neo-Marxist theory contains within it a variety of schools of thought, in essence the central message remains much the same; namely, that the patterns of development can best be explained within a generic model of capitalist development on a world scale.[3]

These two perspectives represent opposite positions ideologically – the former espousing a so-called liberal standpoint and ultimately believing in the benefits of gradualism and the trickle-down effect, and the latter taking a so-called radical stance and viewing development as an inherently unequal process involving the continued exploitation of peripheral societies. Yet, on another level, the two models are similar in that both see development and social change emanating primarily from centres of power in the form of intervention by state or international interests and following some broadly determined developmental path, signposted by stages of development or by the succession of dominant modes of production. These external forces encapsulate the lives of people, reducing their autonomy and in the end undermining indigenous or local forms of co-operation and solidarity, resulting in increased socio-economic differentiation and greater centralized control by powerful economic and political groups, institutions and enterprises. In this respect it does not seem to matter much whether the hegemony of the state is based upon a capitalist or socialist ideology: similar tendencies towards increasing incorporation and centralization occur.

Both models then are tainted by determinist, linear and externalist views of social change.[4] Our summaries of their viewpoints simplify and perhaps caricature their arguments, but a careful reading of relevant literature will, we believe, bear out the conclusion that they share a common set of paradigmatic beliefs. This contention is also supported by a recent analytical comparison of the commercialization (i.e. modernization) and commoditization schools in the study of agrarian development (see Long and van der Ploeg 1988; Vandergeest 1988).

An actor-oriented paradigm

Although less well articulated in the literature on development until relatively recently, there has always been a kind of counterpoint to structural analysis. This is what we call the actor-oriented paradigm. Underpinning (either explicitly or implicitly) this interest in social actors is the conviction that, although it may be true that certain important structural changes result from the impact of outside forces (due to encroachment by the market or the state), it is theoretically unsatisfactory to base one's analysis on the concept of external determination. All forms of external intervention necessarily enter the existing life-worlds of the individuals and social groups affected, and in this way are mediated and transformed by these same actors and local structures. Also to the extent that large-scale and remote social forces do alter the life-chances and behaviour of individuals, they can do so only through shaping, directly or indirectly, the everyday life experiences and perceptions of the individuals concerned. Hence, as James Scott (1985) expressed it:

> Only by capturing the experience in something like its fullness will we be able to say anything meaningful about how a given economic system influences those who constitute it and maintain or supersede it. And, of course, if this is true for the peasantry or the proletariat, it is surely true for the bourgeoisie, the petite bourgeoisie, and even the lumpenproletariat. (Scott 1985: 42)

A more dynamic approach to the understanding of social change is therefore needed which stresses the interplay and mutual determination of internal and external factors and relationships, and which recognizes the central role played by human action and consciousness.[5]

One way of doing this, perhaps, is through the application of actor-oriented types of analysis that were popular in general sociology and anthropology around the late 1960s and early 1970s. Actor-oriented approaches range from transactional and decision-making models to symbolic interactionist and phenomenological analysis. One advantage of the actor approach is that one begins with an interest in explaining differential responses to similar structural circumstances, even if the conditions appear relatively homogeneous. Thus one assumes that the differential patterns that arise are in part the creation of the actors themselves. Social actors are not simply seen as disembodied social categories (based on class or some other classificatory criteria) or passive recipients of intervention, but active participants who process information and strategize in their dealings with various local actors as well as with outside institutions and personnel. The precise paths of change and their significance for those involved cannot be imposed from outside, nor can they be explained in terms of the working out of some inexorable structural logic, such as implied in de Janvry's (1981) model of the 'disarticulated periphery'.[6] The different patterns of social organization that emerge result from the interactions, negotiations and social struggles that take place between the several kinds of actors. These latter include not only those present in given face-to-face encounters but also those who are absent but who nevertheless influence the situation, affecting actions and outcomes. Having said this, however, it is necessary to underline the shortcomings of several kinds of actor-oriented approach promoted in the 1960s and 1970s, especially by anthropologists (see Long 1977: 105–43). In an attempt to combat simple culturalist and structuralist views of social change, these studies concentrated upon the innovative behaviour of entrepreneurs and economic brokers, on individual decision-making processes or on the ways in which individuals mobilized resources through the building of social networks. Yet many such studies fell short because of a tendency to adopt a voluntaristic view of decision-making and transactional strategies which gave insufficient attention to examining how individual choices were shaped by larger frames of meaning and action (i.e. by cultural dispositions, or what Bourdieu (1981: 305) calls *habitus* or 'embodied history', and by the distribution of power and resources in the wider arena). And some studies foundered by adopting an extreme form of methodological individualism that sought to explain social behaviour primarily in terms of individual motivations, intentions and interests.[7]

Another brand of actor-oriented research – especially prevalent among political scientists and economists, but also taken up by some economic anthropologists (such as Schneider 1974) – is that which uses a generalized model of rational choice based on a limited number of axioms, such as the maximization of preferences or utility. While the above types of actor analysis tend to treat social life and especially social change as essentially reducible to the constitutive actions of individuals, the rational choice approach proposes a universal model whose 'core features encode the fundamental properties of human behaviour' (Gudeman 1986: 31). The principal objection to this, of course, is that it offers an ethnocentric western model of social behaviour based upon the individualism of 'utilitarian man' which rides roughshod over the specificities of culture and context.

The central importance of the concept of agency

In an attempt to improve on earlier formulations, many writers have turned back to reconsider the essential nature and importance of human agency. This notion lies at the heart of any revitalized social actor paradigm and forms the pivot around which discussions aimed at reconciling notions of structure and actor revolve. But before recounting these discussions, it is important to stress that the question of agency has not simply been confined to a circle of theorists and their sociological audience but has also penetrated recent empirical work in anthropology

(Smith 1989), political science (Scott 1985), policy analysis (Elwert and Bierschenk 1988) and history (Stern 1987).

In general terms, the notion of agency attributes to the individual actor the capacity to process social experience and to devise ways of coping with life, even under the most extreme forms of coercion. Within the limits of information, uncertainty and the other constraints (e.g. physical, normative or politico-economic) that exist, social actors are 'knowledgeable' and 'capable'. They attempt to solve problems, learn how to intervene in the flow of social events around them, and monitor continuously their own actions, observing how others react to their behaviour and taking note of the various contingent circumstances (Giddens 1984: 1–16).

Giddens (1984: 9, 14) points out that agency refers not to the intentions people have in doing things – social life is full of different kinds of unintended consequences with varying ramifications – 'but to their capability of doing those things in the first place. ... Action depends upon the capability of the individual to "make a difference" to a pre-existing state of affairs or course of events'. This implies that all actors (agents) exercise some kind of power, even those in highly subordinate positions; as Giddens (1984: 16) puts it, 'All forms of dependence offer some resources whereby those who are subordinate can influence the activities of their superiors'. And in these ways they actively engage (though not always at the level of discursive consciousness) in the construction of their own social worlds, although, as Marx (1962: 252) cautions us, the circumstances they encounter are not simply of their own choosing.

It is important to emphasize that agency is not simply an attribute of the individual actor. Agency, which we recognize when particular actions make a difference to a pre-existing state of affairs or course of events, entails social relations and can become effective only through them. Agency therefore requires organizing capacities; it is not simply the result of possessing certain cognitive abilities, persuasive powers or forms of charisma. The ability to influence others or to pass on a command (e.g. to get them to accept a particular message) rests fundamentally on 'the actions of a chain of events each of whom translates it in accordance with his/her own projects . . . and power is composed here and now by enrolling many actors in a given political and social scheme' (Latour 1986: 264). In other words, agency (and power) depend crucially upon the emergence of a network of actors who become partially, though hardly ever completely, enrolled in the projects and practices of some other person or persons. Effective agency then requires the strategic generation/manipulation of a network of social relations and the channelling of specific items (such as claims, orders, goods, instruments and information) through certain nodal points of interaction. Clegg (1989) puts it thus:

> To achieve strategic agency requires a disciplining of the discretion of other agencies: at best, from the strategist's point of view, such other agencies will become merely authoritative relays, extensions of strategic agency (Law 1986:

16). Whatever interests such relay-agencies might have would be [in an extreme case] entirely those that they are represented as having by the strategically subordinating agency. (Clegg 1989: 199)

In order to accomplish this, it becomes essential for social actors to win the struggles that take place over the attribution of specific social meanings to particular events, actions and ideas. Looked at from this point of view, particular intervention models (or ideologies) become strategic weapons in the hands of the institutions and personnel charged with promoting development.

Recognizing that actors are loci of decisions and actions, Hindess (1986: 115–19) takes the argument one step further by pointing out that the reaching of decisions entails the explicit or implicit use of 'discursive means' in the formulation of objectives and in presenting arguments for the decisions taken. These discursive means or types of discourse vary and are not simply inherent features of the actors themselves: they form part of the differentiated stock of knowledge and resources available to actors of different types. Since social life is never so unitary as to be built upon one single type of discourse, it follows that, however restricted their choices, actors always face some alternative ways of formulating their objectives and deploying specific modes of action.

It is important to note here that the recognition of alternative discourses used by or available to actors challenges both, on the one hand, the notion that rationality is an intrinsic property of the individual actor, and, on the other, the idea that it simply reflects the actor's structural location in society. All societies contain within them a repertoire of different lifestyles, cultural forms and rationalities which members utilize in their search for order and meaning, and which they themselves play (wittingly or unwittingly) a part in affirming or restructuring. Hence the strategies and cultural constructions employed by individuals do not arise out of the blue but are drawn from a stock of available discourses (verbal and non-verbal) that are to some degree shared with other individuals, contemporaries and maybe predecessors. It is at this point that the individual is, as it were, transmuted metaphorically into the social actor, which signifies the fact that social actor is socially constructed rather than simply a synonym for the individual or a member of homo sapiens. One needs also to distinguish between two different kinds of social construction associated with the concept of social actor: first, that which is culturally endogenous in that it is based upon the kinds of representations characteristic of the culture in which the particular social actor is embedded; and second, that which arises from the researchers' own categories and theoretical orientation (also of course essentially cultural in that it will probably be associated with a particular school of thought and a community of scholars).

The social construction of actors is, then, underpinned metatheoretically by the notion of agency. But although we might think that we know perfectly well what we mean by knowledgeability and capability – the two principal elements of agency identified by Giddens – these concepts must be translated culturally if they are to be fully meaningful.

One should not therefore, presume (even if one can, for example, pr)duce evidence of increasing commoditization and westernization) a constant, universal interpretation of agency across all cultures. It is bound to vary in its cultural make-up and rationality. Because of this we need to reveal what Marilyn Strathern (1985: 65) calls the 'indigenous theories of agency'. Notions of agency are constructed differently in different cultures and in different segments of the same society; for example, among peasants and urban populations, or within the bureaucracy, church and army.

Such differences underline the importance of examining how notions of agency (knowledgeability/capability) are differently constituted culturally and affect the management of interpersonal relations and the kinds of control that actors can pursue *vis-à-vis* each other. In the field of rural development, this means analysing how differential conceptions of power, influence, knowledge and efficacy may shape the responses and strategies of the different actors (e.g. peasants, development workers, landlords and local government officers). One should also address the question of how far notions of agency, which differ according to the type of policy being promoted, can be imposed on local groups. Here we have in mind, for example, the concepts of 'participation', 'targeting the poor' or 'the role of the progressive farmer' in planned development.[8]

While the quintessence of human agency may seem to be embodied in the individual, single individuals 'are not the only entities that reach decisions and act accordingly. Capitalist enterprises, State agencies, political parties and church organizations are examples of social actors: they all have means of reaching and formulating decisions and of acting on at least some of them' (Hindess 1986: 115). But, as Hindess goes on to argue, the concept of actor should not be used to cover collectivities, agglomerates or social categories that have no discernible way of formulating or carrying out decisions. To suggest, for example, that 'society' in the global sense of the term, or classes and other social categories based on ethnicity or gender, make decisions and attempt to implement them is to attribute mistakenly to them the qualities of agency.[9] It also tends towards reification of classificatory schemata that form part of an individual's or organization's conceptual apparatus for processing the social world around them and upon which basis action takes place. We should be careful therefore to restrict our use of the term 'social actor' only to those social entities that can meaningfully be attributed with the qualities of agency.

The foregoing discussion has, we hope, clarified why the concept of agency is of central theoretical importance. As we suggested earlier, an actor-oriented approach begins with the simple idea that different social forms develop under the same or similar circumstances. Such differences reflect variations in the ways in which actors attempt to come to grips, cognitively and organizationally, with the situations they face. Therefore an understanding of differential patterns of social behaviour must be grounded in terms of 'knowing, active subject[s]' (Knorr-Cetina 1981: 4), and not merely viewed as due to the differential impact of broad social forces (such as ecological or demographic variation, or differential incorporation into world capitalism). A main task for analysis, then, is to identify and characterize differing actor strategies and rationales, the conditions under which they arise, their viability or effectiveness for solving specific problems, and their social outcomes. The last aspect raises several additional key issues, among others, the need for some notion of emergent structures which come into existence as the combined results of the intended and unintended consequences of social action. We shall return to this later on in the chapter.[10]

The theoretical significance of an actor perspective for the analysis of agrarian development

Applied to the understanding of agrarian change, the actor-oriented approach stresses the importance of giving weight to how farmers themselves shape the patterns of agrarian development. Although their choices are often limited by a lack of critical resources, they should not be seen as the passive recipients or victims of planned change, nor as so routinized that they simply follow laid-down rules or conventions. Like other actors, farmers devise ways of dealing with problematic situations and creatively bring together resources (material and non-material – especially practical knowledge derived from past experience) in an effort to resolve these. They also try to create space for their own interests so that they might benefit from, or, if need be, neutralize, intervention by outside groups or agencies. Indeed, as Goran Hyden (1980) observes for Tanzania, peasant cultivators remain largely uncaptured by the state, since it is extremely difficult for central government to enforce its rule on semi-independent, partly self-provisioning, households (see Moore 1973 and Spittler 1983 for a similar point of view). It is also – as James Scott (1985: 304–5) so colourfully reveals in his Malaysian monograph on peasant truculence, irony and non-compliance – an almost impossible task for dominant classes to impose their own vision of a just social order, not only on the behaviour of subordinate classes, but on their consciousness as well. In short, the latter continue operating their own projects, even if these are merely counter-images of the template propagated by the former.

As we have already pointed out, a common assumption of actor-oriented models of the 1960s and early 1970s was the notion that different social patterns may develop within the same structural circumstances. It was left to later work to show the general theoretical significance of this for the study of agrarian change (see e.g. DeWalt 1979: 9–22; Bennett 1980; Long 1984; and van der Ploeg 1990). The central issue here, as DeWalt puts it in his study of a Mexican *ejido*, is to explain how

intracultural variation in adaptive strategies of production among these people constitutes, in effect, a pool of behavioral possibilities (Pelto and Pelto 1975: 14). Some of these possibilities will become more widespread in years to come, others will disappear completely, and still others will continue to attract a minority of adherents. (DeWalt 1979: 268–9)

It remains the task of the researcher, then, to investigate the reasons for these differential patterns and to pinpoint their organizational and other consequences.

Agricultural development is a many-sided, complex and contradictory process that confronts the researcher with several complicated issues, such as how to relate heterogeneity to the aggregation problem and how to deal with micro–macro relations. In our research programme at the Agricultural University of Wageningen we have been trying over the years to tackle some of these methodological problems.

A key characteristic of our work is that it seeks to understand heterogeneity. It does not, however, analyse variation from the point of view of deviation from some average, optimum or generic model, based either on market principles (as we find in micro-economics, e.g. Bennett and Kanel 1983: 217–31, and also in neo-Marxist theories, e.g. Friedmann 1981; Gibbon and Neocosmos 1985; Bernstein 1986) or on other normative criteria (as in structural-functionalism; see van Velsen 1964 for a critique). In these standard approaches such models are assumed to provide a yardstick for explaining (we would prefer to say explaining away!) the exceptions. Instead an actor perspective starts with the assumption that different farmers (or categories of farmer) define and operationalize their objectives and farm management practices on the basis of different criteria, interests, experiences and perspectives. That is farmers develop, through time, specific projects and practices on how their farming is to be organized. Quite often these projects (which entail models for action) are, as it were, responses to other projects formulated for instance by state agencies or agribusiness. The outcome of this whole gamut of practices reflects itself in the impressive heterogeneity of agriculture, which can be analysed into clusters of specific styles of farming (Hofstee 1985; van der Ploeg 1990), each style being the *opus operatum* of farmers' projects.

A large-scale survey in Italy covering a ten-year period indicated that within homogenous agricultural regions, where the same general economic, institutional, technological and ecological conditions pertained, there was an increasing diversity among family farms. As depicted in Figure 3.1 (which considers the relationship between scale and intensity), some farms realized a persistent (and largely self-sustained) process of ongoing intensification, while others, operating under exactly the same objective conditions, tended towards a gradual increase in scale and relative extensification. An explanation of such striking differences in terms of conventional approaches to the analysis of agrarian structure proved to be unsatisfactory (see van der Ploeg 1986). Instead a more convincing explanation was to be found in the strategic, goal-oriented action of farmers, their organizational responses to everyday life circumstances and to the network of relations that they and other actors constructed between their farming enterprises, markets and

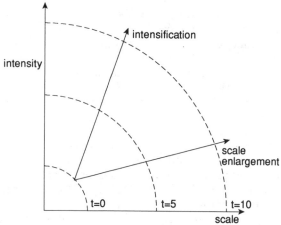

Figure 3.1 Diversity of response among family farms (*Source*: van der Ploeg, 1986).

market agencies. High levels of commoditization and institutionaliz-ation were related to the tendency towards scale enlargement, whilst higher degrees of autonomy *vis-à-vis* the economic and institutional environment were related to intensification of agricultural production grounded mainly on an increase in the quantity and quality of farm labour. Hence it was not markets as such, nor the institutions impinging upon farming enterprises, but rather the multiple and highly variable interrelations established between farms and their economic and insti-tutional environment that turned out to be decisive. Such 'extended' relations of production could not be viewed as a disembodied set of external conditions, since they were the outcome of the ongoing interac-tions and struggles occurring between the specific actors involved.

Styles of farming and classification struggles

Research on Dutch dairy farming highlights a further important point. This is that the articulation of the farm with the politico-economic en-vironment cannot be understood either within a methodological-individualist framework which conceptualizes farmers as independent decision-makers, or within a structuralist framework which gives pri-macy to how external forces shape farming practice. When confronted with questions of scale and intensity, farmers are able – when asked to do so – to make explicit the social distinctions they use to give meaning to the many differences they perceive within local farming practice. Representing these interpretations as a cognitive 'social map' helps us to visualize different styles of farming which are accorded relative pos-itions and given specific verbal categorizations (see Figure 3.2). This social map recalls the earlier, well-known work of Bennett (1980: 210–

16), but with one major difference. While Bennett's (1980: 214) folk classification contained a diagonal 'competence value axis', so that the top-right of the matrix was positively valued and the bottom-left negatively, such a normative ordering was missing among Dutch dairy farmers, suggesting that they considered each style to be equally valid as a model for farming practice.

This is not, of course, to deny that battles are being fought out (openly or in an indirect and implicit way) to advance particular social interests and images (what Bourdieu 1984: 479–84 calls 'classification struggles'). Rather the point is that there is no consensus over 'the best way to farm': most farmers are convinced all styles of farming are legitimate and can generate good incomes and long-term perspectives. They also emphasize that it is above all state policy that is critical for the future of farming in general and for their own farms in particular, and that the main points for debate and conflict are first, how the market as a set of economic opportunities is to be organized, second, how technology development, necessarily involving designs that fit better with particular styles of farming, is to be controlled, and third, how legislation (entailing the specific distributions of rights, benefits, sanctions and hindrances) is to be developed. They are, that is, concerned with issues relating to the interrelations, accommodations and conflicts that arise between their projects and those of the state. Hence they ask themselves such questions as: which farmers' projects correspond best with government plans? Will the organization of markets, technology development and legislation continue to have as its pivotal centre the self-defined 'optimal farmer', or will some differentiation emerge that creates room for manoeuvre for 'pioneers' or 'thrifty farmers' whose farm-development patterns dovetail more adequately with considerations of ecology and landscape preservation?

These, then, are the issues at stake for farmers and farmers' organizations. Needless to say, state agencies and their personnel engage in similar classification struggles in an attempt to promote their own definitions and projects. State agencies tend to be heavily committed to the principles of mainstream farm economics as well as to techno-centrism, making unilinear projections about external parameters such as market expansion, competitiveness, technological progress, scale enlargement and cost reduction.[11] From this they derive the model of the 'vanguard farm', generally identified as the modern, large-scale and highly intensified enterprise, and corresponding closely to the farmers' category of 'optimal farmers'. During the last decades this has become the normative yardstick for the design of agrarian policy and the elaboration of current classification schemes by state agencies in the Netherlands. According to this scheme, vanguard farms are followed by 'medium farms' (which are assumed to be at a midway point on the same growth path as vanguard farms) and an amorphous group of so-called 'small farms'.

Although we cannot enter into details here, the classification schemes applied by state agencies interrelate in specific ways with various farmer projects, while the nature of these relations increasingly becomes an

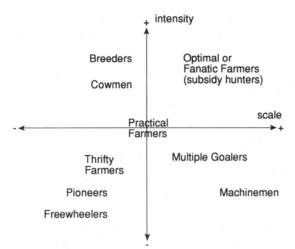

Figure 3.2   A social map of styles of farming (*Source*: derived from studies on dairy farming in the Veenweiden and the Achterhoek in the Netherlands: van der Ploeg and Roep 1990, and Roep *et al.*, 1991).

object of debate and struggle. The classification schemes used by state agencies, which agribusiness also adopts for its own purposes, provide grids for resource allocation among the different farm types. Exercising considerable power – especially when their projects converge and re-inforce each other – state agencies and agribusiness groups funnel resources so as to achieve a positive fit with the patterns or styles of farming they wish to promote. In this way, particular classification schemes promoted by the state and agribusiness (often supported by the agrarian sciences) are turned into socio-political or politico-economic projects aimed at organizing farming practice, internal farm–enterprise relations (de Rooij 1992) and the relationship of farm enterprises to external markets and institutions.

Such projects – which imply specific distributions of potentialities and restrictions (economic, legal, technological and socio-cultural) – have an undeniable impact on the farming population. Especially in retrospect, they seem so strong that they are often elevated or reified to assume the status of a structure *sui generis*. Hence the projects of state agencies and agribusiness are taken for granted (and/or interpreted as an expression of universal processes) and the mechanisms through which they operate are defined as representing a *modus operandi* with the power to deter-mine or shape farming practice. In this way a direct link is posited between 'structure' and 'conduct', policy and outcomes, thus obscuring the important point that particular 'structures' in fact comprise (i.e. are produced and reproduced through) the interlocking of specific projects and practices.

This raises the following important question: do these actively con-structed relationships and mechanisms (mistakenly represented as structure *sui generis*) indeed function as a template? That is do they indeed mould in an unavoidable and determinate way the practice of farming?

Clearly the answer is no. Empirical patterns in agriculture cannot be reduced to a hard, structurally determined core, with certain 'archaic remnants' continuing to induce second order deviations. Heterogeneity in agriculture entails not only the adoption or application of farming models proposed by state and other intervening agencies, but also a wide range of actively generated modifications, transformations, reactions and alternatives, as illustrated in Figure 3.2. These modifications and reactions, as well as the search for new strategies, emerge out of existing styles of farming, farm practices and social relations, which they simultaneously reproduce or transform.

From this highly complex interplay of organizational strategies, particular sets of emergent relationships and properties arise which, in turn, become important boundary-setting and orientation points for the actors involved. These emergent features define elements of the arenas in which particular projects are articulated, and through this articulation, they mould the further development of the projects themselves.[12] This moulding effect should not be visualized as uniform.[13] Nor does it carry within it an intrinsic logic of its own. Rather, it implies the existence of discontinuities that generate a variety of social and cultural forms (see Barth 1981: 129–30).[14] It is here, we believe, that the significance of interface analysis lies (Long 1989: 221–43; see also Hawkins 1991: 279 on interface networks).

It is, therefore, not only the state and agribusiness (macro-actors as Mouzelis (1991: 38) would probably describe them) that develop, promote and try to realize their specific projects. The same evidently occurs, as we emphasized above, among those who, from a structuralist perspective, are considered to be most negatively affected or 'marginalized' by so-called macro-actors. Different styles of farming represent a number of differently constructed farmers' projects. The anticipation of what other actors might do is a central and strategic element in these projects. That is to say, the whole gamut of styles, as they are realized in a particular context, constitutes a kind of cultural repertoire composed of a range of potential responses to trends and changes in markets, technology and policy. Farmers' projects are not just simple reactions to those that are prima-facie imposed by more powerful external actors. They are actively managed as differential responses to the strategies and circumstances generated by others, which they modify, transform, adopt and/or counteract.

It is precisely at this point that the question of power enters into the analysis. Power in fact is intrinsic to the elaboration, adaptation and reproduction of projects, and is a crucial element in strategic action. Projects crystallize along two essential dimensions – the cognitive and the organizational. Moreover, it is in the process of forming coalitions with, or distantiating one's own project from those of others, that power relations become critical.

This leads us to propose a rethinking of the notion of structure along the lines suggested by Berger and Luckmann (1967: 48), namely that relevant structural forms can be identified in the complex encounter of projects (or what they call 'social typifications') and in the variable patterns of interaction actively established between the actors concerned.[15] Let us illustrate this with the example of European farming where nearly all units of production, reproduction and consumption are based on a carefully managed tension between, on the one hand, resources controlled and reproduced relatively autonomously, and on the other hand, resources derived from external markets and hence at least partially controlled by market agencies.

This tension implies not only 'a pool of behavioural possibilities' but also the strategic management of resources which enables farmers to choose to align or distantiate their particular projects with or from those propagated by state institutions and agribusiness. That is the projects and practices of farmers, state officials and representatives of agribusiness can interlock in a variety of ways – both in the conceptualizations that underpin projects and in their enactment. Indeed it is through this highly variable interlocking of projects that agency manifests itself (as we argued earlier, agency signals the capacity to organize social relations in such a way that a pre-existing state of affairs or course of events is reshaped). It is through this interlocking that particular projects become effective and multiple social forms are produced, reproduced and transformed.

Using the folk concepts delineated in Figure 3.2, one could elaborate at length the specific ways in which farmers' and other actors' projects interlock in Dutch agriculture. Suffice it here, however, to offer a few observations (for details, see Roep *et al.* 1991).

'Optimal' or 'fanatical' farmers tend to align their particular projects with those propagated by state agencies and agribusiness interests; that is to quite a large degree they internalize the views expressed by these actors. This is clearly reflected in the parameters used for planning and evaluation at farm level; and the same goes for their farming practices, which are geared towards achieving high levels of intensity and scale enlargement. Congruent with this heavy enrolment in external projects is the folk concept of 'subsidy hunters', a label frequently applied to them by other farmers.

External alignments of this type generate a pattern of necessities and requirements within the farm enterprise. Dependence upon external finance, leading to indebtedness, and reliance on various forms of management and specialized advice (e.g. on cattle breeds) spur such farmers to expand continuously along particular lines, which, in the end, simply reconfirm already established relations and farm practice – even though in itself each farm represents a specific set of adaptive responses. Thus, optimal farmers must not be viewed simply as the captives of an external structure. They engage in a chain of decisions which draws them into specific sets of social relations of production and which ensnares them in particular farming logics. If 'captured', they are captured by the specific projects they themselves have created and by the way they have linked their own projects to those of other actors.

The same holds for multiple goalers, freewheelers, cowmen, and so on, who, in contrast to optimal farmers, actively distantiate their projects from the discourse and strategies of state agencies and agribusiness. They organize their relations with markets, technology development and agrarian policy in ways that differ markedly from the patterns found among their fanatical colleagues. On a material level, the intertwining with markets – reflecting differential levels of commoditization – is strikingly different (i.e. less systematized). And the same is true of the use they make of different forms of socially regulated exchange and resource-mobilization, as well as of the search for and active realization of alternative modes of farming.

To cut a long story short, the existence of widely varying styles of farming within a common context points to the need to acknowledge 'multiple realities' that are embedded in and simultaneously reproduce and transform their own specific 'structures', each being a result of the active linking or distantiation of different projects and practices.

The issue of causation and externalities

Although clear interrelations between styles of farming and specific sets of social relations of production can be discerned, it is nevertheless impossible to construct unilinear causal patterns in which these styles emerge as the direct 'effects' of particular 'causes'. Take commoditization, which is clearly linked to both the direction and rhythm of growth at farm-enterprise level (Long *et al.* 1986).

With high levels of commoditization, as market and price relations penetrate deeply into the core of the process of production, the objects of labour, instruments and labour force appear increasingly as commodities in the labour process itself. Hence, market dependency becomes an empirical phenomenon. The development of highly commoditized farms is not only conditioned by market relations, but also emerges right away as apparently determined by these relations. That is specific styles are indeed grounded in a market logic. But does this imply that the market is to be understood as the cause of these specific styles? And are these styles to be understood as unilinear products of those markets? Evidently this is not the case, since alongside these highly commoditized 'optimal farmers', other styles of farming exist based on greater autonomy *vis-à-vis* the market (van der Ploeg 1986; 1990).

Hence, within a given economic context, several different styles of farming are likely to be found, some closely linked to markets and others sufficiently distanced from them to allow considerable room for manoeuvre. Thus, markets as such are not to be understood as causal factors explaining the particularities of farming practice. Moreover, an increase or decrease in commoditization on the farm can seldom be treated as an 'unintended consequence', let alone the blind result of overwhelming economic forces. Market relations are at least mediated, if not actively sought after and constructed, by the actors themselves. Some farmers actively distantiate their labour process from the market, others engage in, what Ranger (1985) has termed 'self-commoditization'.

That is, the so-called causal links themselves are actively constructed in such a way by farmers so that they fit with given styles of farming.

Thus the explanation for specific social practices and styles of farming inevitably returns to consider these practices themselves. Social practice does not have a clearly distinguishable *explanandum*, nor does it in itself constitute a simple *explanans*. In farming at least, the two fuse: a style of farming is, in the end, its own explanans. It is a socially constructed *modus operandi* and, simultaneously, the *opus operatum*.

The same applies to technology and other possible social relations of production. Introduced technology can be considered and hence treated as a blueprint for an ongoing reorganization of farming so that the latter corresponds with the assumptions and requirements built into the technological design; but it can equally be deconstructed in order to be combined selectively with other, more local elements so as to fit better within a given style of farming (instead of reorganizing farming so as to fit better with the new technology).

We would like to stress here that the foregoing discussion should not be taken to imply that markets, state institutions, technology, ecology and other so-called externalities are irrelevant for the analysis of farming practice and the heterogeneity contained in it. The point is simply that such factors are not relevant as 'determinants' or causes. It depends rather on whether they are considered as self-evident limits beyond which action is judged to be inconceivable or as boundaries that are targets for negotiation, reconsideration, sabotage, and/or change, that is as barriers that have to be moved (Bourdieu 1984: 480). A major complication is that the translation of economic, institutional and technological parameters into specific forms of farm-enterprise development are increasingly the object of interventions aimed at representing these external parameters as indeed self-evident and internalized limits. That is, they are objectified and represented as guiding, if not coercive, structures that form part of the game and that are linked (directly or indirectly) to specific interests and projects.

It is at this point that the agricultural and social sciences come to play a crucial role. The agrarian sciences, for instance, are no longer (as was the case with traditional agronomy) concerned with the knowledge of agricultural production in all its empirical variety. These sciences (including rural sociology) have become increasingly identified with the technological sciences. They are engaged in the production of a continuous flow of models that indicate how farming ought to be (re-)organized, while at the same time showing a chronic ignorance (and delegitimation) of farming as a highly diversified social practice and of the specific empirical agronomic and technical models that accompany it. This makes agrarian science one of the most important forces in the arena of farming. It is through such science that new practices are presented and legitimized as the only correct way, with the consequence that other practices are assessed as less scientific. This is even more the case where scientific designs are adopted by development agencies (e.g. set up by industry, the national state and the EC) as guidelines for their specific actions.

Deconstructing planned intervention

As indicated in the foregoing discussion, the specific 'projects' (using this in the broader sense of models for action) of state agencies often play a crucial role in development processes. Such projects are objectified in many studies as the structural expressions of class relations, of the logic of accumulation or of state–peasant relations. Such interpretations we find extremely simplistic; we have argued that the whole notion of planned intervention needs deconstructing so that it is seen for what it is – namely an ongoing, socially constructed and negotiated process, not simply the execution of an already specified plan of action with expected outcomes (Long and van der Ploeg 1989). Furthermore one should not assume a top-down process as is usually implied, since initiatives may come from below as much as from above.

We argue, therefore, that one should focus upon intervention *practices* as shaped by the interaction among the various participants, rather than simply on intervention *models*, by which we mean the ideal-typical constructions that planners or their clients have about the process. Using the notion of intervention practices allows one to focus on the emergent forms of interaction, procedures, practical strategies, and types of discourse and cultural categories present in specific contexts. The central problem for analysis becomes that of understanding the processes by which external interventions enter the life-worlds of the individuals and groups affected and thus come to form part of the resources and constraints of the social strategies they develop. In this way external factors become internalized and often come to mean quite different things to different interest groups or to the different individual actors, whether implementers, clients, or bystanders.

In 1986 we initiated new field research in order to explore some of these intervention issues. The research focused upon irrigation organization, actor strategies and planned intervention in western Mexico. We aimed to contribute to several fields of practical and theoretical interest: the development of an interface approach which analyses the encounters between the different groups and individuals involved in the processes of planned intervention; the study of peasant-based development initiatives and the ways in which local actors (including 'frontline' government personnel) attempt to create room for manoeuvre so that they may pursue their own 'projects';[16] and the development of an actor-oriented approach to the study of irrigation and water management problems.[17]

The project constituted a co-ordinated team effort, requiring detailed field investigations in different localities and arenas of action. In order to research these themes in an integrated manner, we adopted an actor-oriented methodology.[18] This had certain implications for how we conceptualized the central analytical issues. In the first place, we started with an interest in irrigation organization, not irrigation systems. This implied a concern for how various actors or parties organized themselves around the problems of water management and distribution. It meant going beyond the analysis of the physical and technical properties of the different systems of irrigation to consider how different interests, often in conflict, attempted to control water distribution or to secure access to it and to other necessary inputs for irrigated agriculture. From this point of view, irrigation organization emerges as a set of social arrangements worked out between the parties concerned, rather than simply dictated by the physical layout and technical design, or even by the controlling authorities who built and play an important role managing the system. Irrigation organization, then, is not to be equated with an organizational chart or organigram; it is made up of a complex set of social practices and normative and conceptual models, formal and informal.

The second dimension was the question of actor strategies. This concept was central to our research because we aimed to interpret agricultural and social change as an outcome of the struggles and negotiations that take place between individuals and groups with differing and often conflicting social interests. As we have shown in the European examples given earlier, strategy is important for understanding how producers and other rural inhabitants resolve their livelihood problems and organize their resources. The concept entails that producers and householders actively construct, within the limits they face, their own patterns of farm and household organization and their own ways of dealing with intervening agencies. The same holds true for government bureaucrats or company brokers: they too, attempt to come to grips organizationally and cognitively with the changing world around them by devising strategies for pursuing various personal and institutional goals, and the same applies to day-labourers, even though in their case the constraints on choice may be more severe.

The third issue explored was the nature of planned interventions. This covered both formally organized state-agency intervention and that of the companies and enterprises that attempted to organize and control production and marketing of key agricultural products. As we indicated above, this path of research stressed the importance of looking at the interactions that evolved between local groups and intervening actors. Intervention is an ongoing transformational process that is constantly reshaped by its own internal organizational and political dynamic and by the specific conditions it encounters or itself creates, including the responses and strategies of local and regional groups who may struggle to define and defend their own social spaces, cultural boundaries and positions within the wider power field.

This type of theoretical approach entails an understanding of wider social phenomena, since many of the choices perceived and projects pursued by individuals or groups will have been shaped by processes outside their immediate arenas of interaction. However, it rejects simple causative notions such as the logic of commoditization, the hegemony of state power, the subsumption of the peasantry and the primacy of the laws of capitalist development – and perhaps even the notion of the market itself.

On heterogeneity, 'projects' and the concept of structure

Actors' projects are realized within specific arenas, such as those shaped by market, state/peasant, agribusiness/peasant, or farmer/farmer-representative relations. That is each project is articulated with other actors' projects, interests and perspectives. This articulation is strategic in that the actors involved will attempt to anticipate the reactions and possible strategies of the other actors and agencies. The setting up of coalitions and/or the distantiation of particular actors *vis-à-vis* others is an intrinsic part of this strategic action.

The various arenas in which farming interests are pursued contain what Benvenuti (1991) characterizes as quasi-structures, such as, for example, a centrally regulated structure of commodity relations or particular networks of state agencies commanding authoritative and allocative power. The point, however, is that these 'structures', as they are often called, are not disembodied entities, nor do they have a unilinear and uniform, structuring effect on agricultural practice.

In social science there is a strong tendency to equate the notion of structure with that of the *explanans*, so that structures are conceptualized as specific sets of driving forces, which, it is postulated, 'explain' certain phenomena. Such a procedure is, of course, justified by positing some notion of an abstracted generic mode or set of 'normal conditions'. That such a procedure is basically inadequate (and even more so in times of turmoil and change), we hope now goes without saying.

What is needed, then, is a thorough deconstruction of the notion of structure. Its reconstitution, however, cannot be undertaken in isolation. It necessarily entails explicating the notions of agency (i.e. actors and their projects) and heterogeneity. The first requirement is, as outlined before, a definite adieu to structure understood as explanans. This is especially urgent where 'structure' is visualized as a set of external forces or conditions that delineate and/or regulate specific modes of action, thought to be required or necessary, while other modes are defined as impossible (it is here that determinism is rooted).

The argument applies also to more historical approaches that search for a kind of structural explanation situated in the past. History never relates in a unilinear or uniform way to the present and future. As Kosik (1976) has made clear, their relation is essentially dialectical, involving both the possible and the real. History always contains more than one possibility, where the present is the realization of just one of these. And the same holds for the interrelations between the present and the future. The decisive thing is what Kosik calls *praxis*, or what we have described as the process by which actors' projects and practices interlock and interact to produce emergent forms or properties. It is through this struggle (which involves both strategic actions and the drawing upon a repertoire of discourses and modes of argumentation) that certain possibilities are excluded and others made possible or realized.

It has been argued that an actor-oriented methodology neglects 'social relations' and/or the 'wider structural setting'. This we strongly oppose. What we object to is, as we suggested above, the notion of structure as explanans. Such a notion of structure amounts to nothing more than a reification of what are considered to be 'central tendencies' and, as soon as heterogeneity is introduced into the analysis, this 'structural approach' withers away. On the other hand, it is important to emphasize that our critique does not imply that we deny the significance of social relations of production, or wish to dispense with the concept of social relations of production. Rather our emphasis is on the question of how these specific social relations are constructed, reproduced and transformed. In more substantive terms, structure can be characterized as an extremely fluid set of emergent properties, which, on the one hand, results from the interlocking and/or distantiation of various actors' projects, while on the other, it functions as an important point of reference for the further elaboration, negotiation and confrontation of actors' projects.

Understanding structure in this way, as the product of the ongoing interlocking, interplay, distantiation and mutual transformation of different actors' projects, is not to say that structure should be conceptualized simply as the aggregation of micro-episodes, situations or projects. It would be clearly nonsensical to argue that the operation of, for example, commodity markets or capitalist economic institutions generally could be meaningfully described or accounted for *solely* by observing the behaviour of individual buyers and sellers, or capitalists and international financiers taken individually. Marx rightly emphasizes the existence of certain structural conditions that make possible the processes of capitalist production and exchange. However, it would equally be nonsensical to claim that the operation of such commodity markets and institutions could be accounted for by neglecting completely the actors involved. It is in fact only through the interlocking of specific actors' projects (e.g. simultaneous plans to buy and to sell specific goods or services) that a commodity market as such emerges and is reproduced.

Let us present, for the sake of argument, one recent example. In the years prior to 1985, a large and relatively new commodity market opened up in Dutch agriculture. This consisted of a series of interlocking projects – among them, one of farmers specializing in large-scale milk production (eager to externalize the burdensome task of livestock reproduction), and one of small-scale farmers who, unable to compete on equal terms in the bulk production of milk, decided to specialize in heifer production. However, as it turned out, 1985 marked the end of this circulation of heifers as commodities. New conditions established by the EC for the distribution and reduction of milk quotas led the larger-scale farmers to reconsider their strategy and to use the newly created room to rear their own heifers. The market for heifers thus collapsed as the consequence of a sudden disarticulation of these different farmers' projects.

Leaving aside the details, the crucial conclusion is that what at first sight appeared to be a stable or structural feature, based upon a specific commodity circuit, was in fact dependent upon highly specific farming projects and their interplay. Hence actors' products are not, as it were, simply embedded in structural settings defined by commodity circuits, etc. Instead, it is through the ways in which they interlock that they create, reproduce and transform particular 'structures'.

Actor-oriented analysis, participatory research and intervention

We would like to conclude with some general remarks about how an actor-oriented perspective relates to recent discussions on participatory research and intervention (e.g. farmer-first strategies and methodologies, and work on indigenous or local knowledge *vis-à-vis* scientific knowledge).

We believe that an actor-oriented approach has implications for development practice in that it has a sensitizing role to play *vis-à-vis* researchers and implementors, both of course also being important social actors. It aims to offer a flexible conceptual framework for comprehending development processes – including planned intervention, but not exclusively. However it is important to stress that an actor-oriented approach is not action research, but rather a theoretical and methodological approach to the understanding of social processes. It is concerned primarily with social analysis, not with the design or management of new intervention programmes. Its guiding analytical concepts are: agency and social actors, the notion of multiple realities and arenas of struggle where different life-worlds and discourses meet, the idea of interface encounters and interface in terms of discontinuities of interests, values, knowledge and power and structural heterogeneity. Related concepts include: strategy and 'project', interlocking projects, intermediate and differentiated structures, organizational fields, networks of knowledge and power, and processes of negotiation and accommodation. Implicit in this theoretical perspective is a non-linear and non-deterministic interpretation of processes such as commoditization, institutional incorporation and scientification, and a new understanding of 'structure'.

Although, like many other researchers and development practitioners, we are concerned with the problems and needs of small-scale farmers, an actor-oriented approach should not, we maintain, be embraced as a kind of new panacea for ameliorating the poverty, uncertainties and vulnerabilities of disadvantaged groups. One should therefore not equate an actor-oriented approach with participatory action research or translate it as a methodology for increasing the claim-making capacities of local groups. Nevertheless it does help to identify and explain the nature and degree of social and political space associated with different types of social actor – not only poor peasants and other so-called marginalized populations but also landlords, merchants, extension workers and politicians. We would argue then that it can afford various social actors a useful conceptual framework for analysing their own life circumstances and for assessing possible strategies for action. It may, that is, encourage a certain way of thinking about societal issues and possibilities of change – and one we believe that is much more optimistic than conventional class, dependency or modernization models.

But, like all types of theoretical paraphernalia, it can equally be used against the poor and weak by those in positions of influence or authority. It should not, then, market itself as aligned with either what Richards (1990) has called demand-side or supply-side populism, the former involving the promotion of interests and claims from below by local groups, and the latter, action by progressive scientists, intellectuals and other outsiders (the experts or knowledge managers) whose mission it is to strengthen self-improvement and self-organization among the poor and weak.

An actor-oriented approach must stand or fall by its analytical results. It must not be judged by some pre-given ideological stance or measuring stick. While recognizing that men and women can change their worlds – that is create space for their own activities and ideas – such a perspective does not offer a recipe for 'getting development right'. Indeed it emphasizes the important fact that development discourse and action essentially involves a struggle over images of development and the good society. Hence it is necessary to underline, too, that actor-oriented research should not be seen as support for neo-liberal economic strategies or structural adjustment programmes. Rather such studies should reveal the unpredictable, stochastic, fragmentary and partial nature of planned intervention itself. Particular types of intervention (whether based upon a 'top-down' or 'bottom-up' strategy) must be placed in a broader sociological and historical framework of understanding which identifies the crucial actors, interests, resources, discourses and struggles that are entailed. As we have stressed earlier, planned intervention must be deconstructed to enable us to get away theoretically from certain existing orthodoxies and simplifications concerning the nature and tendencies of structural change and of the articulation between different life-worlds.

Such an endeavour also points to the necessity of developing an actor-oriented sociology of knowledge relating to development processes. As we suggested above, this would question the simple dichotomous distinctions drawn between indigenous/local knowledge and scientific knowledge. Such distinctions, we argue, are problematic because detailed actor-oriented studies not only reveal creativity and experimentation by farmers but also their continuous ability to absorb and re-work outside ideas and technology such that it becomes impossible to characterize a particular element as belonging to people's science or scientists' science. The encounter between different bodies of knowledge involves a transformation or translation of existing knowledge and a fusion of horizons (i.e. the joint creation of knowledge). It also entails the interpenetration of the life-worlds and projects of farmers, extensionists, planners, politicians and scientists. A fresh theoretical look at these interrelated issues of knowledge, power and agency from an actor-oriented perspective could, we believe, revitalize development sociology.

Notes

1. On the other hand, the kind of solution proposed by Giddens (1979; 1984) that collapses actor and structure into one composite entity and therefore fails to specify precisely the relationships between the two remains theoretically problematic.
2. Parts of the chapter draw freely upon previous arguments we have advanced; see Long (1990), Long and Long (1992), van der Ploeg (1990), and Roep *et al.* (1991).
3. We are here of course skating rapidly over all the complexities involved in distinguishing between different structuralist, dependency and neo-Marxist positions. The Latin America literature is especially interesting since it has, from the early 1950s onwards, spawned a rich indigenous tradition of development theory. This includes the structuralist school of Prebisch and others who challenged existing neo-classical economics, various dependency writers (reformist and Marxist *dependentistas*), as well as more orthodox Marxist theorists. Indeed, as Kay (1989: 126) comments, covering the dependency literature – let alone the rest – 'is like being confronted with a Tower of Babel. Any attempt to give a fair account is fraught with difficulties as one is forced to be selective with respect to both issues and authors'. Kay's book on *Latin American Theories of Development and Underdevelopment* (1989) provides an elaborate account of this work from the periphery.
4. No doubt this will be seen by some as an injudicious and far-sweeping statement, since some works may be cited that avoid at least some of these shortcomings. For example, the best neo-Marxist or dependency studies stress the importance of internal patterns of exploitation and class or ethnic relations, give attention to actual (rather than idealized) historical processes, and try to avoid functionalist or determinist formulations. Yet, while recognizing such caveats, the general picture remains, we believe, as we have described it.
5. Although one should perhaps avoid writing about external and internal factors, it is difficult when discussing intervention to expunge completely from one's conceptualization such a dichotomized view since intervention itself rests upon this kind of distinction. For further discussion of this point, see Long and van der Ploeg (1989).
6. For a critical appraisal of de Janvry's logic of capital approach and his argument that the state acts as an instrument to resolve the crises of capitalist accumulation, see Long (1988; 108–14).
7. This position has been sharply criticized, especially by Marxist writers (see Alavi 1973; Foster-Carter 1978: 244).
8. Then we have the extremely difficult epistemological problem, identified by Fardon (1985: 129–30, 1984), of imposing our own analytical ('universal') model of agency on our research data, even if we wish to 'encompass the reflexive awareness and agency of the subjects' themselves. Thus in explaining or translating social action we may displace the agency or intentionalities of those we study by our own 'folk' notions or theoretical concepts.

9. Compare this with what is termed the 'ecological fallacy' whereby statements based on aggregate data concerning geographical areas are extended to make inferences about the characteristics of individuals living in them. For an account of how this can misguide development policy decisions, see Bulmer (1982: 64–6).
10. For a treatment of these essential elements, see Long (1989: 226–31).
11. This, of course, does not imply that one can attribute a uniform project to the state or particular agencies of the state. Government officials try to advance their own political or personal interests, and often adopt a pragmatism aimed at accommodating to competing officials and institutions, to farmer interests and to local circumstances. It is important then to underline the highly differentiated and complex nature of administrative practice and discourse (see Chapter 6 by Arce, Villarreal and de Vries).
12. Although our argument is developed here in relation to agrarian development and styles of farming, the idea of interlocking projects is implicit in an earlier study by Long and Roberts (1984; see also Long 1980) on regional development processes in highland Peru. In contrast to previous work on regional structures which defined regions in terms of certain geographic, economic, marketing patterns and/or administrative criteria, this Peruvian study sought to document the changing interrelations between different sectors of production and between different interest groups – peasants, miners, small-scale entrepreneurs, urban migrants, company managers, state bureaucrats and village politicians – as a means of understanding the patterns of regional development and identity. The mine-based 'regional system of production' – a shorthand for the complex and variegated set of links that emerged as an outcome of the struggles and negotiations that took place between the various social actors involved – looked different from different social locations and at different historical periods, and the form it took was only partly shaped by the actions of the 'powerful' mining enclave. Indeed certain local groups were able to feed off the enclave and pursue 'projects' that significantly affected the strategies and policies promoted by the state and mining company. In this way, the notion of a mine-based regional system served to depict the emergent, highly differentiated and constantly renegotiated sets of interlocking projects involving all those actors directly or indirectly tied to the mining sector.
13. This differentiated pattern is high variable and fluid: as soon as new negotiated interfaces emerge new sets of emergent properties come into existence.
14. According to Barth, 'aggregate' social forms (i.e. encounters, interactions and social interfaces) result from the generative capacity of actors to agree or disagree about what is relevant on a particular occasion and thereby to define or redefine a given situation through the strategies and interpretative modes they adopt.
15. This definition might face the same criticism that Mouzelis (1991: 74) makes of Berger and Luckman's original formulation, that is that it 'neglect[s] the hierarchical aspects of society'. However, we strongly oppose an a priori or fixed hierarchization of macro versus micro actors and agencies. Although the State and its 'ruling' groups are often able to impose their models on others, on other occasions it is members of the so-called "awkward class" that overthrow such models or that create room for manoeuvre in order to implant their own. The issue can only be resolved through an analysis of who precisely emerge as influential actors within particular arenas of struggle. There are no grounds whatsoever for a kind of ontological and a

priori identification of 'hierarchies' or 'structures', since in so far as they manifest themselves as relevant categories for analysis, they must necessarily arise out of an understanding of the intricate ways in which actors' projects interlock – a point which Mouzelis (1991: 32–3) in fact acknowledges indirectly by the examples he presents.

16. See Long (1989) for a first exploration of interface issues and the emergence of 'projects' from below. Several chapters are devoted to Mexican cases.

17. In addition to one of the authors, Norman Long, the field team consisted of Alberto Arce, who specialized in the study of the agricultural bureaucracy; Dorien Brunt, who focused upon household, gender and *ejido* organization in an area of sugar production; Humberto Gonzalez, who investigated the role of Mexican agricultural entrepreneurs and companies in export agriculture; Elsa Guzman, who examined the organization of sugar production and the struggles that occurred between the sugar producers, the mill and government; Gabriel Torres, who studied the social organization, and culture of agricultural labourers; Magdalena Villarreal, who studied three types of women's groups and the issue of countervailing power in an *ejido* community; and Pieter van der Zaag, who was responsible for the technical and organizational analysis of the irrigation systems. After an initial period of fieldwork, Lex Hoefsloot joined us to undertake detailed socio-agronomic studies in a central area of the main irrigation system. In addition, several Dutch and Mexican students contributed to the project. The work was financed bilaterally by WOTRO (the Netherlands Foundation for the Advancement of Tropical Research) and the Ford Foundation.

18. See Long (1989: 245–56) for an account of the types of research strategies and techniques employed. A more complete discussion of the theoretical and methodological underpinning of an actor-oriented approach to ethnography is contained in Long and Long (1992).

References

Alavi H (1973) Peasant classes and primordial loyalties. *Journal of Peasant Studies* I(1)

Barth F (1981) *Process and form in social life: selected essays of Fredik Barth* vol I. London, Routledge & Kegan Paul

Bennett J W (1980) Management styles: a concept and a method for the analysis of family-operated agricultural enterprise. In: Bartlett P F (ed) *Agricultural decision making: anthropological contributions to rural development*. New York, Academic Press

Bennett J W and **Kanel D** (1983) Agricultural economics and economic anthropology: confrontation and accommodation. In: Ortiz S (ed) *Economic anthropology: topics and theories*. New York, University Press of America

Benvenuti B (1991) *Geschriften over landbouw, structuur en technologie*. Wageningen Studies in Sociology 30, Wageningen, Agricultural University

Berger P L and **Luckmann T** (1967) *The social construction of reality: a treatise in the sociology of knowledge*. London, Allen Lane/Penguin

Bernstein H (1986) Capitalism and petty commodity production. *Social Analysis: Journal of Cultural and Social Practice* 20 (December)

Bourdieu P (1977) *Outline of a theory of practice*. Cambridge, Cambridge University Press

Bourdieu P (1981) Men and machines. In: Knorr-Cetina K D and Cicourel A V (eds)

Bourdieu P (1984) *Distinction: a social critique of the judgement of taste*. London, Routledge & Kegan Paul

Bulmer M (1982) *The uses of social research: social investigation in public policymaking*. London, Allen & Unwin

Clegg R (1989) *Frameworks of power*. London, Sage

DeWalt B R (1979) *Modernization in a Mexican ejido: a study in economic adaptation*. Cambridge, Cambridge University Press

Elwert G and **Bierschenk T** (eds) (1988) Aid and development. Special issue, *Sociologia Ruralis* XXVII(2)

Fardon R (ed) (1985) *Power and knowledge: anthropological and sociological approaches*. Edinburgh, Scottish Academic Press

Foster-Carter A (1978) Can we articulate 'articulation'? In: Clammer J (ed) *The new economic anthropology*. London, Macmillan

Foucault M (1972) *The archaeology of knowledge*. London, Tavistock

Friedmann H (1981) The family farm in advanced capitalism: outline of a theory of simple commodity production in agriculture. In Buttel F H and Murphy T (eds) *The political economy of agriculture in advanced industrial societies*. New York, University Press of America

Gibbon P and **Neocosmos M** (1985) Some problems in the political economy of 'African socialism'. In Bernstein H and Campbell B K (eds) *Contradictions of accumulation in Africa: studies in economy and state*. Beverly Hills, CA, Sage

Giddens A (1979) *Central problems in social theory: action, structure and contradiction in social analysis*. London, Macmillan

Giddens A (1984) *The constitution of society: an outline of the theory of structuration*. Cambridge, Polity Press

Gudeman S (1986) *Economics as culture: models and metaphors of livelihood*. London, Routledge & Kegan Paul

Hawkins E A (1991) Changing technologies: negotiating autonomy on Cheshire farms. PhD thesis, South Bank Polytechnic, London

Hindess B (1986) Actors and social relations. In: Wadell M I and Turner S P (eds) *Sociological theory in transition*. Boston, MA, Allen & Unwin

Hirst P Q (1985) Constructed space and subject. In: Fardon R (ed)

Hofstee E W (1985) *Groningen van grasland naar bouwland, 1750–1938: een agrarisch economische ontwikkeling als probleem van sociale verandering*. Wageningen, PUDOC

Hyden G (1980) *Beyond Ujamaa in Tanzania: underdevelopment and an uncaptured peasantry*. London, Heinemann

de Janvry A (1981) *The agrarian question and reformism in Latin America*. Baltimore, MD, Johns Hopkins University Press

Kay C (1989) *Latin American theories of development and underdevelopment*. London, Routledge

Knorr-Cetina K D (1981) The micro-sociological challenge of the macro-sociological: towards a reconstruction of social theory and methodology. In: Knorr-Cetina K D and Cicourel A V (eds)

Knorr-Cetina K D and **Cicourel A V** (eds) (1981) *Advances in social theory and methodology: toward an integration of micro- and macro-sociologies*. Boston, MA, Routledge & Kegan Paul

Kosik K (1976) *Dialectics of the concrete: a study on problems of man and world*. Dordrecht, The Netherlands, D Reidel Publishing

Latour B (1986) The powers of association. In Law J (ed) *Power, action and belief: a new sociology of knowledge?* London, Routledge & Kegan Paul

Law J (ed) (1986) *Power, action and belief: a new sociology of knowledge?* London, Routledge and Kegan Paul.

Long N (1977) *An introduction to the sociology of rural development*. London, Tavistock/Westview Press

Long N (1980) Mine-based regional economies: Andean examples, historical and contemporary. In: Banck G A, Buve R and van Vroonhoven L (eds) *State and region in Latin America: a workshop*. Amsterdam, Centre for Latin American Research and Documentation

Long N (1984) *Creating space for change: a perspective in the sociology of development*. Inaugural lecture, Wageningen Agricultural University. A shortened version appears in *Sociologia Ruralis* XXIV(3/4)

Long N (1988) Sociological perspectives on agrarian development and state intervention. In: Hall A and Midgley J (eds) *Development politics: sociological perspectives*. Manchester, Manchester University Press

Long N (ed) (1989) *Encounters at the interface: a perspective on social discontinuities in rural development*. Wageningen Studies in Sociology 27, Wageningen, Agricultural University

Long N (1990) From paradigm lost to paradigm regained? The case for an actor-oriented sociology of development. *European Review of Latin American and Caribbean Studies* 49

Long N and **Long A** (eds) (1992) *Battlefields of knowledge: the interlocking of theory and practice in social research and development*. London, Routledge

Long N and **van der Ploeg J D** (1988) New challenges in the sociology of rural development: a rejoinder to Peter Vandergeest. *Sociologia Ruralis* XXVIII(1)

Long N and **van der Ploeg J D** (1989) Demythologizing planned intervention: an actor perspective. *Sociologia Ruralis* XXIX (3/4)

Long N and **Roberts B** (1984) *Miners, peasants and entrepreneurs: regional development in the Central Highlands of Peru*. Cambridge, Cambridge University Press

Long N, van der Ploeg J D, Curtin C and **Box L** (1986) *The commoditization debate: labour process, strategy and social network*. Wageningen, Agricultural University

Marx K (1962) (original edn 1852) The eighteenth brumaire of Louis Bonaparte. In: Marx K, *Selected works* 2 vols. Moscow, Foreign Languages Publishing House

Moore S F (1973) Law and social change: the semi-autonomous social field as an appropriate subject of study. *Law Society Review* Summer

Mouzelis N P (1991) *Back to sociological theory: the construction of social orders*. London, Macmillan

Pelto P J and **Pelto G H** (1975) Intra-cultural diversity: some theoretical issues. *American Ethnologist* 2

Ploeg J D van der (1986) *La ristrutturazione del lavoro agricolo*. Rome, La REDA

Ploeg J D van der (1990) *Labor, markets and agricultural production*. Boulder, CO, Westview Press

Ploeg, J D van der and **Roep D** (1990) *Bedrijfsstijlen in de Zuidhollandse Veenweidegebieden: nieuwe perspectieven voor belied en belangenhartiging*. Department of the Sociology of Rural Development, Wageningen, Agricultural University

Ranger T (1985) *Peasant consciousness and guerrilla war in Zimbabwe*. London, James Currey

Richards P (1990) Indigenous approaches to rural development: the agrarian populist tradition in West Africa. In: Altieri M and Hecht S (eds) *Agroecology and small farm development*. New York, CRC Press

Roep D, van der Ploeg J D and **Leeuwis C** (1991) *Zicht op duurzaamheid en kontinuiteit, bedrijfsstijlen in de Achterhoek*. Department of Sociology of Rural Development, Wageningen, Agricultural University

Rooij S de (1992) *Werk van de tweedesoort: boerinnen in de Melkveehonderij*. Assen/Maastricht, van Gorcum

Schneider H K (1974) *Economic man: the anthropology of economics.* New York, Free Press

Scott, J C (1985) *Weapons of the weak: everyday forms of peasant resistance.* New Haven, CT, Yale University Press

Smith G (1989) *Livelihood and resistance: peasants and the politics of land reform in Peru.* Berkeley, CA, University of California Press

Spittler G (1983) Administration in a peasant state. *Sociologia Ruralis* XXIII(2)

Stern S J (1987) New approaches to the study of peasant rebellion and consciousness: implications of the Andean experience. In: Stern S J (ed) *Resistance, rebellion, and consciousness in the Andean peasant world, 18th to 20th centuries.* Madison, WI, University of Wisconsin Press

Strathern M (1985) Knowing power and being equivocal: three Melanesian contexts. In: Fardon R (ed)

Vandergeest P (1988) Commercialization and commoditization: a dialogue between perspectives. *Sociologia Ruralis* XXVIII(1)

Velsen J van (1964) *The politics of kinship: a study in social manipulation among the lakeside Tonga.* Manchester, Manchester University Press

CHAPTER 4

Post-Marxism and post-colonialism:
the needs and rights of distant strangers[1]

Stuart Corbridge

Modernity is changing the locus of belonging: our language of attachments limps suspiciously behind, doubting that our needs could ever find larger attachments.

(Michael Ignatieff, *The Needs of Strangers*, 1990: 139)

Marxist development studies have been subjected to a good deal of critical examination in recent years. Theorists and practitioners of various persuasions have drawn attention to the teleological and economistic logics of structural Marxism, and to the zero-sum tautologies of a less rigorous neo-Marxism. Events, too, have left their mark. The industrialization of some parts of the developing world has dented the most pessimistic recesses of radical development studies. In the mean time, the events of 1989 and 1990 seem finally to have set the seal upon one or more versions of state socialism. There is now a considerable literature which points to the organizational difficulties which must beset socialist planning on a large scale (Nove 1983; Cheung 1986), just as Steven Lukes and others have pointed to an intimate connection between the philosophical and political outlooks of Marxism–Leninism and a local disposition to abrogate the rights of the individual in so-called Marxist-Leninist societies (Lukes 1985; Peffer 1990). The landscapes of the Gulag, of the chaotic terror of the Cultural Revolution, even perchance of Year Zero in Kampuchea, are no historical accidents, no simple errors of a deviant Stalinism. The brutality of Koestler's *Darkness at Noon* is not to be so lightly dismissed (which is not to say that one cannot make a strong case for democratic or market socialism in the developing world).

More recently still, the deficiencies identified in the Marxian project have been expanded as dialectical materialism has come face to face with a renewed empiricism (not least in development studies) and with intellectual postures emanating from post-modernism and post-colonialism.[2] Many development activists are minded to dismiss the irrelevancies of development theory in general and of the Marxian vision in particular. Their faith is placed instead in a series of local struggles and initiatives which build upon the wisdom and resources of local peoples. Interestingly, this populism is closely echoed by the newer and more strident voices of post-modernism and post-colonialism. From the latter quarter comes the charge that Marxism is a child of the Enlightenment which seeks to normalize the Other by virtue of its own, unexamined, Western humanism. Set against this, the demand is floated that humility and not hubris is required; that to prescribe development (or socialism) for others is to seek once more to represent an Other – to speak for and on behalf of a 'Third World' when what is required is a space for the raising of diverse local voices of resistance. Post-modernism, like some versions of feminism, raises the spectre of an oppositional imagination (Cocks 1989) which calls for an end to all universal theories and projects. In place of what may once have seemed to be a certain future and a correct politics, we are now enjoined to celebrate a poetics of difference (see Clifford and Marcus 1986). In place of a materialist epistemology and a transformative ethics we are faced with what Perry Anderson referred to as 'the randomization of history' (Anderson 1983). The very notion of progress is rendered problematic in a way in which it was not previously.

This chapter seeks to intervene in the continuing debates between Marxisms and their critics. More particularly, it aims to take seriously certain of the claims of the populists and the post-modernists, while trying not to lose sight of the claims made by a revitalized post-Marxism. (The chapter does not consider the counter-revolution in development theory and practice: see Riddell, 1987; Toye, 1987). More bluntly still, the chapter wants to reclaim for an account of a radicalized modernity (cf. Giddens 1990) some elements of the critical or deconstructive sensibilities of post-structuralism, while at the same time suggesting that the construction of a truly global space-economy (and 'community') makes necessary a wider transformative politics which is sensitive to the needs and rights of distant strangers. Although the chapter does not develop an account of a 'just society', it does suggest why and how such an argument might be constructed.

Put like this the argument will sound more opaque than I intend it to be. I take seriously the charge that development theory proclaims its seeming irrelevance by virtue of its conceptual gymnastics and tortuous prose. Nevertheless, the argument that I wish to make is a complicated one which at times must resort to an academic shorthand. My main concession to intelligibility is a willingness to develop my arguments at length and in a chapter of four main sections.

In the next section I briefly review the nature of the crises which have beset Marxist development studies (see also David Booth's Chapter 1). I move beyond the conventions of the 'impasse debate' to consider some of the arguments advanced by the populists and the post-modernists. Their voices have not always been central to a consideration of the impasse in development studies.

The third section of the chapter begins with a positive assessment of the populist and post-modernist turns. I acknowledge the power of the post-modernist critique in regard to questions of difference and representation; to the presumptions which so often mark development studies (and not least when it pretends to a value-free content). But most of this section is concerned to make the case for a post-Marxist development studies which would incorporate certain of the insights of post-modernism without surrendering to the latter's nihilistic excesses. I suggest that a sensitivity to the globalizing tendencies of a radicalized modernity should encourage the student of development to confront the moral duties of richer citizens to respond to the claims of distant strangers. I further suggest that while Marxism is not a reliable guide to a prospective socialism (which itself is tied to the modern project), post-Marxism is suited to an investigation of the contradictory logics of modernization and globalization.[3]

The fourth section seeks to return these apparently theoretical concerns to the terrain of development practice. In effect, the chapter raises the old and unfashionable questions of 'what is to be (and should be) done?' I sketch out an argument for linking development theory and practice, the local and the extra-local, the specific and the 'universal', through an account of the needs and rights of distant strangers which are implicit in an interdependent world system. I do not claim a privileged moral position for myself – that would be crass. I simply suggest first, that development studies is deficient to the extent that it does not attend to normative questions, and second, that an ostensibly local development activism cannot avoid an engagement with a series of moral questions – concerning rights and the question of justice – which themselves must have recourse to apparently abstract and generalized discursive claims. The argument is developed with particular reference to the work of Singer, Rawls and Roemer.

The conclusion to the chapter presents a brief discussion of what these claims might consist of in practice (and in respect to arguments about the debt crisis and foreign aid). The conclusion also pays attention to certain objections which might be raised against my arguments.

Revisiting the impasse in Marxist development studies

The impasse debate

The main contours of the impasse debate are well known. In 1985 David Booth published a paper in *World Development* which challenged the terms of reference which had structured a series of exchanges between neo-Marxism and its structural Marxist rival. While sensitive to the differences which define these two schools of thought – the circulationist/autarkic logics of the former contrasting with the productionist/strategic logics of the latter – Booth insisted that all Marxisms share a 'metatheoretical commitment to demonstrating the necessity of economic and social patterns, as distinct from explaining them or exploring how they may be changed' (Booth 1985: 761). Booth further suggested that Marxist development sociology was beset by an unhelpful essentialism, by a tendency to reduce social, cultural and political actions to their supposed economic determinants, and by an unworthy and corrupting epistemological dogmatism.

Booth's diagnosis of a stalled Marxist development studies struck a chord in many of the constituencies to whom his remarks were addressed. In 1986 I published a critique of radical development geography which in some respects was similar to the critique of Marxist development sociology published by Booth a year earlier. The point of focus of *Capitalist World Development* was a radical development geography scarred by four particular (and related) failings: a tendency to oppositionism, a tendency to determinism, a tendency to spatial over-aggregation and a tendency to epistemological confrontation (Corbridge 1986). In place of these failings I urged that development geography should provide an account of development which is sensitive (1) to the shifting production of space under the rule of capital; (2) to the changing sites and temporalities of capital accumulation and crisis formation in the world economy; and (3) to the fragile economic and non-economic conditions of existence of national and international regimes of accumulation. Such an account would need (4) to develop a clutch of meso-concepts (Booth's middle position) which split open the determinism of those theories which seek to read off particular empirical developments from the 'logic of capitalism'; and (5) to eschew forms of reasoning which conceive of capitalism as a totality with functional requirements and necessary laws of motion (Corbridge 1988).

This argument, which depends heavily on the work of Hindess and Hirst, was later generalized into a model of post-Marxism which made particular reference to the work of the post-imperialists and regulation school scholars (Corbridge 1989; 1990). Other prominent contributions to the impasse debate came from Nicos Mouzelis (1988a; 1988b), from Leslie Sklair (1988; 1991), from Jorge Larrain (1989) and from Peter Vandergeest and Fred Buttel (1988). While these various contributions took issue with Booth in respect to details and future scenarios, there was general agreement that Booth had produced a wise and worrying critique of Marxist development studies (for a different view, see Peet 1991). Marxist development studies appeared to have run out of steam because of their internal contradictions, just as some societies constructed in the image of Marxism–Leninism themselves had foundered in the 1980s.

Mention of the context against which the crisis of Marxist development studies emerged, however, only serves to reveal the limitations which marked this first round of debate on the impasse. The reconstruction of eastern Europe has encouraged the view that Marxism is not so much in crisis as dead in the water – a victim of the 'end of history' (Fukuyama 1989). More sober critics note that if Marxism is to have any future it must embrace the market (which itself is an uncomfortable proposition). The only feasible socialism is a market socialism. By the same token, Marxists are urged to repudiate a political philosophy which seeks to privilege the ends over the means. An abstract faith in the innate goodness of socialist men and women is equally to be discarded. Finally, in place of an overriding attention to class and the class struggle, it is suggested that the struggles of women, of ethnic groups, and of those without full citizenship rights cannot be reduced to a set of economic determinants (and so panaceas).[4]

In development studies, this renewed celebration of difference and of polyvocality is beginning to shape a 'new' development theory and practice which is fundamentally opposed to many of the tenets of a once hegemonic Marxist development studies. This much is apparent in David Lehmann's book, which enjoins us to bemove beyond the discourses of *dependencia* and towards a concern for democratization (Lehmann 1990). It is also evident in the practices of what has been called populism, and in the post-modern or post-colonial turn.

Populism and post-colonialism/post-modernism

The populist impulse in development studies is present in the work of Robert Chambers, who asks us to put the last first (Chambers 1983; 1985) and Paul Richards, who celebrates the agricultural knowledges of indigenous peoples (Richards 1985) to name just two exponents of the genre. When pressed to extremes, the populist line supports the conclusion that development studies in general is irrelevant, and that its Marxian lineage is especially so. This is the tack developed by Michael Edwards in his thoughtful paper 'The irrelevance of development studies' (published in *Third World Quarterly* in 1989). Edwards maintains that

> Although some progress has been made in exploring alternative approaches, inspired particularly by the work of Paulo Freire, development studies are still based largely on traditional 'banking' concepts of education. These traditional concepts embody a series of attitudes that contribute to the irrelevance of much of their output to the problems of the world in which we live. Most importantly, people are treated as objects to be studied rather than as subjects of their own development; there is therefore a separation between the researcher and the object of research, and between understanding and action. Research and education come to be dominated by content rather than form or method; they become processes which focus on the transmission of information, usually of a technical kind, from one person to another. (Edwards 1989: 117–18)

These are important claims and I shall return to some of them later. They are important not least because Edwards is able to suggest that 'Development research is full of a spurious objectivity: this is a natural consequence of divorcing subject from object in the process of education. Any hint of "subjectivity" is seized upon immediately as "unscientific" and therefore not worthy of inclusion in "serious" studies of development' (Edwards 1989: 121). Of more direct concern to my argument, however, is Edwards's contention that 'researchers from the political left have been no more successful [in addressing the realities of development] than commentators from the right' (1989: 125). Edwards is dismissive of the way in which most Marxists trade an armchair understanding of development issues for a commitment to local development initiatives born of a participatory research framework. This, I suspect, is the nub of the issue for Edwards, as it is for many others. Edwards voices a reasonable disquiet in the face of development theories which lack applicability, which are inaccessible to the actors for whom such knowledges are intended, and whose *raison d'être* seems to be academic enhancement rather than practical development activity. In place of the general and the abstract – not to mention the unduly pessimistic: Edwards lambasts the usual conclusion of Marxian critiques, 'that "progress" is impossible without revolutionary changes in the structure of (capitalist) society' (Edwards 1989: 125) – the populist/activist urges us to meet local needs with local resources. As Edwards puts it: 'In much current development work, the advice we put forward cannot be used locally because it is manufactured under completely different circumstances. The only way to ensure its relevance is by fostering the participation of poor people in identifying their own problems, priorities and solutions' (1989: 127).[5]

Arguments such as this have an obvious and growing popularity. In certain respects, too, they rub shoulders with a series of arguments which define the post-modern or post-colonial turn – a turn seemingly far removed from the practicalities of everyday development praxis.

The connection is first apparent in the language of post-modernism and post-colonialism (and in the attention of both to language). Simply stated, we might say that post-colonialism is directing our attention to the ways in which the west represents its non-western Others, in the process making possible local structures of colonialism and neo-colonialism. Edward Said puts this argument most forcefully in his book *Orientalism*, when he suggests that, 'without understanding Orientalism as a discourse one cannot possibly understand the enormously systematic discipline by which European culture was able to manage – and even produce – the Orient politically, sociologically, militarily, ideologically, scientifically, and imaginatively during the post-Enlightenment period' (Said 1979: 3). A case, perhaps, of I think, therefore you are.

More recently, Said's work has been criticized and refined by scholars including Homi Bhabha and Gayatri Chakravorty Spivak (Bhabha 1983; 1984; 1986; Spivak, 1985; 1987; 1990; see also Barker *et al.* 1985). Bhabha, in particular, has shown how the discourses of colonialism shift between an overpowering racism and a curious exultation of the noble savage, all the while reflecting a series of deep-seated anxieties in the west's attempts to understand itself. In each case the voice of the post-colonial critic forces the theorist and practitioner of 'development' to come face to face with the logics of empowerment/enslavement which are built into all narratives of 'progress'. In a quite fundamental way, the voices of post-modernism/post-colonialism force us to ask what should be the first question(s) of development studies: what is development? Who says this is what it is? Who is it for? Who aims to direct it, and for whom?

A further affinity between the post-modern and populist turns is their shared concern for a local politics of development. Post-modernism is sceptical of what its adherents refer to as 'metanarratives' (or grand theories which suggest both that we can know about the world and that the 'world out there' is structured by a set of necessary – and thus systematic – relationships).[6] This is not just a question of being against the Marxist metanarrative, although this is an obvious point of focus (Laclau 1990). Post-modernism is radically unsettling because it seeks to challenge the possibility and validity of any foundational logic of understanding or political intervention (Duncan 1991). Its invitations are to a faith in narrative itself (as in the 'new cultural anthropology': Clifford and Marcus 1986; Clifford 1988), to a humbleness which resists the idea of a 'truth', to a willingness to let others speak for themselves, and to a local poetics of resistance. In place of the universalizing assumptions of conventional development theories – free-market, Marxist or modernizing – the post-modern/post-colonial turn threatens development studies with sense of its own arrogance and futility. More so even than populism, post-modernism/post-colonialism would seem to want to dance on the grave of a lifeless Marxist development studies.

Post-modernism/post-colonialism or post-Marxism?

There can be no gainsaying the strengths of the populist and post-modern/post-colonial challenges. Not the least of their virtues is their attempt to re-centre development studies around an insistent critique of what development may be and is taken to mean. In this respect it is significant that both Said and Bhabha have drawn on the work of Frantz Fanon, whose classic text *The Wretchedness of the Earth* remains the most trenchant critique of a persistent ethnocentrism in development thought and practice (Fanon 1967). As Sartre noted in his introduction to that text, in Fanon's work 'the Third World finds itself and speaks to itself through his voice' (Sartre 1967: 9; emphasis in the original). (Fanon puts matters more bluntly when he writes: 'The violence with which the supremacy of white values is affirmed and the aggressiveness which has permeated the victory of these values over the ways of life and of thought of the native mean that, in revenge, the native laughs in mockery when Western values are mentioned in front of him' – Fanon 1967: 33.)

A willingness to contest the west's privileged representation of its Others – its persistent attempts at time–space substitution (Fabian 1983) – is also central to the political programmes of the populists and the post-modernists. But while the populists are concerned mainly to celebrate the voices of the rural poor in the Third World, an emerging post-modernism in development studies is concerned to challenge the possibility of any singular site of representation. The proponent of post-modernism – post-colonialism is minded to celebrate a plurality of voices and representations, in the process inviting those who are most persistently scripted by another to speak for themselves. Peoples who for so long have been defined as marginal to the march of progress are then encouraged to put forward accounts of their own conditions and aspirations. In place of a monolithic politics of modernization or socialist struggle, the invitation now is to a multiplicity of local practices of resistance. These practices will express the needs and experiences of very different social groups: women, the landless, landless women, migrant workers, female migrants, ethnic minorities, women 'natives' (Trinh 1989) and others. In like vein, the sites of such struggles (and such developments) are not confined to the national space-economy. The body, the household, the community and the region each become sites for contested representations of identities and local needs. The effect is to fragment, but to do so in order to enable; to empower different groups to resist those various practices by which they are subjected to the unequal powers of other social groups. The postmodern turn is marked by a continuous and unsettling ability to deconstruct received wisdoms and conventional interpretative practices.

There is, none the less, a problem with deconstruction when it is pressed to its limits. In particular, there is within post-modernism/post-colonialism a debilitating tendency to mistake the word for the World; a tendency to confuse an absence of foundations for knowledge with an absence of certain common conventions or assumptions as to what 'objective' knowledge might look like. This in turn can create the conditions wherein a positive local politics of empowerment slides fitfully into an amoral politics of indifference, or towards a local politics which craves no point of contact with forms of political practice which are connected to global issues and ostensibly 'universal' themes. In the rest of this section (and in the next) I shall develop these points at length. I shall do this by making reference to the work of Marx, Weber and Giddens on modernization and a radicalized modernity, and by citing the work of Singer, Beitz, Rawls and Roemer in regard to questions of justice and the moral community.

Marx, Weber and Giddens

One problem which has afflicted the post-modern turn is the inconsistency which must mark any attempt to argue for a political and intellectual programme which itself is critical of the reasonableness of reason. (My argument assumes a distaste for inconsistency.) Giddens has noted a tendency within post-modern circles to equate the foundational claims of the early Enlightenment with the modern condition itself (cf. Lyotard 1985), in the process forgetting that modernity may best be defined as a chronic restlessness, and that modernism calls to mind a process of reflection by which this dialectic of change is recognized (see also Habermas 1990).

Since the foregoing may not be crystal clear, let me re-phrase it to bring out its implications for development studies. One danger of the post-modern turn is that it may encourage the view that, 'no systematic knowledge of human action or trends of social development is possible' (Giddens 1990: 47). As Giddens points out:

Were anyone to hold such a view (and if indeed it is not inchoate in the first place), they could scarcely write a book about it. The only possibility would be to repudiate intellectual activity altogether – even 'playful deconstruction' – in favour, say, of healthy physical exercise. Whatever the absence of foundation-alism implies, it is not this. (Giddens 1990: 47)

But if this is the case, it follows that a break with foundationalism should not be taken to be equivalent to a break with reason itself (and all that reason makes possible). It is perfectly sensible to accept that our stories about the world are imperfect and do not represent some essential truths, while insisting that some stories are better than others. The possibility of parsimony might reside, for example, in logic itself and/or in the empirical consistency and scope of an argument. The critique of a privileged vantage point need not imply a critique of the possibility of knowledge.

Several propositions follow from this conclusion. If modernism can-not fully be equated with foundationalism, it follows that post-modernism cannot be opposed to modernism in the name of critique versus certainty. More seriously, if modernity is defined by its essential reflexivity – by its capacity to allow the unfettered growth of reason to challenge reason's follies – it follows that so-called post-modernism might better be understood as a radicalized modernity (Giddens 1990: 150). And if this is the case, it follows that the puzzling uncertainties of modernity might reasonably be explained in terms of the discourses of modernism: that is, by going back to the work of Marx and Weber (and Nietzsche and Simmel) – the classic authorities on modernism – in the process adapting their accounts of the modern condition to take note of those more recent tendencies to globalization which help to define a state of high modernity.

Again, we can put the matter more straightforwardly. At one level what is significant about the post-modern turn in development studies is its suggestion that Marxism is unsuited to its tasks because it is bound up with the logics of foundationalism and metanarrative. Marxism might then be seen as disabling rather than as disabling-and-enabling. In place of its supposedly universal propositions and political claims, our attention is turned to a fragmentary and liberating localism. But suppose these oppositions are unfounded. Suppose they are themselves the product of an inconsistent post-modern metanarrative of fragmen-tation. It may then follow that a critique of Marxism/post-Marxism can-not be so lightly made. Indeed, one might want to argue the opposite: that Marxism as critique, as a reading of modernity and modernization, functions so well precisely because it does not support a certain transfor-mative politics (whatever it might claim), any more than Marxism as a guide to modernity eschews reason for a ceaseless deconstruction.

Here, then, is my suggestion. Let us not abandon some aspects of Marxism – let alone post-Marxism – because of the fragility of reason. Rather, let us reclaim from Marx a powerful set of arguments about the dynamics of modernization; a set of arguments which is not always supportive of state socialism, and which is by no means resistant to other accounts of a radicalized modernity (including those of Mann

1986; Unger 1987; Giddens 1990, notwithstanding some obvious points of difference). The nuts and bolts of this proposal can be elaborated upon elsewhere. In the broadest of terms, the argument will take the following shape:

First, notwithstanding the fact that the main object of Marxism is capitalism, Marx provided a powerful account of modernity and modernization which cuts against the grain of some aspects of his work. The gist of Marx's account of modernity is to be found in his suggestion (with Engels) that, under the rule of capital

> All fixed, fast-frozen relations, with their train of ancient and venerable prejudices and opinions, are swept away, all new-formed ones become antiquated before they can ossify. All that is solid melts into air, all that is holy is profaned, and men at last are forced to face . . . the real conditions of their lives and their relations with their fellow men. (Marx and Engels 1975)

Marx's oeuvre is thus a paean to change (Berman 1983); it is a celebration of the powers of capital and modernism every bit as much as it is a programme for their rational re-combination under socialism/communism. For all his disdain of the 'ancient' and the traditional, Marx is able to see that the 'natural state' of the modern world is the antithesis of a Ricardian steady-state. A ceaseless construction and destruction is made necessary by the social relations which define industrial capitalism. The separation of owner from owner, and of the proletariat from the means of production, ensures that an accumulation process is set in motion which is driven by the pursuit of profit and which promotes the commodification of all areas of modern life. Marx, in this vein, is a prophet of the extraordinary time-space compressions which continue to define the modern world. A world which is shrunk first by the canal and the turnpike, and then by the steamship and the railway, will shrink later by inventions which Marx cannot foretell, but whose invention is consistent with his insight that, in the modern era, to stand still is to perish. Globalization, in short, is implicit in Marx's account of capitalism and modernity. What is missing from Marx's work is a clear recognition that the processes of globalization will work very differently in different places, and that a straightforward equation between modernity and progress is problematic. It falls to Weber and to Nietzsche, among others (Simmel comes to mind), to soften the Panglossian tones of Marx's faith in socialism as a form of modernity which might transcend modernity's contradictions.

From Weber, of course, comes a discourse about the alienating effects of the modern, bureaucratic condition. In what is again a western perspective, Weber bemoans the connections between modernization, bureaucratization and the rule over individuals exercised by abstractions. More clearly than Marx, Weber sees that the iron cage of rationalism is the product of industrialization in general (rather than of capitalist industrialization in particular). A transient space of flows necessarily calls forth a compelling machinery of fixity. For Weber, the suggestion that the machineries of state could be smashed by a socialist revolution does not ring true. As Derek Sayer points out:

> Weber's hostility to socialism must be understood in this context. In the political sphere, 'The great state and the mass party are the classic soil for bureaucratisation' [Weber 1970: 209], and socialism elevates both, just as, in the economic realm, the socialization of the means of production would, he believed, merely increase the power of bureaucratised management. (Sayer 1991: 145)

In place of Marx's transformative vision Weber (1970) enjoins us to preserve the pathetic sanctuary of the private life, and to attend to the realm of politics. An abstract morality also becomes important (a point I shall come back to). Weber's vision of modernity and modernization is one in which the death of religion brings with it the death of transcendent meaning. Knowledge and reason are at once the mainsprings of the joys of modernity (especially, we might add, in the west), and the harbingers of what Kundera was later to call modernity's 'unbearable lightness of being'. As Sayer again points out, Kundera draws on Weber and Nietzsche to render unthinkable the faith of most modern Marxists in the possibility of a deep-seated and 'painless' socialist modernization (Kundera 1988). Kundera suggests that while to be modern is to accept that everything is possible, it is also to assent to the pardoning in advance of the excesses of modernity.

It is these moments in the work of Weber (and Nietzsche) which furnish post-modernism with much of its armoury: Weber and Nietzsche as the cynics of reason's capabilities; Weber and Nietzsche as the proponents of the sanctified nature of a banal private life; Weber and Nietzsche as the prophets of depthlessness, of the transitory, the ephemeral and the fugitive. But this is to offer an incomplete reading of Weber and Nietzsche. Not only are both authors the products of modern societies, they are also critical of the powers of pure reason by virtue of reason itself. In this manner, Weber and Nietzsche expose the fateful contradictions of modern life – including the dream of socialism – without succumbing to a fatalism which attends only to the ephemeral, and which thereby forgets the grander forces of accumulation/bureaucratization which help to produce these pathologies.

In what I have called post-Marxism, as opposed to post-modernism, the Janus-faced nature of modernity (post-modernity) is more clearly revealed. Following Marx and Weber, we can say that modernity might indeed be 'meaningless', but that its contours and dynamics are no more resistant to reason than its patterns and projects are closed to transformation. The point, surely, is that it is dangerous to suppose that the contradictions of modernity will easily be evaded (cf. Weber), but this is not to say that particular constructions of modernity (different forms of capitalism, different forms of socialism) will not make a difference to the ways in which these contradictions are revealed and thereby experienced (cf. Marx).

A second reason for not dispensing with some aspects of Marxism concerns the power of post-Marxist political economy to fashion an account of the spatial and temporal logics of modernization (and a radicalized modernity). Again, this is not an argument that can be developed at any length (see Harvey 1989a; Mouzelis 1990). In the present context the main point is that post-Marxism is willing to accept that

> the declining grip of the West over the rest of the world is not a result of the diminishing impact of the institutions which first arose there, but, on the contrary, a result of their global spread. . . . We can interpret this process as one of *globalisation*, a term which must have a key position in the lexicon of the social sciences. (Giddens 1990: 52; original emphasis)

In the wake of recent events in Panama, Iraq and elsewhere we might take issue with Giddens's assumption that globalization necessarily weakens the grip of the west over the rest of the world. But there is no doubting that globalization, or time-space compression, or time-space distantiation, or the disembedding of social relations in favour of such abstract tokens as non-commodity monies, are all motifs of the modern era. Moreover, these motifs are far from transitory or ephemeral, even if their ramifications are always local and contingent. In so far as post-Marxism builds upon Marxian economics, it would understand the dynamics of globalization as a necessary expression of the search by capital for what David Harvey has called the spatial fix (Harvey 1982). In an era of expanded commodity production, in which control over time and space is critical, capital seeks to evade the perils of over-accumulation by purchasing time (with credit monies) and by shrinking space (see Harvey 1989b).

These points should be unexceptionable, even if they are in need of elaboration. Post-Marxism, I have suggested elsewhere (Corbridge 1990), would seek to build into the basic Marxist 'metanarrative' (if there is such a thing) a greater sensitivity to the conditions of existence through which capitalist relations of production are secured at particular times and in particular places. It would further insist that the process of securing such relations is always contingent and is often contested. Post-Marxism would also want to expand the terms in which we seek to understand the dynamics of uneven development in the modern world system. In effect, this returns us to the work of Weber and Nietzsche, and to the work of Giddens, Habermas, Mann and others in the present day. Giddens has argued that historical materialism is deficient to the extent that it focuses only (or mainly) on capitalism as a motive force of modernization (Giddens 1985). Giddens would prefer that modernization and radical modernity be theorized in terms of four sets of processes and contested power relations: those of capitalism, industrialism (transformation of nature, development of the 'created environment'), military power (control of the means of violence in the context of the industrialization of war) and surveillance (control of information and social supervision).

These four institutional dimensions of modernity are clearly not incompatible with a version of post-Marxism: more to the point, they encourage Giddens to build an account of the control of space (including geopolitics) into the more historical concerns of political economy. This has some pressing implication for a post-Marxist development studies, but it also confirms that a meaningful political agenda is possible *and necessary* after the 'death of reason' and the 'death of Marxism'. Once more, it seems, post-Marxism suggests a series of reasons as to why it is to be preferred to some aspects of the post-modern/post-colonial turn. Much the most important of these reasons is its reluctance to substitute a poetics of fragmentation for the sins of the metanarrative. Post-Marxism is rather committed to an understanding of the fragmentary nature of modernity in terms of reason itself. Its 'conventional' account of global-ization/localization – its attempt to map out a new geography – recog-nizes both that modernity is defined by certain common motifs and that these supposed commonalities are always shaped and reshaped in par-ticular places. Post-Marxism seeks to provide a general theory of the local and the extra-local constructions of globalization. This is at some remove from an account which at times focuses on the local and the marginal to the exclusion of those general processes which are embed-ded in the production of differences.

A final reason for not ditching Marxism *tout court* concerns the sensi-tivity of Marxism to a politics of transformation and progress. This might seem like an odd claim given the recent history of the state-socialist world, and certainly it is not intended as an endorsement of the utopian and non-dialectical schemas of Marxism-Leninism. Rather, it is a claim which attends to the suggestion that the uneven development of the modern world is founded in the exploitative and anarchic logics of expanded commodity production. Marx and his followers have consis-tently drawn attention to the ways in which particular groups are disen-franchised by the power of capital. They have also pointed to the ab-sence of any coherent defence of the inequalities thereby produced (other than just deserts arguments). In a quite fundamental way Marx-ism takes the side of the producer and champions his or her right to the unalienated products of his or her labours.

What post-Marxism adds to this agenda is first, an insistent examin-ation of the nature of 'exploitation' in modern societies (replacing the labour theory of value with a conception of exploitation as based on an undefended and unequal distribution of property rights), and second, a sensitivity to the multiple sites of oppression and unfairness which confront modern actors: oppression and unfairness which would relate to questions of gender, ethnicity, age, location and so on. In short, post-Marxism takes from Marxism a commitment to a transformative politics – it accepts a need to attend to the needs and rights of others, even as it accepts that such others must speak for themselves – but it seeks to render problematic the assumption that a correct and/or straightforward politics of transformation can ever be specified. The contradictions of (a radicalized) modernity counsel us against such utopianism.

Once again, this places post-Marxism at a significant remove from post-modernism. Post-Marxism is not concerned to erode a local politics of difference, but it is concerned not to allow a poetics of place to substitute for a related political agenda which reflects upon the nature of responsibility in an interdependent world system. Put more bluntly, it is concerned that there is within post-modernism an affected playfulness which might promote an unhealthy politics of voyeurism. By refusing a commitment to speak for others, post-modernism is in danger of allowing a politics of deconstruction – of pointing up the various linguistic tropes by which the west has imprisoned its Others – to stand in place of (as opposed to in relation to) a more grounded politics of engagement/ transformation. This is the dilemma which stands at the heart of Said's work on Orientalism, and it is not satisfactorily resolved by the later work of Bhabha and others. The suggestion of post-Marxism is that an unwillingness to speak for others is every bit as foundational a claim as is the suggestion that we can speak for others in an unproblematic manner. Here, again, is the tension at the heart of post-modernism: a willingness to use reason to subvert not just other reasons but reason itself; a tendency to confuse the instability of the modern subject with the absence of a subject altogether. Post-modernism can seduce us into believing that the transitory nature of the 'post-modern' world is accessible only to a discourse which seeks to mimic its seeming incoherence. It is a seduction we should be wary of.

The needs and rights of distant strangers

The question is 'how can we resist the seductive charms of post-modernism?' How can we argue for a minimally universalist politics – for a normative development studies – without hitching our stall to an outmoded socialist praxis, and without rejecting the essential insights of post-modernism (that so-called universal claims are often no more than white mythologies which occlude a more purposive politics of local resistance: R Young 1990)?

I certainly do not presume to know the answers to these questions: indeed, the discussion which follows depends heavily on the work of Sen, Beitz, Barry, Singer, Goulet, Held, O'Neill and those few others who have interrogated the boundaries between development studies and moral philosophy[7]. I do believe, however, first, that the facts of globalization compel us to take seriously new ideas on the nature of moral communities and their boundaries (and thus of humanitarian obligations to the needs of distant strangers), and second, that the present distribution of rewards and powers is unjust and can be shown to be unjust in ways which have definite, if not determinate, political implications. This section of the chapter offers a brief discussion of each of these claims. Their relevance to 'development-in-practice' is explored in the conclusion.

The needs of distant strangers

Consider first the issue of humanitarianism and the question of our responsibilities to the needs of distant strangers. The starting-point for a discussion of this issue remains the work of Peter Singer – both his book, *Practical Ethics* (Singer 1979), and an earlier paper entitled 'Famine, affluence and morality' (Singer 1972).

Singer offers a simple and yet compelling case for the delivery of aid to poorer countries from the richer nations. The premisses of his argument are twofold (after Barry 1991). The first premiss is 'that suffering and death from lack of food, shelter and medical care are bad' (Singer 1972: 231). The second is that 'If it is in our power to prevent something bad from happening, without thereby sacrificing anything of comparable moral importance, we ought, morally, to do it' (Singer 1972: 231). (A weaker version of this claim is that 'if it is in our power to prevent something very bad from happening, without sacrificing anything morally significant, we ought, morally, to do it' – 1972: 231.) Singer proceeds to argue that 'an application of this principle [the weaker version] would be as follows: if I am walking past a shallow pond and see a child drowning in it, I ought to wade in and pull the child out. This will mean getting my clothes muddy, but this is insignificant, while the death of a child would presumably be a very bad thing' (1972: 231). If we add to this principle three further principles – that the second premiss is unaffected by considerations of cultural of physical distance, that the child does not wish to drown, and that there is no 'distinction between cases in which I am the only person who could possibly do anything and cases in which I am just one among millions in the same position' (1972: 231) – we are then committed, says Singer, to the proposition that people in richer countries have a moral obligation to help those in distress in poorer countries.

Now there are several objections which can be raised against Singer's thesis and it is as well to consider some of these before drawing from his work certain conclusions which are germane to this chapter. Singer's argument depends first upon the presumption that it is morally correct to save a drowning child. This seems unexceptionable, although moral cynics might dispute the claim that such an action is 'moral': it might be that by saving another we are saving ourselves, in the sense of setting up a future and reciprocal claim on the child's family or on society generally. Altruism then does not enter into it. (Some post-modernists might also take exception to the presumption of a universal morality. To my mind this tells us more about the tendency to agnosticism of some versions of post-modernism than it does about anything else.)

A second objection would be to note that while 'the child may be supposed not to be responsible for his plight . . . countries [may be] responsible for their economic problems' (Barry 1991: 184). But as Barry himself notes,

> even if it were true that death by disease and/or starvation of somebody in a poor country were to some degree the result of past acts or omissions by the entire population, that scarcely makes it morally decent to hold the individual responsible for his plight; nor, similarly, if his predicament could have been avoided had the policies of his government been different. (Barry 1991: 184)

A third objection concedes that there is a moral case for giving alms, but disputes that international aid is a sensible or efficient vehicle for meeting this obligation. Again, this argument falls down if and when we recognize that the international aid industry is contributing imperfectly but positively to development (say in terms of health and nutrition) in most poor countries. A more reasonable conclusion is not to give up on aid, but to seek to improve it. (This conclusion assumes that there is no obvious alternative to aid as a means of meeting the basic needs of people in distress. The precise form in which aid will be delivered remains a matter for empirical discussion: Riddell 1987; Mosley *et al.* 1991.)

Finally, there is the question of distance. Perhaps the most telling rejoinder to Singer is that his argument-by-analogy is a false one to the extent that it presupposes the existence of a moral community (the global community) which does not exist. This would be a fairly standard response of New Right authors, who tend to internalize in their work a distance-decay model of morality (charity begins at home if it has to begin anywhere). It would also be the response of communitarians like MacIntyre and Taylor and, we may presume, many post-modernists (Taylor 1985; MacIntyre 1988). Communitarians deny that the principles beloved by modern liberals can transcend the particular contexts and communities in which they are forged and interpreted.

My question, simply, is 'why not?' Why make morality a prisoner of distance in this way? If morality is defined here in respect of an extreme event – the death of a child by drowning or by hunger – and 'we' can make a difference to each outcome, why let geography serve this disabling role? Why not, instead, embrace geography and make it a party to a normative development studies and praxis? Why not learn from geography, and from the dynamics of globalization, and make the argument that our lives are not that distinct from the lives of distant strangers? Why not say that because we are in part responsible for the lives of others elsewhere we must bear a responsibility for the needs of distant strangers in times of distress? (Note how this argument depends upon a prior account of a radicalized modernity and modernization – hence my attention previously to the work of Marx, Weber and Giddens. Note also how an apparently academic study of globalization (or development studies) is then a precondition for a moral argument with practical implications. To the extent that we can show that our lives are radically entwined with the lives of distant strangers – through studies of colonialism, of flows of capital and commodities, of modern telecommunications, and so on – we can argue more powerfully for change within the global system. 'Theory' (but not certainty) is ever a condition of existence of action.)

Beitz puts this argument more formally when he notes that

> Particularism draws its appeal from three observations about the nature of morality as a social institution. First, moral beliefs are inevitably *learned* within the roles we occupy in a particular community [cf MacIntyre] and interpreted in light of its conventions. Secondly, the rules of morality, as they are under-

stood in a community, are only *justifiable* in terms of values that are acknowl-edged as values within that community. Third, the *motivation* to be moral is only likely to be effective if it is reinforced by the expectations of those with whom one has significant, continuing social ties. (Beitz 1991: 252; emphasis in the original).

Set against this, the conception of morality put forward by Beitz and myself makes reference to the concept of a moral subject as an abstract individual. Beitz concludes, however, that the fact that relationships and commitments form a basic element of one's personality and sense of being does not entail 'a particularist understanding of the moral point of view' (Beitz 1991: 253). There is no necessary inconsistency in recogniz-ing that 'our communal relationships play . . . a constitutive role in defining us as moral agents', while recognizing that we are capable 'of achieving the degree of detachment or objectivity that the notion of impartial judgement requires' (1991: 253). In short, Beitz believes that there is no logical reason to suppose that moral boundaries should coincide with the boundaries of our everyday community: not least because these latter boundaries are themselves not closed, but rather are defined in part by an increasing set of exchanges with distant strangers.

The rights of distant strangers

Arguments in favour of the relief of distress are not the only arguments which can be made in support of a minimally universalist politics which links the local to the distant. Far more pressing are a series of arguments which presume to deal with the question of justice. Once again, this is not the place for a detailed exposition of a wide range of arguments about the good society. I shall instead suggest that arguments for trans-national justice embrace a more or less minimal, or a more or less maximal, conception of justice–injustice which ranges, crudely, from the work of social democrats like John Rawls through to the work of John Roemer and the analytical Marxists. (I do not consider the just deserts arguments of the New Right. Nor do I consider the case of Marxism–Leninism, which rather neglects a concept of justice in its accounts of and for socialism. Finally, I do not here consider the argu-ments of Michael Walzer (1983) and Iris Marion Young (1990), each of whom explores the relationships between justice and the politics of difference.)[8] I shall further suggest that each of these accounts of justice makes reference to apparently abstract claims in a manner which can empower supposedly local struggles for development.

A Rawlsian account of justice has been called upon surprisingly little in the context of development studies. This may be because the Rawl-sian model offers a prospectus for modern western democracies which may not be appropriate in other contexts. It might also be felt that the Rawlsian account of justice is indeterminate (and thus not policy rele-vant), that it embodies an unwarranted individualism, and/or that its terms of reference are avowedly national and not international.

Each of these points has some substance to it. Rawls's classic text, *A*

Theory of Justice (Rawls 1972), is clearly intended as an intervention in the arena of contemporary American politics. As Alan Ryan describes it:

A Theory of Justice sets out to discover what rights we have against each other. . . . What is distinctive about it, and what accounts for its wide influence, is that in doing so, it defends what we might for shorthand call 'American welfare state liberalism' – the view that governments must open up to their citizens the widest possible range of civil rights and opportunities. (Ryan 1885: 105)

It is true also that Rawls's work seeks to privilege a principle of liberty (where each person is to have an equal right to the most extensive liberty compatible with a similar liberty for others) over a principle of difference (such that social and economic inequalities are to be arranged so that they are both (1) to the greatest benefit of the least advantaged, and (2) attached to positions and offices open to all under conditions of fair equality of opportunity). For Rawls, 'freedom may never be sacrificed for an increase in material well being' (Miller 1991: 422). (Compare this to the adage in the old Oxfam poster: 'Freedom begins with breakfast'.)

Notwithstanding these objections, the work of John Rawls surely does have a relevance for development theory and practice. Most signally, Rawls provides a theory of justice which is critical of the utilitarian assumption that the interests of particular individuals can be sacrificed to the aggregate welfare of the whole. Rawls is sensitive to the citizenship rights of those at the bottom of the pile; to their rights to shelter and to work, and to their rights not to have their bodies violated by death squads. The Rawlsian difference principle is also a powerful exposition of the argument that 'there but for the grace of God go I'. Rawls forces us to put ourselves in the position of those people who are less well off than ourselves for no good reason.

Rawls does this by means of an appeal to 'the original position', or what he calls 'the veil of ignorance'. Imagine that the principles of a just society are to be drawn up by agents who are 'deprived of knowledge about their talents and abilities and about the place they occupy [and will occupy] in society' (Miller 1991: 422). Imagine, in other words, that the rich and the powerful are not already the rich and the powerful, and that the chance of becoming one of the rich and powerful is far less than the chance of becoming one of the poor and the dispossessed. In such a situation – where on present odds one's chance of being born into a middle-class family in the USA are much less than the chance of being born into destitution in the developing world – the rational actor would want to (re)arrange society so that at least minimal standards of freedom and livelihood are guaranteed for all. In this manner Rawls provides an account of a just society from first principles. Rawls presents an abstract model of justice which is based precisely upon a reasoned command to think that the needs and rights of strangers could easily – and but for the accident of birth – be the needs and rights of ourselves.

Now there are problems involved in trying to operationalize the Rawlsian prospectus and in trying to extend it to the global stage or community. In respect to practical political and economic arrangements, it is clear that Rawls's account of a just society is compatible with a range of institutions ranging from market socialism to a 'market economy in which material inequalities serve as incentives, increasing the stock of goods available for distribution' (Miller 1991: 422–3). Although the Rawlsian prospectus does imply a strong measure of progressive tax-ation and state spending, it is by no means an invitation to socialism. The exact institutional form that a Rawlsian society might take will vary from place to place and can be determined only empirically. There are also problems in seeking to globalize what for Rawls is avowedly a western and national account of justice. Again, the most obvious objec-tion comes from the communitarians and from others who would point to the logical and institutional (as well as moral) problems implicit in the very concept of a global community. Nevertheless, in principle at least, and for its value in helping to create an idea of an expanded moral community, the Rawlsian argument may be considered at the inter-national scale. In this venture I would join Beitz and others in commend-ing the work of Rawls because it suggests a series of reasons for building political programmes and institutions which are fired by the idea of securing for distant strangers their basic needs not as alms but as of right.

A Rawlsian theory of justice, in conjunction with a globalist critique of communitarianism, provides people in the lands of the haves and the have-nots with arguments for change which are not easily dismissed.[9] Rawlsians are not alone, however, in providing such arguments. All manner of socialists continue to offer accounts of the rights of poor and dispossessed peoples which go well beyond the individualizing and minimax solutions devised by the social democrats.

Some of these arguments take one back to the work of Emmanuel and others in the 1970s (Emmanuel 1972). Thus a consistent refrain of some on the Left is that international trading practices are exploitative and unjust. The concept of justice referred to here is a concept of justice as requital, or the belief that a fair day's work is deserving of a fair day's pay. (A radical tinge is given by an appeal to a concept of exploitation.) Empirical points of reference for this argument would include transfer or over-pricing by transnational corporations, and the tariffs and quotas set up by the most powerful nations in defiance of GATT rules.

Still other arguments on the Left seek to rework Marx's account of exploitation and to tie such a new account to a more radical prospectus for redistribution and justice. A paradigm case is the work of John Roemer (Roemer 1981; 1982; 1988). Roemer has produced an incisive critique of the theory of exploitation in Marx as it derives from the labour theory of value. In its place he has proposed a general theory of exploi-tation wherein

> when exploitation is an injustice, it is not because it is exploitation as such [in the technical, Marxian sense, which can be insensitive to local variations in the disposition to work and save], but because the distribution of labor expended

and income received in an exploitative situation are the consequences of an initial distribution of assets that is unjust. (Roemer 1988: 57)

This is an important argument. Not only does Roemer reject the view that exploitation in itself is always bad and demanding of an ameliorative reversal (let us call it socialism); he further suggests that exploitation as injustice can only be recognized as such on the basis of a prior judgement as to the rectitude of an initial distribution of society's assets. What makes Roemer's work radical is his presumption that most existing forms of property distribution are indefensible – both because of their emergence through systems of primitive capitalist accumulation, and because Roemer rejects the so-called 'talents' effect' (whereby we assume that those with talents are reasonably rewarded by high wages and dividends). Roemer is able to argue an egalitarian case without having to resort to traditional Marxist accounts of exploitation and without having to endorse the allegedly non-exploitative nature of socialist societies. (Note that Roemer may have to depart from Rawls's determination to privilege a liberty principle over a difference principle.) But what also marks out Roemer's work is his willingness to make a case for a version of 'socialism', while making reference to at least parts of the arguments of social democrats like Dworkin and Rawls (see also Osborne 1991). Thus, although Roemer is committed to a political project which involves the public ownership of the means of production – and not least, one supposes, in the developing world – he can see that there is within the arguments of some social democrats a radical challenge to ideas which celebrate the right of an individual to the fruits of his or her 'own' labours. In this vein, Roemer confirms that one can engage in a radical political project without seeking to reinvent the landscapes of eastern Europe. (Whether Roemer is sufficiently attentive to questions of liberty and incentives is another matter.)[10] Perhaps more importantly, the arguments of Singer, Beitz, Rawls, Roemer and others – for all of their differences – each confirm that an activist commitment to political or developmental localism need not be pursued to the exclusion of a wider politics of development informed by the 'abstract' concerns of moral philosophy.

Conclusion

I am aware that the arguments of this chapter may seem unduly abstract. The development 'activist' may still be wondering about the relevance of a so-called moral and political philosophy. What, precisely, can be learned from the work of Rawls and Roemer, and what practical conclusions remain to be drawn?

My response to these questions is threefold. First, I shall insist that a mistrust of grand political projects and their associated 'metanarratives' should not encourage us to betray reason and the claims of justice entirely in favour of a political localism which is at best activistic and at worst deconstructive to the point of voyeurism. This chapter has struggled to argue the opposite case: that the complexity and evident fragmentation of the modern world should not be captured in thought and in (in)action by a parallel rejection of reason itself and of the transformative politics to which it might give rise. I find myself in agreement with Richard Kearney when he observed that: 'If deconstruction prevents us from asserting or stating or identifying anything, then surely one ends up not with "difference", but with indifference, where nothing is anything and everything is everything else?' (Kearney 1984, cited in Dews 1987: 231). It is for this reason that I am not willing to deconstruct further certain minimally universalist claims, of the type that involuntary death from hunger, or involuntary malnutrition, or involuntary homelessness, or slavery, or torture are bad things which must be struggled against. At the same time, I have not specified the forms which such struggles must take (which is an empirical matter); nor have I sought to offer any further 'universalist' claims beyond this Rawlsian minimum (although I would be happy to argue for more radical claims in particular contexts).[11]

This may still not satisfy the activist. My second point is that the seductions of post-modernism should be resisted precisely because the fragments and instincts which they celebrate are the fragments of a radicalized modernity which can be recognized by those many discourses of modernism which are dialectical, and which do have a sense of the strangeness of the modern world. But this too is a complex point. In making this claim I do not only suggest that the landscapes of a radicalized modernity are open to reason; I also suggest that the facts of globalization demand that we engage in a development praxis which does not confine itself to the local and the populist. More exactly, I do not believe that an avowed development activism can usefully be divorced from a wider vision of social and economic transformation. To seek to empower local people by 'putting the last first' is to make a judgement about society and to put into circulation certain claims about its inequalities and injustices. Very often these judgements will derive from the discourses of feminism, or environmentalism, or social democracy, and even from Marxism, and this in part empowers a local activism and local struggles. The capacity to act locally depends upon an ability to first think globally and locally: to recognize a need for change and to think through what such changes should consist in. For this task we need sound theory.

Third, I would argue that an interrogation of the boundaries between moral and political philosophy and development studies does point up some particular and exciting issues for development praxis. The examples of aid and debt may demonstrate what I have in mind (without being exhaustive). Both of these issues involve questions of the responsibilities of Northerners to distant strangers and both are issues wherein current practice is informed strongly by the punitive disciplines of the New Right. The main points I want to make are as follows.

First, it is important that an IMF-style policing of the debt crisis is resisted, and that the downgrading of official aid budgets is quickly repaired. Second, to contest current practice is to have resort to an account of our responsibilities to the claims of others in an interdependent global community. I have tried to show how such an account might be constructed. Third, what this *might* mean in practice is first, a demand that governments in the North commit themselves to delivering to governments in the South (or to some agreed agency: there is an important argument about sovereignty at stake here) an annual sum of money, goods and services equivalent to 5 per cent of gross domestic product; and second, a demand that the debt-cum-banking-cum-import crises should be policed such that a philosophy of just deserts and moral hazard (the idea that Third World debtors are responsible for their own plight and must pay up: Buiter and Srinivasan 1987) does not override a commitment to ensure that the human and civil rights of distant strangers, howsoever defined, are not undermined by massive resource outflows from their countries.

In other words, and in each case, a line is struck: first, which is committed to a development praxis which accepts that many 'local' conditions are manufactured extra-locally; second, which seeks to demonstrate that the global distribution of local conditions is unjust (if sometimes the result of local actors and actions); and third, which urges that actions can and should be taken in support of the needs and rights of distant strangers, by virtue of guidelines on the just society which emerge in various forms from political philosophers and others. These three claims in turn might form a minimum prospectus for development studies.

Finally, let me deal with some objections to this response to a mythical development activist. A first objection might be that my arguments are too vague. I concede this: the arguments are made in principle only and need to be fleshed out empirically. A second objection might be that my arguments are too abstract, with the result that the chapter still leans to development theory and not to development practice. To this objection I shall assent in part, while noting that even simple arguments need to be made at length, and while insisting that development theory and practice are not so easily separated. The one argument I will not bow to is a third one, which says that my arguments are idealistic or that they are 'unreal'. This, for me, is the heart of the matter. I accept that it is unlikely that an appeal to justice based on the new geography of globalization (and the global community thereby created) *will* call forth a politics of international development which agrees to write off debts in favour of development, and which agrees to tax Northern citizens sharply in order to give more aid to the South. My point, though, is that while policies do not so easily emerge from 'abstract theories', without such abstract theories they will not emerge at all.

Keynes put this very well in the 1930s when he noted that 'Practical men [in authority], who believe themselves to be quite exempt from any intellectual influences, are usually the slaves of some defunct economist' (Keynes 1936: ix). More recently, I would point to feminism as an exemplar of my argument. Feminism has been effective not only because it encourages women to define themselves (albeit differently in different contexts), but also because it has provided a vocabulary which helps us to re-think old practices and to think through new ones. It is precisely because most forms of feminism are committed to one version or another of a transformative politics that certain issues defined by and for feminists become, through struggle, accepted political issues and even accepted political practices (one thinks of rights to equal pay, child-care facilities, etc.). Feminism as philosophy, as reason, as language, enables and makes possible feminism as praxis (and vice versa).[12]

The same argument holds for development theory and praxis. The way out of the impasse in development studies lies not in a new empiricism, or even (or just) in a committed local activism. The escape route is much more circumscribed. It lies rather in a disposition to learn from local people and to work on their behalf; but to do so in the knowledge that a commitment so to act need not consist only in a Third Worldist activism (and far less in a grandiose socialist politics). A middle and connecting route would make reference to a politics of social justice. It would recognize that local injustices are connected to far wider logics of exploitation and injustice in the global system, and that as such a local activism cannot and should not exclude a responsibility to be active at other levels on behalf of something so 'abstract' as the claims of distant strangers.[13] The fact that these claims are not always clear, or are open to question, or are not recognized as such by most Northern governments, is not the issue here. The point is that to change the world it is first necessary to offer an account of the world and then to put into circulation a blueprint for change. (Compare attitudes to aid in Anglo-America and Scandinavia.) A related point is that a commitment to change the world need not take the form of a presumption to act for others on the grounds that we know what is best. The post-modern dilemma is avoided as and when we accept that certain human needs and rights, at least, can be taken to be 'universal', and when we learn that in attending to these needs and rights we are not so much dictating to others as dictating to ourselves.

Notes

1. A version of this paper was published in *Society and Space* in 1993 by Pion Limited.
2. In lumping together post-colonialism and post-modernism I do not mean to imply that all of the authors discussed under this sign subscribe to a singular critical position. That would be to fail to understand the purpose of both sets of discourses and to fail to understand the main charge of the post-structuralist turn to which both post-modernism and post-structuralism are indebted. I lump them together for convenience and to indicate a common mistrust of the (so-called) totalizing and normalizing ambitions of Marxist and other Enlightenment discourses. Post-modernism reflects this mistrust, very often, by its 'quest for the singular, the contingent event which by definition refuses all conceptualization, [which] can clearly be related to the project of constructing a form of knowledge that

respects the other without absorbing it into the same' (R Young 1990: 10). The post-colonial critic is likely to take a similar stance (see Spivak on Habermas: Spivak 1990: 72), but his/her point of focus is more specifically on the connections between discourse analysis and the colonial projects.

3. Post-Marxism is an elusive term. It will be used here to signal a set of discourses which share with Marxism a materialist ontology, and a commitment to causal analysis and a concept of determination. It further accepts that the 'economy' is structured by a systematically unequal distribution of assets and powers which leads to contradictions in the process of accumulation; post-Marxist political economy seeks to understand these processes, antecedents and effects. Post-Marxism departs from some traditions of Marxism: first, by opposing a methodological exclusivism born of the dogmatic privileging of certain concepts; second, by opposing propositions which speak of the necessary primacy of the economy (as an epistemological protocol); third, by attaching itself to a generalized theory of exploitation and class which is at some remove from the labour theory of value; fourth, by opposing functionalist accounts of power, the state and civil society; and fifth, by opposing those dualisms which oppose capitalism-in-general to socialism-in-general. It is a moot point whether the emphasis should be laid on 'post' or 'Marxist'. When this chapter was first drafted I assumed that the emphasis would be on the second word; in the light of some searching questions put to me by Tony Giddens and Geoff Hawthorn (in particular), I am no longer so sure. Either way, I *am* happy to acknowledge that the final version of the chapter owes a good deal to the comments of these two colleagues, and to comments from David Booth, Meghnad Desai, John Harriss, Gerry Kearns, Doreen Massey and Andrew Sayer. My thanks to them.

4. In presenting these polemical charges I do not presume that most Marxists are unaware of them, or are not responding to them: see Wood (1987); Watts (1988).

5. It should not be thought that Edwards is against theory *per se*; rather he is against irrelevant theory. Edwards cites with approval the suggestion by Cheryl Payer that 'Armchair radicals like myself . . . can perhaps make a modest contribution to international solidarity by performing scholarly tasks for which revolutionaries on the spot have no time and few resources' (cited in Edwards 1989: 1,130). My point is that it is necessary to interrogate these 'modest contributions' in order to see what their practical relevance might be and to assess their theoretical coherence. Once again, the theory/practice divide is not so easily made.

6. I am grateful to Geoff Hawthorn for advice on this point.

7. The work of Barry, Beitz and Singer is referred to in the text. Equally valuable is the work of Sen (1984; 1989); O'Neill (1986, 1991); Goulet (1989); Held (1991). See also Crocker (1991).

8. In this chapter my attention is confined to questions of distributive justice. Walzer and Young consider the question of justice in a much wider sense, in each case – but differently – connecting a powerful argument about justice to arguments for pluralism and for actions which affirm rather than suppress social group differences. I shall return to their critiques of the distributive justice paradigm on another occasion.

9. Again, I am not proposing a Rawlsian 'solution' to the development impasse; I am proposing it as an example of the sort of argument one might wish to see constructed to begin to depart the impasse. An important critique of Rawls's work from a Left modernist perspective is Heller (1989).

It should also be noted that the Rawlsian position has changed over the years.

10. As for Rawls (footnote 8), so for Roemer. For a critique of Roemer's work see Wood (1990).

11. For an important analysis of Chinese socialism between 1949 and 1976, see Sen (1989). Sen points out that 'the remarkable success of the Chinese economy in raising life expectancy at birth, from a figure close to forty years just after the revolution, to a figure close enough to seventy years just prior to the economic reforms, was built on paying attention to public delivery systems involving food, health care and related necessities' (Sen 1989: 779). Although this is a strong argument for a version of 'developmental social-ism', neither Sen nor myself would wish such an emphasis upon positive freedoms to be divorced from an analysis of the abuse of negative freedoms in China over the same period (Amnesty International 1978). Further, I would not want to assume that such an argument would hold, a priori, in other places, or in China at different times. The possibility that this version of socialism might give way to 'capitalism' or to 'market socialism' in China is not unthinkable. (This last point is consistent with Rawlsian arguments which note that the size of a cake can matter as much as the way in which it is shared.) Finally (and relatedly) I continue to follow Hindess and Hirst (1977) in preferring to speak of various relations of production and their conditions of existence (as opposed to capitalism in general, or socialism in general).

12. In citing feminism in this context I do not mean to occlude the connections between feminism and post-colonialism/post-modernism. Many feminists are concerned to argue against the normalizing assumptions of develop-ment studies (white male mythologies) and to point to the fragmentary nature of the self and the self-in-society. More prosaically, most feminists are aware of how difficult it is to engage in a 'universalist politics' except of a very basic order (such as I have described it in this chapter). The issue of female circumcision, for example, raises particular questions about the siting or 'worlding' of white, western feminists in relation to gendered cultural practices elsewhere. (At the same time this issue illustrates how a willingness to respect 'differences' can slide easily into a passive, if unin-tended, 'indifference'. It is a difficult and instructive issue.)

13. The chapter talks mainly, and as a point of focus, about the needs of distant strangers. It should not be thought, however, that the main propositions of the chapter are relevant only to a distant politics which engages with issues of aid delivery and debt management. I mean to imply, also, that concepts of justice and democratization (or even 'socialism') can empower suppos-edly local new social movements in the periphery. David Lehmann has discussed this relationship in respect to Catholic theology and *basismo* in Latin America (Lehmann 1990). In India, movements including the Chipko movements and the Jharkhand movements are each empowered in part (and given points of connection to one another) by political agendas which advance certain claims relating to local rights, moral economies, sustain-ability, the rights of women and so on (Guha 1989; Shiva 1989; Corbridge 1991). Finally, and to head off one last criticism, I do not believe that the provision of legal rights to justice and citizenship (howsoever defined) will suffice as political objectives. Such rights have of necessity to be struggled for and are given meaning, locally, by related actions to empower local people. 'Rights without resources' is not a practical proposition (Onibokun 1990).

References

Amnesty International (1978) *Political imprisonment in the People's Republic of China.* London, Amnesty International Publications

Anderson P (1983) *In the tracks of historical materialism.* London, Verso

Barker F et al. (eds) (1985) *Europe and its others,* 2 vols. Colchester, University of Essex Press

Barry B (1991) *Liberty and justice.* Oxford, Clarendon Press

Beitz C (1991) Sovereignty and morality in international affairs. In: Held D (ed) *Political theory today.* Cambridge, Polity Press

Berman M (1983) *All that is solid melts into air.* London, Verso

Bhabha H (1983) The other question. *Screen* 24

Bhabha H (1984) Of mimicry and man: the ambivalence of colonial discourse. *October* 28

Bhabha H (1986) Remembering Fanon: self, psyche and the colonial condition. Foreword to Fanon F, *Black skins and white masks.* London, Pluto Press

Booth D (1985) Marxism and development sociology: interpreting the impasse. *World Development* 13

Buiter W and **Srinivasan T N** (1987) Rewarding the profligate and punishing the prudent and poor: some recent proposals for debt relief. *World Development* 15

Chambers R (1983) *Rural development: putting the last first.* Harlow, Longman

Chambers R (1985) Putting last thinking first: a professional revolution. *Third World Affairs* 4

Cheung S (1986) *Will China go capitalist?* 2nd edn. London, Institute of Economic Affairs

Clifford J (1988) *The predicament of culture: twentieth century ethnography, literature and art.* Cambridge, MA, Harvard University Press

Clifford J and **Marcus G** (1986) *Writing culture: the poetics and politics of ethnography.* Berkeley, CA, University of California Press

Cocks J (1989) *The oppositional imagination: feminism, critique and political theory.* London, Routledge

Corbridge S (1986) *Capitalist world development: a critique of radical development geography.* London, Macmillan

Corbridge S (1988) The 'Third World' in global development. In Pacione M (ed) *The geography of the Third World: progress and prospect.* London, Routledge

Corbridge S (1989) Marxism, post-Marxism and the geography of development. In: Peet R and Thrift N (eds) *New models in geography* vol 1. London, Unwin Hyman

Corbridge S (1990) Post-Marxism and development studies: beyond the impasse. *World Development* 18

Corbridge S (1991) Ousting Singbonga: the struggle for India's Jharkhand. In: Dixon C and Heffernan M (eds) *Colonialism and development in the contemporary world.* London, Mansell

Crocker D (1991) Toward development ethics. *World Development* 19.

Dews P (1987) *Logics of disintegration: post-structuralist thought and the claims of critical theory.* London, Verso

Duncan N (1991) Postmodernism in geography. Mimeo, Department of Geography, Syracuse University, New York

Edwards M (1989) The irrelevance of development studies. *Third World Quarterly* 11

Emmanuel A (1972) *Unequal exchange.* London, Monthly Review Press

Fabian J (1983) *Time and the other.* New York, Columbia University Press

Fanon F (1967) *The wretched of the earth.* Harmondsworth, Penguin

Frank A G (1972) *Lumpenbourgeoisie and lumpendevelopment*. London, Monthly Review Press

Fukuyama F (1989) The end of history? *The National Interest*, Summer

Giddens A (1985) *The nation-state and violence*. Cambridge, Polity Press

Giddens A (1990) *The consequences of modernity*. Cambridge, Polity Press

Goulet D (1989) *Incentives for development*. New York, New Horizons

Guha R (1989) *The unquiet woods: ecological change and peasant resistance in the Himalaya*. Delhi, Oxford University Press

Habermas J (1990) *The philosophical discourse of modernity*. Cambridge, Polity Press

Harvey D (1982) *The limits to capital*. Oxford, Basil Blackwell

Harvey D (1989a) *The condition of postmodernity*. Oxford, Basil Blackwell

Harvey D (1989b) *The urban experience*. Oxford, Basil Blackwell

Held D (1991) Democracy, the nation-state and the global system. In: Held D (ed) *Political theory today*. Cambridge, Polity Press

Heller A (1989) *Beyond justice*. Oxford, Basil Blackwell

Hindess B and **Hirst P** (1977) *Mode of production and social formation*. London, Macmillan

Ignatieff M (1990) *The needs of strangers*. London, Hogarth Press

Kearney R (1984) *Dialogues with contemporary continental thinkers*. Manchester, Manchester University Press

Keynes J M (1936) *The general theory of employment, interest and money*. London, Macmillan

Kundera M (1988) *The unbearable lightness of being*. London, Faber

Laclau E (1990) *New reflections on the revolution of our time*. London, Verso

Larrain, J (1989) *Theories of development*. Cambridge, Polity Press

Lehmann D (1990) *Democracy and development in Latin America: economics, politics and religion in the postwar period*. Cambridge, Polity Press

Lukes S (1985) *Marxism and morality*. Oxford, Oxford University Press

Lyotard J-F (1985) *The post-modern condition*. Minneapolis, MN, University of Minnesota Press

MacIntyre A (1988) *Whose justice? Which rationality?* London, Duckworth

Mann M (1986) *The sources of social power* vol 1. Cambridge, Cambridge University Press

Marx K and **Engels F** (1975) *The Communist manifesto*. Harmondsworth, Penguin

Miller D (1991) John Rawls. In Miller D (ed) *The Blackwell encyclopaedia of political thought*. Oxford, Basil Blackwell

Mosley P, **Harrigan J** and **Toye J** (1991) *Aid and world power: the World Bank and policy-based lending* vol 1. London, Routledge

Mouzelis N (1988a) Sociology of development: reflections on the present crisis. *Sociology* 22

Mouzelis N (1988b) Marxism or post-Marxism? *New Left Review* 167

Mouzelis N (1990) *Post-Marxist alternatives: the construction of social orders*. London, Macmillan

Nove A (1983) *The economics of feasible socialism*. London, Allen & Unwin

O'Neill O (1986) *Faces of hunger: an essay on poverty, development and justice*. London, Allen & Unwin

O'Neill O (1991) Transnational justice. In: Held D (ed) *Political theory today*. Cambridge, Polity Press

Onibokun A (1990) Poverty as a constraint to citizen participation in urban redevelopment in developing countries. *Urban Studies* 27

Osborne P (ed) (1991) *Socialism and the limits of liberalism*. London, Verso

Payer C (1982) *The World Bank: a critical analysis*. London, Monthly Review Press

Peet R (1991) *Global capitalism: theories of societal development*. London, Routledge

Peffer R (1990) *Marxism, morality and social justice.* Princeton, NJ, Princeton University Press

Rawls J (1972) *A theory of justice.* Oxford, Oxford University Press

Richards P (1985) *Indigenous agricultural revolution.* London, Hutchinson

Riddell R (1987) *Foreign aid reconsidered.* London, James Curry

Roemer J (1981) *Analytical foundations of Marxist economic theory.* Cambridge, Cambridge University Press

Roemer J (1982) *A general theory of exploitation and class.* Cambridge, Cambridge University Press

Roemer J (1988) *Free to lose.* Cambridge, MA, Harvard University Press

Ryan A (1985) John Rawls. In: Skinner Q (ed) *The return of grand theory in the human sciences.* Cambridge, Cambridge University Press

Said E (1979) *Orientalism.* New York, Vintage Books

Sartre J-P (1967) Preface. In: Fanon F, *The wretched of the earth.* Harmondsworth, Penguin

Sayer D (1991) *Capitalism and modernity: an excursus on Marx and Weber.* London, Routledge

Sen A (1984) *Resources, values and development.* Oxford, Basil Blackwell

Sen A (1989) Food and freedom. *World Development* 17

Shiva V (1989) *Staying alive: women, ecology and development.* London, Zed Press

Singer P (1972) Famine, affluence and morality. *Philosophy and Public Affairs* 1

Singer P (1979) *Practical ethics.* Cambridge, Cambridge University Press

Sklair L (1988) Transcending the impasse: metatheory, theory and empirical research in the sociology of development and underdevelopment. *World Development* 16

Sklair L (1991) *Sociology of the global system.* London, Harvester-Wheatsheaf

Spivak G C (1985) Can the subaltern speak? Speculations on widow sacrifice. *Wedge* 7/8

Spivak G C (1987) *In other worlds: essays in cultural politics.* London, Routledge

Spivak G C (1990) *The post-colonial critic: interviews, strategies, dialogues.* London, Routledge

Taylor C (1985) *Philosophical papers,* 2 vols. Cambridge, Cambridge University Press

Toye J (1987) *Dilemmas of development: reflections on the counter-revolution in development theory and policy.* Oxford, Basil Blackwell

Trinh T M (1989) *Woman, native, other: postcoloniality and feminism.* Bloomington, Indiana University Press

Unger R (1987) *False necessity.* Cambridge, Cambridge University Press

Vandergeest P and **Buttel F** (1988) Marx, Weber and development sociology. *World Development* 16

Walzer M (1983) *Spheres of justice: a defence of pluralism and equality.* Oxford, Basil Blackwell

Watts M (1988) Deconstructing determinisms. *Antipode* 21

Weber M (1970) *From Max Weber.* Eds Gerth H and Wright Mills C. London, Routledge

Wood E M (1986) *The retreat from class.* London, Verso

Wood E M (1990) Rational choice Marxism: is the game worth the candle? *New Left Review* 177

Young I M (1990) *Justice and the politics of difference.* Princeton, NJ, Princeton University Press

Young R (1990) *White mythologies: writing history and the West.* London, Routledge

Part II
Reconnecting theory and research: new perspectives on the struggle for development

Studies of development issues by sociologists, social geographers and political scientists have often suffered from both premature generalization and a narrowly economistic approach to the explanation of development processes. Ironically, those supposedly specializing in the study of socio-cultural, spatial and political dimensions of development were until recently among the most firmly committed to dryly typological approaches to the study of social relations, to theories of global process lacking all sense of place, and to society- or economy-centred accounts of the state. In practice (although this was always denied in principle) there was little room for the sort of analysis in which institutionalized patterns of politics, or cultural, spatial, environmental and other influences on the evolution of social relationships, figure as *explanatory variables*, accounting for significant differences in outcome between otherwise similar settings.

The three chapters in Part II illustrate well both the progress that has been made and the major tasks that remain in liberating the agenda of social development research from these kinds of shackles. Chapter 5, by Nicos Mouzelis, provides a fresh and accessible statement of what some would regard as one of the most important contributions to the rethinking of macro-sociology in the west since the late 1960s.

Mouzelis's analytical focus is the fundamental issue of the relationship between political and socio-economic processes and structures in the context of development. Like the somewhat better known writings of Theda Skocpol, but from a different and independent starting-point, his books and articles have placed (or perhaps re-placed) the study of the state and political institutions at the very centre of inquiries into the mainsprings of national economic development and underdevelopment.

As with Buttel and McMichael in Chapter 2, Mouzelis wishes to continue to occupy the neo-Marxist terrain of historically oriented macro-sociology. His method, like theirs, is the properly contextualized comparative study of different developmental trajectories at the nation-state level. His particular concern is the experience of what Albert Hirschman once called 'late late' development, especially in the Balkan region of south-eastern Europe and in the southern cone of South America (understood broadly so as to include Brazil). What he succeeds in showing for these particular country cases is, nevertheless, richly suggestive of illuminating approaches to the study of social sources of economic development and stagnation in other times and places.

Drawing on and further elaborating the thesis of his 1986 book on the subject, Mouzelis argues that the Balkan and Latin American countries he is concerned with share a common historical heritage based on the triple foundation of a colonial legacy of centralized patrimonial rule; the 'early', that is to say pre-industrial, introduction of parliamentary government; and extensive 'late' industrialization on an import-substitution model. Comparing the trajectories of these countries with those of other 'small', late-developing states such as Norway, Finland, New Zealand and Australia, he maintains that their relative lack of successful economic development is attributable ultimately not to the sorts of general economic constraints and local institutional barriers emphasized by world-system theorists and orthodox Marxists of different stripes (as well as, we might add, by most versions of 1960s modernization theory), but to specific features of the structure and functioning of their *states*. The argument develops as follows.

For the Balkan and Latin American cases, a review of agricultural change and industrial growth between the mid-nineteenth and mid-twentieth centuries reveals a common pattern of missed opportunities; state-sponsored reforms and regulative activities that proved effective elsewhere were neglected or delayed, both in Greece and Argentina, and in Bulgaria and Chile. Contrary to established wisdoms, however, what was chiefly responsible for this failure was the way the framework of political life (the 'mode of domination') evolved during the era following the dissolution of the Iberian and Ottoman empires. By the beginning of the twentieth century, the interaction between the patrimonial legacy and an oligarchic form of parliamentarism had created a system in which the substantial resources generated by commercial agriculture and mineral exports flowed not into the further modernization of agriculture or industry, but into the growth of 'a monstrous state apparatus, whose dynamism obeyed imperatives emanating from the polity rather than from the economy' (p. 137).

The broadening of political participation that followed in the early twentieth century resulted in the modification, not the overthrow, of clientelistic political practices, partly on account of inauspicious timing (it preceded large-scale industrialization and the growth of relatively autonomous mass organizations). Both the limitations in economic-development performance and the political upheavals that have typified these countries in the post-war period are to be explained primarily by the contradictions of this mode of political domination as it evolved into a system of 'guided democracy' based on a mixture of exclusionist and incorporative controls.

The notion that differences in developmental outcomes in otherwise similar settings may be more due to differences in state structure and political arrangements than to anything else, is now far more widely accepted than when Mouzelis and Skocpol first articulated it. Mouzelis is perhaps unduly pessimistic when he writes here that attempts to 'bring the state back in' to the development literature have not taken root (p. 127). For example, nearly all of the best recent writing about the subject he ends his chapter with – the success stories of South Korea and Taiwan – may be said to be informed by insights of this sort. The influence of similar ideas in recent literature on South and South East Asia is strongly reflected in the chapter by John Harriss (discussed below). On the other hand, there is no faulting his claim that given their commonness 'the cases where the holders of the means of domination/ coercion have the upper hand over the holders of the means of production . . . and where very often considerations related to the logic of domination prevail over the logics of the market and of all other institutional spheres' (pp. 126–7) have not yet received sufficiently serious attention.

As Mouzelis makes clear in the concluding paragraphs of his contribution, there is more at stake here than at first meets the eye. The implications of further research at this level may turn out to be relevant not only to the reconstruction of development theory but also for the practice of international NGOs and other agencies, whose campaigns and interventions often carry explicit or implicit messages about the causes of national economic backwardness that may turn out to be barely justified. As he puts it:

> If I am right about the profoundly anti-developmental character of most Third World state apparatuses, neither more favourable world market mechanisms nor less exploitative centre–periphery relations will enable peripheral countries to achieve a semi-peripheral status. . . . Another way of putting this is to argue that the highly unequal distribution of wealth on a world scale should not be seen primarily in terms of the structure of world markets, or of the shortsightedness or self-orientation of the core. Instead it should be viewed as the result of an inter-state system in which the majority of members have administrative structures which systematically prevent them from taking advantage of the developmental opportunities that the changing world economy constantly generates. (pp. 146–7)

Mouzelis's arguments here and in his other writings make a seminal contribution to the new directions in social development research by placing the analysis of state structures at centre stage. The chapter which follows, by Alberto Arce, Magdalena Villarreal and Pieter de Vries, marks out another intellectual terrain which while undervalued by much previous social development theorizing is today the subject of a vigorous research programme. Here the argument *begins* with the centrality of the state.

Taking the conclusions of Skocpol (and by implication, Mouzelis) as a point of departure, Arce, Villarreal and de Vries explore approaches to the analysis of state-sponsored programmes for rural development in Latin America, drawing illustrations from their own field research in Mexico and Costa Rica. They adopt Skocpol's conceptualization of the state as a specific type of organization whose relationship with social and economic forces and structures, including classes, is to be determined empirically. However, they are concerned that in correcting the previous tendency of western liberal and Marxist social science to reduce the state to society, the newer 'state-centred' forms of analysis are sometimes guilty, if only by default, of exaggerating the capacity of states to penetrate societies and enforce their policies. Empirical research is needed not merely at the comparative-historical level, to establish broad patterns of variability in state forms, but also at the level of the formulation and 'implementation' of various sorts of policy within particular historical settings. The task is to explore the range of factors operating across the 'interface' between the state and society which have an influence on the outcomes of state-sponsored change.

Developing the general theme that rural development outcomes are to an important degree socially constructed, Arce, Villarreal and de Vries draw attention to affinities and implicit linkages between the actor-oriented 'interface analysis' promoted by Norman Long (for example in Chapter 3 of this book); the arguments of the late Bernard Schaffer about the 'room for manoeuvre' in the design of rural development programmes, and the writings of Raymond Apthorpe, Geof Wood and others on the relationship between 'discourse' and power in such settings. One of the things that these contributions have in common is that they entail critiques both of official ideologies and self-conceptions of government and international agencies involved in the rural development 'business' and of certain social-science views of the policy process. They involve what Long and van der Ploeg in Chapter 3 refer to as 'deconstructing planned intervention'.

However, Arce, Villarreal and de Vries are not merely concerned with pointing to the fallacies and elements of self-interest in received thinking about rural development. They believe it is important to build up a body of detailed studies of what they call 'the social life of rural development', gathering empirical material on the elements of *dis*organization and *in*coherence which enter the picture on the side of the intervening agencies, and on the sometimes hidden resources available to the 'beneficiary' groups. For them, the processes by which local people are able to steer official programmes in different directions are as interesting as the more easily assumed ability of the powerful to manipulate the weak.

These kinds of dimensions of the reality of rural development become visible, the authors argue, only when the fieldworker gets close enough to the subjects of the research to be able to record the way public programmes enter the 'life-worlds' of different individuals and groups on both sides of the agency/beneficiary interface, and then become the object of different personal and group 'projects'. From the study of such situations it becomes clear that poor people are often capable of making remarkably effective use of the limited power within their reach (as emphasized by James Scott and discussed further by John Harriss in Chapter 7); there is also evidence, confirming recent suggestions from the sociology of knowledge, that power is a resource that within certain kinds of dynamic settings is capable of being 'manufactured' and/or 'destroyed' within comparatively short periods.

These claims are supported in the chapter by three independently recorded empirical accounts. Pieter de Vries carried out a detailed ethnographic study of the work of a government land-settlement and development agency on the Atlantic coast of Costa Rica in Central America. From this fieldwork he has extracted an account of the way the public field trials and ceremonies organized by the agency became vehicles of struggles for legitimacy and effective power between competing factions within both the official government sphere and that of organizations representing beneficiary groups. In the space available it is not possible for de Vries to explore the kinds of eventualities that are possible within such situations, but the implication seems to be that, at the local level at least, outcomes will be characterized by a comparatively high level of unpredictability and, hence, 'room for manoeuvre'.

The empirical stories drawn from the Mexican studies by Arce and Villarreal illustrate different aspects of the way power relations can be altered in the sorts of practical situations from which rural development is built up. Arce reports an incident in 1987 in one Mexican community which may (and may not) be typical of the localities involved in the spectacular growth of export-oriented agriculture in Mexico in recent years. Despite the initially impressive backing for the paternalistic and, in the context, conservative position of the local agricultural officer, the activities of a single representative of the small growers in the area were sufficient to turn the situation around and produce an outcome favourable to the reestablishment of links between local producers and US-based marketing firms. Arce presents the episode as illustrative of the 'fluidity' of power at the micro level, although it could clearly also be read as indicative of the local effects of changes in macro-policies and power relations in Mexico in an era of economic liberalization.

In her short account of a women's beekeeping project in the same part of Mexico, Villarreal reinterprets Scott's 'weapons of the weak' with a focus on gender relations. In so doing, she provides a nice illustration of the trend of recent research and action on gender issues in the Third World. In the early days of women-and-development research, it was often assumed that observed patterns and trends of change in relations between women and men had immediately appreciable and univocal significance, reflecting as they did the impact of certain general and well-understood socio-economic processes. In more recent years, both the simple evaluative judgements and the mechanical quality of the imputed causality in these early studies have been increasingly challenged. Villarreal's questioning of standard assumptions about female 'autonomy' as a yardstick of women's emancipation in rural Mexico is informed by this newer approach, in which the observer is careful to explore all the complex interactions involved before reaching conclusions about the significance of changes for the people concerned or for the wider society in which they live. Without necessarily acceding to the views of some 'post-modernist feminists' according to which general concepts relating to women's oppression come to be regarded as illegitimate *per se*, Villarreal follows most of those working in this field today in recommending a strong dose of the 'listening and reflection' that is the stuff of good ethnography.

In Chapter 7, by John Harriss, we are treated to a style of analysis of rural social change that is actor-oriented in this important latter sense, but which is also careful to root itself in an appreciation of the relatively immutable, 'structural' features of the research setting. Drawing on an empirical case study that is remarkable for its combination of 'thick description' of local social relationships with historical depth gained from repeated visits to the same locality over two decades, Harriss asks why the results of 'green revolution' agrarian change in this district of southern India have been different from those that he and nearly everyone else expected. He also wants to know why, in general, results have differed so much between the various districts that have been the subject of serious studies in different parts of India.

In providing answers to these important questions, Harriss steers a course 'between economism and post-modernism' in several senses. Expectations among social researchers about the likely impact of technological change on incomes and patterns of social inequality in India in the 1970s were influenced by a number of alternative visions of the future dynamic of economic class relations in the countryside. These contending views formed the stuff of the important Indian branch of the once generally celebrated 'mode of production controversy'. Harriss believes that the Marxist debate about the proper characterization of 'peasant' petty commodity production under capitalism did ultimately produce a resolution, in the sense of an acceptable account of the economic character of peasant production. What it did not and could not provide, given its fundamentally economistic character, is a framework for understanding or predicting the direction and pace of agrarian change within given social formations. For, at this level, politics, culture and ideology are critical influences that we ignore at our peril.

Contrary to expectations and despite high initial levels of social differentiation, agricultural development in North Arcot District did not come to a halt after the spurt caused by the green-revolution innovations in the early-to-mid-1970s. Economic growth continued, and there were 'widely distributed though very modest increases in real incomes' (p. 179). The causes that seem to have contributed to this relatively happy outcome are a mixture of 'conjunctural factors', including technological issues and features of the wider political economy of the region (which tend to get abstracted-away in a 'mode of production' analysis of rural social relations), and state-level economic and social policies reflecting the populist political complexion of Tamil Nadu during this period.

Agrarian change in India in recent decades seems to have produced a number of distinct patterns of change rather than a single central tendency with mere local variants, making the country a fascinating laboratory for all those interested in the sources of developmental diversity. As Harriss shows, recognizing the centrality of politics in economic change gets us some way towards a better understanding of this issue, but at least in the Indian context, it is hardly possible to separate politics from questions of ethnicity, caste and cultural identity. At the local level, this includes what has been discussed as 'the moral economy of the peasantry' or what Harriss himself presents as the culturally embedded 'construction of class relations'. Moreover, comparison of evidence from three parts of India in addition to Tamil Nadu does seem to provide significant support for Harriss's claim, in the final section of the chapter, that divergences in trends of agrarian change reflect to an important extent differences 'in the ways class relations are constructed' (p. 191).

The point here about post-modernism is that there is no need for insistence on the cultural construction of class relations to lead to the conclusion that class divisions do not exist or are unimportant 'objectively' to the kind of future that rural people in India or elsewhere look forward to (no more than for recognition of the constructedness of gender relations to imply that the idea of gender oppression has no general validity). Research on rural development needs to be capable of showing 'respect for and understanding of people's own understandings', without abdicating responsibility for distinguishing, 'ideas and actions in terms of their efficacy in relation to the transformation' of people's circumstances (p. 192). In this sense, at least, the future of social development research should be neither actor-oriented nor structuralist, but must involve an effective marriage of indispensable elements of both traditions.

CHAPTER 5

The state in late development:
historical and comparative perspectives

Nicos Mouzelis

This chapter examines, from a historical and comparative perspective, the relationship between state and the economy in 'late-late'[1] developers. Although my main focus will be on the developmental trajectories of some Balkan and Latin American societies, less systematic references will be made to other cases as well. The major thesis of the chapter is that in those countries which tried to 'catch up' with the west at the end of the nineteenth and in the twentieth century, it is the structure and functioning of the state which primarily explains both the failures and the relatively few success stories.

One reason why this point has not received sufficient attention in the development literature is that all the major theoretical approaches neglect to deal with the state in a systematic and theoretically rigorous manner. This is not only true of the market-oriented neo-classical approach; it is equally true of the culture-oriented modernization/neo-evolutionist theories, as well as of the various neo-Marxist dependency approaches to development.[2]

The Marxist approaches to development do, of course, refer to the state incessantly. However, even when Marxists cease to view the state as an epiphenomenon or as the instrument of the bourgeoisie, even when they proclaim the relative autonomy of the political, the state is always conceptualized in a way that systematically ignores cases where the logic of domination prevails over the logic of economic distribution or production.

More specifically, the 'relative autonomy of the state' thesis has not led to the creation of new conceptual tools, in the sense that Marxists continue to define the state in economic terms (i.e. in terms of its contribution to the reproduction of capital, as an instrument of the dominant classes, as an arena where class struggles take place, etc.). But if the state in capitalist societies is defined as serving capital or capitalists, this very definition rules out an open-ended investigation of the cases where the holders of the means of domination/coercion have the upper hand over the holders of the means of production; or cases where state policies obstruct rather than promote the extended reproduction of capitalism. It is precisely, as I shall argue in this chapter, cases like these which are very common in late developing countries, where civil society in general and classes in particular are weakly organized and where very often considerations related to the logic of domination prevail over the logics of the market and of all other institutional spheres.

Given that Marxist political theory pushes under the carpet this type of case, it is not surprising that the obviously negative, obstructionist role (*vis-à-vis* the expanded reproduction of capitalism) that the state is playing in many Third World countries is not taken very seriously into account. Consider, for instance, Marxist writings that view Third World formations as an articulation of modes of production within which the capitalist mode dominates but takes a 'restrictive form' (in the sense that non-capitalist modes persist on a large scale). In trying to account for this characteristic of late capitalist development Marxists have hardly bothered to investigate the role of the state in creating and sustaining this type of restriction. The marked persistence of pre- or non-capitalist forms has been variously explained by the machinations of metropolitan capital (Taylor 1979: 220 ff); in terms of the profit requirements of indigenous capital (Wolpe 1975); or as a result of the nature of Third World pre-capitalist economies (Rey 1971). In none of these attempts have any questions been asked about the extent to which at least the internal obstacles to an expanded reproduction of capital in the Third World may be political rather than economic. The organization of the Third World state and its often obstructive, anti-developmental intervention in the economy have been similarly neglected.[3]

Of course, Marxism is everywhere on the decline now. Still, given that it has not been replaced by a more adequate holistic framework; given also its pervasive (if often unacknowledged) impact on all social scientists concerned with the overall reproduction and transformation of complex societies, its reductive treatment of the state continues to affect even those who do not consider themselves Marxists. Moreover, recent attempts to combat economic reductionism, and to 'bring the state back in', as far as the literature on development is concerned, have not taken root. They have brought no radical reconsideration (such as the elaboration of new conceptual tools or new development policies) of the role of the state in the development process. In brief, this neglect of the political as a major, if not *the* major, base for explaining the varied capitalist trajectories of late-late developers, constitutes the Achilles' heel of all development theory.

The above argument becomes quite obvious in the light of Gerschenkron's thesis (1962) on European industrialization. This is that the later a country joins the development race, the more it requires guidance from 'above', chiefly from the state or other centralized institutions.[4] What I would like to add to Gerschenkron's very plausible thesis is that certain states are better than others at drawing up and implementing development strategies, and that it is in fact the actual structure of the state that is the most crucial aspect for understanding why late developers with comparable starting-points and resources have performed so unevenly within the world economy.

A look at countries that began their industrialization relatively late, but which have managed to become more or less part of the so-called developed or 'first' world (e.g. Norway, Finland, New Zealand, Australia), usually reveals

1   successful agricultural modernization, resulting not only in increased productivity but also in a certain rural egalitarianism capable of engendering an important home market for industrial goods
2   strong links between the primary and secondary sectors, and more generally the creation of an industrial sector with, sooner or later, its own niche in the world market and competitive in certain limited areas[5]
3   a state apparatus playing a crucial role in the modernization of agriculture as well as in its effective articulation with industry.

In the case of relative failures, on the other hand, the state either did not succeed in breaking up traditionally organized big landed estates (as in Latin America), or if it did (as in the inter-war Balkans), it neglected to provide the resulting smallholders with the kind of assistance agricultural modernization entails. Either case could mean only feeble development of the domestic market, and weak or permanently negative linkages between industry and agriculture.

One of the most important effects of such unsuccessful economic development is the impact it has on the state. The failure to modernize agriculture and to articulate it effectively with industry usually leads to an over-inflation of the state apparatus, and to an accentuation of its clientelistic and 'corrupt' features. In other words, it creates a vicious circle. The more the state fails to modernize agriculture, the more it acquires 'anti-developmental' features – that is, features that prevent the rationalization both of itself and of the overall economy.

Barrington Moore (1969) has argued that failure among the early developers to modernize agriculture usually led to a revolutionary mobilization of the peasantry, as both landlords and the state tried to squeeze resources from the direct producers that a non-modernized agriculture was quite unable to provide. In contrast to this, the failure of late developers to modernize agriculture does not necessarily lead to a revolutionary situation, since massive urbanization operates as a safety valve by siphoning people away from the countryside. At the same time, a massive influx of former agricultural producers into cities with weak or non-existent industrialization unavoidably brings an over-inflation of the state apparatus, and this in turn, instead of helping, becomes the major obstacle to development. I shall try to demonstrate these points by looking, from a historical and comparative perspective, at the developmental trajectories of Balkan and southern-cone Latin American societies.

There are significant parallels in the development of the Balkan and southern-cone Latin American societies, their geographical distance from each other and very different cultural and historical backgrounds notwithstanding. Until the beginning of the nineteenth century all of these societies were parts of huge patrimonial empires (Ottoman and

Iberian respectively). For all of them, independence came in the nineteenth century, and they all instituted parliamentary forms of political
rule. Unstymied by constant malfunctioning, these parliamentary institutions manifested quite remarkable resilience. From the second half of
the nineteenth century they managed to maintain themselves more or
less intermittently until, in the case of the northern Balkan societies, the
1930s, and until the rise in the 1960s and 1970s of military authoritarian
regimes in the case of Greece and the southern-cone countries. Moreover, as is evident from what followed the eventual collapse of these
regimes, the interval of dictatorial rule did not automatically entail the
irreversible demise of parliamentary democracy.

With respect to the economy, again all the societies under review did
manage – despite their relatively late start and their failure to industrial-
ize in the nineteenth century – first, to provide themselves with a considerable economic infrastructure, and then, between the wars and after
the Second World War, to achieve an impressive degree of industrialization. For the sake of convenience I shall call these societies (correctly
described as 'late-late' industrializing capitalist societies with early and
persistent quasi-parliamentary politics) the *parliamentary semi-periphery*.
Since the Latin American societies have been given greater coverage in
the development literature than those of the Balkans, my examination of
the role of the state in late development will be rather more detailed for
the latter. The Latin American discussion will be restricted to Argentina,
Chile and Brazil.

The development of agriculture

As mentioned already, all successful cases of late development were
grounded in the modernization of agriculture and other primary sectors
of the economy. This generally involves effective agrarian reforms,
which result in both an increase in productivity and a certain egalitarianism in the form of a broad diffusion of agricultural income to the majority of the direct producers.

The Balkan experience

In the post-independence Balkan societies, unlike those of southern-
cone Latin America, big landownership was not very strong. In places
where the Ottoman landlords were obliged to leave rather abruptly (as
in southern Greece and Bulgaria), the big estates they left behind were
taken over by the direct producers or by the state (which eventually
handed them over to the direct producers). In places where the Turkish
withdrawal was more gradual (as for instance in central and northern
Greece), the Turkish landlords could arrange to sell their estates to well-
off Christians – who, however, never had as strong and secure a hold
over their new acquisitions as did their Latin American counterparts.[6]

To take Greece as an example, the rich diaspora Greeks who bought ex-Turkish estates in Euboea, Attica and Thessaly never managed to get the hold on the state apparatus that Chilean or Argentinian landlords enjoyed in nineteenth-century Latin America. In consequence, they were not able to put up any serious resistance when agrarian reforms were introduced during the inter-war period. These reforms, not only in Greece but in the northern Balkans as well (with the partial exception of Romania), established small-peasant ownership as the dominant form of cultivation.

What needs stressing here is that, despite the weakness and irreversible decline of big landed property in the inter-war Balkans, and despite the relative rural egalitarianism it entailed, there was no effective agricultural modernization. Instead, increasing land fragmentation,[7] and the state's inability to put a stop to it and more generally to assist the small producers by making available cheap credit, technical knowledge, education, etc., resulted in a situation of relative backwardness. This meant that the growing integration (from roughly 1850 onwards) of Balkan agriculture into the world market, and the considerable income obtained from exports of primary products (agricultural and mineral), were not used for modernizing the primary sector and articulating it effectively with industrial production. They simply bloated further an already over-inflated service sector, within which the state, with its rapidly growing administrative and military apparatuses, occupied the dominant position.

Another way of putting this is to say that a considerable surplus was extracted from the small cultivators (via innumerable merchant intermediaries/exporters, very high indirect taxation, 'price scissors' favouring industrial goods, etc.) without much being returned to them in the form of technical assistance, cheap credit, reasonably priced fertilizers, tools and so on.[8] This of course meant the persistence of low productivity and agricultural backwardness, and in consequence the very slow development of a home market. Such a situation severely hampers and drastically reduces the likelihood of relatively balanced growth.

The situation of Balkan agriculture in the post-war period was, of course, anything but uniform. In Greece[9] it continued in the form of petty-commodity production, whereas in the northern part of the peninsula it had become thoroughly collectivized. Even though the results of collectivized agriculture were much more disastrous, both cases stand in dramatic contrast with other small European countries whose primary sectors were also integrated into the world market, but which managed to use the considerable resources derived from primary exports in a more egalitarian as well as more efficient manner. So in Denmark or Sweden, for instance, a combination of successful state policies favouring medium-sized farms and strong co-operative organizations meant that the

export income went into the pockets of family farmers. This in turn provided them with the means to modernise agriculture and to pay for mass consumer goods. Both would not have been possible if land had been splintered or heavily concentrated. If very small farms had dominated, whether rented or owned, their surplus and therefore the means to invest would have been low. (Manzel 1990: 36)

The Latin American pattern

In Latin America the basic parameters were quite different, but the end result was not much more encouraging. Having developed a considerable economic intrastructure in the second half of the nineteenth century, the southern-cone countries managed to adjust their export economies to the 1929 Depression and switched to large-scale import-substituting industrialization. This did not bring any radical change in the relations of production in the countryside, however. The populist leaders who came to power as a result of the rapid rise of the middle classes and the development of urban populism, did not implement serious agrarian reforms once they were elected. While the traditional export/landowning interests did lose the oligarchic control over the state they had enjoyed in the nineteenth century, given that (for a variety of historical reasons) they were much more powerful than their Greek counterparts,[10] they successfully resisted trenchant changes in the highly inegalitarian and largely archaic agrarian structures. In all three countries – Chile, Argentina and Brazil – a more or less implicit deal emerged between urban populist leaders and the landowners. This on the one hand institutionalized the broadening of political participation and the entrance of 'new men' into the national political arena, and on the other left the landowners free to deal with their rural subordinates in the traditional manner.

To take Chile more specifically as an example, the considerable hold of the traditional *hacendado* over his *inquilinos, peons* and *empleados* persisted long after the end of oligarchic politics. Although the crumbling of Chile's oligarchic parliamentarism, together with the subsequent world economic crisis, certainly contributed to weakening the landowners' hold over the peasantry, the effect on the traditional control mechanisms was very slow to show itself (Bauer 1975). It was not until well into the 1950s and the early 1960s that Chilean landlords began to lose their grip on the political support of their rural subordinates. One major reason for this is that the 1925 Constitution (and particularly the manner of its implementation) overwhelmingly favoured the rural elites.[11] There was another and even more important reason why the upper classes in rural Chile were so very slow to lose their electoral pull. This was the existence of a social pact between landowners and urban political groups, which successfully staved off unionization of the rural labour force until the 1960s (Loveman 1977: 257 ff).

Although in Brazil and Argentina the circumstances were very different from those in Chile,[12] these countries too saw no serious efforts at radical agrarian reforms, either before or after the 1929 world economic crisis. If, therefore, agricultural modernization in the Balkans failed because of state incompetence, in Latin America state incompetence was combined with strong landowners' resistance to any serious transformation of the minifundium–latifundium complex that still marks large ar eas of the Latin American countryside.

The development of industry

Industrialization before and after 1929

While Balkan exports during the second half of the nineteenth century did provide the necessary resources for the creation of a rudimentary economic infrastructure (roads, ports, etc.), very little money was spent either to modernize agriculture or (as was done in northern Spain and Italy) to develop a substantial industrial sector. Despite a certain amount of proto-industrialization, and some timid attempts to promote an industrial take-off, industry in the nineteenth-century Balkans was insignificant in terms of both labour employed and contribution to the gross national product (Berend and Ranki 1982). The industrial process in the peninsula did not acquire any real momentum until the period of the Balkan Wars and the First World War. This process was then dramatically accentuated when, in the wake of the 1929 Depression, the Balkan states adopted highly protectionist policies and a programme of import-substituting industrialization (Berend and Ranki 1974).

The pattern was quite similar in the southern-cone countries of Latin America. There, strong western demand for agricultural and mineral products and the settlement of large numbers of south European immigrants had contributed to the rapid commercialization of agriculture and the growth of social overhead capital, but not to the development of big industry. Even in Argentina, by far the most industrialized of the pre-war Latin American countries, the pre-1929 industrial activities were closely linked up with the export sector, and consisted of processing local raw materials and semi-manufactured imported consumer goods. Moreover, the vast majority of Argentina's industrial establishments (like those of the Balkans) were made up of artisanal units employing no or very few wage labourers (Diaz-Alejandro 1970: 209 ff; Furtado 1970: 108).

In both the Balkans and the southern-cone countries, it was in the period after 1929 that large-scale, state-guided industrialization gained momentum. In neither the one nor the other area was the post-1929 drive for import-substituting industrialization crowned with much success. In both cases the government's introduction of measures for the encouragement of industrial investments merely created a number of highly inefficient, privately owned firms, which operated almost entirely on borrowed capital but continued to survive, even after the world economic crisis was long over, due to highly protective tariff walls. This was in part because the creation from above of a class of industrial capitalists was founded on state policies that were both non-discriminating and particularistic. They were non-discriminating because the favourable measures were not applied selectively to industries which, for instance, could have created strong links with other sectors of the economy. They were particularistic in that the criteria for allowing credits were clientelistic/political rather than technical/economic.

The results of such policies was industrial sectors that were neither competitive internationally nor strongly articulated with local agriculture and the various countries' mineral resources. This lack of articulation was expressed in

- relatively slow growth of a home market for consumer goods, which set serious limits to industrial expansion
- continued export of relatively unprocessed primary products
- an industrial sector marked by 'restricted' capitalist development, i.e. by a 'dual' environment, consisting of relatively few, large capitalist enterprises set against a plethora of low-productivity, artisanal units engaged in simple-commodity production[13]
- a general lack of integration of all economic sectors.[14]

In the post-war period – leaving aside now the northern Balkan societies where central economic planning brought disaster – both Greece and the southern-cone countries experienced an exhaustion or crisis of the inter-war import-substitution model of industrialization. During the 1960s, however, and until the 1974 world economic crisis, some of the bottlenecks created by this situation were momentarily eased through the influx of multinational capital, which boosted investments in the high-technology sectors and the export of industrial products.

In spite of all this, it has become increasingly obvious, and particularly so since 1974, that the export-oriented industrialization led by foreign capital that typified the 1960s and 1970s suffered from severe limitations. Even if it did partly overcome some of the difficulties of the earlier import-substitution phase, it created new and more severe blockages, which resulted in extremely incapacitating balance-of-payments problems as well as growing socio-economic inequalities.

Contrasting trajectories

It has been argued by neo-Marxist dependency theorists that late developers, given their politically and economically subordinate position within the international arena, have no chance of avoiding the type of bottlenecks that plagued the pre-war Balkans and post-war Greece – especially when the country is small and poor in terms of natural resources. All the same, equally small and poor European countries, facing a similar international environment and having similar starting-points, did manage to do a great deal better.

Consider Norway, for example. A small European country like Greece or Bulgaria, Norway too was integrated into the world market in the nineteenth century. She too had been relatively late in industrializing, yet she managed to create industries that were both internationally competitive and closely linked to her primary exports (fish and lumber). So, for instance, her fish was salted, dried, frozen or canned by means of machinery that was in part indigenously produced. The lumber was exported in the form of planks, pulp and in later years paper products. Moreover, Norway used her considerable water resources for the production of a type of fertilizer (the 'saltpeter' of Norway) that became very popular on the world markets. In this way the country not only achieved a more integrated economy, but also succeeded in finding a niche in the world economy for both her primary and her industrial products (Nordhaug 1970; Aubert 1989).

It will have become quite clear by now that in certain respects the Balkan and southern-cone developmental projects have been relatively unsuccessful – especially when compared with other late developers. In contradiction to the axioms of early dependency theory, such lack of success does not (at least as far as Greece and the southern-cone countries are concerned) necessarily lead to economic stagnation or to conditions of absolute poverty.[15] It simply leads to a type of development which, in relative terms, is insufficiently integrated or self-centred, and so systematically generates bottlenecks that result in peripheralisation. Whether one calls this state of affairs backwardness, underdevelopment, or dependent development is of little consequence. There is no point in debating whether countries like Greece or Argentina are developing or under-developing. What does count is that nation-states engaged in modernisation can respond in radically different ways to the emerging opportunities and crises, and that their different responses lead to qualitatively different developmental trajectories (Senghaas 1985).

If the relative failure of the Balkan and Latin American developmental projects is conceded, I would suggest that in each of these cases it is the state which must be held chiefly responsible for that failure. The obvious question is then: why did the state perform so badly? In brief, the answer is that the development of both its administrative apparatuses (i.e. its political technologies), and its mode of controlling these apparatuses (i.e. its relations of domination),[16] have systematically led to a situation where the particularistic prevails over the universalistic, and the political over the economic or the social. I shall develop this key point in the next section.

The development of the state

Origins

The first point to stress about the state in the Balkans and the southern cone of Latin America is its patrimonial/despotic origin. Historically, the Balkan and Latin American states never experienced the western-type European absolutism, with its unique balance between monarchy and aristocracy which, from very early on, led to the constitution of autonomous *corps intermédiaires* between the crown and the people (Anderson

134

1974: 397 ff). Instead, the Ottoman state approached very closely to the extreme patrimonial structure that Weber has called *sultanism* (Weber 1978: 281–2). Such a structure is characterized by the total subservience of the nobility and high state-officials to a despotic ruler, with the arbitrary relationships and the high corruption this entailed (particularly during the late Ottoman period) strongly stamped on all authority echelons from the *Porte* to the minor village official.

To be more specific, the Ottoman patrimonial system of power was organized with a view to preventing the creation of a strong landed aristocracy that might have challenged the sultan's absolute authority. In contrast to western-European attitudes to landownership, the Ottoman empire saw all land as belonging, in theory at least, to Allah and his representative on earth, the sultan. Despite the *de facto* existence of private lands, generally speaking all cultivated land came under the *timar* landholding system – a system resembling more the Carolingian benefice than the medieval fief. Timar holders (the *spahis*) enjoyed no ownership rights over the land; they simply had a non-hereditary right to a portion of the produce, in exchange for which they were obliged to provide administrative and military services to the *Porte*. During periods of decline, officials would of course manage to acquire *de facto* ownership of their timars, but such ownership could not be legalized.

When the state was strong, therefore, sultanic despotism kept in check not only the aristocracy's aspirations to landownership, but equally so any designs it might have on controlling the state apparatus. The appointment of slaves, eunuchs, Jews, Christians generally and Greeks in particular (instead of nobles) to key administrative posts further ensured total subservience to the sultan's wishes (Stavrianos 1958: 122 ff).

Iberian rule in Latin America set no such restrictions on landownership, and this difference is relevant for understanding the post-independence trajectories in the two cases. However, imposing the traditions of absolutist rule (developed in the motherland) in a colonial context, where *political* feudalism was absent, eventually resulted in a type of state centralism that was unwilling to tolerate the emergence of autonomous groups and associations. As Claudio Veliz put it: 'In the Indies the fledgling Renaissance state of the crown of Castille was able to bring in a centralised political structure without the hindrance of feudal traditions or the opposition of a baronial periphery' (Veliz 1980: 10).

There is a considerable literature on the negative impact of the Iberian patrimonial/despotic legacy on the functioning of parliamentary institutions in Latin America (Sagatti 1966; Morse 1973; Wiarda 1973). Some of the writers in this tradition emphasize the cultural/ideational aspects of Iberian patrimonialism, while others focus rather on more structural features, such as the corporative/vertical character of state controls. Whatever one's position *vis-à-vis* the validity of purely cultural explanations (more on which below), there is no doubt that Latin American societies, just like the Balkan ones, had state structures in their pre-independence period that were more despotic and arbitrary than those of western Europe.

'Precocious urbanization' and the growth of the state

As historians and social scientists have pointed out repeatedly, the despotic features of Ottoman and Iberian patrimonialism did not disappear
after the countries under consideration had gained their independence.
They persisted and coexisted uneasily with the legal-bureaucratic administrative frameworks and the parliamentary democratic institutions
that 'modernizers' had imported from the west. As a matter of fact, the
nineteenth-century parliamentary regimes in both the Balkans and
southern Latin America were based on very restricted popular participation, and on an authoritarian, particularistic state controlled by a
handful of notable families. These families were able to keep the parliamentary system functioning in a relatively stable manner by manipulating the electorate through a variety of legal and illegal means.

In the Balkans (as noted already) the nineteenth-century political oli-
garchy in control of the state did not base its power on land. Oligarchic
families derived their authority partly from the leading role they had
played – as military chieftains and notables – during the war of independence. As far as Greece is concerned for instance, with big-landowner
status relatively inaccessible to them, they turned

> to the professions (to preserve and perpetuate their power) and, above all, to
> the state itself as politicians, state officials, academics, lawyers and tax
> farmers. Moreover, clientelism proved a remarkably effective strategy, which
> turned universal suffrage to their lasting advantage. Ultimately, the state
> budget itself became their principal economic base. (Mavrogordatos 1983: 123)

Given the above-outlined relative autonomy of the political, it has to be
stressed that, in both the Balkan and Latin American cases under consideration, the state was used not so much as a means for realizing
collective goals or a class-hegemonic project; it was used rather as a
means for consolidating and expanding patronage networks via the
huge distribution of spoils. The dominance of this type of particularistic/
clientelistic orientation becomes more evident if it is remembered that in
all these societies massive urbanization preceded the large-scale development of capitalist industry.[17]

In such situations of 'precocious' urbanization, the state tends to swell
enormously. This is due not only to its being obliged to make vast
expenditures to ensure a modicum of municipal facilities, but also to the
fact that expanding state employment is an easy way of reducing the
massive urban unemployment that is created by the rural influx in
conditions where industry is weak or non-existent. Moreover, state
employment is as early granted as sought, as a means of enhancing the
patron's political position. In other words, in a context of clientelistic
parliamentary politics, an industrial sector with low labour-absorption
capacity in conjunction with a massive population influx into the cities
makes the over-inflation of the state apparatuses a foregone conclusion.

In view of all the above, it is not surprising that in Greece during the

136

1870s the number of civil servants per 10,000 of the population was approximately seven times higher than in the United Kingdom (Dertilis 1975: Table XIV); and that another calculation for roughly the same period gives a quarter of the non-agricultural labour force as being employees of the Greek state (Tsoukalas 1977: 13). The situation is similar in all the other countries under study. For instance, while in the United Kingdom (1911) the proportion of civil servants to the total labour force was 1.1 per cent – and in Germany (1907) and France (1911) 1.4 per cent – in Argentina (1914) it was 3.3 per cent and in Chile (1920) 1.8 per cent (League of Nations 1928: Table 7).

A comparison of state tax-raising capacities, that is of the state's ability to extract resources from civil society, gives a similar picture. So in 1913 the United Kingdom government revenue per capita of the population was equivalent to US$20.14; in France at roughly the same time it was $24.23, in Germany $13.34, and in Sweden $12.73 (Banks 1971: segment 3). In Latin America and the Balkans, on the other hand, during roughly the same period – that is, at a time when their industrialization was still rudimentary – state revenue was similar to or even higher than that of the already industrialized west. This being so, J Lampe's assessment of the economic role of the Balkan state before 1914 could conclude that 'The state drew more human and fiscal resources away from productive investment than it itself contributed' (1975: 83).

Apart from pressure from the urban centres, another reason for the rapid growth of the state in Latin America and the Balkans was the attempt by the respective governments to imitate the institutional structures of the already industrialized western European parliamentary democracies. As Stavrianos has put it in his historical analysis of the Balkans:

> State structures developed in the West naturally and harmoniously with the growth of economic life. But in the Balkans the machinery of government was copied from the West and was superimposed with all its elaborateness and costliness upon an underdeveloped agrarian economy. . . . The result was that all the Balkan bureaucracies became grotesquely overstaffed. Many more officials per capita were to be found in the Balkan states than in the Western ones, despite the weakness of the Balkan economies. (Stavrianos 1958: 607)

What all the above boils down to is that during the last quarter of the nineteenth and the first of the twentieth century, the considerable resources generated in the parliamentary semiperiphery by the commercialization of agriculture and the boost given to primary exports were used neither for the modernization of agriculture nor for the development of industry. All these resources went instead towards furthering the expansion of a monstrous state apparatus, whose dynamism obeyed imperatives emanating from the polity rather than from the economy. It is precisely in that sense that the state in societies with late industrial development can become an obstacle, a hindrance to balanced growth.

137

The demise of oligarchic parliamentarism

In both the Balkans and the southern-cone countries, oligarchic parliamentarism declined in the 1920s and 1930s, and political participation broadened markedly as new political elites entered the parliamentary game, and as political clubs of notables had to give way to more centralized and less loosely organized national parties. This shift from oligarchic to post-oligarchic politics took different forms in the countries under consideration.

In the northern Balkans, where the landowners and the urban middle classes were both relatively weak, oligarchic parliamentarism was undermined by the rise of massive, populist peasant parties. In the southern Latin American countries, where urbanization was more advanced and landowning/export interests more powerful, it was through the populist mobilization of the urban masses that the demise of oligarchic politics was achieved and consolidated. Finally in Greece, where landowners, as in the rest of the Balkans, were weak but where urbanization was relatively advanced, the broadening of political participation did not entail any populist mobilization in either the countryside or the towns; it was brought about much more 'smoothly' by the expansion and broadening of the already existing clientelistic parties and organizations.[18]

It has to be emphasized here that, notwithstanding the wide variations in the mode of transition among the different countries under review, the demise of oligarchic parliamentarism occurred uniformly before these countries' large-scale industrialization (which came after 1929). This means that the opening-up of the political system was not, as in several western European societies, marked by the active participation of the industrial classes (particularly by massive and relatively autonomous working-class organizations). Instead, the new participants and their organizations were brought into the political arena in a more dependent/vertical manner, and this genre of political inclusion did nothing to eliminate the particularistic/personalistic features of parliamentary politics; neither did it check the despotic and anti-developmental tendencies of the state. Moreover, when in the period after the 1929 Depression industrial capitalism gained momentum in the parliamentary semi-periphery, its timing and structure not only led to a disarticulated type of development (as argued already),[19] but also reinforced the authoritarian and particularistic features of the state.

A comparison with cases where industrialization preceded rather than followed the broadening of political participation may be useful here. In several western European societies, working-class movements appeared at a time when advanced industrialization had resulted in a massive industrial labour force, which could effectively resist state attempts at manipulation and repression More than that: working-class organizations contributed in various ways to the rationalization of politics. To take England as an example, the fact that the Labour Party's strength was from the start based on the large number of its followers rather than on their wealth and social prestige, resulted in a highly centralized and bureaucratized party structure. This structure in turn was suitable for the organization of large numbers of people in less vertical and more horizontal manner. That such a mode of integration discourages particularistic and clientelistic political practices is a point well established in the relevant literature (Alford 1964: 33 ff).

The Labour Party's mode of creation, as well as the development of massive trade unions several decades earlier, not only enhanced the autonomy of the working-class movement *vis-à-vis* the state, but also contributed to the weakening of the parochial, clientelistic practices of the more traditional parties. The latter had to take up the challenge presented by the labour movement, and themselves began to adopt more bureaucratic and universalistic principles of organization. Moreover, they not only had to change their mode of political operation, but also were forced to change their goals and to become more receptive to ideas of popular welfare, collective bargaining, and so on.[20]

The above comparison clarifies the contrast with the countries under consideration where, given the broadening of political participation/ inclusion *before* the advent of large-scale industrialization (as well as the pre-independence patrimonial/despotic legacy and the 'restricted' nature of their capitalist trajectory), particularistic party practices and the state's patrimonial and authoritarian features have persisted up to the present. It also makes it easier to understand why the logic of the party quite systematically prevails over the logics of the market and of all other institutional spheres.

The fact that the broadening of political participation preceded major industrialization does not, of course, by itself, explain the widespread persistence of particularistic/clientelistic politics in the countries of the parliamentary semi-periphery. After all, countries like Australia and New Zealand also experienced a broadening of political participation before developing any large-scale industry, yet both of them subsequently achieved a 'First World' profile in economic as well as political terms. In the Balkans and Latin America, however, this (from the point of view of the development of a strong civil society) unfavourable timing of political broadening was combined with a deeply rooted, centuries old patrimonial-despotic legacy that persisted even after political independence was won. It is this combination, the conjunction of pre-independence legacy and inauspicious timing, that provides a somewhat more satisfactory explanation of the malfunctioning of parliamentarism in the countries under examination.[21]

Let me add weight to this crucial point by making a brief comparison between inter-war Australia and Argentina. In the first quarter of the twentieth century both of these countries saw the development of radical populist movements (the Radical Party in Argentina and the Labour Party in Australia) which undermined oligarchic politics and brought about a broadening of political participation prior to any major industrialization (Alexander 1988).

Australia's conservative political forces reacted to the 1929 world economic crises by seeking a peaceful accommodation with the Labour Party and sorting out their economic-policy differences in the electoral arena. The conservative reaction in Argentina was quite different. Here General Justo's 'Liberating Revolution' in 1930 forcibly removed the Radical Party's leader, Yrigoyen, from power, and established the army as the main guardian of a highly repressive, pseudo-parliamentary system (Goldwert 1972: 68 ff). Although this system did not take the country back to nineteenth-century oligarchic structures of domination, it effectively restricted political participation by the widespread and systematic use of illegal and quasi-legal means of political exclusion. In this sense it did revive, and at times even accentuated, the most particularistic and undemocratic features of oligarchic politics.

In fact, ever since 1930 the military have been the decisive force and main regulator of Argentina's political life. Before 1930 it was the civilian politicians who had the upper hand when they were soliciting military support; since 1930 the situation has been the reverse, with the civilians as the subordinate partners in civilian-military ventures (Potash 1968; Goldwert 1972: 35 ff; Rouquié 1978).

In this situation too, of course, there are structural rather than cultural factors that help to explain the ultra-authoritarian reaction of the Argentinian conservative forces. But if it is taken into account that first, in all of the countries of the parliamentary semi-periphery, the inter-war transition from oligarchic to post-oligarchic politics was marked by overt of covert military interventions that seriously disrupted the parliamentary game, and second, there were far fewer, if any, such interventions in the originally Anglo-Saxon ex-colonial settlement societies, then the argument of the pre-independence legacy makes a great deal of sense.

For all that, one should beware: 'cultural' explanations of this kind – in so far as they portray, *à la* Parsons, 'core values' or traditions as disembodied entities mysteriously determining everything on the social scene – are more often than not methodologically dubious. But when values or persisting cultural traditions are located within specific structural situations, when they are linked to actors playing specific games within specific institutional contexts, then they must be taken very seriously into account.

Bureaucratic-authoritarianism

Concerning finally the post-war years – and once more leaving aside the northern Balkans, where the political trajectory took a totalitarian turn – the 1960s and 1970s in both Greece and the southern-cone countries of Latin America witnessed the rise of military dictatorships. These, however, despite attempts at permanent institutionalization, did not manage to destroy irreversibly the long parliamentary traditions of these societies.

It has been argued that these dictatorial, 'bureaucratic-authoritarian' regimes in the parliamentary semi-periphery could be viewed as more or less deliberate attempts at easing the bottlenecks created by the inter-war and early post-war model of import-substituting industrialization. They should be seen, it is suggested, as attempts to restrict working-class demands for higher wages, and to create a favourable climate for the attraction of multinational capital – this being much better able than indigenous capital or the state to 'deepen' the industrialization process.[22]

For a variety of reasons (which I have explained elsewhere)[23] I consider the above explanation of the rise of military regimes too economistic. A more adequate explanation should be sought less in the state's supposed drive for economic modernization, and more in contradictions and struggles within the political sphere itself. To be more specific, all these semi-peripheral countries experienced a system of 'guided democracy' in the early post-war period, which consisted of a mixture of exclusionist and incorporative controls that prevented the more autonomous integration of the popular classes into the rapidly expanding political arena. Within the apparatus of 'guided democracy', the military occupied a dominant position.

This system of 'guided democracy' was undermined in the 1960s by rapid processes of industrialization and urbanization which, by generating huge economic and political inequalities, created very high levels of popular mobilization and radicalization in both towns and countryside. As the contradictions kept growing between the exclusionist/incorporative system of controls and the high levels of mass mobilization, different political forces in these various countries posed a serious threat to the 'guided-democracy' system. This threat was felt most particularly by the military, who were playing the chief monitoring role. From this perspective the establishment of military-dictatorial regimes could be more correctly regarded as an attempt by the army to counter the threat to their dominant position that was emanating from the massive popular mobilization (Mouzelis 1986: 97 ff).

Therefore, although economic considerations do have indirect relevance to the issue, the underlying reasons for the rise of bureaucratic authoritarian regimes in the parliamentary semi-periphery were political rather than economic. They had much more to do with the military's attempt to preserve a mode of domination that gave them a privileged power position, than with any effort by the bourgeoisie or the state to resolve economic bottlenecks and promote industrialization.

With respect to the thesis of this chapter, the salient point here is that neither the military dictatorships nor the subsequent, post-dictatorial parliamentary regimes effected any basic change in the features of these countries' state apparatuses. Both before and after the military interventions, these features did and do point to an over-inflated, highly corrupt and inefficient state apparatus, which is controlled by forces (military, civilian or a mixture of both) whose concerns for political survival and consolidation more often than not undermine attempts at political and economic modernization. So if in the western capitalist democracies those who control the means of domination operate in a context that encourages them to adopt policies favouring the expanded reproduction of capitalism, in the parliamentary semi-periphery the powerholders operate in contexts that encourage them to adopt policies favouring a highly restricted and unequal type of capitalist growth.

Conclusion

Summing up

In the foregoing, the argument has been that the Balkan and Latin America's southern-cone countries have failed to use the resources generated by their export-oriented, nineteenth-century agrarian economies in order to modernize their agriculture, or to create an industrial sector well articulated with the primary and tertiary sectors. The major reason for this failure must not be seen in imperialist exploitation, in the 'comprador' nature of these countries' bourgeoisies, the malfunctioning of markets, or lack of entrepreneurial skills and personalities; it must rather be located in the structure and functioning of their states. Given the late-late character of their industrialization, their only chance of integrating their peripheral economies into the world system in a more self-centred manner was from above. The state would have had to intervene flexibly and selectively – not in order to destroy or supersede private initiative, but so as to bolster and direct it towards the modernization of agriculture and the creation of strong linkages between the countries' industries and their agricultural and mineral resources.

Such strategic monitoring of development the Balkan and Latin American states were unable to provide in the past, and remain unable to provide in the present. Some of the reasons for this incapacity have to do with the following:

1 their pre-independence patrimonial/despotic legacy, and its persistence in the post-independence period
2 the fact that these states acquired enormous dimensions before the large-scale development of capitalist industry
3 the way the semi-periphery's state-led industrialization generated state-dependent industrial classes which were unable to check state authoritarianism and the particularist/clientelistic tendencies of the major political-military actors
4 the fact that the enormous state apparatuses were, and are still, controlled by parties of a predominantly clientelistic or populistic character, or more generally by forces (civilian or military) whose interests of self-preservation and expansion systematically contradict requirements for the expanded reproduction of capitalism or the modernization of non-economic institutional spheres
·5 the prevailing relationship between the economic and the political, in which, wherever there is incompatibility between the two spheres, the logic of the latter *systematically* prevails over that of the former.

Given all this, the state in the parliamentary semi-periphery resembles a colossus with feet of clay, a shapeless monstrosity incapable of reacting and adapting intelligently to a rapidly changing international environment. Whenever there has been a crisis or a challenge – like the need to modernize agriculture in the late nineteenth and early twentieth centuries, the need for effective import-substitution industrialization after the 1929 Depression, or the need for intelligent direction of multi-national and indigenous capital in the post-war conditions of the new international division of labour – at every one of these critical junctions, the rigid, over-politicized and particularistic orientations of the semi-peripheral state have made it act in ways that perpetuate these countries' peripheral status in the world economy and polity.

Needless to say, if one looks at late-developing countries (LDCs) with even weaker civil societies than those examined here (at African polities, for instance), the obstructive, anti-developmental character of the state is even more pronounced. This frequently takes the form of a straight-forward and systematic plundering of national resources, by a clepto-cratic state that is controlled by politico-military elites whose overriding concern is the transfer of indigenous national resources into deposits in privately held foreign bank accounts.

East Asian contrasts

The question that the above analysis raises is to what extent the over-inflated and anti-developmental state is an inevitable consequence of late-late development – at least for countries lacking the western European socio-cultural background of societies like Australia and New Zealand. I would say that the connection between late-late development and the anti-developmental character of the state is very strong, but there are instances where the connection does not hold. These are of course the cases of Taiwan and South Korea.

To account very briefly for their exceptional development, one has to note that the inter-war situation in these two East Asian countries was very markedly different from that in our Balkan and Latin American societies. Both Taiwan and South Korea were occupied at the time by Japan, which was trying to turn them into an agricultural hinterland to her own rapidly expanding economy. Although by ruthless exploitation they effected vast transfer of resources to the metropolis, the Japanese also introduced a number of changes that were later, in the post-war, post-colonial period, to assist decisively in the achievement of a relatively balanced economic growth.

For one thing, the Japanese occupation undermined the local landowning elites, and so set favourable preconditions for post-liberation agrarian reforms. In both Korea and Taiwan these brought a drastic reduction in the number of big estates, and an impressive increase in agricultural productivity. The Japanese also generated considerable development of social-overhead capital as well as of industrialization. Despite the fact that both of these were due to Japanese capital and informed by Japanese needs and interests, they created a firm foundation for the countries' post-war industry which, with much help from the United States, progressed spectacularly from 1960 onwards, especially in terms of industrial exports. A third important legacy of the Japanese occupation has been a strongly authoritarian state apparatus committed to economic planning and to a highly selective, flexible and efficacious regulation of the overall economy.

Finally, the recent industrialization of Taiwan and South Korea, like that of Greece and Latin America, was promoted by multinational capital. The structure of the two Asian states seems, however, to have lent itself to a greater steering of foreign investments as well as of indigenous capital (the former more limited than in the Latin American cases). In this way export-oriented industrialization could combine with a more balanced overall economic growth. Their developmental trajectories have suffered relatively little from severe bottlenecks, and could profit from mechanisms ensuring that the fruits of rapid growth (particularly since the early 1970s) were more widely spread in both the countryside and the urban centres. Although wages continue to be relatively low, neither of these two countries has anything like the degree of marginalization that prevails in the Latin American societies.[24]

These results have been achieved with a highly *dirigiste* state that keeps a close watch on capital (indigenous as well as multinational) without strangling private initiative. It also handles the trade unions – in an admittedly highly repressive manner – and keeps down wages, or more recently, ensures that wage rises are closely linked to productivity increases. There can be little doubt that the, by Third World standards exceptional, structure of the state seems to be the key to the East Asian success story. As a student of Taiwanese development puts it:

> If development strategy in Taiwan has been defined by state officials, if state officials have stressed market forces so as to create the kind of production structure which they think Taiwan should have, then the question of the basis, organisation and operation state authority becomes exceedingly important. Given that not a few states are little more than instruments of plunder on behalf of the small group of officials, politicians and the military, why has the state in Taiwan deployed its power benignly rather than malignly? How has the use of public power been disciplined? . . . My concern has been to show that these questions do have to be addressed if Taiwan's remarkable industrialisation is to be understood, because the neo-classical explanation in terms of self-regulating markets is not adequate. (Wade 1985)

Implications

I am without both the space and the expertise to explain why the state in Korea and Taiwan has managed to develop an interventionist public administration which, without avoiding entirely the particularistic and 'corrupt' features typical of Third World states, has largely escaped or mitigated the kind of bottlenecks that the great majority of late developers are experiencing today. Nevertheless, there are two points that emerge very clearly from the above analysis. First, the highly exceptional circumstances that have resulted in the Korean and Taiwanese success stories demonstrate once again how difficult it is to escape the bottlenecks typically entailed by late development. Second, the key issue for late-late developers is not whether to have state intervention or not. The key issue is *effective versus ineffective* state intervention.

In other words, the challenge for late developers is not to 'roll back' the state, as neo-liberals keep advocating. If Greece and the southern-cone countries cannot avoid peripheralization as long as the present features of their state apparatuses persist, neither can they avoid it by merely freeing their markets. The only possibility of clearing the way forward is through measures that aim, first, at a drastic rationalization of the state's administrative apparatuses, and second, at a radical change in the relations of domination, so that balanced socio-economic development is no longer systematically sacrificed on the altar of particularistic politics.

This is easier said than done, of course. But any attempt to resolve the bottlenecks that late development creates by bypassing the state is doomed to failure. This does not mean that aid schemes cannot be effective or useful that, for instance, seek to escape the suffocating controls of the central state bureaucracy by direct investment in local projects that are geared to the satisfaction of basic needs. But such strategies do not work on the more general, national level. There the state as the major co-ordinator of all developmental efforts, cannot be sidestepped. It is precisely for this reason that *state rationalization* (implying both improvements in administrative efficiency and the demise of anti-developmental relations of domination) is the make-or-break factor for all late developers.

I conclude with a final note on the policy implications of the above analysis. Although this seems to bring us back to the Marxist idea that the solutions to the developmental bottlenecks of late developers are more political than technical, there is a significant difference: the 'political' obstacles that I have been pointing out are not those of imperialism or of a dominant capitalist class preventing socialist transformation. The 'political' problem here does not entail, as suggested by Frank's early work, opting out of the world capitalist system, or changing the capitalist relations of production in any given country. Solving the political problem demands changes in the relations of domination, changes in the way the state apparatus is organized and controlled.

Marxists will maintain that the nature of the dominant classes is highly relevant for understanding the malfunctioning of the state in the countries of the parliamentary semi-periphery. My answer to this is that, although class is relevant and the state quite obviously is not classless, the malfunctionings I have been talking about are not class-specific; they continue to operate whatever the class composition or the origin of the ruling elites. In other words, whatever the social background of politico-military elites, once in control of the state, they tend to promote the interests they perceive as closely associated with their own politically dominant position, rather than those of the class they are supposedly 'representing'. In that sense, neither the abolition of the dominant relations of production (as the northern Balkan experience has clearly demonstrated), nor a change from a conservative-upper class to a 'progressive'/working-class government (as the rule of Papandreou's socialist party in post-dictatorial Greece has shown) will necessarily lead to the type of state rationalization that I have been discussing.

One can of course develop a similar argument *vis-à-vis* the Marxist or *marxisant* thesis (still very influential in Wallerstein's world-system approach) that focuses not on the dominant classes at the national level, but on capitalist relations at the world economy level. Here, relations between central, semi-peripheral and peripheral nations are held to reduce drastically the chances of most Third World countries moving from the periphery upwards. It seems to me that in so far as the world system approach sensitizes the student to the importance of viewing nation-states, not in isolation, but in the context of the rapidly changing world capitalist economy, its usefulness is undeniable. But in so far as it claims to provide not only a conceptual framework (i.e. what Althusser would call generalities II), but also a set of substantive propositions (generalities III) about how world market mechanisms change the over-all trajectory and the internal structures of peripheral and semi-peripheral societies, its theses are much more problematic.

To argue, for instance, that the world capitalist system operates in such a manner that it creates a centre/semi-periphery/periphery struc-ture, and that this structure retains its tripartite character despite limited possibilities for a few nation-states to move upwards or downwards, is true but trivial. It is as trivial as to argue that one can always divide a population into upper, middle and lower status categories according to a variety of criteria (wealth, power, prestige, etc.).

On the other hand, there is the more interesting substantive prop-osition (often encountered in the world systems literature) that the re-lations between central, semi-peripheral and peripheral nations have a *zero-sum* quality – in the sense that the movement of a few countries from the periphery upwards makes it more difficult for other peripheral countries to do the same, or that 'a worsening of conditions of periph-eral states as a group is a requirement of the success of semi-peripheral states' (Arrighi 1990: 18). However, this type of thesis is not at all con-vincing. More often than not the proposition is simply advanced as an obvious feature of capitalist markets, without any systematic effort to provide the reasons or mechanisms which bring about such a zero-sum situation on the level of the world economy. But in any case it is not clear why mechanisms of this sort need to be assumed. For it may be that the reason why the tripartite periphery/semi-periphery/centre structure is not pear-like (that is, the reason why it does not have a narrow base and a broad middle) has less to do with the world market and more with the *internal* organization of peripheral states.

If I am right about the profoundly anti-developmental character of most Third World state apparatuses, neither more favourable world market mechanisms nor less exploitative centre–periphery relations will enable peripheral countries to achieve a semi-peripheral status. In other words, if the tripartite stratification of present-day nation-states in terms of wealth for instance has a 'Brazilian' rather than a 'Swedish' profile, this may have little to do with the nature of the world economy and much more to do with the way states in the periphery articulate with economies and with civil societies. Another way of putting this is to argue that the highly unequal distribution of wealth on a world scale should not be seen primarily in terms of the structure of world markets, or of the shortsightedness or self-orientation of the core. Instead it

146

should be viewed as the result of an inter-state system in which the majority of members have administrative structures which systematically prevent them from taking advantage of the developmental opportunities that the changing world economy constantly generates.

Notes

1. The 'late-late' label is used extensively in development theory to make a distinction between the (in comparison with England) relatively late western European industrializers (e.g. Germany), and those societies that experienced *large-scale* industrialization only in the post-1929 period. See on this point Hirschman (1970: ch. 3).
2. See on this point Mouzelis (1988).
3. For the problems created by Marxist economic reductionism in the study of developments in the Balkan and southern-cone Latin American countries, see Mouzelis (1986: 199–205).
4. For criticism of Gerschenkron's thesis see Berend and Ranki (1982: 64).
5. For both (a) and (b) see Senghaas (1985).
6. See Stavrianos (1958: 2–4, 593–4).
7. Land fragmentation was due not only to the agrarian reforms, but also to lack of primogeniture in the Balkans. For a relevant comparison between Greece and Norway (which does have primogeniture), see Aubert (1989: 46–66).
8. For an extensive discussion of this point in the case of Greece, see Vergopoulos (1975).
9. One might, of course, point out that during the 1980s the unfavourable position of the small Greek cultivator was finally reversed by Andreas Papandreou's government, which heavily used EC funds to improve the lot of agricultural producers. However, these funds were distributed in such a way that, in most cases, they led to individual enrichment without corresponding structural changes leading to productivity increases. So it is not surprising that, in terms of productivity, Greek agriculture (together with that of Portugal) lags far behind that of all other EC partners. See Maraveyias (1989).
10. For some of the reasons for this, see pp. 134–5.
11. Rural over-representation in Congress surviving right up to the military coup of 1973 is shown, for example, by the fact that whereas in the congressional elections of 1973 the minimum number of votes for electing a deputy in the Third District of Santiago was 73,143, in Aysen (southern Chile) it was only 3,918 votes (Caviedes 1979: 53).
12. Argentina's countryside being relatively unpopulated, the Argentine conservatives did not have the large rural constituencies at their disposal that, as demonstrated by post-oligarchic Chile, are so easily amenable to landowners' clientelistic control. But this did not mean that the landowning classes were without political influence. Their considerable economic power and their cultural hegemony enabled them to exercise control over political developments, or at least to resist successfully any attempts at agrarian reform.
13. One of the most striking characteristics of peripheral and semi-peripheral industry is the persistence and even proliferation (especially in the more traditional industrial branches) of small, inefficient units that do not use wage labour on a large scale (i.e. which are not capitalist), existing side by

side with large capitalist firms. Although this type of industrial structure can also be found in First World economies, it is much more accentuated in peripheral and semi-peripheral capitalist countries.

As far as the parliamentary semi-periphery is concerned, in the middle of the 1960s Chile's industrial establishments employing more than 100 workers amounted to 6 per cent of all firms with over 5 workers, and to 10 per cent in Argentina. In both countries these relatively large units contributed more than 65 per cent of the total industrial value-added (Lambert and Martin 1971: 325). The situation in Greece is similar. In the inter-war as well as the post-war periods, a few big firms have coexisted with a plethora of small, family-based, artisanal units. For a variety of reasons, any increase in the demand for indigenous industrial products has generated a proliferation of additional small units (Ellis *et al*. 1965).

14. Let us take Greece as an example. If one looks, for instance, at railway construction in the nineteenth century, Greece saw a marked discrepancy between supply and demand in the transport services. Whereas in western Europe railway construction met the growing demand for transportation by an already formed national market and a rapidly growing capitalist economy, in nineteenth-century Greece the absence of a national market and the relative immobility of her pre-capitalist economy meant that 'the supply of a modern means of transport met a demand that was practically non-existent' (Papayiannakis 1984: 120, my translation).

Moreover, given the weak linkages between Greek industry and railway construction, the country had to spend large amounts of foreign currency to import not only cereals but also railway equipment. It is not surprising, therefore, that shortly before the turn of the century Greece was forced to declare bankruptcy.

Shipping, finally, provides another example of disarticulation. It is true, of course, that after a prolonged period of crisis, Greek shipping rapidly developed again towards the end of the nineteenth century. However, during this period control over shipping had passed from the local ship-owners of Ithaca, Galaxidi and the Aegean islands to diaspora Greeks, who gave it a more international orientation (Dertilis 1984: 31 ff). This disconnected it from the other sectors of the Greek economy, which did not profit much from its growth. Greece did not have

> the stable and long-term connections that prevailed in nineteenth and twentieth-century Norway, for example, between shipping, commerce, ocean fishing, and related industries. (Dertilis 1984: 35–6, my translation)

Similar types of malintegration of sectors are to be found in all the other cases under consideration here.

15. Greece, in contrast to some Latin American countries that have achieved high rates of industrialization in the 1960s and 1970s, has not only eliminated absolute levels of poverty, but also avoided the creation of widespread slums in her major urban centres (see on this point Mouzelis 1978).

16. For the concepts of political technologies and relations of domination, see Mouzelis (1990: ch. 4).

17. For comparative data, see Mouzelis (1986: 9 ff).

18. For an analysis and explanation of the different routes to post-oligarchic politics, see Mouzelis (1986: ch. 1).

19. For the concept of disarticulation, see Amin (1970).

20. See on this point Kircheimer (1966). The emergence of a strong working-class movement does not automatically bring about the end of clientelism,

neither was it the only factor responsible for the demise of particularistic/ clientelistic politics in the United Kingdom. The introduction of the secret ballot, large constituencies and stiffer penalties for corrupt political practices such as vote buying, as well as broader developments such as educational reform – all these helped to effect a change in public attitudes and the emergence of a new and more democratically oriented public opinion.

21.   Apart from considerations of timing and the patrimonial legacy, another important factor relevant for understanding the weakness of working-class organization in the parliamentary semi-periphery is the highly *restricted* character of capitalism, both in agriculture and industry. It is restricted in the sense that, even after the dominance of the capitalist mode of production, capitalist enterprises proper (i.e. economic units employing large numbers of wage-labourers) constituted mere islands in an ocean of small units employing only a few wage-labourers or none at all.

Such economic organization is not very conducive to the development of autonomous, large-scale trade-union movements. See on this point Mouzelis (1986: 113 ff).

22.   See O'Donnell (1973). O'Donnell's work has generated a great deal of research and debate. See for instance articles by F H Cardoso, J Cotler, A Hirschman, R R Kaufman and others in Collier (1979).

23.   See on this point Mouzelis (1986: 179 ff).

24.   On the last point see Morawetz (1977: 40).

References

Alexander M (1988) Conservatism, counterrevolution and semi-peripheral politics: Australia and Argentina in the interwar period. Paper presented to the Political Economy of the World System Conference, Emory University, Atlanta, Georgia

Alford R (1964) *Party and society*. London, Murray

Amin S (1970) *L'Accumulation à l'échelle mondiale*. Paris, Anthropos

Anderson P (1974) *Lineages of the absolutist state*. London, New Left Books

Arrighi G (1990) The developmentalist illusion: a reconceptualization of the semiperiphery. In: Martin W G (ed) *Semi-peripheral states in the world economy*. New York, Greenwood Press

Aubert V (1989) Notes on Greece and Norway. *Sociologi i dag*

Banks A S (1971) *Cross-polity time-series data*. Boston, MA, MIT Press

Bauer A (1975) *Chilean rural society: from the Spanish Conquest to 1930*. Cambridge, Cambridge University Press

Berend I and **Ranki G** (1974) *Economic development in East-Central Europe in the nineteenth and twentieth centuries*. New York, Columbia University Press

Berend I and **Ranki G** (1982) *The European periphery and industrialisation: 1780– 1914*. Cambridge, Cambridge University Press

Caviedes C (1979) *The politics of Chile: a socio-geographical assessment*. Boulder, CO, Westview Press

Collier D (ed) (1979) *The new authoritarianism in Latin America*. Princeton, NJ, Princeton University Press

Dertilis G (1975) Social change and military intervention in politics: Greece 1881–1928. PhD thesis, University of Sheffield

Dertilis G (1984) *The Greek economy and the industrial revolution: 1830–1910* (in Greek). Athens, Sakoulas

Diaz-Alejandro C F (1970) *Essays on the economic history of Argentina*. New Haven, CT, Yale University Press

Ellis H et al. (1965) *Industrial capital in the development of the Greek economy* (in Greek). Athens, Centre of Economic Research

Furtado C (1970) *Economic development of Latin America*. Cambridge, Cambridge University Press

Gerschenkron A (1962) *Economic backwardness in historical perspective*. Cambridge, MA, Harvard University Press

Goldwert M (1972) *Democracy, militarism and nationalism in Argentina 1930–1966*. Austin, TX, University of Texas Press

Hirschman A (1970) *A bias for hope*. New Haven, CT, Yale University Press

Kircheimer O (1966) The transformation of European political parties. In: Lapalombara J and Weiner M (eds) *Political parties and political development*. Princeton, NJ, Princeton University Press

Lambert D and **Martin J** (1971) *L'Amérique Latine: économie et société*. Paris, Armand Colin

Lampe J (1975) Varieties of unsuccessful industrialisation: the Balkan states before 1914. *Journal of Economic History* 35 (1)

League of Nations (1928) *Statistical year book 1927*. Geneva, League of Nations

Loveman B (1977) *Chile*. New York, Oxford University Press

Manzel U (1990) The experience of small European countries with late development: lessons from history. Paper presented at the International Symposium on the Functions of Law in the Development of Welfare Societies, Oslo

Maraveyias N (1989) *The accession of Greece to the European Community: the impact of agriculture* (in Greek). Athens, Institute of Mediterranean Studies

Mavrogordatos G (1983) *Stillborn republic: social coalitions and party strategies in Greece: 1922–1936*. Berkeley, CA, University of California Press

Moore B, Jr (1969) *The social origins of dictatorship and democracy*. Harmondsworth, Penguin

Morawetz D (1977) *Twenty-five years of economic development 1950–1975*. Washington, DC, World Bank

Morse R M (1973) The heritage of Latin America: the distinct tradition. In: Wiarda H J (ed) *Politics and social change in Latin America*. Amerst, MA, University of Massachusetts Press

Mouzelis N (1978) *Modern Greece: facets of underdevelopment*. London, Macmillan

Mouzelis N (1986) *Politics in the semi-periphery: early parliamentarism and late industrialisation in the Balkans and Latin America*. London, Macmillan

Mouzelis N (1988) Sociology of development: reflections on the present crisis. *Sociology* 22 (1)

Mouzelis N (1990) *Post-Marxist alternatives: the construction of social orders*. London, Macmillan

Nordhaug K (1970) Politics of development and underdevelopment within the European periphery: political regimes and economic transformations in Scandinavia and the Balkans before 1940. Paper presented to the International Symposium on the Function of Law in the Development of Welfare Societies, Oslo

O'Donnell G (1973) *Modernisation and bureaucratic authoritarianism: studies in Southern American politics*. Berkeley, CA, Institute of International Studies, University of California

Papayiannakis E (1984) The Greek railways 1880–1910. In Tsaoussis D (ed) *Aspects of nineteenth-century Greek society* (in Greek). Athens, Estia

Potash R (1968) *The army and politics in Argentina 1928–1945*. Stanford, CA, Stanford University Press

Rey P-P (1971) *Colonialisme, néo-colonialisme et transition au capitalisme*. Paris, Maspéro

Rouquié A (1978) *Pouvoir militaire et société politique au République Argentine*. Paris, Presses de la Fondation Nationale des Sciences Politiques

Sagatti M (1966) *Spanish bureaucratic patrimonialism in America*. Politics of Modernisation Series no. 1. Berkeley, CA, University of California

Senghaas D (1985) *The European experience: a historical critique of development theory*. Dover, Berg

Stavrianos L S (1958) *The Balkans since 1453*. New York, Holt, Rinehart & Winston

Taylor J (1979) *From modernisation to modes of production*. London, Macmillan

Tsoukalas C (1977) The reforms of Trikoupis. In: *History of the Greek nation: modern Hellenism 1881–1913* (in Greek). Athens, Ekdotiki Athinon

Veliz C (1980) *The centralist tradition in Latin America*. Princeton, NJ, Princeton University Press

Vergopoulos C (1975) *The agrarian problem in Greece: the issue of the social incorporation of agriculture* (in Greek). Athens, Exantas

Wade R (1985) State intervention in outward-looking development. In: White G and Wade R (eds) *Developmental states in East Asia*, mimeo. Brighton, Institute of Development Studies

Weber M (1978) *Economy and society*, edited by Roth G and Wittich C. Berkeley, CA, University of California Press

Wiarda H J (1973) Toward a framework for the study of political change in the Iberian-Latin tradition: the corporative model. *World Politics* 25

Wolpe H (1975) The theory of internal colonialism: the South African case. In: Oxaal I *et al.* (eds) *Beyond the sociology of development*. London, Routledge

CHAPTER 6

The social construction of rural development:
discourses, practices and power

Alberto Arce, Magdalena Villarreal and Pieter de Vries

This chapter is concerned with knowledge, human agency and power in the context of state-sponsored programmes for rural development in the Third World. Our starting point is a critique of those views of the state and the institutional framework of rural change that exclude on a priori grounds investigation of the ways that social actors interact and negotiate the outcomes of rural development processes. Rejecting the structural conception of state intervention as a set of more or less inflexible constraints upon action, we suggest that policy formulation and implementation are best analysed as processes through the detailed study of what may be called the social life of rural development.

Understanding rural development, we believe, involves both serious empirical (ethnographic) work at the local level and a wider sociological framework of analysis capable of dealing with specific configurations of administrative practice, the elaboration of 'discourses' of development and the ways that policies and programmes are 'internalized' by the various actors concerned with them. It has often been observed that there are substantial variations between societies in the way that formally similar state-sponsored programmes are organized and implemented. To explain why this is the case, it is important to investigate not only the discourses and practices which constitute the reality of rural development, but also changing forms of power and authority, especially new patterns of 'discretion' arising from the interaction of different personal and group projects which cannot be accounted for simply in terms of economic or political structures.

The notions of power and authority introduced in the chapter are borrowed from recent developments in the sociology of knowledge and may be unfamiliar to some readers. As well as using concepts like 'discourse' whose credentials are now reasonably well established in rural research, the chapter trespasses across several conventional academic boundaries, especially those between development studies and a variety of areas of general micro-sociology.

The chapter uses case studies drawn from fieldwork in Mexico and Costa Rica to explain why we see the way forward in the micro-sociology of rural development in a knowledge-interface framework. In this limited context, we put forward a proposal for a new agenda for social researchers concerned with development issues. We remain unconvinced of the possibility at this stage of the 'impasse' debate of reaching a new theoretical consensus drawing on elements of Marxist structuralism as well as on phenomenology and the new tendencies in microsociology. Nevertheless, we agree that if the will for a more integrated agenda is present among the different sectors of the development research community, the benefits are potentially very large.

The chapter begins by reviewing established and new approaches to what we call the social construction of rural development, beginning with basic concepts for the analysis of the state and state intervention. The arguments are then illustrated and elaborated with reference to case studies drawing on the work of the three authors.

State intervention and the rural development interface

Theda Skocpol's path-breaking contribution to the sociology of the state is a natural starting point for any discussion of state intervention in development processes. Directing her criticisms against both Marxist and liberal positions, Skocpol (1979; 1985) made a decisive stand against the simple conceptualization of the state as a reflection, or arena, of conflicts between social and economic interests. In her view the state is to be conceived as a 'set of administrative, policing, and military organizations headed, and more or less well coordinated, by an executive authority' (1979: 29). The main objectives of this 'macro-structure' are the extraction of resources from society and the deployment of these to create and support coercive and administrative organizations. Although embedded in class-divided socio-economic structures and an international system of states, state organizations are seen as having a powerful capability to rebuild themselves in the wake of revolutions and other social upheavals.

One of Skocpol's most important contributions is to identify the contradictions inside the organization of the state as a critical point of departure for the analysis of social transformations, including both social revolutions and large-scale reforms. In the study of rural development, bringing the state's organizational contradictions into the analysis provides a valuable framework with which to understand processes of policy formulation and policy implementation. However, we want to suggest, an analysis that is 'state centred' in this sense need not and should not be insensitive to the impact of societal forces on policy processes.

The focus on the state as a specific organizational form leads to the view that, although a particular state style of governance may be influenced by class and other economic interests, this is far from universally the case. The activities of states are regulated first and foremost by interests arising within the state itself. But this does not mean that the state necessarily enjoys great power in relation to society. In fact, in Third World contexts the state's legitimacy is seldom sufficient on its own to compel people to follow a particular development programme or ideology. The outcomes of state intervention in rural development have a socially negotiated character, and in reality no state policy is free of elements of social construction. In summary, the relationships between state and society should not be collapsed into a single form of explanation. The state is not a mere expression of contradictions in society; but neither are the results of state intervention simply reflections of the political and economic 'needs' of the state.

Recent work on development administration and the state takes us some way towards a proper recognition of these issues. Leaving behind tired discussions about the degree of relative autonomy of the state, authors such as Grindle (1980; 1986) and Migdal (1988) have adopted an organizational approach to the state as a set of agencies and governmental institutions each with its own history, operational styles and ways of dealing with people. In these studies, the problematic shifts away from the role of the state in the process of capital accumulation or economic modernization, to the various ways in which state leaders attempt to shape society by establishing powerful departments and agencies with the view to controlling sectors of the population. However, as these authors argue, state centralization is often thwarted owing to the tendency within the process of policy implementation for resourceful agencies to establish special relationships with particular groups in society, while at the same time developing their own distinct interests. In this way they become a threat to the unity and effectiveness of the state. Consequently, the history of intervention is often that of the rise and fall of agencies and their associations, resulting in a proliferation of resource-poor agencies. In Midgal's view, the result is that states tend to grow weaker and society stronger (1988).

Although this type of analysis is helpful in focusing on the dynamics of bureaucrats' interactions with societal forces, the view offered of local organizational dynamics is often shallow. Relationships between state representatives and the population are seen in terms of 'traditional' power relationships, with rural producers appearing as the last link in a chain of patron–client relationships (Grindle) or, in the case of Migdal, as operating within the 'moral economy' of traditional communities. The latter position is highly problematic in our view, but our concern here is more with what such over-simplifications may reflect, namely the continued tendency of scholars working in this tradition to conceive state activity as basically an enclosed sphere, insulated from society.[1] The danger is that by conferring on the state too much of an endogenous dynamic responding to the attempts of state leaders to shape society, we may lose sight of the effects of local negotiations between state representatives and other actors.

The important role that is sometimes played by such processes is illustrated by the study of the dynamic of knowledge interfaces in rural Mexico by Arce and Long (1987). In this case, a variety of social actors –

bureaucrats, peasant producers and other parties – are shown to be involved in the social construction of policy implementation, in such a way that the apparently 'external' and 'internal' domains of the state intervention process are merged within an arena of struggle and nego- tiation. These negotiations, it must be stressed, are not only related to the distribution of resources, but also concern the degree of legitimacy and credibility accorded to the state by its subjects. Following Foucault (1979), strategies of accommodation, avoidance and penetration in the face of state authority are viewed as part of the mode of operation of power in society. The study of development interfaces (Arce and Long 1987) provides insight into the strategic ways in which actors deploy development *discourses*. It also throws light on the ways in which they develop organizational *practices* within the implementation setting, shaping particular styles of intervention at the local and institutional level.

Other studies of public policy (for example Schaffer 1984) have emphasized that policy is something other than a rational exercise in resource allocation with a view to reaching objectives of growth or redistribution. This perspective argues that institutional procedures and the social practices of bureaucracies in implementing policies are more significant than those considered rational by the established theoretical models of policy practice. Schaffer's position signals the need for studies of the actual practice of development policies. These studies should explore possible alternatives to attempting to shape or influence policy, by identifying 'other openings and possibilities'. The focus should be on the 'room for manoeuvre' arising in the intermediate ground between the choices that emerge from the activities of state institutions and the forms of negotiation pursued by the other actors participating in the development process.

At the centre of Schaffer's concept of room for manoeuvre is the premise that policies can make a difference in developing countries, and that the process and practice of government is a fundamental area for social research. The interface and room for manoeuvre approaches therefore both lead to the view that the analysis of state intervention needs to focus on the actual content of administrative practices, on the capacity of the various actors to internalize the technical and political factors embodied in a policy process and the various negotiations and interactions among the different categories of actors.

The process of policy implementation

Practices, representations and knowledge

Policy implementation is the sphere in which state representatives move and which they seek to manage. It is the social space where the official must mediate between the appropriate general administrative rules and what s/he can do 'in the field'. Rural development interfaces are 'critical point[s] of intersection or linkage between different social systems, fields or levels of social order where structural discontinuities, based upon differences of normative value and social interest, are most likely to be found' (Long 1989: 1–2). In rural development, the concept of interface implies face-to-face encounters between state representatives and rural people. In these encounters the reality of policy is circumscribed by the existence of different interests, strategies and thought-styles. This diversity is an expression of the range of choices open to the social actors, and at the same time, a manifestation of the complex social world that development policy has to contend with.

The study of practices involves analysing the ways that people operate in their everyday life. However, when we study actors' everyday activity we realize that each individual is a locus of an often complex set of social relations. This is the setting in which knowledge ('traditional', 'modern', 'expert' and 'local') influences the form and content of representations, and in turn provides the freedom for actors to manipulate features of the context of policy implementation. Knowledge thus becomes a relation of power (Fardon 1985), not just a link between the 'life-worlds' (Schutz and Luckmann 1974) of those individuals participating in development, but an important organizational resource in the strategies, conflicts and negotiations that emerge during the process of policy implementation. The dynamics of knowledge do not stem simply from the contrast between the perspectives of rural producers and those of bureaucrats, but from the ways that different knowledge processes interrelate, and thus reinforce or transform each other, across the rural development interface. This creates the conditions for communication between different social actors and for the emergence, through the action of rural producers, politicians, bureaucrats, farmers' associations, women, youth, etc., of the distinctive properties of the social field of rural development.

Agency, discourses, interests and identities

The concept of human agency starts from the notion that the individual has the knowledge and capability (see Giddens 1984) to understand social experiences and to solve the riddles of everyday life. The individual recognizes himself/herself in his/her social practices within specific situations. In these operations, discourses are one crucial form of practice, because it is in the domain of discourse that interaction between knowledge and power accords validity to images of 'reality'. It is through discourse that individual properties and beliefs are transmuted into actions that contribute specific definitions of the world in which the actor attributes values to material resources (e.g. social interests) and to non-material resources (e.g. identity).

A useful contribution in this connection is the work of Apthorpe (1986) on discourse in politics. Apthorpe argues that ' "discursive practice" can be taken as an example of the capture and exercise of power by some sort of people, arguments and organizations against others through specific happenings, in particular arenas, over various periods of time' (1986: 377). For Apthorpe the deconstruction of policy discourse is not simply an intellectual exercise; it has a constructive purpose: that of reminding us that 'facts never speak for themselves, they are bespoken and spoken for'. The contribution of Apthorpe's discussion of discourse is to stress that in development there are always alternatives, and hence contradictions and conflicts, in the actual practice of public policy (Apthorpe 1984).

Continuing with this line of analysis, Schaffer (1985) and Wood (1985) argue that development intervention goes together with forms of labelling which stigmatize people – as poor, resourceless and dependent – and hence reduce their capacity to engage in independent organization. In their view the administrative project model serves mainly to legitimize state intervention and de-politicize the role of the state. This is apparent when people are forced as 'clients' or a 'target population' to adopt the discourse of administrators in order to express their needs. Development administration, then, is not a factor that is external to the problem of rural development, but itself forms part of it. Schaffer argues that scarcities in development are constructed through discourses of development along with administrative practices, and that they lead to a specific mode of social control and legitimacy.

Through their critiques of development discourses and the evasion of responsibilities in administration, Schaffer and Apthorpe have contributed notably to the analysis of these issues, but neither of them follows the discussion through to the *field* level of implementation. At this level a different dynamic seems to emerge, where discourses of the kind discussed by Schaffer and Apthorpe are being put to different uses by different actors, producing what may be quite different effects in the actual process of policy implementation.

Agency and discourse, we have argued, are important notions in any analysis of agrarian change. However, discourses cannot be viewed independently of specific, situated practices and experiences. Therefore what needs attention is the strengths and weaknesses of particular discourses in generating social networks that can organize representations of what rural development should be about. This activity requires a number of skills from actors, such as persuasion and argumentation, and the ability to translate the needs of others in delineating particular problems (MacDonell 1986). As an element of social practice, discourse encompasses, first, the experiences and skills necessary for setting up a legitimate argument that can generate a flow of communications between rural producers and government officials, and second, the discursive skills required for putting experience and knowledge to use in particular settings.

Up to this point, there is a close parallel between our position and that of Long and van der Ploeg (see Chapter 3). However, we have borrowed heavily from the work of Foucault (e.g. 1973; 1982), thereby extending the discussion to cover the importance of studying the sources of power (techniques/modes) and legitimation available to social actors participating in rural development. In what follows we take this argument a step further, drawing on recent work in the sociology of knowledge and power.

Power, discretion and social order

Foucault's insights into the constitution and importance of discourses, power and knowledge in society have important implications not only for debates concerning European societies, but also for the present situation of the Third World (Escobar 1984–5). In anthropology, Foucault's ideas have been treated as important springboards to a fresh appraisal of the theory of ideology implicit in both 'structural functional and interpretative frameworks' (Fardon 1985). The challenge that remains is, as Fardon suggests, how not to 'dissolve the agent' when we study what are labelled dominant ideologies.

Significant advances have been made in this vein within the sociology of knowledge. For instance, Barnes (1986) has introduced the useful notion of discretion, which he depicts as the 'room' whereby people can exercise their capacity to make decisions in situations. This leads him to explore the different practices of 'authorities'. Barnes identifies verbal rules or instructions as the main device used by certain types of agents ('authorities') to restrict other actors' discretion. Knowledge and power, culture and social structure, reveal themselves not as distinct phenomena, but as phenomena constructed from different points of view. At this point the study of action merges with the study of belief, and vice versa. Thus, according to Barnes, any account of communication 'is also a prototypical theory of cognitive order and of social order; and vice versa' (1986: 187).

Barnes proceeds by comparing the traditional perspectives of macro-sociology and micro-sociology on these issues. The former assumes that rules or instructions can be made clear and definite to people, and that discourses have the ability to constrain the actions of actors receiving them. The latter argues that verbal formulations 'have neither fixed logical implications nor fixed semantic implications', allowing total freedom to the agent. According to this point of view, actors retain complete discretion and their use of discourse(s) does not restrict their will to act; hence they remain unconstrained and powerful. Barnes notes that a macro-sociological position allows for a notion of authority, as he has defined it, while a micro-sociological perspective allows only room for power. Barnes acknowledges the latter's contribution to understanding more 'flexible' discourse formulation, but as he points out, in the end, this perspective dissolves the social in the mist of atomic individual beliefs and acts.

Starting from Barnes's preoccupation with 'the production of passive agents', Callon (1986) is concerned with the actual process of (reduction of) discretion among actors. Using what he calls an actor-network approach Callon views actors' struggles with one another as the means by which they construct their identities. Unlike Barnes, Callon is concerned with the analysis of how authorities become constrained by the strategies of other actors. In this sense power is seen, not as a fixed property, or a possession of any particular actor, but a consequence of micro-social negotiations. This is consistent with much of Foucault's thinking and with Latour's (1986) thesis 'that power cannot be stored'.

Within this general perspective, we wish to suggest that an analysis of power in rural development should be based upon recognition of the following major factors:

1 The study of state intervention practices in rural development requires a close examination of the ways in which relevant authorities (a) condition rural actors' responses, and (b) affect their discretion through discourses.
2 Development situations are not only shaped by but also help to shape power relations. Given the fact that actors' everyday practices involve struggles against different forms of domination and subjection, it is important to study the polycentric local representations of power, and at the same time, the ways that actors' projects interlock in the construction of future social configurations.
3 The study of state intervention in rural development should be partly concerned with the generation of counterdiscourses and people's resistance; these localized struggles can be traced back to a wide range of local and extra-local discourses and processes such as democratization, state intervention, gender and political repression, issues of local knowledge, intermediate technology, and the internationalization of agricultural products. This search for the 'genealogy' of local discourse formation highlights the importance of knowledge interfaces and of actors' capacities to internalize and translate discourses at the level of the ordinary person, in order to negotiate the meanings of their local reality with others.

However, a crucial objective of such studies is to reveal the actual composition of power that results from intervention situations and the degree to which, under particular circumstances, people acquire power to keep, ignore, subvert, resist or change the prevailing social order.

Rural micro-sociology: issues and cases

The first sections of this chapter have provided a general framework for analysing policy implementation in rural development, drawing on issues relating to discourse, practice and power. Contradictions within the state, we suggested, are an essential departure point for the investigation of rural transformations. However, these contradictions have to be followed through and analysed at the level of actual policy implementation. The interface between state representatives and local actors is central to understanding not only actors' representations of policies and programmes, but also the ways in which actors' projects interlock diverse interests, thus constructing a chain of interrelated rural issues. The actions of those responsible for policy implementation, and the negotiations between rural producers and state representatives, are important because neither group are passive subjects of their administrative or local contexts. In short, state intervention requires an understanding of diverse practices in rural development.

At the same time, we have shown, all practices have a political dimension associated with the (re)definition of relations between persons, or what Foucault calls 'modes of objectification'. The study of knowledge interfaces provides a social window through which one can analyse choice and the constitution of power at the local level. The exercise of authority, whereby the discretion of others is constrained or enhanced, and people's capacity to bring about significant changes in the distribution of power, are two main dimensions of this central issue in contemporary rural development.

In the next section of the chapter we illustrate the complex interrelations between state intervention and policy implementation in rural development. Three cases are offered to suggest how social construction takes place in development situations, especially how rural people and bureaucrats cope with situations in which specific development discourses are rendered. We focus on how confrontation of meanings affects the content, representations and construction of social interests, restricting the degree to which actors retain their discretion, while at the same time providing opportunities for actors to exercise their power, transforming or reinforcing existing social relations and systems of knowledge.

The material for the case studies presented here was collected by the authors of this chapter during the late 1980s in Costa Rica and Mexico respectively. Pieter de Vries's research in Costa Rica concerned state–peasant relations in the context of a USAID-financed settlement programme in a part of the Atlantic Zone that had earlier been subject to land invasions organized by peasant unions. He undertook an analysis of the Land Development Agency, the institution in charge of managing and developing the settlement area. The first illustration we present in this chapter is part of that experience. This contribution is concerned with arenas of legitimation, that is with issues of power and authority within state agencies. De Vries shows how bureaucrats have to negotiate with producers the rights and obligations of state rural intervention. His analysis of public ceremonies illustrates issues of representation within the state, and he argues that practices within the state are not radically different from the practices that take place in society at large.

The second and third illustrations are the fruits of a research programme on Mexican agrarian development initiated by the Agricultural University of Wageningen in the Netherlands in 1986 and supervised by Professor Norman Long. Empirical research was carried out in Jalisco, western Mexico. Alberto Arce studied the relationship between state representatives and local farmers, applying an interface methodology, while Magdalena Villarreal studied three women's groups and explored issues of power, identity and gender relations in an *ejido* community in the same district.

Arce's case provides the second illustration in this chapter. It describes the local political struggle that developed in the district over the prospect of a revival of export-oriented fruit and vegetable production. It shows how state authority can be challenged and eventually subverted by the skilful political practices of a single local actor. Arce's story shows how an actor can make him/herself indispensable to others, lock these others into his or her project, construct a powerful network and thereby redefine the roles of actors with authority within the process of rural development. This brings us very close to Callon's (1986) analysis of how 'passive authorities' are created. The case illustrates a specific instance of room for manoeuvre at local level, and shows how communication and the circulation of knowledge among different actors constructs a social field of rural development.

Magdalena Villarreal presents the experience of women of a community in the valley of Autlán-El Grullo in the same part of Jalisco. Her case study analyses the wider social implications of change for a group of peasant women who have undertaken a beekeeping enterprise under government sponsorship. Villarreal provides insight into the life-worlds and dynamic social positions of these women, suggesting that women's practical discourses at the level of the household and community as well as in their interactions with state representatives, do not necessarily render women passive victims of gender oppression. On the contrary, these discursive practices reveal women's discretion and their capability, as individuals and as a group, to exercise a degree of power.

Arenas of legitimation: land development in Costa Rica

In Costa Rica, de Vries studied how front-line agricultural extension officers dealt with farmers, accompanying them in their work to observe how they interacted with their 'clients'. He found that in the administrative setting of the Land Development Agency office and in the 'field', contrasting realities prevailed. The agricultural extension officers in the field were subject to pressures from clients to deliver services, while at the same time, as representatives of the state, they had to ensure that the settlers would comply with the policies and rules of the programme. In implementing this latter task the government workers had to negotiate their credibility and legitimacy as state-representatives *vis-à-vis* producers and also in relation to other bureaucratic factions involved in the programme.

An important feature of the programme in the area were the various public 'encounters' or events organized by bureaucrats. These included, in the first place, on-farm trials and field-days (*días de campo*), and publicity, extension and promotion activities in which settlers and front-level bureaucrats were involved. Such public activities were organized for extension purposes, in order to present a new export crop, to recruit farmers for a new production programme, or to announce a campaign against illegal purchase of land. Another type of public encounter involved politicians, planners, implementors, managers, researchers and, sometimes but not always, settlers. These two types of public encounter involved different sorts of bargaining relationships and had different implications for rural policy implementation.

Assessing 'los días de campo'

Días de campo (field-days) were organized to involve peasants in the assessment of various local programmes. The whole organization of these events involved social practices expressing the existence of power relations between state representatives and settlers. For instance, government officials constantly feared that dissidents would transform these events into a political platform for criticizing the various programmes, or worse, into a tribunal, in which the performances and commitments of particular bureaucrats would be judged and the whole process of state intervention assessed. Thus meetings with relevant groups of peasants were tightly scheduled and controlled. Extensionists were always anxious that a dissident group of peasants might take over the meeting and dwell on the failures and shortcomings of the programme, eventually accusing them of being agents of the state apparatus exploiting the peasantry. These extensionists usually tried to pre-empt this possibility by asking the public for 'constructive criticisms': as one extensionist used to say, 'let's accompany every criticism with a realistic proposal to overcome the problem; let's forget the past and look to the future'.

Despite such admonitions, public encounters provided an arena in which various actors put forward their claims. There was, for example, much talk about the value and importance of the interpretative modes used by extensionists and farmers. Settlers would argue that the extensionists' knowledge was bookish and theoretical, and that theirs was 'real' and suited to the locality. Extensionists would deplore the settlers' ignorance and unwillingness to adopt modern agricultural practices. The subject of one ongoing debate was farmers' practice of applying fertilizers much less intensively and over a larger area than was recommended by the extensionists. According to the farmers, output per hectare was lower but total output considerably higher using this approach, whereas the extensionists saw it as an inefficient use of land. For the farmers, this was a way to counter yield variability, offering them more opportunities in regard to labour force deployment (e.g. off-farm work).

These debates embodied not only technical disputes, but also conflicts of interest. Extensionists were obliged to implement a policy of reducing the total maize area. In line with the state policy of *agricultura de cambio* ('farming for change') extensionists were promoting a shift towards non-traditional crops, that is from maize to new export crops, such as tubers for the North American market. Farmers, however, had previously had bad experiences with these new crops, especially with respect to their marketing, and so their main concern was to obtain increases in the maize prices established by the marketing board. These opposing interests were expressed in alternative discourses concerning agricultural technology and production practices. In public encounters peasants and state representatives engaged in a continuing negotiation over the meaning of 'progress' in the locality and the desirability of different paths of technological advance. Both parties understood clearly that their disputes over matters of knowledge entailed fundamentally conflicting claims over the aims of rural development.

Public ceremonies and state authority

The second important type of public encounter consisted of ceremonies such as the inauguration of an agricultural store or a piped water system, the distribution of land titles or the closure of a rural development project. Such ceremonies were tightly structured. The persons involved varied according to the occasion. When land titles were to be distributed, the President of the Republic would be present and would give a speech. At other ceremonies (such as the state Institute's annual party) only selected farmers would be invited to give a small speech of gratitude to the Institute.

On these occasions the proceedings started invariably with the national anthem. Sometimes a peasant artist would then sing a few songs about the pride that fills the peasant who tills his own land, or bemoaning the exploitation of the moneylender. Peasants would present themselves as 'backward' and 'ignorant' people, reinforcing their stereotypical identities in front of the state officials. Speeches would be repetitive, and common themes referred to the solidarity between the Institute and the peasantry, and the need to preserve the national democratic political system and the peaceful traditions of Costa Rica. The need to reject 'foreign ideologies' such as Communism was frequently stressed. Official speeches from state officials would support those peasant organizations that had thanked their agencies individually, and would always make special mention of the President of the Republic for his commitment to the peasant cause.

These ceremonies might be seen as ritualistic, as events underwriting a common moral order through the use of collective representations. However, to the informed observer, hidden messages could be detected in many of the speeches, and there were a few unexpected turns. For example, one peasant representative interrupted the usual routine by reminding those assembled of the need to improve institutional efficiency and to overcome unfortunate legacies of 'bureaucratic traditionalism'. He went on to refer to events taking place in a neighbouring country where a civil war was going on. This, the speaker argued, could be the fate of Costa Rica if 'the state was not capable of resolving the land issue'.

More generally, these ceremonies provided an important setting for directors of institutes, local politicians and other influential people to meet and to hold all sorts of negotiations. What seemed in the first instance to be exercises in institutional legitimation were in fact significant episodes where distribution of power was negotiated among different institutional factions operating in the field of rural development. Within the programme, several factions were fighting among themselves for credibility. It was important for these factions to mobilize people (peasants, local politicians and local institutional managers) in a public way in order to demonstrate both their ability to represent 'other' people from society, and their capacity to extend the influence of the st: te into the countryside. In other words, these ceremonies had a lot to do with the positioning of bureaucratic factions aimed at limiting the discretion of other agencies, while maximizing their own power so as to retain authority to organize rural intervention.

La Lima: the social construction of an irrigation system

In August 1987, rumours started to circulate among the small farmers of the *ejido* of La Lima, Jalisco, Mexico. It was reported that water would soon be available from a new government-constructed irrigation system. This was good news for some producers, but for others it revived their worst fears, the residue of their previous 'rip-off' at the hands of dishonest US brokers (Heijdra 1988; 1989). For the Mexican state officials of the Ministry of Agriculture and Water Resources (SARH), the rumour foretold troubles ahead. In practical administrative terms, irrigation meant reorganizing the boundaries of their field units, deploying new personnel and taking on new responsibilities. The SARH fieldworker in charge of La Lima was convinced that agro-export companies could return to take advantage of the new irrigation system, depriving local producers of the expected economic benefits.

Working in favour of an association between local interests and agro-export companies were the intriguing activities of one of the economically better-off small farmers in the area, who was also the manager of the idle local packing plant. This person became very active overnight, looking into possible solutions for the reactivation of the plant and suggesting the need to establish commercial contacts with 'reliable US companies'. He organized a visit to explore contacts with some US companies and started to enrol some of the other local producers in his scheme. At the same time, he arranged personal interviews with the district authorities at the Ministry of Agriculture and Water Resources (SARH) and with the relevant fieldworker. The field official felt that it was his responsibility to inform local producers about the risks involved in this type of venture. According to the fieldworker, producers had always been victims of ignorance or misinformation and trickery.

On the other hand, the packing plant manager saw in the reactivation of agro-export activities the only way for local producers to pay back the costs of the irrigation programme and its future conservation. He argued that a successful export-oriented agricultural season could restore local confidence in government programmes and in the international market. Part of his strategy was to involve the US companies in financing the process of production, so as to reduce the risk to the producers. He wanted government support to consolidate this venture, but he was careful to seek the support of district officials rather than their direct involvement.

At one of the regional SARH meetings, the head of the district finally made the announcement that the water was coming to La Lima, initially on an experimental basis. The government wanted to test the system and see how producers were going to respond to the new opportunities it created. This announcement set in motion an intense process of social interaction and construction of alliances through which the loyalties and identities of the different actors were renegotiated. These local processes of association and disassociation established, in action, what we may call the social construction of the irrigation system.

The SARH fieldworker, who was following the events closely, proposed a first meeting with all the farmers who were members of the packing plant co-operative to explain the new situation to them. The plant manager countered by suggesting a meeting of only those producers who were 'active members'. After a process of negotiation the two agreed to call a general meeting. After this first informal conversation they set a date and time for the general meeting. When Alberto Arce, the sociologist, arrived with the field official – at the time, day and place agreed – none of the producers was there.

The fieldworker was visibly upset. However, after further discussion at the plant manager's house, a meeting was eventually convened in the local sports centre. The thirteen producers present were all active members of the packing plant co-operative and, according to the manager, they wanted the plant reopened. The fieldworker opened the meeting saying: 'This is not an official meeting. You have not worked the plant for the last three years. Therefore the government wants to help by providing producers with irrigation. We are going to irrigate a small area, so we need only those producers who want to work hard'.

The officer established in his discourse the centrality of the government's role, weaving subtle notions into the information he provided, thus planting the idea that no producer could cultivate a crop without authorization from the government. He then pointed to the range of problems that had existed in the past with regard to the marketing of fruit and he asked the producers to analyse their failures, learn from experience, and collectively decide on a course for action.

Worried about the turn of the discussion, the plant manager argued that the US companies were the only market for their agricultural products. He reminded his listeners of the role of local corruption and maintained that not all US companies could be characterized as dishonest. He spoke about his conversation with a Texas company and added that this company could provide inputs for the producers. At the local branch of the UNPH (National Union of Horticultural Producers) there was a list of honest US companies, a list which had been approved by the government. If something were to go wrong, it would be the UNPH, the responsible organization, which would enforce the payment to the producers.

The government official replied in a similar manner. How many of the packing plants and associations that existed here three years ago were still working today? Where were these located and to whom did they belong? They were all moneylenders and speculators from Autlán (a nearby town), brokers of US companies, blood-suckers of the independent producers! These people were linked to the local, regional and national association (UNPH). Producers in other areas realized that this organization was no guarantee for them. It was merely the political and economic expression of power in the region.

The meeting had become a contest of knowledge and discourse credibility. It ended with the formation of two committees. One group was given the task of visiting the government's district office to find out which plots were going to receive water. The second group was to explore alternatives for marketing. This was to be a process of learning from experience and would be headed by the local government official. For him, it was clearly a device to protect the producers from repeating their past mistakes. The official's objective was to make producers aware of the potential dangers in this economic venture. Deeply entrenched in his approach was distrust of the market system and of the leadership of the local producers.

The packing plant manager went to the district and obtained information about the land. However, he probably discovered something else too, because after the fieldworker had managed to organize two meetings, the latter's situation was suddenly undermined. A direct instruction came from the head of his field unit informing him that the reopening of the La Lima packing plant was an issue to be handled directly from the offices of the district by the section specializing in producer organization. This *de facto* de-legitimation of the local fieldworker induced some producers to withdraw from the project.

The newly involved district officials, some of whom had personal conflicts with the fieldworker, started the process again from scratch. In their view, any revival of economic activity would be beneficial for the locality. They disregarded the fieldworker's previous work and supported the views of the packing plant manager, agreeing that the local association should be reorganized only with active members. The officials portrayed the connections between the La Lima producers and the Texas companies as an instance of spontaneous local self-organization.

The episode in La Lima illustrates well an aspect of the way that power can be redistributed within a context of state intervention. The actions of the packing plant manager in favour of agro-export agriculture involved high levels of personal and financial risk. His arguments went counter to previous agro-export experience in the locality. Nevertheless he was successful in creating a new network in which US companies, a different section of the Ministry of Agriculture and a handful of small independent producers managed to ensure the viability of the project. He achieved a redistribution of local power and established a new institutional authority. The case shows that power is far from being a fixed structural property that is simply to be invoked to explain particular actors' action. It illustrates the way power is negotiated by actors and can be in practice extremely fluid. It is because of this that success or failure of state intervention is never assured.

Gender and identity: the beekeepers of Ayuquila

In analysing processes of policy implementation, gender relations and their transformations call for special attention. But gender relations involve relationships of power between men and women, and as such they have been subject to the same analytical limitations as other power relations. They still tend to be thought of as structurally given, self-evident and relatively immutable features of social situations. Villarreal's study of a small-scale development project for women in western Mexico (for a detailed analysis of this case see Villarreal 1990) illustrates the value of a more subtle approach which focuses on women's ability to use discourses of accommodation and strategic compliance (cf. Scott 1985) to exploit and enhance their room for manoeuvre in a given situation.

The beekeeping project was considered by many people in the community of Ayuquila to be an issue of secondary importance in the life of the village. Women's work had often being characterized in everyday life as subsidiary to male activities. Most men and women were not keen to consider seriously a project whose main purpose was to involve women in income-generating work. Furthermore, the project involved allotting certain plots of land to the women beekeepers, which many farmers resented greatly. Many claimed that the beekeepers should keep to their household tasks and not stray into 'the men's world'.

The women had particular interests to protect within their social networks and had little influence in established community decision-making spaces. Thus they had to measure their steps carefully and make sure they did not transgress any major community norms; they had to manoeuvre for specific objectives while maintaining an 'acceptable' position as women. Women in Ayuquila were allotted 'gender roles' not only within the household, but also in their different networks in the village, and in their dealings with the representatives of the state.

In their everyday life, the members of the project faced the complex task of managing sets of interlocking relationships in which subordination and compliance were important features. For example, the husband of Petra, the group's leader, accepted that she could engage in her 'hobby', as long as it remained a hobby and did not endanger his position as head of the family. Likewise, the non-verbalized 'conjugal contract' entered into by Rosa, another member of the group, clearly established that she should contribute economically to the household, as well as performing the domestic chores defined as 'women's work', besides accepting that her husband could come home drunk, bringing friends in a similarly inebriated condition. Juana, another beekeeper, admitted she had to give her husband 'his quota of power', and had to comply with unwritten village norms by respecting the authority of her spouse, so that he, in turn, would be respected by his neighbours and kin. However, in all this the women maintained a degree of discretion. This involved controlling whatever aspects of their everyday life they could and enrolling others in their projects, even while subordinating themselves whenever necessary within the domestic or public spheres.

The beekeepers were offered a paternalistic deal both by government agencies and by the head of the *ejido* (agrarian community), who described the group as 'powerless' and as 'people in need of help'. This assessment denied the women authority in the community. Presenting them as helpless implied not only that the government should provide resources (credit) to favour peasant women's 'development', but also that state resources should be directed through the men's institution, the *ejido*, which would support and 'stand up' for them.

To a degree, the women accepted these conditions, according men and the 'authorities' their 'place'. They were willing to enhance the authority of the *ejido* assembly, for example agreeing that the project had come about thanks to men's organizations, but often with their own purposes in mind. Towards male *ejidatarios* they downplayed their capacities as entrepreneurs but then used these same interpretations to push the project forward. Thus, Petra was prepared to accept that, as women, the group were not as capable as men, and that therefore they needed training.

As the project began to show signs of 'success', the women were able to open up more room-for-manoeuvre. For some, the success of the project led to a better bargaining position at home. Thus Petra used her project activity – consciously or unconsciously – to achieve more space within her domestic situation. For Rosa, the argument in her household about her extra work and income ended by giving her more flexibility in other kinds of spaces, for example in her relationships with other men and women.

Other women in the group continued to subordinate themselves in the domestic sphere in order to achieve greater freedom outside it. Juana's conduct towards her husband had the effect of portraying a harmless conventional image of herself, which was necessary so as to create space for her other projects. Sara apparently subordinated her activities to her husband's, taking a hot meal to him in the fields every day and helping out with what she called minor tasks such as weeding and driving the cows home. But, in the end, this proved an effective way to put pressure on her husband to establish clearly what for her was 'proper' work. This provided her with crucial decision-making situations in which she could get her points across. Thus, these women accepted roles for themselves in order to win arguments useful for battles elsewhere.

What this case illustrates is that women are not passive victims of a gender situation. Although it is undeniable that women are constrained and moulded in many ways by circumstances and conditions, some of which they themselves help to re-create, they also have the capacity to manipulate these limitations, using what might be called 'women's weapons' in order not only, as it were, to survive in deep water, but to use the current whenever possible to bring the boat in their direction.

Embodied in this assessment is a critical view of what has been seen as a core issue in many analyses of gender situations: autonomy. To different degrees, it has been usual to describe women as striving for autonomy from male domination. Thus, women are said to be in a struggle to achieve control over their lives, over their bodies and over their projects (Schrijvers 1985). But what does 'control over one's life' amount to in contexts such as Ayuquila?

Autonomy can be a misleading concept. Looking at the boundaries they placed on their projects, at the meanings they accorded their bee-keeping, agricultural and household activities, and at the kinds of roles they were willing to see themselves playing, we have found the women of Ayuquila renewing their bonds with their menfolk, not breaking them unless it is really necessary, while at the same time working to build their other networks and creating new ones. This is not without problems, since one can easily see the constraints faced by these women, among other things, due to their sex, status and economic and political situation. Nevertheless, the case illustrates the importance of understanding the efforts of poor rural women in the creation, appropriation and conservation of space for themselves. The beekeepers provide a clear example of how women manipulate their constraints in their struggle for this space. In the reconstruction of the social worlds, making room-for-manoeuvre involves a degree of independence in certain spheres and a degree of 'dependence' in others. It implies 'enrolment' of other people in one's project. This, in turn, involves not only a 'trade' of images, but also a 'war' of imposing upon others those images which are useful for one's interests. It implies power, negotiation and consent.

Conclusion

This chapter has re-examined some central issues in the analysis of the social construction of rural development. Beginning with the issue of state intervention, we challenged the notion that the state is the main or only institution contributing significantly to rural development out-comes, emphasizing the importance of contradictions and negotiations between state agencies and between state representatives and rural producers. A critical overview of recent work on rural development administration indicated the need for a revised conceptual and empirical agenda. The basis for such an agenda is to be found in two main directions that explore issues of interface and room-for-manoeuvre. Both raise important questions about discourses, practices and power.

Taking up each of these issues, we analysed, first, how knowledge confrontations affect the content of social representations, how actors exercise power and transform or reinforce existing discourses. As we saw, knowledge is a fundamental property of agency which allows actors to construct socially the field of rural development.

Second, we examined the links between human agency, discourses, social interests and identities. Our analysis suggested that discourses can be viewed as important social practices which actors deploy to attribute value to material resources and to define social identities. We accepted the need to study the formation of macro-social discourses, but stressed the importance of examining how actors use discourses in practice, and how this affects the process of policy implementation.

Our last general argument concerned the importance of studying the distribution of power and legitimation in local contexts. We argued on the basis of various recent contributions that power is to be seen not as a fixed property, or as a possession of any particular actor, but rather as a consequence of micro-social negotiations. This position, finally, led us to explore the relation between power and authority in micro and macro situations of rural intervention.

In the latter part of the chapter, we have illustrated in different contexts how disputes over 'knowledge' reflect struggles for legitimacy as well as conflicting interests and visions of the ends of rural development. We have also explored how power relations can be transformed in action at the local level, and the ways in which the discourses and practices of rural women may serve as 'weapons of the weak', thereby sustaining and enhancing their discretion or room for manoeuvre.

Our chapter points, then, to the importance of negotiations and struggles over social interests in the processes of rural development. It also implies a certain view of the role of the state in such processes, which it is well to make explicit before concluding. We believe state intervention has a limited but potentially positive part to play in contemporary rural change. By virtue of policy formulation, policy implementation and administrative practices, the state may be said to filter out some choices open to rural actors but not others. State agricultural policies provide a framework of macro-order in society, favouring certain institutional environments and discourses for social transformation over others, while exerting a diffuse influence upon people's everyday lives. Under these conditions the capacity of the state actually to determine the outcome of the changes it helps to initiate may be quite limited. But so far as rural polices can be put in place that permit diversity and maintain the discretion of rural people, rather than forcing 'good intentions' down on them, state intervention may provide some of the necessary conditions for rural development to take place.

Note

1.   This tendency is clearly present in the work of Grindle and Thomas (1991).

References

Apthorpe R (1984) Agriculture and strategies: the language of development policy. In: Clay E J and Schaffer B B (eds)

Apthorpe R (1986) Development policy discourse. *Public Administration and Development* 6

Arce A and **Long N** (1987) The dynamics of knowledge interfaces between Mexican agricultural bureaucrats and peasants: a case study from Jalisco. *Boletin de Estudios Latinoamericanos y del Caribe* 43

Barnes B (1986) On authority and its relationship to power. In Law J (ed)

Callon M (1986) Some elements of a sociology of translation: domestication of the scallops and the fishermen of St Brieuc Bay. In Law J (ed)

Clay E J and **Schaffer B B** (eds) (1984) *Room for manoeuvre: an exploration of public policy in agriculture and rural development.* London, Heinemann

Escobar A (1984–5) Discourse and power in development: Michel Foucault and the relevance of his work to the Third World. *Alternatives* 10

Fardon R (ed) (1985) *Power and knowledge: anthropological and sociological approaches.* Edinburgh, Scottish Academic Press

Foucault M (1973) *The order of things.* London, Tavistock

Foucault M (1979) On governability, ideology and consciousness. Reprinted in Burchell G, Gordon, C and Miller P (eds) *The Foucault effect: studies in governmental rationality.* Hemel Hempstead, Harvester-Wheatsheaf

Foucault M (1982) The subject and power. In: Dreyfus H and Rabinow P (eds) *Michel Foucault beyond structuralism and hermeneutics.* Chicago, IL, University of Chicago Press

Giddens A (1984) *The constitution of society.* Cambridge, Polity Press

Grindle M S (ed) (1980) *Politics and policy implementation in the Third World.* Princeton, NJ, Princeton University Press

Grindle M S (1986) *State and countryside: development policy and agrarian politics in Latin America.* Baltimore, MD, Johns Hopkins University Press

Grindle M S and **Thomas J W** (1991) *Public choices and policy change: the political economy of reform in developing countries.* Baltimore, MD, Johns Hopkins University Press

Heijdra H (1988) Local organizations, outside interventions and peasant strategies: a case study at the intermediate level in an export-orientated irrigation zone of western Mexico. MSc thesis, University of Wageningen

Heijdra H (1989) Social encounters and interfaces between farmers and intervening actors: the emergence of local organization in western Mexico. In: Long N (ed)

Latour B (1986) The power of association. In: Law J (ed)

Law J (ed) (1986) *Power, action and belief: a new sociology of knowledge?* Sociological Review Monograph 32. London, Routledge & Kegan Paul

Long N (ed) (1989) *Encounters at the interface: a perspective on social discontinuities in rural development.* Wageningen, University of Wageningen Press

MacDonell D (1986) *Theories of discourse: an introduction.* Oxford, Basil Blackwell

Migdal J S (1988) *Strong societies and weak states: state–society relations and state capabilities in the Third World.* Princeton, NJ, Princeton University Press

Schaffer B (1984) Towards responsibility: public policy in concept and practice. In: Clay E J and Schaffer B B (eds)

Schaffer B (1985) Policy makers have their needs too: Irish itinerants and the culture of poverty. In: Wood G (ed)

Schrijvers J (1985) Mothers for life: motherhood and marginalization in the North Central Province of Sri Lanka. Leiden, Research and Documentation Centre

Schutz A and **Luckmann T** (1974) *The structures of the life world.* London, Heinemann

Scott J C (1985) *The weapons of the weak: everyday forms of peasant resistance.* New Haven, CT, Yale University Press

Skocpol T (1979) *States and social revolutions.* Cambridge, Cambridge University Press

Skocpol T (1985) Bringing the state back in: strategies of analysis in current research. In: Evans P B, Rueschemeyer D and Skocpol T (eds) *Bringing the state back in.* Cambridge, Cambridge University Press

Villarreal M (1990) A struggle over images: issues on power, gender and intervention in a Mexican village. MSc thesis, University of Wageningen

Wood G (ed) (1985) *Labelling in development policy: essays in honour of Bernard Schaffer.* London, Sage Publications

CHAPTER 7

Between economism and post-modernism:
reflections on research on 'agrarian change' in India[1]

John Harriss

Sociological research in and on India has had a distinctive pattern of development since the early 1970s. Even though it can be claimed with some justice that 'dependency theory' originated in South Asia – in the work of the Indian nationalist historians of the later nineteenth century – the wave of theorizing sparked off by Gunder Frank and others largely passed India by. On the whole Indian Marxists remained locked in their long-standing debates over the character and role of the Indian bourgeoisie, and on the question of whether or not the main line of struggle in the countryside is still that of opposing landlordism. Indian sociology, meanwhile, remained embedded in structural functionalism, while Indian anthropologists engaged with the different lines of interpretative sociology blazed by Dumont on the one side, and by the Chicago School on the other. Beteille's was a lone Indian voice advocating scholarly engagement with problems of class formation (see Beteille 1974a); and Kathleen Gough's alone among those of foreign scholars (see Gough 1969).

But the fundamental question posed by 'dependency theory', that of whether or not capitalism could develop a former colony, found expression in India in a debate over the character of the mode of production, especially – and this was a crucial limitation upon the debate – in the agricultural economy (for reviews of the debate see J Harriss 1980; A Thorner 1982). It was sparked in part by an interest in the impact of the introduction of new agricultural technology (what came to be called 'the green revolution'), and the question of whether this had called agrarian capitalism into being. The various protagonists all drew heavily on the writings of Marx and Lenin, claiming authority thereby for their differing views of what defines capitalism as a mode of production, drawing then on more or less stereotyped views of the economic history of India to provide evidence of the existence of capitalism thus defined. All grappled with the problem of reconciling the evidently capitalist and apparently non-capitalist features of the Indian economy, and sought either to justify a claim that capitalist relations of production were a reality in Indian agriculture or to explain why they were not.

172

In general the debate was marked by the same features which Booth identified in neo-Marxist development theory and which he believed to have created an impasse:

> a metatheoretical commitment to demonstrating that the structures and processes that we find in the less-developed world are not only explicable but necessary under capitalism. This general formula covers two variants: the type of necessity entailed by the Marxian insistence that the salient features of capitalist national economies can be 'read off' from the concept of the capitalist mode of production and its laws; and another, also inspired in Marx's theory, that involves a system teleology or functionalism. (Booth 1985: 776).

The Indian debate exhibited both variants of the general formula.

For all its limitations the 'Indian Mode of Production (MOP) debate' gave rise to work of enduring significance. In my view the most important contribution to it was that made by Jairus Banaji in a long article entitled 'Capitalist domination and the small peasantry' (1977), based on detailed historical research on the Deccan in the later nineteenth century. Banaji acknowledged the influence of Michael Cowen's Kenyan research and followed Cowen in drawing upon Marx's own analysis of the history of capitalist development which drew the distinction between the 'formal' and the 'real subsumption' of labour under capital. Banaji used these concepts in showing how, historically, 'peasant' production was reproduced in relations with capital. His argument makes use of an ill-considered and teleological notion of 'pre-formal' subsumption of labour (see J Harriss 1982: 290–2), but I believe that the article made an important contribution to clarification of the character of 'peasant' petty commodity production by Bernstein and others; see Bernstein (1977) for the start of a trail which leads through to a recent statement of exemplary clarity in Bernstein (1990). This has at last broken through the stultifying impasse in research on agrarian issues created by opposition of Leninist and Chayanovian views of the peasantry.

But, though I believe that there has been real advance in theoretical understanding of the economic character of peasant production (in India notably in the work of Bharadwaj, e.g. 1985), there have not been comparable advances in analysis of politics, culture and ideology. The problems to which attention was drawn in a particularly sharp way in a paper on Venezuelan coffee producers by William Roseberry (1978) remain. Roseberry had shown the subsumption of what appeared as independent 'peasant' production under capital, but then seemed almost to ask the question 'so what?' so far as understanding of the politics of rural producers is concerned. He argued:

> At the level of the mode of production . . . peasants may occupy a structural position comparable to that of proletarians. As we move toward a concrete analysis, however, a more complex picture emerges [so that] . . . We are forced to conclude . . . that peasants are not proletarians in disguise in Venezuela. A simple abstraction of mode of production might lead us to see peasants and proletarians occupying similar structural positions in a dichot-

omous class model. In this sense they would be paid a 'concealed wage' in their interaction with merchants. Peasants, then, would be proletarians. A more concrete analysis, however, suggests that they occupy and perceive different structural positions. (Roseberry 1978: 10, 15)

And in a collection of his essays the same author, while stoutly defending the value of the concept of 'mode of production' in the historical analysis of class formation, also says that 'when we come to consider culture and politics, we enclose profoundly contradictory social experiences within unproblematic and simplistic class or epochal labels' (1989: ix).

The economistic reductionism which marks the Indian MOP debate and the intellectual traditions of the Indian Left in general meant that the Left was ill-prepared for the actual events of the 1980s. These years saw the rise of what the press called 'Farmers' Movements', more recently described by a leading scholar-activist as a 'new peasant movement' and by implication to be considered among other 'new social movements' (see Omvedt 1988; Lindberg 1990). These movements in India drew very large numbers of rural people, including rich, middle and poor peasants, and sometimes also landless agricultural workers, into often prolonged agitations (notably through Rasta Roko, 'sit-ins' on major roads and railways, immobilizing traffic). They were directed explicitly against the state and in support of demands for higher agricultural prices, lower prices for agricultural inputs, or for such measures as the cancellation of outstanding debts to public sector financial institutions. The organized Left had great difficulty in deciding upon its response to these undoubtedly popular movements. The 1980s also saw a mounting tide of caste and communal conflict for which the Left was equally ill-prepared.

The intellectual space left by the neglect of political and cultural issues in the tradition of Indian radicalism has been filled latterly by the work of the 'Subaltern School' of historians, who originally drew inspiration from Gramsci. Their use of the term 'subaltern' to refer to subordinated groups and classes comes from Gramsci. Latterly the influence of this group has begun to extend directly into sociological research especially through the writing of Ramachandra Guha (1989). As is the case with any 'School' of thought those who are thus labelled are not absolutely univocal, but they all acknowledge the influence of Gramsci and share in a critique of conventional Left and nationalist thought in India, as well as of what they describe as the western historiography of India which they see as being reproduced in nationalist thinking.

The way in which the 'Subalterns' draw out cultural aspects of historical change is shown, for example, in David Hardiman's analysis of rural politics in Kheda District in Gujarat in the 1920s and 1930s (Hardiman 1981). Whereas scholarly debate had focused on the respective roles of rich, middle and poor peasants in political action (in this case their participation in the nationalist struggle), Hardiman, while not at all unmindful of these distinctions, argues that political mobilization was

174

crucially affected by the existence of a sense of caste community and by kinship organization:

> neither the 'rich peasant' nor 'middle peasant' theories shed light on [an] important feature of the movement in Kheda: namely, that although the peasant nationalists were mostly rich and middle peasants, they were also Patidars. Besides being a nationalist struggle, this also became a movement by the Patidars for their self-assertion as a community. (Hardiman 1981: 250)

Another 'Subaltern', Dipesh Chakrabarty, asks in his book *Rethinking Working Class History* (1989) 'what happens when a working class is born into a culture characterised by persistence of pre-capitalist relations – or by the absence of notions of "citizenship", "individualism", or "equality before the law"', given that, in his cogently argued view, 'Marx's discussion of the labor–capital relation as it operated within the capitalist organization of work cannot be placed outside his assumption of a hegemonic bourgeois culture' (1989: 4). Chakrabarty explores the implications of the Subalterns' general position – that colonial capitalism failed to establish the hegemony of bourgeois culture (see Ranajit Guha 1989) – in relation to the formation of a working class in the Calcutta jute industry. He shows how the silences of the historical record reflect the exercise of sardari authority (that of labour contractors) 'which was rooted not in capitalist but in pre-capitalist modes of domination'. He suggests that the militancy but lack of organization of the jute workers may be explained as the outcome of the way in which unions were set up and led by Left intellectuals of the Bengali middle-class, who though 'Intellectually committed to developing trade unions based on the democratic, contractual and voluntary procedures of organisation that their theory of trade unionism entailed [actually] . . . related to the coolies through a hierarchy of status'. And he explains the susceptibility of jute workers to ideological manipulation by ethnic leaders.

The 'Subalterns' thus address questions of culture and politics which have been neglected, assumed to be unimportant, or relegated to the box of 'false consciousness' in the mainstream of work on the sociology of development in India. Their work, in turn, has been criticized in a variety of ways, though perhaps nowhere with more vigour than in an article by Tom Brass, a sociologist who has undertaken field studies especially of rural labour in Peru and in India. Brass tries to establish the continuities between the arguments of Wolf and Alavi on the political roles of middle peasants; Scott's arguments about the 'moral economy of the peasantry' and more recently on the forms of peasant resistance; analysis in Latin America of the so-called 'new social movements'; and the ideas of the Subalterns. He suggests that they 'provide Chayanovian theory about the peasant economy with its missing politico-ideological dimension' (Brass 1991: 174). By implication, he suggests, therefore, that just as Chayanov's theory attempts to show how 'people's capitalism' is possible (in spite of the real impossibility of capitalism without inequality and hierarchies of power), Scott, the Subalterns and others similarly suggest a future for peasants which involves 'resistance' to capitalism and to the state, but which, because it has no positive project of change and offers only a return to the past (of the mythical 'moral economy'), in practice must assist the reproduction of capitalism.

Chakrabarty, in the Preface to his book, provides a striking example of the Subaltern dilemma which would seem to justify Brass's critique. Chakrabarty agonizes over the tensions between his opposition to western capitalism, his awareness of the injustice inherent in the old order of Hindu culture and polity, and his belief that, none the less, there is a future in the old institutions of community: 'The question is this: Can we . . . build democratic, communitarian institutions on the basis of non-individualistic, but hierarchical and illiberal, precapitalist bonds that have survived and sometimes resisted – or even flourished under – the onslaught of capital?' Brass thus argues that those scholars who have latterly made such powerful contributions to the study of peasant politics and culture – Scott, Ranajit Guha, Ramachandra Guha – by sharing in the post-modernist rejection of the concept and project of progress, are in the end profoundly conservative in spite of their original professed intention of identifying with the oppressed 'subalterns' of history.

The sociological study of development in India, and specifically the study of 'agrarian change' (a shorthand term referring to agrarian structure – structures of social relationships based on relationships to land – and the changes which may come about in it in the course of the development of capitalism), seems therefore still to be stuck in an impasse. On the one hand there is a mode of analysis which, in spite of the advances which it has marked in understanding of rural production, is frankly economistic. On the other there is a growing literature which is concerned with politics and culture/ideology but which seems to entail an epistemology which rejects the possibility of 'development'.

This is the theoretical context in which, in this chapter, I reflect upon my own research into agrarian change in India. This started in the early 1970s and was stimulated by an interest in the broader social implications of 'the green revolution', so that it was, inevitably, concerned with the questions which were also addressed in the Indian MOP debate. Whereas the contributors to that debate, however, drew mainly on empirical reference to (often stylized) historical or statistical 'facts' about the Indian agrarian economy, my research has always been based upon fieldwork, with the limitations and the advantages that this implies.

Agrarian structure and agricultural development: the significance of politics

The introduction of the new agricultural technology (higher-yielding varieties of the principal foodgrains and complementary inputs of agro-chemicals) entailed an intensification of the process of commercialization. An argument about the impact of commercialization appears in analyses of the agrarian economies of North Arcot District in Tamil Nadu, and of Birbhum District in West Bengal, by Barbara Harriss and myself (B Harriss 1981; 1983; J Harriss 1982; 1983; 1985). Rather comparable analysis appears in work on Bangladesh by Wood (1981) and by Westergaard (1985). I shall summarize our arguments about North Arcot as a paradigmatic case.[2]

Socio-economic inequality

North Arcot has an agrarian structure characterized by high incidence of landlessness (30 per cent of rural households). Altogether about 80 per cent of households are insufficiently endowed with means of production as to be able to produce their own livelihood requirements. A small class of rich peasants and small landlords, who make up 5 to (at most) 10 per cent of households, is able to dominate labour, money and product markets as well as land. Through this domination they extract surplus in the forms of absolute surplus value derived from their own production, profits from usury, and from speculative trading.

Their control now exists in much the same way that it did a century ago, according to Washbrook's analysis of the agrarian economy of this part of Tamil Nadu in the later nineteenth century (e.g. Washbrook 1976). The agrarian structure is closely comparable with that recently described by Athreya, Djurfeldt and Lindberg from a region further south in Tamil Nadu. In their study Athreya *et al.* (1990) established that only 4 per cent of households in 'dry' (i.e. non-irrigated) villages were of 'surplus appropriators', and they show that 'The majority of the middle peasantry is pushed below the level of autonomous production and depends upon non-farm sources of income for their reproduction' (1990: 233).

'Compulsive involvement' in markets

There is, necessarily, in these circumstances, a high level of what Krishna Bharadwaj calls 'compulsive involvement' in markets, or what Amit Bhaduri refers to as 'forced commerce' (see Bharadwaj 1985; Bhaduri 1986). These authors argue that when the process of commercialization takes place in circumstances in which there is already inequality in the ownership of assets, so that people don't actually enter the market on equal terms, even those who lack true marketable surplus find themselves necessarily involved in the market. This comes about for reasons which include seasonal irregularities in flows of income and demands for cash, and what Bernstein describes as 'the simple reproduction squeeze' – arising from a shift in the terms of trade between those products which are sold and those which producers need to buy in order to survive and carry on their production (see Bernstein 1977).

'Compulsive involvement' of this type is on terms which are extremely adverse so that what they produce is substantially appropriated by dominant owners of means of production and/or by merchant capital. Such relationships are at the same time the reason for the continuing underdevelopment of the mass of rural producers – in the sense that they are unable to improve their productivity and incomes – and the base of what may be, from the point of view of the dominant economic agents, an efficient mode of surplus appropriation.

There is resonance between this argument and the results of recent historical scholarship, reviewed by Washbrook. He argues that capitalism flourished in nineteenth-century India. The dynamic of its expansion, however,

> came not from the 'dangerous' entrepreneurship of capital but from the pressure of social necessity which forced previously 'unproductive' groups and groups productive in now unviable sectors onto the land to work. This pressure, by increasing the competition for land and for subsistence, also increased the dominance of capital and enabled it both to claim a progressively higher share of the social product and to cast off more and more of its responsibilities for the social reproduction of the labour force. (Washbrook 1988: 87)

In North Arcot District now, most producers have no alternative but to sell their paddy or groundnuts at harvest, and then to draw loans for subsistence and for the renewal of production. Such compulsive involvement was increased in the late 1960s and early 1970s by the introduction of 'green revolution' technology. Small producers' accounting is in terms of the total product of grain rather than profit. The goal of increasing the number of bags of paddy from the field made the new rice varieties attractive to such producers and they would borrow to purchase the necessary seeds and other inputs. It is easy to understand how this could, in many cases, given the riskiness of agricultural production, lead to increased debt and further 'compulsive involvement'.

The 'built-in depressor' and after

For surplus appropriators and those with money, moneylending, trade and non-agricultural production were more profitable than investment in agricultural production. Such monied capitalists thus profited from the compulsive involvement in the market of the mass of producers. In more abstract terms merchant capital was dominant and acted as a 'built-in depressor' (in a phrase of Daniel Thorner's – Thorner 1956) in economic development. The advent of the 'green revolution' and of higher land productivity resulting from it had given the system a little kick by 1973–4, and brought about some increase in production, but it did not appear at all likely to be a sustainable effect, because it was simply not profitable enough for the surplus appropriators to be encouraged to continue investing directly in production.

In fact, follow-up research in 1983–4 showed that we were wrong and that the 'built-in depressor' did not operate in the way in which we supposed. Agricultural production had continued to grow, exceptionally for Tamil Nadu, at more than 3 per cent per annum through the 1970s and early 1980s; cultivation of HYVs (high yielding varieties) had increased from less than 20 per cent of the paddy acreage to more than

90 per cent; investments in groundwater irrigation and in fertilizers had increased from what were already comparatively high levels; and there were widely distributed though very modest increases in real incomes. What had happened to offset the effects of the depressor? What was involved was basically a set of conjunctural factors and state interventions lying (in Ronald Herring's (1984) way of putting it) 'beyond the reach of local power structures' which are what is emphasized in the notion of 'the depressor'.

The conjunctural factors were first, the chance that the variety IR20 was well suited to local agro-climatic conditions, proving higher yielding than local varieties even in moisture-stressed and low fertility conditions; second, the equalization of prices between local and modern varieties which occurred in the mid-1970s; and third, the expansion of employment locally and in more distant towns and cities, not linked to local agriculture, but playing a significant part in the 'tightening' of the local labour market (as demand for labour more nearly matches supply), which helped in turn to account for the modest increases in real incomes of landless agricultural workers in particular.

The state interventions were first, those which continued the expansion of the supply of cheap formal sector credit, legislated against (supposedly) usurious private moneylending and sought to regulate agricultural marketing; second, those which subsidized the supply of electric power – and thus helped to sustain the expansion of groundwater irrigation – and, for a time at least, maintained the fertilizer/paddy price ratio; third, land reform legislation which, though not at all effective in bringing about much redistribution of land, has limited the accumulation of land in large holdings and provided some allotments for landless people, thus improving their creditworthiness even if not supplying them with a livelihood holding; and fourth, welfare interventions, notably a very large-scale supplementary feeding programme, the Nutritious Noon Meals Scheme for children, which has had some impact upon living standards, and also contributed to the generation of off-farm employment in the public sector. This is another factor involved in the tightening of the local labour market.

The centrality of politics

These interventions have come about because of the nature of politics. The regime, in the state of Tamil Nadu, as in the Indian union, is one in which no single class exerts economic or political dominance, and neither is there a state organization which is powerful in relation to society. In a context of parliamentary electoral politics the maintenance of power had come to depend on a precarious trading of concessions to different social groups, including the rural poor as well as those whom I have described as 'surplus appropriators'. As Kohli says:

> The state is highly centralised and omnipresent, but the leverage of its leaders
> . . . has diminished. The main reason for this is that authority has seldom run
> deep, and the authority structures have in recent years fallen into disrepair.

> As a result, state authorities have little ability to persuade people to support government initiatives. . . . It has become a vicious circle: Weakness in the authority structures makes it difficult to solve precisely those problems whose solutions could strengthen authority. (Kohli 1990: 16)

The weakness and ineffectiveness of political organization is associated with the practice of populism, and with personalization of power (exemplified *a fortiori* in the regime of the film star politician M G Ramachandran in the state of Tamil Nadu), which has happened along-side the mobilization of previously passive groups in electoral competition. The vicious circle of which Kohli speaks is intensified. Its outcomes include the sorts of interventions which have recently been significant in North Arcot.

In short, as Venkatesh Athreya and his co-authors have put it in describing their very comparable empirical findings: 'relations of production in themselves do not explain agrarian change. Several state interventions have proved strategic . . . and analysis [points to] the fundamental role of politics for economic change' (Athreya *et al.* 1990: 17). Debates over agrarian structure and agrarian change in India have tended to ignore their context in larger political economic forces. Local power structures are themselves influenced by circumstances such as demographic change, price levels and legislative interventions which are beyond their reach (Herring 1984), and which are significant in determining productivity and patterns of growth and change. It is also true, of course, that the state is influenced by local processes, but it can never be simply an aspect or reflection of them. The nature of the state and the relations between state and local society exercise a powerful influence upon agrarian structure and processes of agrarian social differentiation.

In the case of Tamil Nadu, the Dravidian parties which have been in power – save for two short periods of President's Rule – since 1967, have managed political support and sought to maintain their legitimacy by the pursuit of populist politics. This has encouraged the adoption of costly welfare programmes, and made them susceptible to pressures like those for the continued subsidization of rural electricity and rural credit, even at the cost of industrial accumulation in the state. Political management does not depend upon local 'big men' or faction leaders but upon ideological and material appeals to 'the Tamil people' and to different groups among them. It has thus encouraged the mobilization of broad-based demands from rural people such as have been championed by Farmers' Movements, and so helped to blunt, though not to eliminate, polarizing tendencies in the countryside. The structure of agrarian social relations would be different in the context of a different sort of regime with another style of political management – as in the case of Bangladesh, for example, where according to Cain's analysis the political system allows for and even encourages the continuing accumulation of land by local bosses (Cain 1981).[3]

The study of agrarian change in India thus points to the limitations of conventional Marxian political economy because of the way in which, by its reduction of politics to economics, it consistently fails to account for politics. There is an interesting convergence between this argument (which appears also in studies of agrarian transitions in South East Asia in Hart *et al.* 1989) and some recent developments in the different tradition of rational choice theory (as in the work of Robert Bates, who explains public policy regarding agriculture in Kenya as 'the choices resulting from a struggle among competing interests that takes place within a setting of political institutions rather than markets' – Bates 1989). Further fruitful theoretical development is likely to come from comparative study of political regimes and their relationships with economic and social development.

The construction of class relations

Even a fairly casual acquaintance with India in the recent past suggests that 'caste wars' are endemic in some parts of the country. The electoral success of the Bharatiya Janata Party, with its appeals to Hindu nationalism, shows that it has found some fertile ground in villages as well as in towns, while there has unquestionably been an extraordinary political mobilization of 'farmers' in a number of states, partly because of the way in which ties of caste and kinship bridge other differences between people. Events themselves seem to underscore the importance of various ethnic identities, rather than of class.

The argument which follows is founded upon the view that class relations exist, in the sense that there are definite relationships between individuals and groups of people that come about in the process of the production, distribution and consumption of the goods and services that are required for social reproduction to take place. Such relations include essentially those entailed by the division of labour in production and the way in which appropriation of surplus occurs. But these relationships do not exist independently of the meanings they have for people themselves. My argument from my fieldwork is that class relations are constructed by village people in terms of caste and of a model of community which is aptly described as that of a 'moral economy'. The long-running debate about the 'class view' of Indian society as opposed to the 'caste view' thus strikes me as being a nonsense. To say that class relations are thus constructed (in terms of caste and moral economy) does not mean to imply that there is a single agreed view of them. There are different versions of the constructions held by different actors, and there is continual negotiation between them.

Moral economy: a defence

The idea of 'moral economy', certainly as it was used by James Scott in his book *The Moral Economy of the Peasant* (1976), has attracted so much criticism that a preliminary word of defence and clarification is in order. Much of the criticism of Scott is quite misplaced (including even the most celebrated – that of Samuel Popkin) because it attributes to him, quite unjustly in my view, a simple structural-functional model of a village community, as if 'moral economies' really exist. I think that it is clear that Scott uses the term to refer to ideas about what is right and just to which people sometimes appeal, or which some actors may seek to enforce, and which may (or probably more often not) be respected.

There is room no doubt for a great deal of discussion and criticism of the adequacy of Scott's use of the idea of 'moral economy' in accounting for peasant rebellions in South East Asia. But this is not to deny the impressive volume of historical evidence which he and others (not least of course E P Thompson, who inspired Scott's use of the idea) have amassed to substantiate the view that many people in different times and places have thought about their circumstances in this sort of way (see Scott's more subtle recent developments of his idea – Scott 1990). It is also a travesty to suggest, as Brass has done, that Scott 'does not subscribe to a concept of an internally differentiated peasantry' (Brass 1991: 198) and that he depicts peasants as archetypal middle peasants who are 'actively and continuously engaged in covert struggle to remain middle peasants' (1991: 183). Such judgements take no account of the careful analysis of a differentiated peasantry, and of the process of differentiation following from 'the green revolution', which appears in Scott's study of north-west Malaysia (in *Weapons of the Weak*, 1985). This is about rich peasants and landlords, and about the efforts of those who are heavily dependent upon wage labour to get a better deal for themselves.

Brass's judgements also fail to recognize that Scott does not attribute a single view of their possible futures to rural people, even if their 'working the system to their minimum disadvantage' (Hobsbawm 1973: 7, quoted Scott 1985: 301) does mean that some of them sometimes appeal to a model of the past. There is nothing in the account to suggest that peasants won't make a fast buck when they can, or rationally calculate a strategy of accumulation. Indeed there is only a problem about the 'moral economy' because some peasants quite clearly do act in these sorts of ways, causing others to appeal to the idea of community/'moral economy' as they struggle to improve their lot.

Constructions of class in North Arcot

North Arcot District, in northern Tamil Nadu, the region to which I have already referred, has now – as apparently for a long time – very little tenancy. The relations of production therefore entail relations between cultivating peasants and a small number of small landlords, and labour. The forms of labour contracts involved are essentially of three types. First, there is casual, daily-paid wage labour (the most frequent), paid a standard wage in cash or (for harvesting and threshing work) in kind, which differs between men and women, and involves a contract between individual cultivators and individual labourers. Second, there is casual labour employed on a contract basis, at a piece-rate, involving a contract between an individual cultivator and a group of labourers. Third, there is the employment of regular farm servants, known locally as padials, on a seasonal or annual basis for a wage paid in kind, or cash and kind, and usually involving both the full commitment of the labourer's time to the employer and regular 'gifts' from the employer on festival occasions.

This last type of employment has not decreased in importance in the recent past, as (for example) in the village I know best the number of padials increased from thirty-seven to forty-six between 1974 and 1983. Whether or not such labour contracts should be described as labour bondage is a somewhat vexed question. I have found a range of degrees of freedom and unfreedom. In some cases padials are bound by long-term debts, which may be transferred from employer to employer and from generation to generation. But this is certainly not always the case.

Between 30 and 40 per cent of households are landless, or very nearly so, a majority of them Paraiyans (one of the principal 'untouchable' castes among Tamils), while most Paraiyans are landless. Among the remaining, landed, households only about half are primarily dependent upon cultivation; and as I explained earlier, 10 per cent at most may be described as 'surplus appropriators'. Thus the majority of peasants are engaged not only in their own cultivation but also undertake other kinds of work. A large number engage some of the time in wage labour for others. The class structure is thus complex and overlapping; the ambiguities which this complexity must introduce into the expression of resistance are compounded by cleavages and alliances that run across potential class divisions – notably those of kinship and caste.

Specifically, who employs who, and how (type of contract) tends to vary according to caste. Members of locally higher-ranking castes, when they seek agricultural employment, are likely to work only for other members of their own caste, or (especially if it is outside their own villages) for members of higher-ranking castes. Thus in the village I know best, Yadhava Pillais, the second-ranked landholding caste community, who include mostly middle and poor peasants, mainly exchange labour among themselves as well as employing Paraiyan labour. It would be deeply shameful for a member of a higher-ranked caste to work for a Paraiyan landholder. Members of the locally dominant castes – especially Agamudaiyan Mudaliars – mainly employ Paraiyan and other such 'untouchable' caste labourers; these labourers are employed mainly by members of the dominant caste. Those who are employed as padials are usually such 'untouchable' people, and are employed mostly by dominant caste landholders. Thus the least ambiguous or diffuse class relations are those involving the employment of 'untouchable' Paraiyan labourers by dominant caste landholders – rich peasants or landlords. So class relations are experienced as part of a wider structure of relationships between castes.

The ideas in orthodox Brahminical Hinduism which find expression in caste relationships depend crucially upon power, because of the necessity that what is thought of as pollution should be devolved on to others (see J Harriss 1989 for a short introductory account of theories about caste). The devolution of pollution downwards through the social hierarchy requires the services not only of such religious specialists as barbers and washermen, but also of scavengers (from among the 'untouchable' groups). In a more general way avoidance of polluting substances may also make it desirable for those who are or would be high ranking to minimize their involvement in the physical labour of tillage. There is in this culture a religious sanction for what is surely a general tendency for rank to be associated with avoidance of physical toil.

Specifically, in this region of northern Tamil Nadu, there is still a system of relationships known locally simply as *talaimurai*. The word *murai* is glossed by the Tamil lexicon as having the connotations of 'order' (note that the word is also used to describe the system of allocating water from the village irrigation tank in times of scarcity – in principle if not in contemporary practice. This system is an order, a system of rotation between kinship groups); but also of 'birth', 'manners', 'relationship', 'justice', 'fate' and 'nature'. *Talai* means literally 'head' or maybe 'person'. *Talaimurai* refers to the allocation of particular quantities of paddy by landholding members of the upper castes to the different specialists after harvest (i.e. what anthropologists have usually, if misleadingly, described as 'the jajmani system').

Among those who are the recipients of these payments are the *Vettiyan* (a Paraiyan who acts as a kind of graveyard superintendent, responsible for cremations and burials), the *Talaiyari* (who may be described as the village messenger, also a Paraiyan), and the *Tootti*, elected in turn from each of the kottu, kinship groups among the Paraiyans attached to a particular village, for a period of a year to perform duties as a watchman. The *Tootti* is responsible for the behaviour and attendance of the Paraiyan drummers who are needed at all village funerals and festivals. In principle one of his most important functions is that of overseeing the distribution of water from the tank. His services can also be called upon by any cultivator in the village, without cash payment, and he is paid by every landholder a fixed amount of grain per *kaani* (a unit of area). These specific roles of Paraiyans within the system described as *Talaimurai* symbolize their relationships as menial servants to other, higher-ranked castes, within the village community as a whole. The system is also a specific working out of some of the principles which give rise to caste relationships.

Class relationships are thus not distinguished from the wider system of social relationships which we describe as 'caste'. And these relationships are associated with religious ideas which offer a clear explanation for the different roles that people have in their present lives. These ideas therefore constitute a powerful ideology legitimizing actual inequality. We know, especially from Moffatt's work (1979), that the system of caste relationships is reproduced, as it were in miniature, even among those classified as 'untouchable' within the system as a whole. The indigenous theory of caste thus seems to constitute an hegemonic ideology.

Yet, as I have explained in some detail in my monograph (J Harriss 1982), though Paraiyan labourers are aware of and do sometimes – in response to deliberate questions – articulate a version of the caste explanation for their situation (deeds in past lives, etc.) the same individuals are perfectly well aware of 'class'-based explanation for their status, and in some cases, of alternative religious beliefs. Paraiyans generally take great delight in such acts as my own eating with them, as a challenge to the caste order and an expression of an alternative principle of equality between people (which is found both in non-Brahminical Hinduism and in the ideologies of modern political parties). The dominant ideology is certainly contested in private utterance.

The wider system of ideas and relations in the context of which class relationships are experienced implies a 'moral economy' or a bounded community of people among whom 'moral economy' principles apply. The system of *Talaimurai* is a model of redistributive patronage (cf. Epstein's classic paper on the *jajmani* system, 1967); and village social relationships are extensively influenced by ideas and expectations of such patronage, which satisfies moral economy principles. There is a strong sense of the village as a 'community', reflected in many casual comments about the character or ethos of 'our village' compared with others, and shared to some extent also by members of the untouchable hamlet (the *cheri*) associated with each caste village (*ur*).

I saw this, for example, when, on a pilgrimage to a distant temple, the dominant-caste people I was with welcomed to the group a man from 'our *cheri*'. As we returned, the closer we got to the village the greater the distance grew between the group and the local Paraiyan. Remarks and statements made on both sides of the divide between *ur* and *cheri* express the ambiguities of belonging/not belonging of the *cheri* people to 'our village'/'our place'. But in this region of South India still in the mid-1980s festivals dedicated to the principal village deity, the goddess, involve members of the *cheri* as well as of the *ur* in the sequence of ritual. On the several occasions when I have witnessed the possession of low-caste women by the goddess, at such festivals, and the goddess has spoken through them, her utterance was a complaint about the dilapidated state of her temple. Her threats that if something wasn't done about it then evil would follow, might be understood as an expression of concern about the stability and continuity of the village 'moral economy', for the state of disrepair of the temple certainly did reflect the increasing tendency of wealthier higher-caste people to withdraw from involvement with the village affairs, and from support through their patronage for the poor.

'Moral economy' ideas and expectations also inform the day-to-day interactions of cultivators and labourers. Relations of patronage do obtain between some rich peasants and landlords, and labourers; and there are close relationships of this kind between most of the richer households and particular households in the *cheri*. I have heard it said quite spontaneously by labourers that 'so-and-so Udaiyar is mother and father to us'; I am equally aware of rich peasants whose own ideas about their status and the respect which they believe is due to them, are bound up with notions both about their right to command Paraiyan labour and their duty to provide for 'the deserving poor'.

It is stinginess – for which Tamil has a rich vocabulary – rather than exploitation which is the subject of complaint in this context. The

Yadhava Pillais, the second-ranked landholding caste, are generally notorious as 'misers'. Even the rich Yadhavas are said to eat only one rice meal a day and their stinginess is the subject of jokes in both *ur* and *cheri*. The reputations of different individual rich peasants are the subject of much gossip among labourers; while among the wealthy gossip distinguishes between the 'deserving' and the 'undeserving' poor, essentially according to the extent to which particular individuals are compliant and respectful.

Thus I believe that the idea of 'moral economy' is not a romantic notion dreamt up by conservative intellectuals but one which is effective among Tamil village people; it is backed up by those religious ideas which give rise to caste differentiation. But none of these ideas is uncontested. There are religious beliefs and practices – notably those of devotional religion – which challenge the orthodox Brahminical view of life and morality; both cultivators and labourers have alternative understandings of their relationships than those of moral economy paternalism. These alternative constructions are reflected in the differing attitudes of members of the *cheri* to the status of the padial, or of less specific labour attachment – which some value and others resent and scorn bitterly; and in the attitudes of rich peasants, too, to these relationships. Some prefer, if they can get away with it, to employ casual labourers from outside the village precisely so as to avoid long-term commitments to particular individuals; and, probably increasingly, as I shall discuss later, the rich peasants are turning away, outside the village, and wish to cut themselves off from any sense of obligation.

Wars of symbols and everyday resistance

There are then, as James Scott argues (1990), both public and hidden transcripts on both sides of the class relationships of the village. The public transcript of the labourers demonstrates compliance and deference, to the point of willingness, say, to take action against his/her kin in protection of an employer's interests; it may include such statements as the 'mother and father' remark I referred to earlier, in talking of 'our Udaiyar'. But the same individuals have a hidden transcript too, when, in the company of family or close friends or a sympathetic outsider, they will give vent to their suppressed anger. Then the Udaiyar may be described in words which might be glossed as 'mean bastard', his own cringing deference to some outsider big-wig derided, and open pleasure taken in his misfortunes.

Similarly the public transcripts of the rich peasants are likely to include statements of duty towards the *cheri* people in general, and expression of paternalistic friendliness towards individual labourers. Those from the dominant caste may feel bound to maintain both seigneurial generosity and occasional displays of command by violence. Their 'hidden transcripts' are likely to include references to 'thieving bastards' and 'idle sods', and reasons for evading the claims of the poor. We have no reason for saying that one or other of these different and conflicting versions of class relations and of the idea of the community as a 'moral economy' is 'true' and the other 'false'. The statements have equivalent veracity as comments upon essentially contested constructions.

Jan Breman and I, with others, have been derided by Tom Brass for taking patronage at its face value: 'Harriss laments the break-down in patron–client relationships since this deprives clients of subsistence, rather than recognising the object of these debt–bondage relations as being to deprive clients (= bonded labourers) of a capacity to secure better returns in exchange for their labour power' (Brass 1986: 70). I think this is just as one-sided a suggestion as I believe mine would have been had I said that patronage is really about moral economy rights to subsistence and nothing else. Certainly I believe that it abstracts the class relationships of cultivators and labourers from their broader social and cultural context. The discussion above represents these class relations and the ideas in terms of which they are constructed as being continually contested. There is no doubt in my mind that, as Scott puts it in *Weapons of the Weak*, 'The occasional benevolence of the wealthy farmers is not so very different from a protection racket' (1985: 278).

There is not only a war of words and symbols between upper caste, rich peasant cultivators and Paraiyan labourers. There is also much everyday resistance. Petty pilfering is as endemic in villages in northern Tamil Nadu as I guess it is in poor villages anywhere else. Groundnut crops especially are at risk from pilferage, and their protection is such a headache for wealthier peasants that it is not worth their while to cultivate distant rainfed plots at all intensively. Palmyra palms, their leaves and fruit, are similarly exposed. Thefts of this kind are seen by the poor as morally justified – as a kind of *inam*, or charity, which has been begrudged by the rich.

Some observers of rural Tamil Nadu in the early 1970s (at a time when it was widely supposed that 'the green revolution was turning "red"') were convinced that a revolutionary upsurge of the labour class was on its way because they saw groups of labourers in the fields vociferously disputing with their employers, or sometimes, apparently, engaged in go-slows or strikes. These observers failed to appreciate that such behaviour is part of everyday life. Negotiations over wage rates, standard for a particular operation at a particular time, never take place very directly. There is considerable mutuality among labourers, and rather than enduring the shame of rate-busting locally labourers who are desperately in need of employment prefer to go outside to try to find it. Outside their own villages they perhaps will feel able to work for a lower rate. (The employment of outside labour by landholders has sometimes led to bitter confrontations such as that which brought about the terrible incident at Kilvenmani in Tamil Nadu in the late 1960s when untouchable labourers were burnt to death in their huts.)

The mutuality which exists among labourers locally is a general feature of rural labour markets in India and accounts for what Dreze and Mukherjee (1987) have identified as their most distinctive characteristic – and the one which is most difficult to explain in terms of the economists' models – the 'stickiness downwards' of agricultural wage rates. 'Stickiness downwards' depends on the mutuality which can only exist among labourers in a restricted, local labour market, so that it is associated with another general feature of labour markets over most of India – the fact that they are fragmented or parcellized with, *inter alia*, different wages obtaining for the same tasks even in villages (or perhaps sections of big villages) which are very close to each other. Ashok Rudra, in an essay describing such parcellization, argues that neither the analytical tools of neo-classical economics nor those of Marxist theory are adequate to explaining these characteristics of rural labour markets. His own attempt at explanation advances the view that 'Even when labourers are not organised in unions they have a sense of community and an under-standing of collective self-interest which is an integral part of the ethos of village society' (Rudra 1984: 265).

On the basis of this kind of mutuality labourers may at some point let it be known that they are reluctant to work at the going wage rate, for example by being late for work, or by sending messages to say that they are tied up with 'personal work'. Or there may be a lot of generalized grumbling, to the point of the kinds of vociferous outbursts which deceived observers in the early 1970s. This is the way in which 'nego-tiations' over wage rates generally take place. It reflects a kind of trade unionism even in the absence of trade unions and is part of the continual contestation of production relations.

Some will say, no doubt, that this sort of action also represents 'trade union consciousness' rather than 'true' class consciousness or class re-sistance, and ultimately reflects accommodation with the facts of power. I agree strongly with Scott that there is, however, a serious problem with this sort of argument which lies

> in what is ultimately a misleading, sterile and sociologically naive insistence upon distinguishing 'self-indulgent' individual acts (like the thefts of ground-nuts in North Arcot villages) . . . from presumably 'principled', self-less, collective actions . . . and excluding the former from the category of real resistance. To insist on such distinctions as a means of comparing forms of resistance and their consequences is one thing, but to use them as a basic criterion to determine what constitutes resistance is to miss the very well-springs of peasant politics. (Scott 1985: 295).

These are aimed, much of the time, at 'working the system to their minimum disadvantage' (in a phrase of Eric Hobsbawm's).

Class construction and 'agrarian change'

What have been described as 'trends of agrarian change' are outcomes of the ways in which class relations are constructed. Key elements in recent economic changes in the Indian countryside are, as we have seen, first, the increasing importance of cash inputs and the consequent vulner-ability of production to market fluctuations;[4] second, the tightening of rural labour markets (rather widely reported in India; see Jose 1988); and third, the greatly increased extent of state intervention in welfare oriented programmes, which, in spite of the massive leakages of funds from them, have had an impact on levels of welfare, so that to a limited extent the 'countervailing power' of poor rural people has been enhanced.

The circumstances of the increased commercialization of agriculture and of state intervention, together with the overlapping of interests and cross-cutting social ties among peasants, account for the agrarian politics which emerged so forcefully in the 1980s – politics which have reflected mobilization against what has been represented, explicitly by leaders of the 'Farmers' Movements', as exploitation of peasant production. These movements, and what the Rudolphs refer to as 'the new agrarianism' in Indian politics (Rudolph and Rudolph 1987, especially Chapter 13), are clearly driven by the interests of more highly commercialized cultivators,[5] and to this extent they may fairly be described as 'rich peasant movements'. But such an analysis underestimates the extent to which the mobilization of different social groups and classes behind the movements depends upon shared experience of exploitation in markets, and shared experience of confrontation with the state over payments for inputs, access to credit, and resistance to taxation. In addition to cross-cutting ties of caste and kinship, and an idea of moral community,[6] the sharing of experience facilitates the formation of a multi-class coalition around the idea of 'Bharat' – the notion (potential 'imagined community') of the nation of toilers on the land, as opposed to the modern urban nation of 'India'.

The other important set of changes that has been taking place concerns agricultural labour. Cultivating peasants have confronted a costs–prices squeeze in circumstances, often, of tightening labour markets in which the mutuality that exists among labourers continues to apply. There have been several, not necessarily exclusive, responses, which, however, constitute different patterns of agrarian change resulting from variations in the way in which class relationships are constructed.

First, one response has been to re-forge attached labour relationships, or what Brass rightly argues should be referred to as 'labour bondage'. Brass has provided detailed accounts of deliberate 'deproletarianization', through the creation of debt-bondage, in the 'green revolution' heartland of Punjab and Haryana. He argues of this:

> in Haryana unfreedom constitutes a central component in the struggle between landholders and agricultural workers. In a context where alternative and better-paid employment is available, and labourers are as a result capable of sustaining their unwillingness to enter attachment at any price, landholders have not only to make labour power available but also to make it available cheaply. Both these objectives are realised through the operation of the debt bondage mechanism, which constricts or eliminates the free movement of labour in the market. (Brass 1990: 55).

In circumstances like those of northern Tamil Nadu, however, where historically the supply of labour has been much more abundant, but where there are still pressures associated with control over labour in the conditions of the costs–prices squeeze, landholders have not had to resort to the creation of debt-bondage as a mechanism for attaching labour but have continued to operate through the institutions and ideology of the 'moral economy'. Here, as Ramachandran has put it in his account of labour relations in another Tamil village (Ramachandran 1990), labourers are willing to submit to patronage 'in order to book a place'. In these circumstances, certainly, in those of Haryana less surely so, we might expect to find that the public transcripts of the moral economy, and the institutions and rituals associated with it, are still valid.

A second response, reported in vivid detail by Jan Breman from the region in South Gujarat which he has studied for a quarter of a century, is that of deliberately smashing the moral economy. His monograph, *Of Peasants, Migrants and Paupers* (1985) shows how

> Over the last two decades agriculture has become a dynamic industry (on the South Gujarat plain) which in addition has created a number of new economic activities in the countryside itself. Together these ensure great pressure of work nearly the whole year round. But it is precisely in Surat District, where intensification and diversification of production has been most rapid, that this development has led to growing unemployment amongst the local landless. (Breman 1985: 343).

Alongside this unemployment of local labour there exists substantial seasonal migration of labour from outside. The reason for such an apparently odd situation is that outside labourers are more amenable to control: 'In contrast to the Halpatis the seasonal workers *cannot retreat to a milieu of their own* in order to make a stand against the farmers' dominance' (my emphasis). The rural labour market is thus characterized by the deliberate exclusion of local labour, with the result that an area of accelerated economic growth has seen the progressive impoverishment of local labourers. In a somewhat similar way 'untouchable' labourers are excluded from the rapidly growing handloom silk industry in part of North Arcot (Harriss and Harriss 1984).

Another kind of response again is what might be described as the 'exit' option. In northern Tamil Nadu – and, apparently, from observations reported by others from across a much wider area of South India – there is a tendency for many of the dominant landholders to seek to leave the village and even to get out of agriculture. This is reflected in an analysis of the determinants of wages in different villages across a broadly homogeneous region in North Arcot (J Harriss, 1991). My conclusion, tested successfully by econometric methods by Peter Hazell *et al.* (1991), was that wage rates are most significantly influenced by caste structure – specifically wage rates are higher in villages in which the dominant caste attempts to pursue a seigneurial lifestyle, leaving as much of the toil of cultivation as possible to others. This notable instance of the social determination of wage rates also reflects the declining interest in cultivation and in their villages among Agamudaiyan

Mudaliars especially. The present generation frequently seek whenever they can to enter employment outside the village and outside agriculture. Their willingness to participate in the institutions and rituals of the moral economy is clearly limited and declining.

Thus in different circumstances, in which class relationships have been constructed in different ways, similar economic trends may be expected to have a different impact upon the directions of agrarian change. In some cases we might expect the institutions and ideas of moral economy to persist; in others that they will be increasingly questioned or simply destroyed. Given the common experience of production relations in terms of kinship and caste, and the morality of community ('the moral economy'), it is not at all surprising that the 'imagined communities' of 'We Tamils', 'We Hindus', 'We Dalits' or 'We Vanniyas' should have become the dominating bases of identity and action in contemporary Indian society. Only, it seems, in rather exceptional circumstances, such as those, notably, in which there is a significant overlap between 'class' identity and another, more powerfully experienced sense of identity, as in the 'community' of Paraiyans in Eastern Thanjavur (according to the accounts of Beteille 1974b; Bouton 1985), has political class mobilization come about.

Conclusion

In the first section of this chapter I have shown the limitations of the approach to agrarian change characteristic of the mainstream of research in the sociology of development in India, which privileges the economic as a determinant of social process, and focuses narrowly upon the relations of production. My own experience of research aimed at understanding change in part of northern Tamil Nadu leads me to the conclusion also reached in research on South East Asia by Gillian Hart. She argues that 'The neglect of power and politics results in an almost exclusive focus on commercialisation and technology as the main sources of rural change and portrays agrarian change as a unilinear process leading to a determinate outcome' (Hart 1989: 31). My research shows that the reliance of state regimes in India on a precarious effort of satisfying different interests, and of managing electoral support by the pursuit of populist policies, even though they continually undermine the capacity of the regime, have led to a range of interventions which have crucially affected agrarian change. A different type of regime, with different kinds of organization, practising other methods of regime maintenance, would allow different agrarian outcomes.

Political institutions, obviously, are influenced by economic factors; but, equally clearly, politics have their own dynamics – which stand to be illuminated by more comparative and theoretical work such as that which Mouzelis has undertaken in studies of Argentina, Chile and Greece (1986). Research of a similar nature in the Indian context (though it is theoretically less ambitious) has been undertaken by Atul Kohli (1987). He shows how different regimes at state level, having differing degrees and types of authority, create different outcomes in very comparable economic contexts.

The second section of the chapter aimed to show the importance of the cultural context of production relations, and the third the ways in which differences in these constructions may result in distinct patterns of agrarian change. The chapter thus acknowledges explicit continuities with the work of some members of the Subaltern School of Indian historians and with that of James Scott. The approach, like that of Ramachandra Guha, the Indian sociologist who, in his study of resistance to ecological change in the Himalaya, explicitly situates himself as a 'Subaltern', is intended 'to avoid the pitfalls of an exclusively "interpretive" approach' (1989: 5) which downplays the material base of human society. The intention is to understand the relations of culture and material practice, by paying attention to cultural differentiation – to ways in which social actors' different understandings of the world are affected by historically constituted social and political inequalities – as well as by allowing for the way in which cultural categories 'construct' the experience of class (cf. also Chakrabarty (1989) on working-class history).

But given its professed filiations and influences, this chapter stands square in the sights of Brass's attacks. I have referred earlier to what seem to be misrepresentations of some of the work of which he is critical in Brass's article. That article also deliberately privileges class as an analytical category, and rests its whole argument on the concept of 'false consciousness'. This is an important but highly problematical notion in sociology, suggesting that people's ideas about their circumstances and interests may be based on a faulty understanding. It can be used in a dismissive way which really assumes away what has to be explained – forms of consciousness such as caste and ethnicity. Brass tends to this position in his polemics.

But the idea of 'false consciousness' is still an important one because it is a way of distinguishing between ideas which are effective in transforming people's circumstances and those which are not. Of course it is important to respect and to try to understand people's own ideas, but even a Weberian sociology does not reject the potential in etic analysis as well as in emic understanding. And this, it seems to me, is a crucial limitation of the work of Scott and others. Scott is a sophisticated and subtle writer and he does not, for example, fail to distinguish between petty pilferage and collective action. But he is, apparently, relatively uninterested in the consequences of resistance, celebrating the fact of the 'weapons of the weak' and leaving one in no doubt as to where his sympathies lie, but ultimately pessimistic about the possibilities of change.

The strength of Brass's position is in his willingness to make the judgements which are necessary in distinguishing between ideas and actions in terms of their efficacy in relation to the transformation of the circumstances of subordinate people (the 'subalterns'). The strength of Scott's position – and, I believe, of that taken in this chapter – is in their respect for and understanding of people's own understandings. Making progress with the political project of human development – the liberation of human potentials – stands to be assisted by such interpretive analysis of the ways in which people themselves comprehend the production relations in which they are involved.

Marxism, like the rest of nineteenth-century social theory, is remarkably silent about nationalism, racism and other forms of ethnicity, which have been, and remain, the dominant social forces of this century. The material bases of the politics of nationalism and ethnicity are illuminated by Marxian analysis, which has shown how, for example, states may build hegemonic 'imagined communities' based on multi-class coalitions (cf. Roseberry 1989: Chapter 8). But it is not then very helpful to dismiss them as manifestations of 'false consciousness' – when they are so palpably the springs of action and 'class', more often, is not. In the Indian context this point has been seized by those radical activists who have argued that the struggle of Dalits ('untouchables', or Harijans in the polite euphemism of modernizing India) against caste oppression is immediately more salient than class struggle.

The insistence in this chapter on the importance of understanding the ways in which class relationships are culturally constructed clearly owes something to the influence of post-modernist 'deconstruction' of concepts such as that of class. I want finally, therefore, to enter on to terrain which I believe that I share with Brass – which is a terrain of hostility to the implications of the further developments of this 'deconstructionism' as we see them in the more recent writings of members of the 'Subaltern School' in India.

I referred in my introduction to work such as that of Dipesh Chakrabarty, who writes a history of class formation in the context of an hierarchical culture. But Chakrabarty is surely so uncritical in his acceptance of a Dumontian view of 'traditional' Hindu culture as 'hierarchical', as to warrant the description of 'Orientalist' (a way of thinking which has, supposedly, been demolished by post-modernist deconstruction!). My own account of the ideas and actions of village people clearly shows their awareness of egalitarian and individualistic ideas and values as well as those of hierarchy. There is strong textual evidence of the existence of elements of 'equality' and 'individualism' as well as of 'hierarchy' in the Hindu tradition (see e.g. Holmstrom 1968; Ramanujan 1973). Is there any reason to suppose that such elements were not also present in the ideal worlds of Calcutta jute workers earlier in the twentieth century? I think not; and I believe that in his concern to avoid Euro-centred ideas and interpretation of history Chakrabarty becomes so unself-critical as to have presented, ironically, an Orientalist interpretation himself.

But there is a more serious side to this, which is brought out in Chakrabarty's question to himself: 'Can we build democratic, communitarian institutions on the basis of non-individualistic, but hierarchical and illiberal, precapitalist bonds that have survived . . . the onslaught of capitalism?' He provides no satisfactory answer to this question, and finally leaves open the possibility that what is actually celebrated is a thoroughly conservative restatement of the values of a traditional, illiberal, inegalitarian society. In this way intellectuals such as Chakrabarty serve the ends of such conservative political forces as the Hindu nationalism of the Bharatiya Janata Party.

Notes

1. I am grateful to participants in the departmental seminar in the Department of Anthropology at the London School of Economics where an earlier version of this chapter was read in February 1991; to David Booth for his scrupulous and sympathetic editing; and to David Booth and David Washbrook, of the Department of History at the University of Warwick, for helping me to avoid some of the more atrocious failures of judgement which appeared in earlier versions. Those that remain are my responsibility alone.
2. The argument that follows appears also in J Harriss (1992).
3. See Hart (1988) for comparison of Bangladesh with Java which makes general points comparable with those advanced here.
4. In particular cereal agriculture, especially rice cultivation, has been subject to a costs–prices squeeze and continuing problems of profitability.
5. Whether 'small', 'medium' or 'large' in terms of acreage operated – as emerges from Nadkarni's (1987) analysis of the farmers' movement in Karnataka.
6. Which certainly do bring together people from different class positions, as Omvedt (1988) has shown in the case of Maharashtra.

References

Athreya V, Djurfeldt G and **Lindberg S** (1990) *Barriers broken: production relations and agrarian change in Tamil Nadu*. Delhi, Sage

Banaji J (1977) Capitalist domination and the small peasantry: Deccan districts in the late nineteenth century. *Economic and Political Weekly* 122 (33–4)

Bates R H (1989) *Beyond the miracle of the market: the political economy of agrarian development in Kenya*. Cambridge, Cambridge University Press

Bernstein H (1977) Notes on capital and peasantry. *Review of African Political Economy* 10

Bernstein H (1990) Taking the part of peasants? In: Bernstein H *et al.* (eds) *The food question: profits versus people?* London, Earthscan

Beteille A (1974a) *Studies in agrarian social structure*. New Delhi, Oxford University Press

Beteille A (1974b) Agrarian relations in Tanjore District. In Beteille A (1974a)

Bhaduri A (1986) Forced commerce and agrarian growth. *World Development* 14

Bharadwaj K (1985) A view on commercialisation in Indian agriculture and the development of capitalism. *Journal of Peasant Studies* 12 (4)

Booth D (1985) Marxism and development sociology: interpreting the impasse. *World Development* 13 (7)

Bouton M (1985) *Agrarian radicalism in South India*. Princeton, NJ, Princeton University Press

Brass T (1986) Unfree labour and capitalist restructuring in the agrarian sector: Peru and India. *Journal of Peasant Studies* 14 (1)

Brass T (1990) Class struggle and the deproletarianisation of agricultural labour in Haryana (India). *Journal of Peasant Studies* 18(1)

Brass T (1991) Moral economists, subalterns, new social movements, and the (re-) emergence of a (post-) modernised middle peasantry. *Journal of Peasant Studies* 18 (2)

Breman J (1985) *Of peasants, migrants and paupers: rural labour circulation and capitalist production in West India.* New Delhi, Oxford University Press

Cain M (1981) Risk and insurance: perspectives on fertility and agrarian change in India and Bangladesh. *Population and Development Review* 7 (3)

Chakrabarty D (1989) *Rethinking working class history.* Princeton, NJ, Princeton University Press

Dreze J and **Mukherjee A** (1987) Labour contracts in rural India: theories and evidence. Discussion Paper no. 7, Development Research Programme, Suntory Toyota International Centre for Economics and Related Disciplines, London School of Economics

Epstein S (1967) Productive efficiency and customary systems of rewards in rural South India. In R Firth (ed) *Themes in Economic Anthropology.* London, Tavistock

Gough K (1969) Peasant resistance and revolt in South India. *Pacific Affairs* 41 (4)

Guha Ramachandra (1989) *The unquiet woods: ecological change and peasant resistance in the Himalaya.* New Delhi, Oxford University Press

Guha Ranajit (1989) Dominance without hegemony and its historiography. In: Ranajit Guha (ed) *Subaltern studies VI.* New Delhi, Oxford University Press

Hardiman D (1981) *Peasant nationalists of Gujarat: Kheda District 1917–1934.* New Delhi, Oxford University Press

Harriss B (1981) *Transitional trade and rural development.* New Delhi, Vikas

Harriss B (1983) Paddy and rice marketing in a Bengal District. *Cressida Transactions* 2

Harriss B and **Harriss J** (1984) 'Generative' and 'parasitic' urbanism? Some observations from the recent history of a South Indian market town. *Journal of Development Studies* 20 (3)

Harriss J (1980) Contemporary Marxist analysis of the agrarian question in India. Discussion Paper, Madras Institute of Development Studies

Harriss J (1982) *Capitalism and peasant farming: agrarian structure and ideology in Northern Tamil Nadu.* Bombay, Oxford University Press

Harriss J (1983) Making out on limited resources, or what happened to semi-feudalism in West Bengal. *Cressida Transactions* 2

Harriss J (1985) What happened to the green revolution in South India? Economic trends, household mobility, and the politics of an awkward class. Discussion Paper no. 175, School of Development Studies, University of East Anglia

Harriss J (1989) Knowing about rural economic change: problems arising from a comparison of the results of 'macro' and 'micro' research in Tamil Nadu. In Bardhan P (ed) *Conversations between economists and anthropologists.* New Delhi, Oxford University Press

Harriss J (1991) Population, employment and wages: a comparative study of North Arcot villages 1973–1983. In Hazell P and Ramasamy C (eds) *Green revolution revisited.* Baltimore, MD, Johns Hopkins University Press

Harriss J (1992) Does the 'depressor' still work? Agrarian structure and development in India – a review of evidence and argument. *Journal of Peasant Studies* 19 (2)

Hart G (1988) Agrarian structure and the state in Java and Bangladesh. *Journal of Asian Studies* 47 (2)

Hart G (1989) Introductory essay in Hart *et al.* (eds)

Hart G, Turton A and **White B** (eds) (1989) *Agrarian transformations: the state and local processes in Southeast Asia.* Berkeley, CA, University of California Press

Hazell P *et al.* (1991) Changes in village household welfare. In Hazell P and

Ramasamy C (eds) *Green revolution revisited*. Baltimore, MD, Johns Hopkins University Press

Herring R (1984) Economic consequences of local power configurations in rural South Asia. In: Desai M *et al.* (eds) *Agrarian power and agricultural productivity in South Asia*. New Delhi, Oxford University Press

Hobshawm E (1973) Peasants and politics. *Journal of Peasant Studies* 1(1)

Holmstrom M (1968) Moral and religious changes in an urban village of Bangalore, South India. Unpublished DPhil thesis, University of Oxford

Jose A V (1988) Agricultural wages in India. *Economic and Political Weekly, Review of Agriculture* June

Kohli A (1987) *The state and poverty in India*. Cambridge, Cambridge University Press

Kohli A (1990) *Democracy and disorder*. Cambridge, Cambridge University Press

Lindberg S (1990) Civil society against the state: farmers' agitations and new social movements in India. Paper to the Seventh Annual Conference of the Nordic Association for Southeast Asian Studies, and the XII World Congress of Sociology, Madrid

Moffatt M (1979) *An untouchable community in South India: structure and consensus*. Princeton, NJ, Princeton University Press

Mouzelis N (1986) *Politics in the semi-periphery*. London, Macmillan

Nadkarni M V (1987) *Farmers' movements in India*. New Delhi, Allied Publishers

Omvedt G (1988) The 'new peasant movement' in India. *Bulletin of Concerned Asian Scholars* 20 (2)

Ramachandran V K (1990) *Wage labour and unfreedom in agriculture: an Indian case study*. Oxford, Oxford University Press

Ramanujan A (1973) *Speaking of Siva*. Harmondsworth, Penguin

Roseberry W (1978) Peasants as proletarians. *Critique of Anthropology* 3 (11)

Roseberry W (1989) *Anthropologies and histories: essays in culture, history and political economy*. New Brunswick, NJ, Rutgers University Press

Rudolph L I and **Rudolph S H** (1987) *In pursuit of Lakshmi: the political economy of the Indian State*. Chicago, IL, Chicago University Press

Rudra A (1984) Local power and farm level decision making. In: Desai M *et al.* (eds) *Agrarian power and agricultural productivity in South Asia*. New Delhi, Oxford University Press

Scott J C (1976) *The moral economy of the peasant: rebellion and subsistence in Southeast Asia*. New Haven, CT, Yale University Press

Scott J C (1985) *Weapons of the weak: everyday forms of peasant resistance*. New Haven, CT, Yale University Press

Scott J C (1990) *Domination and the arts of resistance: hidden transcripts*. New Haven, CT, Yale University Press

Thorner A (1982) Semi-feudalism or capitalism? Contemporary debate on classes and modes of production in India. *Economic and Political Weekly* 17 (49–51)

Thorner D (1956) *The agrarian prospect in India* (2nd edn 1976). New Delhi, Allied Publishers

Washbrook D A (1976) *The emergence of provincial politics: the Madras presidency 1870–1920*. Cambridge, Cambridge University Press

Washbrook D A (1988) Progress and problems: South Asian economic and social history *c* 1720–1860. *Modern Asian Studies* 22 (1)

Westergaard K (1985) *State and rural society in Bangladesh: a study in relationship*. London, Curzon Press

Wood G D (1981) Rural class formation in Bangladesh 1940–1980. *Bulletin of Concerned Asian Scholars* 13 (4)

Part III
Linking theory, research and practice: the issue of relevance

To what extent is the achievement of greater 'relevance', a closer relationship with the worlds of development policy and practice, a possible and desirable goal for those engaged in social development research in the 1990s? What are the implications for the design of research projects, and for the reconstruction of social development theory, of an orientation towards the requirements of practice and practitioners? And what are the specific issues raised by the new importance of nongovernment organizations (NGOs) as users (and indeed subjects) of social development research? These central questions have already been addressed in various chapters of this book. As we saw in Part I, the suggestion that social development research and theory should be governed by the search for greater relevance is far from uncontroversial. No consensus was arrived at there as to possible designs for more relevant research projects or on the implications for theory of trying to reconnect development theory and development practice.

These issues are taken up in Part III by three chapters which share a positive, though not uncritical, commitment to the idea of relevant research. The chapters by Anthony Bebbington, Tony Barnett and Piers Blaikie, and David Hulme, both exemplify and reflect upon the trend of recent social development research towards more practice-oriented and even 'applied' concerns. Bebbington's contribution draws on research carried out in close cooperation with Latin American NGOs and financed jointly by a North American NGO think-tank and the UK's official aid agency, the Overseas Development Administration (ODA). Barnett and Blaikie reflect upon a project commissioned directly by ODA, while Hulme is the author of several recent studies undertaken on behalf of or in collaboration with NGO sponsors. The three chapters nevertheless vary considerably in their subject matter.

In Chapter 8, Bebbington provides a fascinating exploration of the theme of indigenous alternatives to top-down development with particular reference to Andean peasants and peasant organizations. He shows how a piece of donor-funded research (the term 'applied research' should be used more restrictively, he believes) can be both intellectually challenging and relevant in the sense that it is 'of interest' to peasant, non-governmental and public-sector organizations and capable of informing strategies that are 'viable and practical' for them (p. 202). In the process he offers a number of insights of wider relevance to the discussion in the book, about actors and structures, and about realism and choice.

Among the ideas about Third World rural development that have gained ground most rapidly since the early 1980s are those suggesting a radical re-evaluation of traditional agricultural knowledge and farming practices in relation to the knowledge-base of modern scientific agriculture. It is a trend of thought that has strong affinities with the general precepts of some of the leading international NGOs. However, critics regard some of the best-known programmatic statements favouring peasant-based or 'farmer first' strategies for technological change in agriculture as dangerously naïve about prospects for change within local and regional structures of power. More generally, it is suggested that the new populism of indigenous agriculture illustrates the tendency for local 'actor-oriented' studies which are not firmly rooted in an understanding of wider, structural issues, to lack the realism that practitioners as well as academics are entitled to expect.

In the province of Chimborazo in the Ecuadorian Andes, Bebbington shows, Indian peasant organizations are building an 'alternative' as they see it. Yet, in terms of the programme of the technological populists, the main line of advance is a thoroughly conventional one. Even though local NGOs and church organizations provide support in principle for a variety of technological strategies, and there is some diversity of approach among the different peasant federations, the dominant trend is towards agricultural 'modernization' – that is intensified use of commercially supplied, laboratory- and factory-produced inputs. Understanding why this happens involves appreciating the way that technology issues are bound up historically and in the contemporary society and politics of Ecuador with the peasants' claims in the areas of identity, citizenship and civil rights.

Bebbington's study shows how in reality local decisions about technology-choice cannot be studied separately from decisions about organization and political strategy, based on the structural position of the Indian peasantry within the broader (regional and national) processes of Ecuadorian society. In so doing, the chapter provides further support for the general methodological point that the actor/structure question, although it may appear as a dilemma in some contexts, is not in practice an either/or issue. In Bebbington's perspective, agency and structure represent two necessarily related aspects of any imaginable research topic in development. The exaggerated theoretical posturings of the exponents of 'indigenous agricultural revolution' on the one hand and 'political economy' on the other, may have their place in academic debate; but in the interests of relevance social researchers should be challenging such polarizations of approach, injecting into development work stronger doses of both realism and humility.

If Bebbington is concerned to illustrate some of the features of 'relevant' academic research, Chapter 9 by Barnett and Blaikie is more in the nature of an academic reflection on what the authors themselves see as a wholly applied piece of work. The chapter is an attempt to 'pick apart' a completed research project (now the subject of an important monograph) and to dwell a little on what it has involved in terms of the received canons of scientific method as well as the perspectives on social development theory and research adumbrated in this book. The subject matter is how rural people have been coping with AIDS in one of the worst-hit areas of southern Uganda.

Barnett and Blaikie admit that in carrying out their research they both made intellectual compromises ('ignoring the wider picture') and set about answering a set of analytical questions which they formulated in advance. They did not, for example, analyse the class structure of southern Uganda, or the nature of the Ugandan state. They asked instead: What was the evidence of 'exceptional demographic change' as a consequence of AIDS? How did AIDS compare with other 'disasters'? In what ways were individuals and groups 'coping' with the disease and its effects, and what factors influenced the capacity to cope? Did the epidemic in Uganda have a socio-economic history? And what was likely to be the impact on 'farming systems'?

But what *sort* of questions were these, in what senses did the attempt to answer them involve 'doing theory' and were the results theoretically coherent? In direct dialogue with the perspectives on theory and practice advanced in Part I by Buttel and McMichael, Barnett and Blaikie rebut the suggestion that applied research is particularly susceptible to overgeneralization, 'paradigm filling' and other defects of the 'Grand Theory' tradition in sociology and development studies. These tendencies, which they agree have been characteristic of social development theory in the recent past, stem not from the pressures of applied work but (sheer ideology and politics apart) from a conception of theory as a completely articulated deductive system, characterized by a high level of logical and conceptual coherence.

Having entered this proviso, Barnett and Blaikie freely admit that their work did not achieve 'theoretical coherence'. On the other hand they did use theoretical categories, and despite considerable eclecticism in their choice of analytical tools they succeeded in telling a 'coherent story' to a particular audience whose major interest lay in practical intervention in the situation. Their results, they imply, are not only of interest to a particular grouping of practitioners; they may also 'feed back into theoretical work', though not in the form of large generalizations or striking conceptual innovations. This combination of practical orientation and theoretically unambitious analysis may be the best and most important thing to be achieved by the present generation of social development researchers – or at least by those, like the writers, who are unashamed to call themselves 'jobbing social scientists'.

David Hulme in Chapter 10 concerns himself specifically with the relationship between social research and the important constituency of development practitioners within the NGO movement, or what he prefers to call the 'third sector'. The chapter contains a well-informed and richly illustrated introduction to what the third sector consists of, why it is important and where it is heading. While social scientists in general may not be entirely ignorant of the emerging reality described here, Hulme is no doubt right that current conceptions often underrate 'the multiplex, and often contradictory, relationships that local, national and international NGOs have with each other, with the state, with those in opposition to the state, with different segments of civil society and with wider international forces' (p. 252). He makes a compelling case for considering the third sector, its growth and contradictions an excellent point of entry for social researchers interested in development in the 1990s, as well as a major topic in its own right.

But Hulme's argument faces both ways at the same time. He is equally concerned to demonstrate to an NGO audience that *they* need social research. The discussion passes, explicitly in places and almost imperceptibly elsewhere, from issues of interest to the student of the NGO movement, or to the citizen or donor concerned about NGO accountability, to issues coming to the attention of NGOs themselves, especially in their drive to 'scale-up' their operations and provide checks on their effectiveness. The theme of the relevance of social development research to the current concerns of the third sector (taken a few steps further by Michael Edwards in the Afterword to this book) is an important source of balance in Hulme's chapter, and it enables him (and indeed Edwards) to separate the good sense from the polemical exaggeration in some of the earlier debate about 'relevance'.

If social researchers are to study NGOs, or work with or for NGOs, they *are* going to have to abandon those 'extractive' attitudes towards the acquisition of knowledge, and dilettantism about opportunities for action, that have so irritated some practitioners. As Bebbington also argues, the goal should be a style of research that consciously thinks through the implications of the understandings that are produced for the actors involved. 'Researchers must explore the opportunities for practitioners to modify strategy, or even subvert existing strategies, before they opt for radical pessimism (individuals can do nothing), or radical jest without action (shoot the landlords)' (p. 252).

On the other hand, NGO staff may not be the best judges of the kind of research that they are going to need in the coming period. Action research and other approaches that involve the 'subjects of development' (i.e. project beneficiaries) in learning processes related directly to their own empowerment have an important special place in the repertoire of development research. However, this is not what is meant by relevance, and it would be unfortunate if researchers committed to relevance were to adopt innovative micro-level work to the exclusion of more conventional approaches. In view of Hulme's analysis of the current difficulties and dilemmas facing the third sector on a global scale, there is a strong case for an intensification of responsible research on the sector itself relating micro-level activities to macro-level processes. For example 'southern NGOs' (and, we might add, social movements and significant actors of many kinds) 'require study to determine the ways in which their relationships with the institutions of the state, political parties, external financiers and civil society constrain or expand their "room for manoeuvre"' (p. 252).

CHAPTER 8

Theory and relevance in indigenous agriculture:
knowledge, agency and organization[1]

Anthony Bebbington

Jeeps and pickups dotting the agricultural landscapes of many poor countries mark the presence of new actors in rural social life. These are the ever more numerous development organizations, governmental and non-governmental, membership and non-membership: the 'new institutions of civil society' as one Bolivian commentator calls them (Durán 1990).

Many of these organisations claim to be building models of rural development upon peasants' own indigenous agricultural knowledge (IAK) as a basis for locally appropriate, indigenously conceived strategies for agrarian and social change. Because they have this orientation, some analysts have begun to argue that such non-governmental organization (NGOs) are legitimate and important allies of the peasant centred social development researcher, and that, as such, any research interest into the conditions, nature and possibility of what Paul Richards (1985) has termed an 'indigenous agricultural revolution', ought be made relevant and available to them (Chambers 1989). Conversely, as actors in rural development, these NGOs should not simply be *clients*, but also *objects* of research (Bebbington and Thiele, 1993; Farrington and Bebbington 1993). What does it mean, then, to do relevant research on IAK for organizations that are also implicated in its construction and its change?

A reflection on relevance

Relevant research is not applied research. Applied research is done to address a particular problem set by the needs of a particular client – research that often not only 'ignores the wider picture' as in Barnett and Blaikie (Chapter 9), but also the rather more local picture.[2] Relevance is less limiting, and should not mean that we do research on *specific* field problems suggested by these peasant, non-governmental and public sector organizations. Instead, to be relevant implies that the research we do be of interest to these organizations, and that the strategies that might lead on from it be viable and practical. Among other things, this means that its conceptual basis and analytical focus should offer 'entry points' that correspond with field experiences, rather than float unconnected to everyday life as so many actor-less structural analyses of agrarian change have done. Indeed, in the near future such relevance may be a prerequisite for these organizations participating in, and permitting, a research project. This means taking 'lay concepts', people and places seriously; it means understanding what local organizations themselves mean by an indigenous agricultural revolution, why they have developed that particular understanding, and how they are acting upon it.[3] As a corollary it means avoiding over-indulgence in elitist, separatist language.

'Relevant' research can problematize, theorize and question in a way that 'applied' research does not. It was on these terms that the research discussed in this chapter sought to be 'relevant'. The study dealt with how and why local organizations and indigenous farmers were responding to trends of technological, economic, and socio-political modernization in Ecuador. Although it clearly had implications for what should be done, my concern was not prescription but rather to analyse the significance of what was being done. This being the case, the ideas resulting from the research may not help NGOs or peasant organizations in solving particular problems. Their relevance lies instead in promoting reflection in these organizations regarding their strategy and impacts.

In this vein, a central theme in the study was how these local organizations, the 'clients' of relevant research on IAK, are themselves part of the social processes in which peasants' agricultural technologies and socio-political strategies are being constructed. NGOs and government projects have worked on and reworked local IAK, promoting their own ideologies about what it is and should be, to such an extent that peasants and their organizations have themselves taken in these institutional actions and discourses, disagreed with some of their themes, and continued to rework and act on others, frequently changing their meaning and effect in the process.

This in itself is cause for reflection, but there is a related reason for these organizations to reflect. For, however local their work, these organizations have to be viewed as responding to, and being part of, more structural processes and changes in society. By extension, the impacts they have on local knowledge systems are also part of, although not necessarily determined by, economic, political and social dynamics that go beyond the bounds of the locality. Aside from influencing local IAK, these wider relations set constraints and conditions on what local action, organized and everyday can achieve. These constraints would ultimately have to be addressed in any locally grounded strategy for social development. Relevant research ought then address both the local and the non-local, the spatially present, and the absent but influential (Giddens 1981).

This concern for the relationship between local and non-local, possibility and constraint, takes us to the heart of the academic literature on indigenous agricultural revolutions: for in broad terms, this literature falls into two camps. Some authors, at times specifically in the name of relevance, focus on the local and technological dimensions of IAK (although they recognize the importance of political economy and cultural politics). Others recognize the importance of peasant technical creativity, and of what it might achieve at a local level, but focus on wider questions of commoditization, accumulation and peasant–state relations, and on the socio-political and cultural dimensions of peasant agency.

The following section discusses a selection of writings on IAK from these two broad perspectives. On the one hand, I refer to the polarizations that have been drawn in that debate – in this regard, what follows is not a literature overview but a discussion of two poles in a debate. On the other hand, I point out that the different sides in the debate often refer to the importance of strong local organizations in bringing about the technological, institutional and socio-political changes that these authors' respective theoretical analyses lead them to identify as indispensable. Yet the nature and actions of these organizations receive limited treatment.

Case study material from a region of Ecuador is then used to elaborate the actions of local organizations, showing how they are fashioning their own indigenous agricultural development, and are both constructed by and drawing on the resources that history, modernization and development institutions have brought to their locality. I argue that their actions and perspectives cast light on the questions of relevance in theoretically grounded research, for they suggest that the (occasionally acrimonious) polarizations in the literature are often unhelpful and overdrawn. Instead the organizations are concerned to identify appropriate technological responses to peasant conditions; but at the very same time, the concept of an indigenously conceived agricultural development strategy resonates for them with questions of cultural identity and civil rights in an emerging democratic state, and so necessarily speaks of social and political strategy. The agrarian programmes of the indigenous peasant organizations and NGOs reviewed in this chapter explicitly relate agricultural technology to the concern for broader ranging strategies pressing for deeper social changes, and demanding citizenship rights for indigenous peasants, claiming a greater role in the administration of the rural state and rural space. As one Indian[4] leader commented in a related context, these strategies constitute

> The search for our own identity, or rather, the forging of an identity that continuously adjusts itself to this society and this proposed democracy which as yet does not exist. (Mario Fares, interview in Dinediciones 1990:3)

This field reality challenges us to build bridges between the different sides of the academic debate, increasing the relevance of our theoretical elaborations. Let me simply say here that on the one hand these concerns suggested the utility of concepts of agency and structure from structuration theory for combining action, structure and history in analyses of IAK (Bourdieu 1977; Giddens 1979). The theoretical subtext of this chapter thus shares many of the perspectives of Long and van der Ploeg (Chapter 3), while erring more towards the terminology of structures and social histories than they would probably wish. On the other hand, the question of relevance suggested the importance of considering these peasant organizations and NGOs as objects of the theoretical analysis – to understand in what sense they are becoming part of processes of rural social change, and how, as such, their future agrarian activities will be enabled and constrained by the 'rules and resources' inhering in those processes (the terminology is from Giddens 1979).

Indigenous agricultural revolutions in academic debate: a review and an elaboration

The agrarian populists: reaching for relevance

The view that indigenous agricultural knowledge is of high technological quality and ought to play a leading role in designing agrarian futures is not a new theme; while it has only recently been popularized, the terms of the debate have shown much continuity. I take two examples, one from the 1940s, the other from the 1980s.

As it was setting the bases in the 1940s for what was to become the 'green revolution', the Rockefeller Foundation hired Carl Sauer as a consultant to advise on how the Foundation should begin a programme of agricultural research in Mexico (Jennings 1988). Sauer cautioned against a policy of rapid technological modernization, arguing that any programme of technology generation should begin with traditional peasant knowledge and build on this (Sauer 1941). Such a strategy would both draw on peasant farmers' skills and preserve cultural diversity. The Foundation, however, saw Sauer as a type of radical indigenist whose approach would not solve problems of food supply or poverty – either rural or urban (Jennings 1988). It therefore opted for the path of high yield, high input technologies.

The resulting green revolution produced much food, and, as a by-product, significant academic and development debate. This debate has revolved around several critiques emerging since the early 1970s:

1 a technology bias critique, to the effect that certain crops and types of environment have been under-represented in the research done
2 a political-economy critique, developing the socio-economic causes and consequences of this bias against peasant farmers
3 a cultural critique suggesting that the introduction of modern technologies has eroded local cultural practice and identity
4 an environmental critique, that the technologies have created ecological problems
5 a macro-economic critique, that the technologies have generated costly import dependencies
   (Griffin 1974; Hewitt 1976; de Janvry 1981; Altieri 1987; de Walt 1988;

Lipton and Longhurst 1989; Bebbington and Carney 1990; Biggs and Farrington 1991).

In each of these critiques, traditional agricultural knowledge has been presented as central to any solution. As the knowledge of peasant farmers, so the argument goes, it is oriented toward their interests, is appropriate to their production conditions, uses no external inputs, and is environmentally friendly and adapted (e.g. Altieri 1987). It should, therefore, be the basis of future agricultural strategies: Carl Sauer once again. Two particularly influential authors in this version of agrarian populism (Richards 1985: 15–17) have been Robert Chambers (1983; Chambers et al. 1989) and Paul Richards (1985), and I shall discuss their work below, but consistent arguments from Altieri (1987), Biggs (Biggs and Clay 1981; Biggs 1989), Conway (1985) Rhoades (1984; Rhoades and Booth 1982) and the team at the International Institute for Environment and Development have among others also played important roles in promoting the 'farmer first' argument.

Chambers has targeted his work directly on the problem of relevance to the rural poor, and is highly critical of 'negative academics' for a tendency to 'lose touch with reality and practice' (1983: 33), and to overemphasize failures and constraints. Counterposed to this negativism, his overall project has been to promote actions that will change agricultural institutions so that they build on the needs, ideas and knowledge of the rural poor. His pursuit of this strategy has several bases: a particular interpretation of the failures of the green revolution; a belief in low-risk political strategy; and a certain conception of human agency. Ironically, however, in stressing the urgency of relevant research and action, repeatedly arguing that 'it is action that matters' (Chambers 1983: 216; also 1989: 193–5), the basis for knowing exactly how to act and what to do is left underdeveloped. This is because his sense of urgency appears to draw him away from historically grounded and theoretical elaboration of the origins and nature of the social and institutional problems he clearly wishes to resolve.

For Chambers, the failings of the green revolution inhered in its institutions and attitudes, and in the general idea that technology should be transferred from centres of modern science to the rural poor. 'Normal' agricultural professionals and their institutions demonstrate a bias for the 'exotic rather than indigenous, mechanical rather than human, chemical rather than organic, and marketed rather than consumed' (1983: 77). They have ignored what Chambers calls 'rural people's knowledge' (1983: 83), and have failed to talk as equals with the rural poor. Yet the rural poor create, see and know things of importance to them that 'normal' agricultural professionals simply do not look for. The way forward in rural development is, he argues, to begin with this knowledge, and see the rural poor as the main resource for development, not the problem (Chambers 1987). He is aware that IAK can be overvalued and romanticized (1983: 84), but at times he suggests that indeed its quality ought to be overstated as a counter to the more frequent overstatement of the validity of 'modern' technologies and ideas.

This requires institutional changes. He accepts that power relations and entrenched interests are a grave obstacle to such change, and that the organization of the rural poor is a *sine qua non* for protecting their interests (1983: 163–7). However, he criticizes harshly the social scientists who propose politically impractical strategies aimed directly at usurping these power relations. Such strategies involve risk for the rural poor, and it is hence ethically questionable for an outsider to recommend them (1983: 193). Because of the risks involved, and the likelihood of failure, they are not to his mind particularly relevant.

So, while acknowledging that institutional change will require pressure from civil society (such as from peasant organizations), his preferred approach to relevance is to focus on the 'room for manoeuvre' (Chambers 1983: 192) for changes from inside dominant institutions. While this leads Chambers to concentrate his attention on how to change development institutions, he tends to leave aside the question of peasant organizations except to stress their importance (1983; 1989).

Chambers is cautiously optimistic that the necessary institutional changes for a 'farmer first' development (Chambers *et al.* 1989) can be achieved. He stresses again and again the validity of a strategy of 'small steps and little pushes' (1983: 192) seeking to change authoritarian bureaucracies and rural social structures by entering at the 'soft spots' (1983: 212; 1989: 186–95) and changing people's values, attitudes and behaviour. The importance of introducing methodological change in agricultural development institutions in order to promote a new peasant-centred style of professionalism is a recurrent theme (Chambers 1987), and he has himself dedicated much effort to the reorientation of professional training.

Such changes require us to know how to act, and Chambers does operate with a conception of action. It is a conception 'based on the premise that individual behaviour is not fully determined' and that when 'social and economic forces . . . are dissected . . . we come to individual people who are . . . deciding what to do and all are to some degree capable of changing what they do. What varies is the scope they have to act differently and the extent to which those different actions can change what happens' (1983: 191). But his is not a *theory* of action, nor is it a theoretically grounded analysis of the relationship between actions and institutional change. This lack of theory, unfortunately, leaves us without the means to understand what action would be appropriate, where those institutional 'soft spots' are, and what the unequal distribution and limitations of IAK might be. Similarly, while Chambers points us towards the importance of peasant organizations and NGOs, we are left without much basis on which to understand what their actual contribution to an indigenous agricultural revolution has been and could be. His point about the dubious ethics of conducting research that can only lead to the recommendation of risky strategies is important – but if these same NGOs and peasant organizations are acting politically, is it not relevant to contribute research that assists in those actions, without advising (see e.g. Posey 1989)?

In some respects, rather than theory, Chambers's work is advocacy based on a wealth of personal experience which should be taken very seriously. Richards's (1985; 1986) fine studies of West African peasant farmers move well beyond advocacy, and provide a detailed empirical and historical demonstration of peasant research and innovatory capacities. They have become perhaps the main touchstone of the populist cause, as well as an exemplary case of how to do research on technological aspects of IAK. His argument, more theoretical than Chambers's, questions the generalization and implicit model of cultural evolution that inhere in both the theory and practice of agricultural science and agrarian modernization (including Marxist variants – Richards 1985: 138). He demonstrates that diversity, heterogeneity and complexity are the ecological characteristics of West African farming systems. These give rise to locally specific, and so spatially varied, farming practices, and require locally specific strategies in any attempt to increase food supply (Richards 1986).

This is 'relevant academic research' – it treats a conceptual and theoretical problem (the relationship between science and development), but in a way that provides provocative entry points for policy and practitioners. Presenting the case for 'ecological particularism' (1985: 12), Richards argues with much evidence that the top-down, centre-out model of the green revolution will never work in West Africa. An 'indigenous agricultural revolution' based on the knowledge and adaptations of peasant farmers is, however, possible: 'peasant enterprise has already laid the basis for an agricultural revolution in West Africa' (1985: 14).

Having set out the entry points (such as technical practices, places, institutions) he lays down certain principles for action to move towards this revolution. In this he echoes many of Chambers's comments. He presents the case for a decentralized research and extension system, and for the importance of attitudinal change so that researchers and extensionists take IAK more seriously and let peasants take the lead in development strategies beginning with IAK and combining it with outside western science (1985: 142–58). His argument is less clear on how this will happen. He comments that one of the two key factors for a successful participatory research programme is 'the existence of strong local organizations capable of formulating tractable problems, and of carrying out much of the necessary R & D (research and development) for themselves' (1985: 154). But again how those organizations will come into being, how their dynamics will influence the sorts of technology they want, how they will combine technological and other activities, and how they will pressure formal institutions to decentralize remains to be treated in depth. One assumes there would be much heterogeneity in this also.

Clearly, Richards (1985) speaks of localities in his work and stresses the importance of cultural politics and specificity. Indeed, his is explicitly a case against evolutionary Grand Theories (1985: 138). His admiration for peasant creativity is clear but as he rightly extols it, the image of the essentialized 'knowledgeable peasant' using (and wanting to use) environmentally adapted, low input technologies, rises from the text. As with other studies of IAK, and although Richards counters any such claim, one leaves the book with the image that all peasants are constantly creating and deeply knowledgeable of their environment. Many bibliographic references to his work clearly recognize this message. Indeed he argues that the general principle of his analysis is 'relevant to a wider audience . . . [sharing] a common interest in the methodological issues raised by ecological particularism' (1985: 12–13).

It is at this point that it becomes important that Richards's avowed interest is in the 'ecological aspects of the populist case' (1985: 17), and that the book is not concerned with the 'politics, sociology and economics of agrarian populism' (1985: 17). This is not Richards's fault: all authors write within limits, and he himself draws attention to these (1985: 162). Yet because the very title generalizes (*Indigenous Agricultural Revolution*), it may have lent itself to more universal applications than are appropriate. Specifically, the variability of social context (that he notes as important) will influence the possibility and the nature of appropriate institutional responses to peasant science. Similarly, context may well influence the nature of viable technical responses and peasant ideas and knowledge about what is viable and desirable. These will depend on the prior social, cultural and agro-ecological history of the peasants and region in question.

The implication is that Richards's approach is be emulated but not necessarily generalized, and that 'indigenous agricultural revolutions' will take different paths in different locations, and that to understand those paths it is important to address not only the ecological, but also the socio-historical particularism of the case.

A political-economy perspective on relevance

Although these arguments have received harsh criticism, from Marxists above all, the line of the agrarian populists is a carefully chosen one, designed to gain an audience rather than repel it. There are subtexts to the populist argument: that research and development institutions must be opened up to peasant participation; that peasants must be recognized as competent and skilled individuals; and that sensitivity to local knowledge will help preserve local culture. These are points that have to be made in policy debate through the back door, so to speak. They ride on a claim for the technological rationality of traditional knowledge: the claim to which the makers of food policy are most likely to listen.

While this argumentative strategy is understandable, it is potentially problematic. The voluntarist turn in much writing on peasant knowledge pays more attention to the creativity of farmers than to the possibility that their actions are influenced by a multitude of 'acknowledged' and 'unacknowledged conditions', and themselves have 'unintended consequences' (Giddens 1979; Gregory and Urry 1985). Such voluntarism overstates the ease with which 'farmer first' conditions might be instituted – as one suspects Chambers would indeed admit. While cultural ecological analyses of IAK are not so voluntarist in that they state agro-ecological conditions of, and constraints upon, farming practices – Richards (1985; 1986) is not the only example; see also Denevan and Padoch (1987); Wilken (1987); theirs is a conception of peasant agency that is primarily bio-physically knowledgeable and constrained. Yet the rules and resources (Giddens 1979) of peasant agency are not only agro-ecological – they also lie in socio-economic, cultural and political realms. The social history of agrarian change would tell something of the formation and nature of these rules and resources.

Developing this line of critique, some geographers (sometimes adopting the label 'political ecologists') and social anthropologists have drawn on various formulations of radical political economy to stress impacts of the state, economy and wider systems of social relationships on this peasant agency (Watts 1983; 1989; Grossman 1984; Blaikie and Brookfield 1987; Redclift 1987; Bassett 1988; Carney 1988; Hecht and Cockburn 1989). It is in their writings that the debate about indigenous technology is most thoroughly engaged with social theory. Since the early 1980s this social theory has incorporated the peasant as human agent to ever increasing degrees – consequently it has become easier to see relevance in their writings, as the concepts and empirical material become more pertinent for the question of actual political strategy.

Writing on 'sustainable development' Redclift (1987: 150–9) agrees with the populists on the central role for IAK in development strategies. His difference, however, is in the emphasis and starting-points of his analysis (Redclift 1991). Redclift stresses that 'our first task must be to recognize the links between environmental rationality and the political economy which has contributed to its formulation and intellectual genesis' (1987: 202) – a political economy which sets the political realities by which development institutions operate and which will typically undervalue indigenous knowledge. The obstacles to an indigenous agricultural revolution here are cast in socio-political terms, and Redclift talks much more of the important role that social movements have to play in contesting and changing development paths than he does of the need to change attitudes and behaviour in the bureaucracy (also Redclift 1988). In this analysis, the extent to which there is a peasant-centred environmental rationality underlying development strategies, and the possibility of furthering this, depends on the strength of representative forces in civil society to challenge the prevailing political economic formations that mould dominant rationalities.

In this vein, the contributions of Michael Watts are also important, not least because he has dedicated several statements to specific criticism of Richards's populism (1983; 1987a; 1987b; 1989). For Watts, the populist approach is theoretically deficient because it fails to analyse how political economy is interwoven with power relations at different levels of society producing 'local complexities of resource access and control' (Watts 1987b: 223) – without such analysis, he argues, little can meaningfully be said about environmental management. He claims that 'questions of ecological regulation are . . . shaped by property rights' (1989: 15) rather than simple peasant experimentation. This theoretical deficiency inevitably leads into a practical deficiency, Watts argues, because Richards 'appears less concerned with the rough and tumble of peasant political economy' (Watts 1987b: 223). Consequently, one might expect Watts to argue that Richards's recommendations are politically naive and, consequently lack relevance. What one considers relevant depends on one's theory.

Watts keeps hold of Marxism, class and materialism as organizing concepts (1989: 4, 5). He continues to argue that 'agriculture must be situated within capitalist accumulation as a whole in order to identify the general features of particular forms of agrarian change' (1989: 31), and points to the 'structural equivalences' in different agrarian transitions (1989: 30). None the less, Watts himself argues against structural proclamations of generalized crisis in African agriculture in which 'History is conducted behind the backs of peasants who appear as residues of a hegemonic world system' (1989: 11). Thus, like Richards, Watts is interested in peasant agency and heterogeneity in agricultural systems.

Watts's agency, however, is one of everyday and organized local struggle, of peasant strategy and political intention, rather than one of technical creativity. This reflects a belief that any analysis of African agriculture must begin with two assumptions: that it is shaped by states with interests, and mediated by locally complex agrarian structures – the final effect of which is a heterogeneity of local outcomes, a 'multiplicity of agrarian strategies and struggles' (1989: 12). Consequently he and his colleagues, such as Judith Carney (1988), deal with the construction and change of local meanings, labour organization and land and crop rights as they treat the peasant agency that would underlie any 'indigenous agricultural revolution'.

Watts's writing represents a body of work that is primarily theoretical. For this reason it, and research in a similar vein, has been criticized for its self-contradictory tendency of using 'elitist' language to express ostensibly democratic sentiments (Tuan 1989). This, says Tuan, is analysis 'for mandarins – not for Gambian peasants or even for run-of-the mill geographers' (Tuan 1989: 379). None the less, by speaking of peasant agency, it does keep one eye cocked towards relevance – a relevance for an appropriate political strategy for particular agrarian and national social structures.

Of course, it is precisely the nature of an 'appropriate' political strategy that begs the question. For Chambers, a strategy entailing great risk would not be appropriate. As Scott (1985) has so clearly demonstrated, daily forms of peasant resistance can be more effective and less dangerous ways of coping with and manipulating local social relationships. Indeed, much recent writing on peasant political agency has focused on such subaltern, everyday resistance, and the 'daily texture of local power relations' (Fox 1990: 3).

However, as Fox (1990) notes, there are limits on what individualized acts of 'everyday resistance' can achieve, and it is necessary to understand the actual and potential relationships between local, regional and national political changes. What confronts us then is the 'challenge of rural democratization', the strengthening of rural civil society as an arena for organized political expression and negotiation, whose very organization can reduce the risks involved and expand the frontier of the achievable (Fox 1990). Simultaneously, this organization can strengthen local capabilities for self-administration – in short, for drawing on local knowledge.

Bridging the gap: structures, actions and relevance

Two common themes emerge from these different discussions: one theoretical and (not independently) the other thematic. The first is that theoretical analyses of agrarian change must take agency seriously in relation to both peasants and development organizations. Such agency should be conceived as at once technologically creative and socio-politically oriented. The different perspectives also agree that this agency must be in some sense situated (Gregory and Urry 1985): in local agro-ecological context as well as within a regional (and national) political economy. Farmers may be analysed as 'human beings [who] reflexively monitor their conduct *via the knowledge that they have of the circumstances of their activity*' (Giddens 1979: 254, my emphasis), but the distribution of that knowledge and these circumstances will be spatiotemporally and socially differentiated (Marcus and Fischer 1986: 94). This suggests that the parameters of any future strategy for indigenous agriculture with technical and socio-cultural relevance and meaning to peasants, will depend on local *and* agro-ecological history. Appropriate and viable strategies will not be the same everywhere.

The second theme cutting across these different analyses is the role of local peasant and development organizations – or the strengthening of rural civil society – in pursuing both the technological and administrative aspects and the socio-political dimensions of a peasant-centred agrarian programme. Thus, Watts's analysis leads him to identify the urgent 'need to develop social democratic forces through farmers, groups, trades unions and political parties' (1989: 29) in order to negotiate relationships within and between society and the state. Richards (1985: 152–4) and Chambers (1983: 166) emphasize strong local organisations as a necessary prerequisite for the administration of a successful indigenous agricultural revolution based on peasant technical knowledge.

Yet, despite the importance accorded to it, the theme of local organizations remains underdeveloped. It has several implications. One is theoretical: that if such organizations are to be the agents of a strategy, then it is necessary for reasons just noted to understand the conditions that will structure the possibilities and tendencies of that agency. Another returns us to the question of relevance: that relevant research must allow entry points to these organizations. One important starting-point would then be to understand, within the theoretical concerns outlined here, how local organizations themselves resolve what is relevant to their goals, and most appropriate to their local conditions. This speaks of the importance of understanding indigenous agricultural strategies within the relationship between technical and socio-cultural change in a particular region. It is to an attempt to begin such a line of research that I now turn.

Agrarian change, peasant strategies and institutional models in the Central Ecuadorian Andes

The case study comes from the *cantons* of Colta and Guamote, and the adjacent parish of San Juan in the province of Chimborazo in the central Andes of Ecuador, an area of well-organized indigenous peasant farmers with a long history of daily Indian subversion and resistance to domination.[5] This has been a resistance of both momentous mobilizations, and daily 'resistant adaptation' (Stern 1987a): coping with, manipulating and surviving in the face of parasitic and repressive external social systems. This speaks both of resistance itself, and of a determination for ethnic and cultural survival. This resistance also draws attention to a long history in which indigenous people in the Andes have always understood themselves as a cultural group negotiating a relationship with an external institution: be it the *kuraka* (the regional ethnic leader), the hacienda, or now the state. This theme of negotiating and resisting external forces in order to survive culturally recurs in current agricultural projects of indigenous organizations.

Our story (or their story), revolving around the question of land and territory in this long history of resistance, begins in the mid-twentieth century when large rural estates still dominated Colta and Guamote. Indigenous farmers, directly or indirectly tied to the haciendas, farmed in textbook agro-ecological style. On their small plots they had to meet family food needs, and produced little for the market place: a production system without agrochemical inputs and using a range of local crops and varieties. In Chambers's already noted terms (1983: 77) this was indigenous, human, organic and consumed. Alongside them, the hacienda introduced limited 'exotic' innovations, marketed its surplus and kept large lots in pasture on which Indians were allowed to keep their animals.

The social relation underlying these production systems was, however, contested. A steady strategy of Indian peasants to recover Andean space from the hacienda, expanding their plots by a furrow at the start of each crop cycle, or invading parts of the hacienda, took on more organized form by the 1940s and 1950s (Sylva 1986). Influenced by trade union experiences and a national Indian movement related to the Communist Party,[6] the local peasantry mounted co-ordinated labour withdrawals and land invasions. Facing problems of labour discipline and consequent falling profits, some haciendas subdivided their lands. As local subversion intensified, the central state, already concerned that the hacienda was an obstacle to modernization, was pulled deeper into Chimborazo's conflicts (Haney and Haney 1989). The fear of unbridled peasant radicalism led the state to declare the province the priority zone for the application of land reform legislation in 1973 and rapidly the hacienda all but disappeared from these two *cantons* (Sylva 1986; Bebbington 1990).

And along with it, disappeared the conditions sustaining organic indigenous production. Hacienda pastures were subdivided, Indian animals were sold to acquire land, and the source of organic matter underlying Indian production systems was rapidly diminished, albeit at different rates in different localities reflecting differing levels of population pressure on the haciendas – which has its own historical explanation (Sylva 1986). In the absence of other local sources of off-farm work (an effect of regional underdevelopment), increasing demographic pressure has contributed to progressive land subdivision, reduction of fallow periods and resource degradation increasingly necessitating the use of agrochemicals to offset yield declines and crop loss. In parallel, seasonal migration to urban areas has intensified, something indigenous people associate with social problems and cultural degradation in their communities: the import of urban pathologies of petty theft, bad manners and petty violence; and the weakening of family ties, community relationships, and participation in and support for communal activities are all associated with this migration.

The new institutions of civil society in Chimborazo and the construction of indigenous development

These material and social changes have contributed to current perceptions of a possible and desirable future for indigenous agriculture. But the changes in rural civil society fostered by the agrarian reform (Casagrande and Piper 1969; Muratorio 1981) have similarly contributed to these perceptions, and to the strategies based upon the perceptions. Mention must be made of the discourses and actions of government rural development agencies, the Christian church and NGOs. These institutions have each promoted conceptions of Indian identity in modern Ecuador, and of desirable indigenous agrarian practice in the zone. In the process they have influenced the political and technological programmes of peasant federations.

The state and rural development

In many countries throughout Latin America land reform has been followed by rural development programmes aimed at the modernization of peasant agriculture (de Janvry 1981; Barsky 1984; Grindle 1986; Jordan 1989). In Chimborazo these programmes began in the 1960s, have intensified since the mid-1970s, and carry on through to the present. Projects deliver inputs, credit, infrastructure, education and technical assistance to rural areas. In line with the Chambers critique, little attention has been paid to local knowledge and rarely has allowance been made for indigenous participation (although certain conjunctures and individuals have facilitated this – see Bebbington 1990). Programmes are staffed almost entirely by whites and *mestizos* on the grounds that indigenous people lack the necessary knowledge of modern science and administration.[7] Yet the state's very inefficiency in these programmes (Jordan 1988) undermines this justification, contributing to a growing Indian belief that 'we can do it just as well as they' and that the state should therefore hand over to them the resources and responsibility for rural development.

Rural development programmes lend themselves to political patronage (Grindle 1986), and government has presented itself in rural areas as the 'concerned' deliverer of services and modernization to the indigenous peasantry. This has contributed to a rhetoric of state obligation to rural areas. The generation of young indigenous adults now leading most community councils has grown up with a significant state presence in their communities. This helps create the sense that the reproduction of indigenous agriculture will necessarily be mediated by the state. It also fosters the belief that it is the state's duty to give this support, and these leaders increasingly turn the rhetoric of obligation back on the state:

> The [rural development project] must complete the planned works mentioned in this letter. It can not offer written or spoken words alone but must realize the projects that we need in the peasant communities of Chimborazo. . . . It must work in *all* communities that need the support of Public Institutions and not only assist those places in which it prefers to work. (Letter from the community Santa Martha de Sablog to the DRI-Guamote, 8 December 1982)[8]

The changing church and the NGOs: discourses on Indian identity, agrarian change and democratic rights

In both liberation theological (Catholic) and evangelical guises, the churches' allegiance with the indigenous peasantry predates land reform; indeed the Catholic Church was active in the struggle for land. Playing an important role in rural social life, the churches have had significant impacts on peasant strategy.

Despite their obvious theological differences there are important similarities in the orientations of the two most influential Christian tendencies. Both have sought high levels of Indian participation in the administration of the church and its social development projects. Each stress that indigenous people are equals with all other Ecuadorians and therefore should claim equal rights from the state – they too are turning the rhetoric of development back on the state. Finally, both emphasize the validity of indigenous people maintaining and asserting a cultural difference from white-*mestizo* society (e.g. CEP 1979; Muratorio 1981).

The tension inhering in these propositions is between claiming the resources and rights of modernity and sustaining a cultural identity. In the agrarian sphere, the Gospel Missionary Union, an important voice for the evangelical church, resolves this by favouring agricultural modernization ('the knowledge, resources and skills available to more fortunate people in the world' as one evangelical agronomist puts it), and asserting cultural difference in other spheres: language, dress and high levels of indigenous organization and indigenous control of rural space. It has decentralized the location and control of churches *into* the community. Its agrarian projects involve high levels of decision-making and execution by indigenous people (e.g. as extension agents): new forms of indigenous social management of technical resource systems.

In discourse, liberation theologians question agrarian modernization, preferring the recovery of indigenous practices as an element in an indigenous political and economic strategy (Amboya 1989: 28; Proaño 1989: 40). In practice, however, the Catholic church has fostered agricultural change and innovation, through credit and input distribution projects: similar to the evangelical church.

These two discourses separate agricultural technology out of the essentials of cultural identity, while presenting its adoption as the claim of a democratic right. In both approaches, what becomes more important than the technical practice is the control of the modernization process.

While these ecclesiastical changes predate the rise of NGO activity, there are close ties between these two social and institutional changes. The NGOs have tried to draw out far more explicitly the implications of these social messages for the development of indigenous agriculture (e.g. CESA 1980; 1987).

With the decline of the hacienda, and the increase of foreign finance for NGOs, these organizations have proliferated in the region, especially in the 1980s. Not surprisingly, the proliferation implies a diversity of strategies. The difference of discourse on modern and traditional technologies parallels that in the church, with many more hues of variation. There are NGOs that promote wholesale technical modernization and others that seek agro-ecological alternatives (contrast CESA 1980 and FEPP 1990). The latter have more difficulty in transferring their technologies, being often told by farmers that they are not a viable alternative in current conditions.

While the technological differences among the NGOs are important, of more significance are the common threads in their visions, rhetoric and strategies. The NGO discourse speaks of indigenous farmers having the same rights as other Ecuadorians to decent social conditions. It places confidence in indigenous peoples' ability to administer projects and tries to pass this administration on to them. While the details and effects of their strategies may differ, the principle has been common throughout. Furthermore, while some NGOs strengthen and create indigenous organizations to be vehicles not only of administration but also of socio-political mobilization to petition the state, others avoid criticism of the state for marginalizing indigenous people. None the less, the very presence of these others in areas where the state is weak, and their far more generous (sometimes reckless; CEPLAES 1984) disbursement of resources to communities, constitute implicit criticism of the state. Indeed, peasants compare the state negatively with these NGOs.

Indigenous organizations: technological innovation, cultural identity, political strategy

In this ferment of institutional discourse and action, and of agro-ecological and socio-economic change, the organized peasantry has sustained an active search for social and agrarian change – showing both change and continuity in regard to its earlier militant actions over land, and incorporating ideas and administrative models from these other institutions. Indeed, peasant organizations have frequently formed in the context of NGO and church activity.

For Ramón (1987; 1988), the steady recommunalization of Andean space holds the key to understanding long-term Indian political strategy, but here I shall focus on a different level of peasant organization which suggests a peasant search for a more regionally integrated control of territory. These supra-communal forms of social organization in the case study area, known as 'second-order organizations', are federations of anything from nine to forty communities. They are usually spatially coherent, often following parish or county boundaries. They have an elected governing body (although there is a tendency to re-elect the same leaders for several years), weekly meetings, and a central office in one of the member communities or, more frequently, in a small village at a focal point of the micro-region the federation covers.

One group of these federations was formed in a process of explicit struggle (over land, wages, transport costs, and so on), frequently has links with the radical church and Marxist Left, and presents a more radical, anti-capitalist orientation and rhetoric (e.g. UCASAJ 1989). Another group of more reformist 'second generation' federations have been created to negotiate the increasingly available resources for indigenous development (cf Chiriboga 1987). While these organizations all manage several activities (health projects, education, agriculture, rural infrastructure, and so on), the projects for the adaptation and dissemination of agricultural technology are always among the most important. As projects designed and implemented by indigenous peasants, they may be considered an institutionalization of local conceptions of indigenous agricultural strategies.

The technological bases of these projects show the same diversity mentioned above. The more radical organizations have talked about recovering traditional Indian agrarian technologies. This approach is justified as: a rejection of white and capitalist culture; an affirmation and validation of indigenous identity; and a means of reducing market dependence, costs of production and environmental pollution (MICH 1989: 199). However, promoting traditional technologies in a context of land degradation combined with market-oriented production has proved difficult. The membership of the federations has not accepted these initial justifications, and the organizations have moved towards strategies based on partial modernization of productive practices.

This takes them towards the strategies of the 'developmentalist' federations for which technological modernization, along with the promotion of non-traditional cash and food crops, are explicitly seen as a means of cultural *survival*. The argument is that indigenous cultural identity hinges not so much around maintaining traditional technologies but around remaining in rural areas, a residence which in turn protects local forms of social organization (family, fictive kin, group work and the community). Indigenous culture, it is implied, must adapt to survive, and this survival depends above all on retaining the cohesion of the group. Such a strategy is also encountered in other (but not all) regions of Ecuador (Ramón 1988: 24–5).[9]

Beyond such differences are more significant shared rationales for these agricultural programmes. The first is a concern to strengthen indigenous organization in order that Indians are better able to push for deeper social changes to change the context within which they have to farm. An indigenous agricultural future will involve peasants claiming their rights, as full Ecuadorian citizens, to the services of the state. It will not be, and should not be expected to be, an entirely autochthonous strategy (cf. Blauert 1988). 'If other social groups have not had to be self-reliant, why should indigenous peasants be expected to be so?' goes local talk.

Second is the insistence that the organizations control the administration of resources for development projects in their territory, adapting them to the needs of their membership, and showing, via the success of the organization, that indigenous peasants are quite as able as *blanco-mestizos* to use and manage modern administrative methods, and modern technologies. Finally, though they may have differing strategies for doing so, all stress that their agrarian projects seek so sustain the social and cultural integrity of their membership.

How far these rationales are shared by the membership is debatable, but there are certain common interpretations and a recent experience that suggests some congruence.[10] 'Traditional' technologies are often associated by peasants with the subjugated forms of living associated with the hacienda, and thus speak of social relations to be rejected. Embracing modern technologies of the type that were used on some of the old haciendas, and now associated with modernized white farmers, is also to make a statement that indigenous peasants are equal to these farmers and are claiming the access to technology that whites have always had (cf. Bourdieu 1990: 155). This use of modern technology in turn speaks of a far broader set of rights that this peasantry is steadily claiming in Ecuadorian society. The discourse of citizenship rights has thus been taken up into the interpretation of technologies (cf. Lehmann 1990).

The administrative structure of the projects is also politically symbolic. It and project implementation are *in form* very similar to those of the state's and NGOs' agricultural development programmes (research and extension; seed distribution; input distribution, etc.). The *practice*, however, is quite different. Almost everything is executed and administered by indigenous people selected by their communities.[11] Consequently projects are more responsive to the preoccupations of local peasants than are the state's, because leaders and workers live in the same rural areas as the members, and are already caught up in the existing structures and methods for exercising accountability, however imperfect these may be.

In technical terms this means a more efficient project. In political terms it is increasingly interpreted by indigenous people as the demonstration of an Indian capacity to organize rural development that is at least equal to the state's ability (Bebbington 1989 discusses evidence of this ability). The further implication is that indigenous people should have a very prominent part in all rural development planning and implementation. This experience, building on and coupled with the experience of projects with NGOs in which indigenous people also have more control in the planning and administration of the project, feed into an implied and felt criticism of the state for not allowing such peasant participation.

As spatially defined administrative units, the federations implementing rural development are one of a number of changes in Colta and Guamote that speak of the increasing indigenous control of rural space. For the first time now indigenous people are being elected to local government positions in the Ecuadorian state (Sánchez Parga 1989; Bebbington 1990). As white and *mestizo* presence in rural areas declines every year, rural space is being returned to, or taken back by, indigenous people as an arena in which to practise indigenous culture and agriculture.

The political impact of the federations goes beyond the symbolic. In June 1990 the national umbrella organization for regional indigenous peasant groups, the Confederation of Indigenous Nationalities of Ecuador (CONAIE), called on Indians of Ecuador to participate in 'The First Indigenous Uprising' as a protest at the failure of the government to attend to the needs of the countries' indigenous peasantry. Between 4 June and 8 June indigenous peasants closed roads, prevented the free circulation of food products, refused to sell their agricultural products, and, by controlling rural space, threatened to precipitate food shortages in urban areas (CEDIME 1990; MLAL-Abya-Yala 1990).

One of the strongest centres in this uprising was Colta, Guamote and San Juan. Now, the area has always been politically active, and the federations must be seen as part of this political history; but they also contribute to its reproduction and adaptation, and in June 1990 they were one of the vehicles for mobilizing the local peasantry. More significantly, and more tentatively, I would also suggest that in their more daily practices of rural administration, of petitioning the state, and of asserting the possibility of an indigenous control of development they provided a bridge between local experience and CONAIE's more distant demands, and provided tangible experiences suggesting the feasibility of sustaining CONAIE's claims. In their administration of agricultural

219

projects they constitute a space for peasant socialization into a sense of the politically possible.

A final note of caution is needed, however, for the uprising takes us back to consider the interests entrenched in the state and dominant society, leading us to reflect on Chambers's admonitions about political risk. For, while the government agreed to negotiate with CONAIE, little has yet been achieved. Worse still, rural self-defence squads have emerged, armed by landowners or local authorities concerned about and feeling threatened by this Indian militancy. And they have intimidated and killed Indians. Guamote and San Juan now know a military presence in their communities under the cloak of doing 'social work'! The army has sought to place soldiers in community schools to give educational and agricultural assistance to supposedly 'backward' Indian farmers – but the real reason for their presence is obviously to feel the pulse of Indian politics, and to identify local leaders should they ever need to be arrested in order to prevent future mobilizations.[12] In a very cruel way these experiences remind us that relevant analyses must also consider the limits of the politically possible, for the limits are very real.

Conclusion

The earlier suggestion that peasant agency must be taken seriously in studies of agrarian change is amply supported by the experience in Colta and Guamote. Peasant organizations there are vehicles for both political expression and the administration of agricultural projects, and they have had some success in each of these arenas. Moreover, they themselves clearly see a relationship between the two: organizing around an agricultural project is one of several practices for strengthening the organization as a socio-political agent. At the same time one of the purposes of the technologies that these organizations handle is to sustain the presence of indigenous peasants in rural Chimborazo in order that they can continue to reproduce that peasantry as a culturally cohesive group with political potential.

The technologies these organizations work with, the meanings they ascribe to them, and the socio-political goals towards which their promotion is directed are, however, all in some sense products of the region's history and political economy. The rural poor continue to work with these products even as they reproduce, contest and change the physiognomy of this political economy. This is important, for the argument here is in no way meant as a defence of agrochemicals and a rejection of agro-ecologically sound strategies grounded in past practices. It is simply to say that local histories can lead to situations in which local groups decide that agrochemicals have an important and appropriate place in their repertoire of technologies. In Colta and Guamote, peasant farmers are taking in green revolution technology and turning it into something it was never intended to be: a sign of democratization and a material basis for possible politics. Similarly, from their experiences of state rural development, they are not being simply integrated into Ecuadorian society,[13] but are developing a sense of the *rights* to rural development they should claim as a consequence of being part of that society, and are forging an alternative vision of organizing that development.

These experiences suggest that any theoretical concept of indigenous agricultural revolution must have technical, cultural and political aspects – because that is quite simply how the rural poor live. They seek social change, but worry about food production to sustain them as they search for change, and, as reflexive actors, are always interpreting their life-worlds. The complexity, creativity and conflict inhering in this process suggest the importance of being circumspect about simple generalizations. This, in turn, leads to the more generalizable conclusion that any intervention, for research or development, must take the ideas and actions of local people and their formal and informal institutions very seriously. It is in these institutions that many of the building blocks for a locally appropriate, organizationally sustainable indigenous agricultural revolution will be found.

Of course, my research was influenced by a predisposition to connecting different lines of theory, and in particular by a wish to do justice to peasant agency while being serious about constraint. This does not need to imply theoretical eclecticism. Rather, the conception of agency and structure that conceives 'constraints' as being simultaneously 'resources' provides a sensible bridge. The experience of seeing Chimborazo's peasantry in action only confirms me in this belief: for, more or less consciously, they work with the resources that social and agro-ecological history has placed at their disposal, use them, make sense of them, take pride in what they achieve, and frequently discuss what to do about the obstacles to social change they have not yet surpassed. They, and the research, both vindicate and qualify the postulations of the populists and the political economists, suggesting that one very important role of research in the ongoing formulation of theory is to challenge our oppositions, qualify our generalizations, and humble our academic pride.

Notes

1. Material for this chapter was collected during research periods in Ecuador funded by the InterAmerican Foundation, Washington, DC, Fundagro, Quito, and the Overseas Development Institute, London. I am grateful for their support, as well as for that of the Centre of Latin American Studies at Cambridge University, where I worked at the time of writing this chapter. Comments from Simon Batterbury, Paul Richards and other contributors to this book were very helpful. The opinions are my own.
2. This is not at all meant to imply that applied research is undesirable: it is simply that it asks a more limited set of questions.
3. Interestingly, this conception of 'relevance' seems not so very far away from Giddens's (1991: 155–6) recent formulation of the requisites of a critical theory: namely, that it be 'alert to immanent institutional transformations' in society, be politically 'tactical', build 'models of the good society', and link 'emancipatory politics' with a 'life politics' (Giddens 1991: 155–6).
4. In the text I use the words 'indigenous' and 'Indian' interchangeably.

Although the word 'Indian' has often had derogatory implications in Ecuador, I have used it because indigenous people appear once again to be applying the label to themselves in the context of the social and political claims they are currently making against the Ecuadorian state.

5. For Ecuador, see Sylva (1986), Sánchez-Parga (1989) and Bebbington (1990). See Scott (1985) for the seminal statement.

6. The Ecuadorian Federation of Indians, formed in 1944 (Barsky 1984).

7. *Mestizos* are mixed race Spanish-Indian who identify culturally and politically with whites more than Indians.

8. These quotations come from my own field notes.

9. Ramón's (1988) example is of 'the initiatives of the Otavaleños [commercial textile producers] or the onion producers of Cangahua, who, on the basis of controlling land resources or artisanal production, have developed marketing networks, and increased their share in the proportion of value added in production, which in turn enables the sustained reproduction of the ethnic group' (Ramón 1988: 24–5).

10. Moreover, one must recognize that there are varying interests among the membership, of gender, wealth, and age for example. Although not discussed here, some of these interests are represented within the organizations, in particular women's groups.

11. 'Almost' because they have all at some time had a part or full-time white or *mestizo* agronomist.

12. As Giddens (1985) notes, surveillance is an important element of state power.

13. The titles of the first rural development loan from the Inter-American Development Bank was precisely 'The Integration of the Peasantry' (Barsky 1984: 32–3).

References

Altieri M (1987) *Agroecology: the scientific basis of alternative agriculture.* Boulder, CO, Westview Press

Amboya C (1989) 'Como Fui Conociendo al Monseñor'. In: CEDIS-FEPP (ed) *Monseñor Proaño: Luchador de la Paz y de la Vida.* Quito, CEDIS-FEPP

Barsky O (1984) *La reforma agraria Ecuatoriana.* Quito, Corporación Editora Nacional

Bassett T J (1988) The political ecology of peasant–herder conflicts in the northern Ivory Coast. *Annals of the Association of American Geographers* 78 (3)

Bebbington A J (1989) Institutional options and multiple sources of agricultural innovation: evidence from an Ecuadorean case study. ODI Agricultural Administration (Research and Extension) Network Paper 11, London, Overseas Development Institute

Bebbington A J (1990) Indigenous agriculture in the central Ecuadorian Andes: the cultural ecology and institutional conditions of its construction and its change. PhD dissertation, Graduate School of Geography, Clark University, Worcester, MA

Bebbington A J and **Carney J** (1990) Geographers in the international agricultural research centers: theoretical and practical considerations. *Annals of the Association of American Geographers* 80 (1)

Bebbington A J and **Thiele G** (1993) *Non-governmental organizations and the state in Latin America: rethinking roles in sustainable agricultural development.* London, Routledge.

Biggs S (1989) Resource-poor farmer participation in research: a synthesis of experiences from nine national agricultural research systems. OFCOR Comparative Study Paper no. 3, The Hague, International Service for National Agricultural Research

Biggs S D and **Clay E** (1981) Sources of innovation in agricultural technology. *World Development* 9 (4)

Biggs S D and **Farrington J** (1991) *Agricultural research and the rural poor: a review of social science analysis.* Ottawa, International Development Research Centre

Blaikie P and **Brookfield H** (eds) (1987) *Land degradation and society.* London, Methuen

Blauert J (1988) Autochthonous development and environmental knowledge in Oaxaca, Mexico. In: Blaikie P and Unwin T (eds) *Environmental crises in developing countries.* Monograph no. 5, Developing Areas Research Group, Institute of British Geographers

Bourdieu P (1977) *Outline of a theory of practice.* Cambridge, Cambridge University Press

Bourdieu P (1990) *In other words: essays towards a reflexive sociology.* Cambridge, Polity Press

Carney, J (1988) Struggles over crop rights and labour within contract farming households in a Gambian irrigated rice project. *Journal of Peasant Studies* 15 (3)

Casagrande J B and **Piper A R** (1969) La transformación estructural de una parroquia rural en las tierras altas del Ecuador. *América Indígena* XXIX (4)

CEDIME (1990) El levantamiento indígena. *Punto de Vista,* special edition, 2 June

CEP (1979) *Leonidas Proaño: 25 Años Obispo de Riobamba.* Lima, Centro de Estudios y Publicaciones

CEPLAES (1984) *Visión mundial y su actividad en el sector rural del Ecuador.* Quito, Centro de Planificación y Estudios Sociales

CESA (1980) *Un apoyo al desarrollo campesino: C.E.S.A.* Quito, Central Ecuatoriana de Servicios Agrícolas

CESA (1987) *Formas de participación de la mujer en cinco zonas rurales del Ecuador.* Quito, CESA

Chambers, R (1983) *Rural development: putting the last first.* Harlow, Longman

Chambers R (1987) Sustainable livelihoods, environment and development: putting poor rural people first. IDS Discussion Paper 240, Brighton, Institute of Development Studies

Chambers R (1989) Reversals, institutions and change. In: Chambers *et al.* (eds)

Chambers R, Pacey A and **Thrupp L A** (eds) (1989) *Farmer first: farmer innovation and agricultural research.* London, Intermediate Technology Publications

Chiriboga M (1987) Movimiento campesino e indígena y participación política en Ecuador: la construcción de identidades en una sociedad heterogenea. *Ecuador Debate* 13

CONAIE (1989) *Nuestro proceso organizativo.* Quito, Confederación de Nacionalidades Indígenas del Ecuador

Conway G (1985) Agroecosystems analysis. *Agricultural Administration* 20

Denevan W M and **Padoch C** (1987) Swidden fallow agroforestry in the Peruvian Amazon. *Advances in Economic Botany* 5, New York, New York Botanical Gardens

Dinediciones (1990) *Cifra: revista económica* no. 129. Quito, Dinediciones

Durán J (1990) *Las nuevas instituciones de la sociedad civil.* La Paz, Huellas

Farrington J and **Bebbington A J** *with* **Wellard K** and **Lewis D** (1993) *Reluctant Partners: NGOS, the State and Sustainable Agricultural Development.* London, Routledge

Fox J (ed) (1990) *The challenge of rural democratization: perspectives from Latin America and the Philippines.* London, Frank Cass

Giddens A (1979) *Central problems in social theory.* London, Macmillan
Giddens A (1981) *A contemporary critique of historical materialism.* London, Macmillan
Giddens A (1985) *The nation state and violence.* Cambridge, Polity Press
Giddens A (1991) *The consequences of modernity.* Cambridge, Polity Press
Gregory D J and **Urry J** (eds) (1985) *Social relations and spatial structures.* London, Macmillan
Griffin K (1974) *The political economy of agrarian change.* London, Macmillan
Grindle M S (1986) *State and countryside: development policy and agrarian politics in Latin America.* Baltimore, MD, Johns Hopkins University Press
Grossman L (1984) *Peasants, subsistence ecology and development in the highlands of Papua New Guinea.* Princeton, NJ, Princeton University Press
Haney E B and **Haney W G** (1989) The agrarian transition in highland Ecuador: from precapitalism to agrarian capitalism in Chimborazo. In: Thiesenhusen W (ed) *Searching for agrarian reform in Latin America.* London, Unwin Hyman
Hecht S and **Cockburn A** (1989) *The fate of the forest.* London, Verso
Hewitt de Alcantara C (1976) *Modernizing Mexican agriculture.* Geneva, United Nations Research Institute for Social Development
de Janvry A (1981) *Land reform and the agrarian question in Latin America.* Baltimore, MD, Johns Hopkins University Press
Jennings B H (1988) *Foundations of international agricultural research: science and politics in Mexican agriculture.* Boulder, CO, Westview Press
Jordan F (1988) *El minifundio: su evolución en el Ecuador.* Quito, Corporación Editora Nacional
Jordan F (ed) (1989) *La economía campesina: crisis, reactivatión y desarrollo.* San Jose, IICA
Lehmann A D (1990) *Democracy and development in Latin America: economics, politics and religion in the postwar period.* Cambridge, Polity Press
Lipton M and **Longhurst R** (1989) *New seeds and poor people.* London, Unwin Hyman
Marcus G E and **Fischer M J** (1986) *Anthropology as cultural critique.* London, University of Chicago Press
MICH (1989) Movimiento indígena de Chimborazo, MICH. In: CONAIE (ed) *Nuestro proceso organizativo.* Quito, Confederación de Nacionalidades Indígenas del Ecuador
MLAL-Abya-Yala (1990) *KIPU: el mundo indígena en la prensa ecuatoriana 14.* Quito, Abya-Yala
Muratorio B (1981) Protestantism, ethnicity, and class in Chimborazo. In: Whitten N (ed) *Cultural transformations and ethnicity in modern Ecuador.* Urbana, IL, University of Illinois Press
Posey D (1989) Interview with Darrell Posey. In: Hecht S and Cockburn A. *The fate of the forest.* London, Verso
Proaño L (1989) Compartiendo los Sufrimientos y Las Esperanzas de los Pobres. In: CEDIS-FEPP (ed) *Monseñor Proaño: Luchador de la Paz y de la Vida.* Quito, CEDIS-FEPP
Ramón V G (1987) *La Resistencia Andina: Cayambe 1500–1800.* Quito, Centro Andino de Acción Popular
Ramón V G (1988) *Indios, crisis y proyecto alternativo.* Quito, Centro Andino de Acción Popular
Redclift M (1987) *Sustainable development: exploring the contradictions.* London, Methuen
Redclift M (1988) Introduction: agrarian social movements in contemporary Mexico. *Bulletin of Latin American Research* 7 (2)

Redclift M (1991) The multiple dimensions of sustainable development. *Geography 76* (1)

Rhoades R E (1984) *Breaking new ground: agricultural anthropology.* Lima, Centro Internacional de la Papa

Rhoades R E and **Booth R** (1982) Farmer-back-to-farmer: a model for generating acceptable agricultural technology. *Agricultural Administration 11*

Richards P (1985) *Indigenous agricultural revolution: ecology and food production in West Africa.* London, Hutchinson

Richards P (1986) *Coping with hunger: hazard and experiment in an African rice farming system.* London Research Series in Geography 11. London, Allen & Unwin

Sánchez-Parga J (1989) *Faccionalismo, organización y proyecto étnico en los Andes.* Quito, Centro Andino de Acción Popular

Sauer C O (1941) Letter to Rockefeller Foundation, 10 February 1941, Rockefeller Foundation/Reference no. 1.2/3.2/, page 2, Tarrytown, NY, Rockefeller Foundation Archives

Scott J C (1985) *Weapons of the weak: everyday forms of peasant resistance.* London, Yale University Press

Stern S J (1987a) New approaches to the study of peasant rebellion and consciousness: implications of the Andean experience. In: Stern S J (ed)

Stern S J (ed) (1987b) *Resistance, rebellion, and consciousness in the Andean peasant world: 18th to 20th centuries.* Madison, WI, University of Wisconsin Press

Sylva P (1986) *Gamonalismo y lucha campesina.* Quito, Abya Yala

Tuan Yi-Fu (1989) Review of R. Golledge *et al.* (eds). A ground for common search. *Professional Geographer 41* (3)

UCASAJ (1989) *Pueblo indio.* San Juan, Chimborazo, Unión de Cabildos de San Juan

de Walt B (1988) Halfway there: social science in agricultural development and social science of agricultural development. *Human Organization 47* (9)

Watts M J (1983) Populism and the politics of African land use. *African Studies Review 26* (2)

Watts M J (1987a) Drought, environment and food security. In: Glantz M (ed) *Drought and famine in Africa.* Cambridge, Cambridge University Press

Watts M J (1987b) Powers of production – geographers among the peasants. *Society and Space 5* (2)

Watts M J (1989) The agrarian crisis in Africa: debating the crisis. *Progress in Human Geography 13* (1)

Wilken G C (1987) *Good farmers: traditional agricultural resource management in Mexico and Central America.* Berkeley, CA, University of California Press

CHAPTER 9

On ignoring the wider picture:
AIDS research and the jobbing social scientist[1]

Tony Barnett and Piers Blaikie

Doing research is a process of construction. First; a vague 'problem', 'hypothesis', 'area of interest' or 'mere hunch' is discerned. A framework of ideas, notions, theories and concepts is assembled in order to define that problem more closely. Fieldwork is done, human experiences, from conversations in a peasant home or from documents in a dusty archive in a ministry, are transformed into 'data' which are stored in notebooks, as tape recordings, on survey schedules or on computer disks. The whole is painstakingly assembled into a 'coherent' account which in some way relates to the 'problem' from which the journey originated.

Theoretical and empirical coherence

This chapter is an attempt to pick apart a piece of research and to say something of how its 'coherence' was arrived at. The aim is to expose how and why the research was constructed and to draw some lessons from that process. It is an attempt to explain the odd jumble of concepts and frameworks, of *theoretical* incoherences which underlie that apparently coherent *empirical* account. Underlying our depiction of these processes is an argument that what is needed today is not elaborate theoretical work but detailed and coherent analytical description which may contribute to later theoretical work on the one hand while confronting some very serious and weighty policy issues on the other.

The broader research which is reflected upon here (Barnett and Blaikie 1992) was a first attempt to understand some of the downstream effects of the AIDS epidemic on African society and economy. In undertaking this work – which was explicitly concerned with policy – it was often necessary, through pressure of time, to take short cuts, make assumptions, work with inadequate data and, given the extreme sensitivity of the subject, exercise extreme tact. Above all, however, this work has involved operating with a whole range of theoretical discourses, some of

226

which were recognized, some of which the reader will no doubt conclude, remain implicit. Thus, the research was a pragmatic and practical piece of work designed to answer some very specific questions.

There was recourse to 'theory', but not to 'grand theory'; this was because of the policy focus. We incorporated a wide range of theoretical 'insights', 'frameworks', 'reference points' and even just plain 'theories'. But throughout, our intention has been to tell a coherent story, to develop an empirical model, to provide an account or description which would be accessible to policy-makers in Uganda, the Overseas Development Administration, the international agencies and non-governmental organizations, so as to inform their decisions as to whether and how to intervene in response to the downstream effects of the epidemic.

In the great divide between 'Grand Theory' and 'Abstracted Empiricism', we have fallen somewhere in the middle. C Wright Mills's distinction (Mills 1970) was, of course, more a polemical device than an account of how social science research is done. In *practice* (and we use that term advisedly), the activities of 'doing theory' and 'being empirical' are reflexive, and it is this reflexity which is involved in the 'doing' which is one of the focuses of this chapter. Those who 'do theory' as a genus of mind game develop logical/lexical systems which may mislead and discourage innovation (as was the case in the latter days of the hegemonies of 'dependency theory' and 'political economy') as the institutional structure of research encourages paradigm-filling rather than theoretical imagination, testing and development. When this happens, the science rapidly disappears from the social science.

Buttel and McMichael (Chapter 2) make a distinction between 'sociologists of development' and 'development practitioners'. We appear to fall into the chasm between these two positions. We believe that it *is* productive to occupy the middle ground between 'theory' and 'practice'. While recognizing that theory and practice can be conceived of as separate discourses, we do not believe that they should be. Good work in social science comes from the tension between these two ways of operating. Buttel and McMichael argue for a greater separation of 'development sociology' and 'development practice' – which are 'seen as related but distinct areas of work, mainly on account of their different levels of analysis and different problematics' (p. 44). Such manicheism raises acute identity crises for those who see themselves as 'jobbing social scientists' – people who do both, and consider that doing both is what social science can be about.

The problem since the early 1970s has not only been that the search for 'universals' has been urged on by the demands of 'practice'. Any practitioner (colonial administrator, politician, agronomist) would have highlighted the diversity of 'development' to the naïve academic social scientist eager to explain everything (and nothing) by reference to a simplifying general theory. And such a practitioner might also have suggested more or less gently that the lack of practical experience and also of rigorous, empirically informed research (sometimes encouraged by the institutional structure of academic sociology) had led to just the kind of universalism which Buttel and McMichael are so uneasy with.

Hence, we and they agree as to the problem – undue generalization – but differ as to how we would account for this phenomenon.

There is an activity which might be called 'theoretically informed empiricism'. This activity involves the choice, collection and organization of social and economic material with the intention of developing generalized empirical models which can be used to illuminate and explore the complexities of a range of specific social and economic phenomena. Max Weber was perhaps the greatest original exponent of this approach. It is in the processes of choice, collection and organization of data that the main theoretical work is done, and it is in this process that the reflexivity to which we have referred is situated. The output of this activity is the production of a 'coherent story'. It is the role of 'theory' (or, the reader may decide, absence of theory) in one example of this type of research activity which we discuss here. In the next section we briefly outline the broad research problem; in those following, we discuss the way we interpreted the data.

AIDS in Africa[2]

In many parts of Sub-Saharan Africa, the Human Immunodeficiency Virus (HIV) is widespread and many people are currently suffering from Acquired Immune Deficiency Syndrome (AIDS). The number of people with AIDS will increase dramatically in the coming decade given current rates of seropositivity (evidence of HIV infection). In Africa, AIDS predominantly affects men and women aged between 15 and 50. In addition, about 10 per cent of cases are found among very young children who have been infected by their mothers.

The overall demographic impact may be severe, resulting in population downturn (Anderson *et al.* 1991). It is now clear that the local and regional socio-economic impact of the disease is likely to be considerable, particularly in communities which depend very largely on subsistence agriculture for their livelihoods (Abel *et al.* 1988; Barnett and Blaikie 1989). In such societies, a disease specifically affecting the most productive age cohorts will have implications for labour supply to both the farm and the domestic sphere. Studies in Uganda make it clear that the disease has been long established in some rural areas (Government of Uganda 1989; Musagara *et al.* 1989) and is affecting the population structure in some communities. There can be little doubt this is also the case for other regions of Africa.

This is a human tragedy for the victims of the disease and for their families. From a broader perspective, it may also have very profound social and economic implications. Africa has experienced a secular decline in food production per capita since the early 1970s and is therefore particularly vulnerable to further shocks affecting agricultural production. In most African countries subsistence production based on human labour power is the main source of food for the majority of the population. Thus, a disease with an age-cohort specific impact which reduces labour inputs to agriculture may have a disproportionate effect.

While this tragedy might be supposed to result in a stepped reduction of producers and consumers, leaving overall food supply per capita stable, we believe that the cohort specific impact may actually result in disruption of food production systems in some regions and localities as the dependency ratio rises, resulting in reduction of overall food supply. There would also be many other associated negative social and economic effects.

Results from Uganda

In rural areas of Rakai District, Uganda, AIDS-related deaths and illness are having profound effects on the lives of some households and communities. These effects include changes in agricultural practices and in the structure of households. Given the high levels of HIV seropositivity reported from Uganda,[3] and evidence that the disease is now well established in rural areas, it can be assumed that changes such as those currently observed in Rakai District may also be occurring in other parts of Uganda as well as more widely on the continent.

In so far as the most severely affected parts of the Rakai District are characterized by good soils, frequent and dependable rainfall and a large range of food crops, it is likely that other, less favoured, areas of Uganda and Africa may be experiencing, or about to experience, severe pressures on the coping capability of households in both domestic and farm work.

Table 9.1 Rakai District:
Seropositivity by Age
and Gender (per cent)

Age Group	Males	Females
10–14	0.0	5.0
15–19	5.0	30.5
20–24	25.0	42.0
25–29	35.0	31.0
30–34	30.0	22.0
35–39	15.0	22.0
40–44	20.0	20.0
45–49	19.0	15.0
50–54	5.0	14.0
55–59	0.0	9.0
>60	0.0	0.5

Source: Musagara *et al.* (1989)

Comparatively little is known about rates of rural seropositivity in Africa generally. However, the rates shown in Table 9.1 suggest that in this area of Uganda the disease is well established. Given what we know of the progress of the disease, such rates of seropositivity will be matched by a corresponding number of deaths in the future, the timing of these deaths depending upon the mean survival rate after initial infection, which in African circumstances appears to be around five or six years.

Population data from Rakai District suggest that such rates of sero-positivity are matched by under-representation of people in the age cohorts five years ahead of peak recorded seropositivity. Table 9.2 shows the age and gender distribution for five villages. Villages 1 and 2 are in areas widely acknowledged by outsiders and local people to be seriously affected, while villages 3 and 4, although also in Rakai District, are in sub-counties which are said to be less seriously affected, and village 5, in Kigezi, is distant from the main centres of infection. These data describe families rather than households, and thus the under-representation of certain age groups cannot be explained by labour migration or marriage out of the local community.

Table 9.2 shows that there is a marked under-representation of women in the age cohorts 20–24 and 25–29, and of men in the age cohort 30–34 in villages 1 and 2 as compared with villages 3, 4 and 5. In addition, it will be noted that there appear to be more children aged 0–4 in the affected villages than in the 'unaffected' villages. This may be indicative of the presence of unusual numbers of orphans in these villages.

Table 9.2 Age stucture in two sets of villages, males and females

Ages	Males				Females			
	Affected villages (1, 2)		Unaffected villages (3, 4, 5)		Affected villages (1, 2)		Unaffected villages (3, 4, 5)	
	(no.)	(%)	(no.)	(%)	(no.)	(%)	(no.)	(%)
0–4	21	16.8	53	12.7	21	13.8	47	11.5
5–9	18	14.4	58	13.9	19	12.5	59	14.5
10–14	16	12.8	52	12.5	27	17.7	48	11.7
15–19	15	12.0	51	12.3	27	17.7	53	12.9
20–24	18	14.4	38	9.2	12	7.9	46	11.3
25–29	11	8.8	38	9.2	4	2.6	38	9.3
30–34	1	0.8	30	7.2	10	6.6	25	6.1
35–39	4	3.2	20	4.8	10	6.6	29	7.1
40–44	7	5.6	18	4.3	6	3.9	16	3.9
45–49	3	2.4	16	3.8	7	4.6	13	3.2
50–54	6	4.8	13	3.1	2	1.3	10	2.5
55–59	0	0.0	4	0.9	6	3.9	5	1.2
>60	5	4.0	24	5.7	1	0.6	19	0.6
Total	125	100.0	415	99.6	152	99.7	408	99.8

Source: Rakai District

We conclude that these data are indicative of present and future labour loss in some rural areas of Uganda.

Eclecticism, pragmatism or random choices?

The research discussed in this chapter was done under a contract from the Overseas Development Administration. The goal was to provide a coherent account of the HIV impact using the conceptual tools available to us. Given the disciplinary training and experience of the two principal researchers (in sociology/social anthropology/political science and environmental science respectively), together with interdisciplinary constitution of our base at the School of Development Studies, University of East Anglia, such an account was unlikely to be restricted to any one discipline. Rather, it was bound to use concepts and methods as they fitted our attempt to tell a coherent story.

One very simple way of approaching this problem might have been '*merely* descriptive', providing a list of the problems which exceptional demographic change seemed to produce and then indicating the responses which we observed or were told about. However, (apart from our scepticism as to whether 'description' is ever 'simple') we preferred to provide some provisional answers to the following, broader, analytical questions which were of interest to policy-makers.

1   Was there evidence of 'exceptional demographic change'? If so, was it related to the AIDS epidemic?
2   Were there lessons to be learned from 'disaster theory' which might act as a guide to the social and economic impact of AIDS in Africa?
3   What did the concept of 'coping' mean and how could it be operationalized?
4   What was the socio-economic history of the epidemic in Uganda? What could we learn from this?
5   What were the likely effects of the disease on farming systems?

All of these questions relate to the policy issues arising from wanting to do something about a serious threat to people's welfare in a poor and deeply traumatized society. In other words, this work had its origins not only in the world of the academy, but also in ethical concerns related to the world outside the academy.

In the next section, we outline the main conceptual and analytical approaches which were useful in trying to answer these questions. Of course, the research questions were not all posed a priori as the preceding list might suggest. Indeed only some of them were foreseen as research problems. Others came out of the research process as it developed. Looking at this list now, it is apparent that neither the list nor the conceptual framework underlying it is particularly coherent. In some respects, it constitutes an eclectic assemblage (or jumble) of theoretical genres – which could be a definition of post-modernism! Or it might be described as a pragmatic approach – or even just plain random.

The research questions which we considered

Research question 1: Was there evidence of 'exceptional demographic change'? If so, was it related to the AIDS epidemic?

When we began the research in 1987, work by demographers and epidemiologists (for example Anderson *et al.* 1988) was moving towards the view that the epidemic would have major demographic effects, but this view was hedged around with reservations recognizing that there were serious data inadequacies. We had to examine this question in the field and in relation to a small area of Uganda. To this end we collected some very simple population statistics – age and gender distributions in a number of rural communities – and placed these against other data on rates of seroprevalence collected by other researchers. The results of this analysis appear in Tables 9.1 and 9.2.

Although not conclusive (our sample was too small) the close relation between the two tables suggested that we were observing demographic change related to the epidemic. Such a conclusion was supported by other data on the temporal incidence of orphaning in the area (Hunter 1989a; 1989b; Hunter and Dunn 1989).

Research question 2: Were there lessons to be learned from 'disaster theory' which might act as a guide to the social and economic impact of AIDS in Africa?

There were two possible sources for answering this type of question. One was historical accounts of other outbreaks of epidemic disease, the other the experience of other more contemporary 'disasters' such as hurricanes, earthquakes, droughts and famines.

We explored the first part of the question through a search of the historical literature. The result was largely inconclusive as the information available on the two main epidemics which might have been of help (the Black Death in Europe and the Sleeping Sickness epidemic which affected part of Central Africa in the late nineteenth century) did not contain the level of detail which would have enabled valid comparisons to be made.

Our understanding of the mainstream literature about disasters did, however, provide some valuable insights. This literature indicates that 'disasters do not happen, they unfold', which is to say that the structural predeterminants of disasters are formed over long periods and render sections of a population vulnerable to discrete events such as dry periods, earth tremors, and so on. Natural events are to be seen only as a 'trigger' to a disaster and the character of the society and economy in which this trigger occurs is now seen as crucial in understanding its precise impact (Caldwell *et al.* 1986; Cutler 1986; Longhurst 1986; Corbett 1988). We found it useful to adopt this perspective. But, as will become clear in what follows, we made some additions to the existing paradigm. In particular, we consider that there are important differences between the AIDS pandemic and other disasters in that the latter are usually identified by a discrete event, whereas in the case of the AIDS pandemic the early stages cannot be easily identified by the population without recourse to blood tests and wide dissemination of a relatively complex and new set of medical information. Thus we describe the AIDS epidemic as a 'long wave disaster' – one in which the disaster is well established before it is socially identified as a disaster or even as a problem.

The AIDS pandemic differs from other disaster events in two ways. It is slow acting and almost surreptitious, with no clear trigger mechanism. Thus the incremental rate of increased mortality associated with AIDS may mean that communities are not aware of the extent and novelty of the crisis until well into the pandemic. Therefore experimentation in coping with the causes and results of the disease will be delayed. In order to understand these processes, we had to give consideration to the notion of 'coping'.

Research question 3: What did the concept of 'coping' mean and how could it be operationalized?

Here we looked to theoretical perspectives ranging from psychology to anthropology (Murphy and Moriarty 1976; Watts 1988). Crisis events occur from time to time in people's lives and in the lives of whole communities and societies. Such events call for the mobilization of resources to cope with their impact. When people know an event will occur because it has happened in the past, they develop ways of coping with it in advance.

People make their decisions upon the basis of the knowledge that, sooner or later, a particular event will occur and represents a risk concerning which they have some stored subjective estimate and experience of how to cope. For example births, deaths and marriages will occur for all households, and likewise droughts or floods cause widespread loss from time to time to those living in physically hazardous environments. It can be assumed that people do not like conditions of uncertainty where there are no known and familiar ways of coping with a particular unprecedented event.

In situations where communities and households are increasingly affected by illness and death (such as in the AIDS pandemic), the balance is perceived over time to move between the known and the unknown. At the margin, another single death may seem like any other. But when large numbers die, and are perceived to do so as a result of unprecedented causes, established coping mechanisms may begin to show signs of stress. In such circumstances, expectations derived from past experience increasingly become a poor guide to the solution of management problems in the present: coping becomes difficult. The circumstances of everyday life become increasingly uncertain and therefore stressful and puzzling. Confronted by such uncertainty in the decision environment, it is to be expected that a range of 'experiments' will be undertaken by households and communities as their experience of the new situation increases. Such 'experiments' can be seen as attempts to reverse the balance between the unknown and the known in a search for normalization and predictability. In the case of a disease such as AIDS, where the nature and epidemiology of the disease means that the onset of 'abnormality' is very gradual, but where the rapidity of spread increases as a critical mass of HIV+ people is reached, the period of transition and experimentation may be expected to be quite long and delayed. The duration of the crisis, whether long or short, will provide advantages and disadvantages from the perspective of developing coping mechanisms, whether these are local mechanisms (for example new ways of caring for orphans) or society-wide policies (for example developing a health budget which takes into account large numbers of AIDS sufferers).

In order to operationalize this perspective, we identified 'coping' as another word for 'management'. A prerequisite for managing a crisis is that it must be socially recognized. In other words, a household or a community must explicitly define the situation as one which is 'abnormal', and which is not manageable by recognized coping strategies.

In an affected household, illness or death of one member may be accepted as 'normal', but subsequent illness and deaths which follow an unprecedented pattern will force recognition that an 'abnormal' situation has developed. In an affected community, this transition may occur because a large number of households are affected, or because people from outside the community define the situation as unprecedented. Or both of these things may happen at the same time.

In Rakai district, most households have now been forced to recognize that there is a crisis. People are beginning to think about new ways of managing what is now defined as a novel situation. These innovations include: calls for special by-laws to control prostitutes and infected men, the formation of local NGOs to care for orphans, and the restructuring of households. These are examples of experimentation and new forms of action.

Transitions in the coping process
Defining 'coping' as 'management' led us to consider the further question of how coping altered over time, recognizing that there is probably a series of transitions in the coping process. These might include some or all of the following dimensions.

The different levels of coping. Coping strategies will operate at various levels. There is the individual level, based upon the resources which one independent person can mobilize. There is the household level, where typically resources of land, labour, tools and technology along with the parenting, caring and supportive roles of the family are available for disposal among its members. Above this there is the 'community level' consisting of kin, patrons and neighbours. These resources may be mobilized and distributed according to a variety of institutional rules, and they typically involve the provision of employment opportunities, food and labour on a communal basis to assist affected households, and substitution of new arrangements for the various roles of the household as indicated above, when for some reason the household members themselves cannot fulfil them. Above all of the preceding levels lie the national and international levels.

Changes in rules of behaviour. There is usually a set of rules (some explicit, others implicit) which prioritizes people according to their culturally defined access to the different resources which may be available to cope with a crisis. Often there is competition for scarce resources. In the case of famine, men may eat before women and may leave to find alternative employment opportunities sooner than women, children and elderly people, who may be left behind to die. Status within the household is often based upon gender and age. Hence, we had to consider the possibility that the impact of AIDS would be different for men and women, adults and children and for rich and poor households.

Hierarchies of expectation. In any culture people can be assumed to have a hierarchy of expectations which may be subject to change in the face of a crisis. The highest expectation might include self-respect, a sense of worth and the giving and receiving of affection. A lesser expectation may be an acceptable standard of living now and in the future, while lower ones are a minimum food intake, shelter and, at the lowest level, basic physical security and survival in the short term. Usually coping requires the redeployment of resources to maintain the highest level of expectations possible for those groups which hold power. In the most severe crises resources may simply not be available and each level of expectation may sequentially have to be abandoned. In the worst case of famine for example, all expectations of anything but the next meal are long since forgotten.

Perceptions of crisis in Buganda
The area of Uganda known as Buganda is the home of the Ganda people. Prior to colonization by the British this region formed an integrated state ruled by a king, the Kabaka. The strong ethnic identity of the Ganda people and their tradition of statehood meant that they maintained a degree of political autonomy (and at times even sought secession from Uganda) until the late 1960s.

The perceptions of crisis in response to the AIDS pandemic are largely based upon the communal experience of the presence of many sick people and their eventual deaths. Variations in perception from place to place principally reflect the present state of diffusion of infection.

Whether or not there is a 'crisis' is a question of perspective. In some circumstances (such as with AIDS) a crisis may be recognized at an early stage by an observer, while it may not necessarily be recognized by the people directly affected. We suggest that it may be an important characteristic of a long-wave crisis or disaster that recognition may be delayed, masked for those most directly involved by other short-term and more immediate concerns.

Evidence from Buganda suggests, however, that the people most directly involved, those in the rural communities of Rakai where most mortalities have occurred, *do* see themselves as living in a crisis situation. Of course, the evidence of crisis is sickness and death and not levels of HIV. An example of the recognition of this crisis is the way in which the people compare what they are currently living through to their recent experience of war and civil unrest. In contrast to their experiences during the long period of political instability and armed conflict which characterized Uganda during the 1970s and early 1980s, the new crisis is defined by people as a double crisis – a crisis of beliefs and of expectations as to the expected rewards of 'normal' life and what the future may hold.

Thus, for example, one person commented that

> With AIDS we are now on the front line just as we were during the Liberation War of 1979. Then we were prisoners of that war, now we are prisoners of AIDS. Those, of us who are ill are under sentence of death.

In addition, the ways in which the disease is named reflects a sense of its abnormality. It is referred to in the following terms:

- *Mukenena* – the one that drains
- *Lukonvuba* – an incurable disease
- *Mubbi* – the robber.

It is apparent that for many people in most affected areas, the sense of abnormality and therefore uncertainty is very deep. Expectations about the purpose of life, personal fulfilment and relationships with children and grandchildren have all been profoundly disturbed.

Analysing coping strategies
We defined coping as the management of resources under conditions of stress. These conditions often arise and coping mechanisms are devised a priori and activated after a trigger event. Recognized courses of action, based on past experience, are then adopted. However, the AIDS pandemic does not follow the pattern of other types of disasters since its overt symptoms (illness and death) are slow to make their impact in the long initial stages. Repeated deaths and widespread illness gradually impose pressures on accepted and normal ways of coping with these events. A point of crisis is reached when the situation is widely perceived to be abnormal. Past patterns of behaviour and expectations fail to provide a guide to what may be expected in the future.

One area in which we operationalized this perspective was in relation to the ways in which farm households responded to labour loss (others included care of orphans and of the elderly, and funeral arrangements in an environment where there were a lot more funerals than had previously been the case). In order to do this we used the following analytical parameters:

1 AIDS Status

2 Household Development Stage
3 Socio-Economic Status
4 Producer–Consumer Ratio.

We adopted a working definition of a household as 'a group of people, some of whom may be related by a sexual union or by descent and who recognize the common management of their domestic and economic life'. Within this general definition, we allowed respondents to define their household in their own way, accepting their subjective account of the structure of their household. We then considered the ways in which the four analytical parameters appeared to affect household coping.

AIDS Status. We sub-divided households as follows:

1 *Unaffected* These are households in which no member is ill or has died from AIDS and which has not been affected by the illness or death of a member of any related household. Being unaffected can be specified more precisely as a situation in which no additional burden, of either time or economic or financial resources, has to be borne on behalf of a member of this household or another. Of course, in reality, few households in Buganda are totally unaffected by the impact of the disease.
2 *AIDS Afflicted* In this type of household, the impact of the epidemic has been direct. A member of the household is either currently ill or has died from the disease. Resources have to be reallocated in order to deal with the problem.
3 *AIDS Affected* This type of household has been affected by the disease either through the death of a family (not household) member who was contributing cash, labour or other support, or because the death or illness of a family member has meant that, for example, orphans have come to join the household. These are all events which place additional demands on existing resources.

Each of these types of household circumstance will require different general strategies for coping with the AIDS pandemic. There will also be differences within these types. These differences will reflect differing levels of 'vulnerability' as measured by a household's store of assets, production capabilities and position in the market.

Household Development Stage. In normal times, households are established, grow (with the birth of children), and then contract as their members grow older, children leave, and so on. The point at which AIDS intervenes in this process is significant. For analytical purposes, we defined households as 'young', 'mature' and 'in decline'. As a rough indication of this, we used the age of the household head (male or female) as the main indicator. Thus, we may say that in a young household the household head (male or female) is aged less than 30, in a mature household between 30 and 55, in a declining household over 55 years of age. However, this is only a very rough guide. A very old man who has married a young woman and started a new family has characteristics of both a declining and a young household. Indeed we found that one way in which men can cope with old age is to remarry and thus effectively prolong the mature stage of the household.

Socio-Economic Status. We divided households into the three broad categories: rich, middle and poor. These are, of course, relative terms. In practice, we distinguished them as follows:

1 *Rich*   These household will have some or all of the following attributes: adequate or surplus land, ability to hire labour, involvement in trade or other non-agricultural occupation.
2 *Middle*   This type of household may have non-agricultural sources of income, may occasionally employ labour, and will certainly have adequate land or sufficient non-agricultural income to be able to rent land or purchase food.
3 *Poor*   In these households there will be land shortages, labour shortages which cannot be met by hiring, and few if any sources of cash income, or alternatively, the land resources may be so low as to require that household labour is sold.

Combining these criteria produced a matrix of eighteen possible 'types' of household of which twelve are either AIDS affected or AIDS afflicted.

Analysis of case material showed that the impact of AIDS was differentiated between households. The following general conclusions were possible.

1 Consideration of the effects of AIDS deaths and illness must recognize the interrelated nature of farm and household in such communities. Loss of labour affects not only the agricultural work but also the domestic sphere. Thus general household management, nutritional status, hygiene and child care may all be affected.
2 Deaths of adult children may reduce cash remittances to these households.
3 Deaths of urban-based family members may result in additional burdens for rural households as the orphaned children return to their grandparents.
4 The resource endowments of a household as well as its development status are important in understanding its vulnerability to mortality and morbidity.
5 Loss of a household member involves the loss of not only a 'hand' but also a 'head', and thus managerial ability and technical knowledge.
6 In some cases, the agricultural response is to neglect cash crops (mainly coffee in this area) in favour of food crops.
7 One response to labour loss is to reduce the range of food crops being grown, or to retain the range of crops while restricting the cultivated area, sometime by resort to inter-cropping.
8 In this area of high soil fertility and rainfall, some households are having to alter their domestic and agricultural arrangements in response to AIDS.

238

Producer–Consumer Ratio. We used this concept as follows. In most interviews, both men and women were invited to comment on household composition. Detailed interviews were undertaken with a randomly selected sample of 129 households of which 109 were unaffected by AIDS-related illness or death. Eight reported themselves as being affected by AIDS (defined as receiving orphans or other relatives as a result of AIDS deaths in other households, or having lost cash income as a result of the death or illness of a member of the family), eight reported themselves as afflicted (suffering present illness or past death(s)) and four reported themselves as being both afflicted and affected. We use the concept of the producer–consumer ratio as a way of understanding these data.

We plotted changes in producer–consumer (p/c) ratios over the five years up to 1989. These changes include births, deaths from all causes and arrivals/departures of household members for reasons of marriage, employment, etc. The distribution of p/c ratios was divided into three ranges: favourable – where the ratio had become more favourable (the number of producers per consumer had increased); neutral – where the change was insignificant; and unfavourable – where the change had resulted in there being a greater number of consumers than producers.

Of the total of 129 households in the questionnaire-based survey, 48 (37 per cent) had experienced a favourable change in their p/c ratio. 15 (12 per cent) had experienced no significant change, and are said to be neutral, and 66 (51 per cent) had experienced an unfavourable change. Of the 66 households in which the change in p/c ratio was unfavourable, 14 (21 per cent) were households either affected or afflicted by AIDS.

There are of course many reasons other than AIDS which may result in an unfavourable ratio of producers to consumers. But the important point to note is that among all those households which had experienced an unfavourable change in this ratio, 21 per cent also reported themselves as being AIDS affected, AIDS afflicted or both. In contrast, among the 48 households in which the p/c ratio has become more favourable, only 5 (10 per cent) fell into any of these categories. In the 'neutral' range, 6 per cent of households (one case) were AIDS affected, AIDS afflicted or both.

We asked respondents what had been the main effects of the changes in their household composition in the last five years. This section of the questionnaire was not pre-coded and when the responses were analysed they did not indicate any clear difference between the three categories of change in p/c ratio. Whilst the most common responses from all households were that they had less labour on the farm (24 per cent of all households), had more mouths to feed (12.6 per cent of all households), were cultivating less land (12.6 per cent) and now had more work to do on the farm (11.4 per cent of all households), there was no statistically significant difference in response between the AIDS affected, AIDS afflicted and other households. Clearly, other factors since the early 1980s, particularly the deteriorating economic situation and collapse of established marketing networks and the co-operative system has caused hardship to many households, regardless of AIDS.

While it is difficult to distinguish these 'background' effects from the specific impact of AIDS, it *was* observed that among AIDS affected and afflicted households, there was a marked feeling that they had more mouths to feed as a result of the impact of the disease. The detailed response of households to AIDS was elicited by means of an open-ended questionnaire. Interviewees were allowed to list any number of responses, so that the 129 households gave a total of 167 responses concerning how they had been affected by changes in the producer/consumer ratio over the previous five years. Responses were tabulated by the categories *unaffected, affected* and *afflicted* (for more detailed discussion and data on this analysis, see Barnett and Blaikie 1992: 100–4). Although the cell size is usually too small to draw statistically significant conclusions, most of the differences between unaffected households, on the one hand, and afflicted or affected households on the other hand, are marked and in the expected direction.

For example, affected and afflicted households have a higher rate of taking children out of school than do unaffected, because they are forced to pay greatly increased school fees for orphans who have joined the household. Affected households too are most aware that they have more mouths to feed. In the main, hiring in of labour remains within the capabilities only of unaffected households, with the exception of one wealthy household, which although affected and afflicted by AIDS was able to adopt this strategy. Although afflicted households appear to reduce the area of land cultivated for obvious reasons of labour short-age, the percentage of households doing so is no different from that among unaffected households. Thus it is not possible to conclude that the overall cultivated area in this region is declining as a result of the demographic impact of AIDS. Simply, there have been many other disruptive events in recent Ugandan history which have also discour-aged cultivation. Loss of remittances and other cash income is another important impact of AIDS upon households who have both received orphans and lost household members. However, from these data, there is some small, but once again we must emphasize, not statistically sig-nificant, indication that change in the expected direction is occurring, and is manifested in pressure on household resources and attempts to hire labour from other households in the communities.

Research question 4: What was the socio-economic history of the epidemic in Uganda? What could we learn from this?

If disasters do not just happen but are waiting to occur, then the way a particular disease affects a particular society will reflect aspects of that society's sociology, economy, culture and history. In order to pursue this point, we developed the concept of 'risk ecology'.

Much in the AIDS literature employs the concept of 'risk behaviours'. Indeed, the WHO's classification of the epidemic patterns found in different regions of the world is based on type of behaviour (see e.g. Wellcome Foundation 1989). Such a perspective is useful in a brief descriptive typology, but it was limited for our purposes as it tends to individualize the problems underlying epidemiology, according primacy to the act of transmission rather than locating that act within a context and relating it to processes which may mean that a specific act may be high risk in one place but not in another.

The seroprevalence data in Table 9.1 shows that in certain areas of Uganda, sexual intercourse of any kind amounts to risky behaviour; in other places it may not be very high risk behaviour. Such an observation does not tell us a great deal about why heterosexual intercourse has taken on this complexion in this place. More useful is an understanding of the social, economic and historical factors which have produced this particular spatial distribution of risk. In other words, we considered it useful to balance the concept of risky behaviour with that of a risky environment or area.

Adopting this perspective, we arrived at the following analysis. It seems likely that a certain set of conditions may have contributed to the rapid spread of the disease in this area. The immediate causes of the rapid spread of the disease are directly related to the pattern of sexual contact. These can be established only very approximately through epidemiological modelling, but since empirical studies on sexual networks in Africa are even more inadequate that those for Europe and the United States we had no data to go on.

There is still doubt about the relative importance of different parameters, but two are very important. These are the mean rate of sexual partner change and the variance of sexual partner change between sexual activity classes. Also the movement patterns of sexual partners for reasons such as journey to work and seasonal migration constitute another important set of variables which probably help to determine the spatial diffusion of the pandemic. There are other important variables referring to the age of sexual partners of either gender which influence the demographic impact of the disease. As a first approximation, some of the social and economic circumstances lying behind the epidemiological pattern of the disease in Buganda appeared to be: the high mean rate of sexual partner change, in some circumstances a high mixing of partners across sexual activity classes, and a high spatial mixing of sexual partners.

In Uganda, it is very difficult to provide a rigorous account of the impact of social disruption since the early 1970s upon the patterns of sexual activity most associated with the rate of spread of AIDS. Unfortunately, there is virtually no information about the patterns of other sexually transmitted diseases (STDs), so they cannot be used as 'markers' to trace the impact of rapid and disruptive social change upon sexual practice over this period. Therefore, we arrived at a set of reasoned hypotheses concerning four related areas of rapid socio-economic change. Three concern factors which are associated with the decline of the Ugandan state: first, the existence of a lively illicit economy (*magendo* – Southall 1980) beginning during the Amin period but continuing to some extent into the present; second, warfare, and third, general civil unrest. A fourth area concerns the status of women in Buganda.

RETHINKING SOCIAL DEVELOPMENT

We discuss the last point briefly. It seems very likely that women's lack of access to land and other economic resources, except through a relationship with a man, has been of considerable importance. At the height of the *magendo* period the incomes of men (who were the main participants in and beneficiaries of illicit trade) and women became grossly unequal. In order to gain access to the considerable wealth which fell into male hands during this period, women traded sexual favours. In addition, the very nature of *magendo* involved considerable male spatial mobility and resultant disassortative mixing between sexual activity classes. This spatial mobility and disassortative mixing was further increased in the period of the Tanzanian invasion and the civil war.

Research question 5: What were the likely effects of the disease on farming systems?

An important focus in this research was on the ways in which farming systems might respond to labour loss. Briefly, it could be assumed that the more peaked the demand for labour (as determined by climate and soils, and thus crop types) and the smaller the crop portfolio typical of any particular system (again related to climate and soils), the more sensitive or vulnerable a farming system would be to the loss of labour. Thus, farming systems could be described as more or less sensitive to labour loss in the productive age groups.

We defined a farming system very broadly as describing the combination of climate, soils, crops and human resources which characterize the dominant mode of agricultural production in a defined geographic area. We did not include social and cultural aspects. For Uganda, the most comprehensive and up-to-date description of farming systems was to be found in the unpublished work of Johnson and Ssekitoleko (1989).

We then attempted a very broad classification of the farming systems of Uganda and developed a method for assessing their vulnerability to labour loss. However, we were very aware that within any farming system, the socio-economic impact of the disease may be experienced more acutely and earlier by some households than by others. Within 'vulnerable' systems it is poorer and older households which will face economic stress earliest, and that even within the least vulnerable systems the early impact may be felt by a minority of households although not by the generality of them.

The degree to which a farming system is vulnerable to loss of labour depends upon a number of characteristics. How these characteristics are defined may be determined more by the availability of data and the form in which they are collected than by any analytical design. Johnson and Ssekitoleko have defined fifty farming systems in Uganda but recognize that the quality of their data leaves much to be desired.

Bearing this in mind, the following general characteristics were used to assess the vulnerability of a farming system to labour loss:[4]

1 Whether the farming system already has a shortage of energy or

protein. While it may be possible for individual producers to adapt successfully to labour loss in a variety of ways, the existence of systemic food shortage in the first place suggests a lack of access to land, labour, or capital, making adaptations more difficult.

2   Whether labour supply is currently less than demand at any time during the agricultural calendar. The product-mixes of different farming systems vary in their labour demand profile. In general terms the more seasonally peaked the demand, the more vulnerable the system will be to labour loss. Such peaking is, of course, closely related to the rainfall regime in an area.

3   Whether there are substitutable staple crops requiring a lower level of maximum labour input, which will provide sufficient energy and protein.

Applying this approach to the fifty farming systems identified by Johnson and Ssekitoleko, we were able to identify nine as 'very vulnerable', having existing shortages of protein and energy as well as of labour. Seventeen were identified as vulnerable on either the criterion of existing or potential labour shortages or that of existing protein and energy deficits. The remainder were not vulnerable by the criteria adopted in this method.

Discussion

Having outlined the nature of the research, we now consider the ways we used 'theory' in doing it. In particular, we consider two groups of issues: the various forms of 'coherence', the choice of units of analysis and its implications for the development of theory, and the relations between the theoretical choices and political attitudes and beliefs.

Coherence

One important question which must be posed about this research which has been so eclectic in its use of conceptual and theoretical tools, is whether or not it is 'coherent', and if it is 'coherent', for whom is it 'coherent'? 'Coherence' is an important idea implying that an explanation somehow fits together in a 'logical' way, and 'makes sense'. It is one of the goals of theoretical projects and it is also one of the goals of analytical description.

At one level, in an extreme form, 'theoretical coherence' refers to 'a systematically related set of statements, including some law-like generalizations, that is empirically testable' (Rudner 1966: 10). Theories of this type should be logically coherent in the sense that they form a 'completely articulated deductive system' (Rudner 1966: 11). Although this may be the goal of some theoreticians in the social sciences, few of us would now aspire to such rigour except in the most restricted type of theoretical statement. However, at the level of 'Grand Theory' there has been no lack of attempts to develop such all-encompassing, universalistic, conceptual frameworks. The work of the 'schools' of Talcott Parsons and Louis Althusser and the mode of production debate are examples. Often, these have required the development of complex and very specialized lexicons. They have involved the elaboration of specialized discourses, new (or at least lexically new) ways of describing the world – new paradigms.

We believe that in the social sciences the notion of 'theoretical coherence' has most often described the process of lexicalization, and that this language game has often provided a logic which is often more lexical than real in so far as data have frequently been squeezed into the conceptual boxes rather than being used to test their utility. The result has been paradigm-filling at best, and intellectual dishonesty at worst. In particular, this type of language game has sometimes been played to make the data fit the political or ethical orientation of the researcher. The way that for many years some social scientists used the languages of dependency theory and neo-Marxism is a case in point. These 'theories' were able (in most cases) to ignore contrary evidence until the advent of Warren (1980) who chose to use another paradigm which gave weight to contrary evidence. This then made some of us sit up and think anew. For a variety of reasons there did not then occur a paradigm switch; rather we stood embarrassed and bewildered by what we had been doing. This was the essence of David Booth's 'impasse' (Booth 1985) – a retreat from the all-embracing seductiveness and grandiose claims of 'Grand Theory'.

It seems best to see this retreat as leading (for the time being at least) into much more limited projects, projects which bear a resemblance to Merton's 'theories of the middle range' (Merton 1957) or to some of Weber's attempts at constructing ideal types. Such 'theories' offer a different type of 'coherence' from the logical/lexical (and it might be added, political) coherence of 'Grand Theory'. This 'coherence' is the coherence of the analytical description, and it is, we believe, akin to that form of understanding that Weber described as 'causally and meaningfully adequate' (Weber 1978).

Of course, what we should then do with the products of this kind of, empirical modelling is another question. Within the Weberian tradition we should expect to go on to undertake some kind of 'experiment' through comparison. However, mere comparison of units will not be enough – and the suggestion of 'incorporated comparison' (Buttel and McMichael, Chapter 2) seems an interesting one, although very hard to execute in practice. In particular, the implications of this approach are not clear for those who do not wish to take as their empirical focus whole societies or locate their problems in the context of 'the world system'.

There is also the danger that were such a view to become prematurely established as a new 'paradigm' we would find ourselves with a generation of bad historians, rather than one of good social scientists. These might be the postgraduate students produced by an institutional and career structure dominated by such a new orthodoxy, all busy filling out another seductive paradigm at a time when the world we are analysing

ON IGNORING THE WIDER PICTURE

is undergoing profound changes as familiar political and cultural structures dissolve and old certainties, even of a politically correct kind, fall
away.

In what we have been doing in this research, we have most certainly
not achieved theoretical/lexical/discourse coherence – indeed we have
been positively eclectic in our choice of discourses – in terms of both
those we have used and those which we have either chosen to ignore or
not considered as candidates at all. We have, in short, ignored a wide
range of issues by not using certain theoretical concepts.

To take three very important theoretical discourses which we might
have spatchcocked into the analysis, we have not dealt with the issue of
the Ugandan state at all (which is a very interesting question), we have
not looked at the relation between the Ugandan economy and the world
economy, and we have not explored the issue of class relations, using
only the more limited notion of social status. Each of these could have
been used but was not. What we have done is to use a range of dis-
courses/lexicons/theories in order to arrive at some account of the situation for the particular purposes we had in mind. The final product does
not attain coherence at the level of theory. But it does attain some level
of coherence (although unevenly) at the level of analytical description
(the account of the risk ecology, the account of coping strategies) as well
as at the level of meaning (the account of people's experience of crisis).
Thus, the units of analysis we chose were, we would argue, sufficient
for the job in hand.

There is one very important respect in which the results of deploying
these theories and these units of analysis are not theoretically/lexically/
discourse coherent. This is at the level of 'discipline'. This was inevitable
given the interdisciplinary environment in which we work as well as the
fact that we each have very different disciplinary formations. Hence, we
find mixed into one text, discourses drawn from sociology, social
anthropology, agricultural economics, agronomy and environmental
science. How all these different discourses *could* be made coherent is
difficult to envisage except in the context of some unified theory
(General Systems Theory or even Marxism might be candidates). However, an attempt at such theoretical integration was not required by our
sponsors, and would have required attributing primacy to one conceptual framework, and in doing so prematurely closing the analysis. By
adopting an eclectic approach and making our aim coherent description
rather than conceptually coherent theory, we were able to deal with a
wide range of data and suggest how they all related to the analysis of a
problem. This is what the jobbing social scientist should do. In so doing,
differences between social situations (whether whole societies or other
social phenomena) will be brought to the fore, and we will not find
ourselves doing mere paradigm filling.

In the past, attempts at large-scale theory construction have led to
considerable theological (in the sense of filling out paradigms) rather
than scientific work. In short, the premature search for coherence in
social theory has often led social scientists in wrong and unprofitable
directions by closing minds rather than opening them. To use Gluck-

man's vocabulary (Gluckman and Devons 1964), in creating closed theoretical systems we may also have closed minds. This is not to say that theoretical coherence should not be the aim of social science. It is, though, to say that we cannot all be grand theorists all or even any of the time, and also that, in development studies, now is probably not the time.

Theory selection, problematics and beliefs

By now the reader who has stayed the course will be wondering why we actually chose those analytical concepts that we used. Our aim in doing the research was to develop a coherent account of the situation in one country, Uganda, with the intention of indicating areas in which policy intervention might be possible in order to mitigate the worst effects of the epidemic. We were not attempting to make a contribution to the development of social theory. Rather, we were trying to use existing theory so as to make a first stab at illuminating the situation – an enterprise comparable to entering a dark room and shining a very thin torch beam so as to get some idea of the dimensions and main features of the room and some of its contents.

The main analytical concepts that we chose to use were: disaster/ crisis, household, gender relations, coping mechanisms, community, Buganda, Uganda, socio-economic status, household development status, producer–consumer ratio and farming system. In addition, it is worth observing that we also chose to stick to the present apart from a brief excursion into recent history necessary in describing some aspects of the epidemiology of AIDS in Uganda.

These concepts do not naturally form part of any unified theory; indeed they may sometimes be contradictory, most clearly, perhaps, in the simultaneous use of 'the household' and 'gender relations'. The first concept has been criticized for ignoring the importance of gender differentiation, while the latter concept can be seen as deconstructing 'the household', perhaps particularly in the study of Africa where gender roles in household production, reproduction and consumption are so often separate and conflicting. Similarly, the concept of 'Buganda' (used in this research as a description of a culture and a region) conflicts with that of 'Uganda', a nation-state the government of which has actively attempted to dismember 'Buganda', the elite of which, in turn, has at times tried to subvert the state of 'Uganda'. Above all, perhaps, 'socio-economic status' stands out as suspect. There is no more attempt to consider 'class relations' than there is to discuss the relation between Uganda and Buganda. We quite simply did not introduce these issues because they did not seem to offer any marked gain in clarifying and explaining the situation of people trying to cope with the impact of the epidemic.

This list of omissions could be continued. But the point is as follows: each of the concepts contributed to a description. It is not a final description, only a provisional one – all scientific enterprises are provisional; that is the nature of science. It is a description which in its conceptual incoherence (as opposed to its descriptive coherence) opens the way for further questions to be asked. And lastly, it is a description which allowed the clear identification of policy issues which had a chance of being taken seriously by policy-makers. To have entered into an extended discussion of class relationships and of the state, to take two major examples of what is missing from the analysis as it stands, would have weakened the chances of the report being taken into the policy machinery – the introduction of gender as an issue (by white, male foreigners) was sensitive enough. To have effectively threatened some of the administrators and politicians whom we wanted to influence, by discussing the role and nature of the state in all this, might have been scientifically more honest, but would have been less effective.

Inevitably, we omitted to make any explicit political or ethical judgements. This omission was intentional, and should be an important part of the way a jobbing social scientist operates. In this particular case, we chose the problem for very definite ethical reasons, but having done this, we then approached what was a very harrowing research subject as dispassionately as we could using the concepts which seemed best to handle the problem we had set out to analyse and which seemed most likely to be accessible/acceptable to the audiences we were addressing.

However, we were conscious of trying to be good scientists in the sense of collecting/constructing our data with care as well as examining contrary cases and hypotheses. Thus, we tried to avoid the problem so clearly stated by Buttel and McMichael (p. 47) when they say 'We would argue that the problematic or explanandum of development sociology has been shaped so centrally by normative considerations – that is, by an agenda to accomplish certain social goals in the Third World – that its social scientific foundation has been seriously compromised', which we take to mean that people have shaped their conclusions to fit their political/ethical starting-point! We had normative considerations – that the problem was worth researching because it threatened people's welfare. But having made our selection for that reason, we had no political or theoretical axe to grind, our aim being to explain the situation in a way which would be accessible to those in the state (British in the form of the ODA, Ugandan in the form of 'the Ugandan AIDS community') – as well as in the supra-state agencies in the form of the IBRD, WHO, FAO and the NGOs – who were ignorant of the situation.

Such theoretically informed empiricism is in some respects akin to some types of personal therapy. It engages with the realities of social and economic policy, it uses theory in order to make that engagement and to communicate from the academy to the wider world of which it is a part, it is closed in so far as choices have been made as to concepts and discourses, but not as closed as those universalizing theories of an earlier era. Above all it presents a coherent account of a problem to those who have been given (or who have taken upon themselves) the responsibility for confronting such issues, and it may contribute to the clarification of decision processes.

The presentation of such analyses, engaging with both theory and practice, deriving from theoretical work and feeding back into theoretical work, is the task of the jobbing social scientist. While this work is obviously not a foray into 'Grand Theory' and makes no attempt to universalize, it is, we would argue, important work at this stage in the development of development theory.

Notes

1. This research was funded by a grant from the Economic and Social Research Committee of the Overseas Development Administration (ODA). The views expressed are not necessarily endorsed by the ODA or the Government of Uganda.
2. AIDS is not the most serious disease affecting African populations. At present, malaria, bilharzia and diahorreal infections kill more people per year than does AIDS. However, because of the inevitable mortality and the high levels of seropositivity which are recorded or suspected in some African populations, it is a disease which must be taken very seriously indeed. The annual increase in the reported numbers of cases is now very large. It is usual to measure the extent of the disease in cases per million of the population. Rates are reported to the World Health Organization (WHO) by national authorities and published in WHO's bi-weekly report. These statistics have to be treated with caution as they reflect many different kinds of reporting problem, mainly problems of under-reporting. However, it is vital to recognize that while case rates in Africa are often very high, they must be seen against the case rates reported in other parts of the world. Thus, while by December 1991 (reported July 1992) the cumulative number of *reported* AIDS cases (adult and paediatric) in Uganda (population around 16.5 million) totalled 30,190 – 1,830 cases per million – the USA in July 1992 reported a cumulative total of 230,179 cases – 920 cases per million – and the United Kingdom in June 1992 a cumulative total of 6,140 cases – 105 cases per million.
3. In the absence of a detailed serosurvey, estimation of the number of people who are HIV+ in a population is difficult. The 1988 Ugandan National Serosurvey indicated that at that time around 750,000 people were infected. The most recent official estimate of the number of people *seropositive* in Uganda was 'around 1.5 million' in 1991 (statement by Director of the National AIDS Control Programme, July 1991). In comparison, the figure for the USA is an estimate of 'around 1 million' by the Center for Disease Control, July, 1992, while an estimate for the UK is '14,000–15,000' (Department of Health, June 1992).
4. We identified these three characteristics as being the main determinants of the degree of vulnerability to labour loss. However, there are four further local characteristics which can be used to modify the primary classification made on the basis of the characteristics above.

   4 Whether there are significant economies of scale in return to labour involved in major agricultural operations. For example, the transportation of vegetable matter for shifting cultivation, or the herding of cattle, may both have significant economies of scale in return to labour.
   5 Whether there is a marked sexual division of labour, which would accentuate the loss of labour for specific tasks, and how easily and over what time period readjustment of work roles might occur.
   6 Whether there is significant essential maintenance work on conservation

structures such as terracing and bunding (e.g. in the mountainous south-west of Uganda).
7 Whether there is a significant degree of out-migration and non-agricultural remittances, in which case labour losses could be absorbed by either the return of out-migrants and/or the deployment of cash remittances to hire labour.

Unfortunately, we did not have these data to hand, and they are, of course, rarely collected by agronomists concerned with the types of variables we are considering.

References

Abel N, Barnett T, Blaikie P M, Cross J S W and **Bell S** (1988) The impact of AIDS on food production systems in East and Central Africa over the next ten years: a programmatic paper. In: Fleming A F *et al.* (eds) *The global impact of AIDS.* New York, Allan R Liss; Chichester, John Wiley

Anderson R M, May R M and **McLean A R** (1988) Possible demographic consequences of AIDS in developing countries. *Nature* 332

Anderson R M, May R M, Boily M C, Garnett G P and **Rowley J T** (1991) The spread of HIV-1 in Africa: sexual contact patterns and the predicted demographic impact of AIDS. *Nature* 352

Barnett T and **Blaikie P M** (1989) The possible impact of AIDS upon food production in East and Central Africa. *Food policy* 14 (1)

Barnett T and **Blaikie P M** (1992) *AIDS in Africa: its present and future impact.* London, Belhaven Press

Booth D (1985) Marxism and development sociology: interpreting the impasse. *World Development* 13 (7)

Caldwell J C, Reddy P H and **Caldwell P** (1986) Periodic high risk as a cause of fertility decline in changing rural environment: survival strategies in the 1980–1983 South Indian drought. *Economic Development and Cultural Change* 34 (4)

Corbett J (1988) Famine and household coping strategies. *World Development* 16 (9)

Cutler P (1986) The response to drought of Beja famine refugees in Sudan. *Disasters* 10 March

Garine I de and **Harrison G A** (eds) (1988) *Coping with uncertainty in food supply.* Oxford, Clarendon Press

Gluckman M and **Devons E** (1964) *Closed systems and open minds.* Manchester, Manchester University Press

Government of Uganda (Ministry of Health) (1989) AIDS control programme: press release of the national serosurvey for Human Immunodeficiency Virus (HIV) in Uganda. Entebbe, 1 December

Hunter S (1989a) Untitled paper given at the NGO AIDS Coordinating Committee Conference, Institute of Education, University of London, 1 December

Hunter S (1989b) Social aspects of AIDS in Uganda in perspective. Unpublished paper

Hunter S and **Dunn A** (1989) Enumeration and needs assessment of children orphaned by AIDS in Uganda. Poster 292 at the IVth International Conference on AIDS and Associated Cancers in Africa, Marseilles, France, 18–20 October

Johnson D T and **Ssekitoleko Q W** (1989) *Current and Proposed Farming Systems in Uganda.* Farm Management and Economic Research Station, Planning Division, Ministry of Agriculture, Government of Uganda

Longhurst R (1986) Household food strategies in response to seasonality and famine. *IDS Bulletin* 17 (3)

Merton R K (1957) *Social theory and social structure.* Glencoe, IL, Free Press

Mills C W (1970) *The sociological imagination.* Harmondsworth, Penguin

Murphy L M and **Moriarty A B** (1976) Vulnerability, coping and growth. New Haven, CT, Yale University Press

Musagara M, Musgrave S, Biryahwaho B, Serwadda D, Wawer M, Konde-Lule J, Berkley S and **Okware S** (1989) Sero-prevalence of HIV-1 in Rakai District, Uganda. Poster 010 at the IVth International Conference on AIDS and Associated Cancers in Africa, Marseille, France, 18–20 October

Rudner R (1966) *Philosophy of social science.* Englewood Cliff, NJ, Prentice-Hall

Sen A (1981) *Poverty and famines: an essay on entitlement and deprivation.* Oxford, Oxford University Press

Southall A (1980) Social disorganisation in Uganda: before, during and after Amin. *Journal of Modern African Studies* 18

Warren B (1990) *Imperialism: pioneer of capitalism.* London, Verso

Watts M (1988) Coping with the market: uncertainty and food security among Hausa peasants. In: Garine I de and Harrison G A (eds) *Coping with uncertainty in food supply.* Oxford, Clarendon Press

Weber M (1978) *Economy and society: an outline of interpretative sociology,* 2 vols. Berkeley, CA, University of California Press

Wellcome Foundation (1989) *AIDS: a global health crisis.* Berkhamstead, England, The Wellcome Foundation

CHAPTER 10

Social development research and the third sector:
NGOs as users and subjects of social inquiry[1]

David Hulme

The developmental activities of the third sector[2] (local membership organizations, non-governmental organizations (NGOs), international NGOs, social movements, church organizations) have long been a research topic for those interested in social and political change. Activity in this field has intensified in the 1980s as the sector has expanded and found favour with a broad range of supporters. For many concerned with development the third sector has become a source of optimism, promising the 'room for manoeuvre' in development interventions for which they have been searching. There has been an outpouring of academic studies and findings (Johnston and Clark 1982; Tendler 1982; Gran 1983; Esman and Uphoff 1984; Gorman 1984; Hirschman 1984; Uphoff 1986; Elliott 1987a; Korten 1987; OECD 1988; Schneider 1988; Clark 1991).

Increasingly the boundaries between academic research and NGO action have blurred as academics have taken to advising NGOs, taking jobs with NGOs or setting up their own NGOs, and as some practitioners have oscillated between periods in the field and periods of study and reflection. As a consequence of this the direct and indirect mechanisms by which research may influence action, and action may influence research, have become more complex. Despite these interactions, a tension often exists between development 'researchers' and third sector development 'practitioners' who feel that academics have few products that have practical value. As Poulton (1988: 11) puts it 'NGO fieldworkers consider academics to be ignorant of the real world where there is no bookshop, no electricity, no telephones working and frequently no petrol'.

This chapter examines the relationship between social development research and the activities of the third sector and makes proposals about the form that such research should take. Initially it argues that social development research must recognize the relevance of the third sector to its goal of extending the understanding of the processes of economic and social development in the 'Third World' and the consequences of those processes for different groups. This recognition entails greater

251

efforts to develop concepts that can capture the complexity and dynamism of the sector along with more detailed empirical studies. Present
conceptualizations do not permit a thorough exploration of the multiplex, and often contradictory, relationships that local, national and international NGOs have with each other, with the state, with those in
opposition to the state, with different segments of civil society and with
wider international forces.

Subsequently the chapter discusses the relevance of social development research to the third sector, in terms of the capacity of such
research to assist NGOs to achieve the development goals that they
espouse. It accepts that much past academic research has been 'extractive' but contends that relevance could be achieved if in the future
researchers explicitly attempt to link knowledge to action by analysing
the implications of the knowledge they create for the actors involved in
the practice of development. Producing an elegant critique of a development intervention is not sufficient. Researchers must explore the opportunities for practitioners to modify strategy, or even subvert existing
strategies, before they opt for radical pessimism (individuals can do
nothing), or radical jest without analysis (shoot the landlords).

It refutes the claim that relevance can be achieved only by 'action
research' or 'participatory research'. At times such approaches may be
desirable (and may be feasible) but if they were pursued to the exclusion
of more 'conventional approaches' then knowledge which is fundamental not only to the understanding of social and political change, but also
to the selection of strategies by the third sector, would be lost. There is a
distinct likelihood that much of the efforts of this sector, especially in
Asia and Africa, will be of decreasing relevance to development (in
terms of the alleviation of poverty and the strengthening of opportunities for poor people to exercise influence over decisions that affect their
lives) unless the sector is subjected to intensified research that relates
micro-level activities to macro-level processes. In particular, intermediary 'southern' NGOs (SNGOs) require study to determine the ways in
which their relationships with the institutions of the state, political
parties, external financiers and civil society constrain or expand their
'room for manoeuvre'.

The chapter recognizes that heterogeneity is a central feature of the
organization of the third sector, but it attempts to make some broad
generalizations. This is not intended to suggest that the trends identified
are ubiquitous, but rather to promote the more detailed examination of
these trends and their consequences.

The relevance of the third sector to social development research

Those who wish to advance our understanding of the processes of
development must now include within their analytical schema an explanation of why the third sector increased so greatly in size during the

1980s and extended its role from relief and welfare to development and social mobilization.[3] Several reasons can be advanced for social development researchers to conduct a systematic study of the voluntary sector.

Most obvious is the fact that the third sector is now a significant 'player' in terms of attempts to promote development. By 1985 the volume of aid flowing from OECD countries to developing countries through voluntary channels exceeded US$4 billion. This represented more than 13 per cent of total aid flows for that year (van der Heijden 1987: 104) and this proportion increased in the late 1980s. In many countries dense networks of NGOs have memberships that run into millions. For example, in Sri Lanka the Thrift and Credit Movement had a membership of more than 600,000 by 1990 and the Sarvodaya Shramadana Movement operates 9,500 community groups with a membership of the same order of magnitude. The Bangladesh Rural Advancement Committee (BRAC) has similarly impressive figures, while in India the government can barely keep up with the registration of newly formed NGOs. In Rio de Janeiro more than 1,500 spontaneous associations operate (Fuentes and Frank 1989: 184). The situation in Africa is less clear, and varies from relatively well-developed networks of voluntary organizations in some countries (e.g. Kenya) to others where it has been actively discouraged and is negligible (e.g. Somalia). Not only is the third sector operating on a more significant scale, but it is also extending its role in some countries to substitute for government in what might be regarded as classic state functions. In Northern Uganda and Southern Sudan voluntary aid agencies have virtually operated as local administrations, co-ordinating and planning operations across entire districts at times of turmoil. In Bangladesh the government has ceded responsibility for the allocation of newly formed land in some parts of the Bay of Bengal to OXFAM.

Second, this sector merits attention because of the light that it can throw on weaknesses of the state and the market as mechanisms for meeting the needs of society. Its growth, at least in part, is a reflection of dissatisfaction with both state and market. Indeed, its proponents argue that it can function in situations where 'market failure' and 'state failure' have occurred e.g. production credit for micro-entrepreneurs.

Third, a common claim of the voluntary sector, with which most social development researchers would concur, is that poverty is not purely an economic condition but is also a condition of political powerlessness. The sector claims to be able to address this situation through the processes of 'conscientization', 'mobilization', 'empowerment', 'policy advocacy' and, sometimes, 'social transformation'. However, very little has been documented about the ability of the third sector to achieve, or not to achieve, the redistribution of social and political power. Such claims demand analysis by researchers who reject narrow economic notions of development.

Fourth, the sector has managed to gain support (sometimes moral and sometimes material) from a wide range of sources spread across the political spectrum. This ranges from official aid agencies pursuing the policies of market-oriented governments (e.g. USAID and ODA), popu-

253

lists at the political centre (e.g. Korten 1990) and academics of the left (e.g. Fuentes and Frank 1989). It seems unlikely that the values underpinning such a range of political viewpoints can all have converged, and so the phenomenon of the third sector merits attention to understand the role it can play in these differing agendas.

Finally, the sector has a wealth of knowledge about the nature and operations of local elites, about strategies for by-passing, weakening, co-opting or coping with elites and about the responses of those elites to such strategies.[4] For those concerned about social inequality and its perpetuation, the study of these strategies, and subsequent responses, proffers significant insights into micro-level processes of subordination. In sum, the understanding of contemporary development and social change in poorer nations could be extended by a systematic analysis of the third sector and its recent rise. To date, most work on the topic has been of isolated case studies[5] which do not relate third sector activities to their political economies (in social science terms) or to their organizational environments (in management terms).

The relevance of social development research to the third sector

Having made the case for research on the third sector to be accorded some priority it is pertinent to ask would such research be of any utility to practitioners of development? The recent moves by international and indigenous NGOs to establish NGO-controlled research and training institutions provides a strong indication that the social development research outputs of existing institutions are of little utility, as these new institutions are premised on the case that NGOs lack access to relevant theory and empirical analysis. Currently there are plans to establish at least four NGO international research and study centres (personal communication, Alan Fowler) in the UK (International NGO Centre for Research and Development), the Horn of Africa (Centre for the Study of Peace and Development), Eastern Africa (NGO Study and Development Centre) and Spain (*El Taller*, the NGO Workshop).

Edwards (1989) suggests that to date social development research has had limited utility as the 'immense outpouring of information and advice [from writers and researchers on development] is having demonstrably little effect on the problems it seeks to address'. A major reason for this is methodological, 'the absence of strong links between understanding and action' (Edwards 1989: 116–17). This absence is interpreted along Freirian lines with 'conventional approaches' to research devaluing and demeaning the knowledge of the intended beneficiaries of development, denying them a role in the process and defining them as passive and dependent recipients of assistance – 'objects' not 'subjects'. Edwards's solution, weaving Illich's warp to Freire's weft, is to deprofessionalize knowledge creation and return the activity, and its ownership, to those it directly affects, in our case the poor in poorer nations.

These arguments have some weight, particularly if one measures them against personal experiences and specific examples.[6] But, as Edwards acknowledges within his article, the case is overstated[7] and only *some* development studies' and 'development studies of a particular form' are irrelevant (Edwards 1989: 131). Others within the voluntary sector see a much more positive link between theory and action. Indeed Poulton (1988: 11), an experienced field director for an international NGO, has gone so far as 'to highlight some of the theories which have had most influence on NGO thinking over the past twenty years or so'. If we examine the relationships between development knowledge and action, using the third sector as an example, then it becomes evident that these are more complex, and less irrelevant, than Edwards postulates (Figure 10.1).

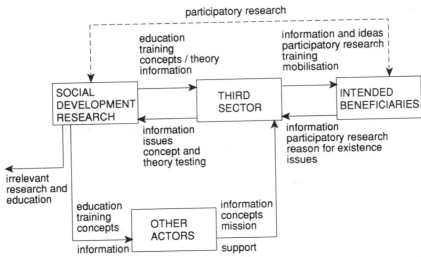

Figure 10.1   Social development research and the third sector.

Focusing on the direct linkages between the knowledge created by researchers and its relevance to third sector action, two 'flows' are of particular importance.

1   Within the ranks of the third sector are a significant number of people educated and trained with the products of social research. 'A new generation of social science-trained graduates has entered the NGO sector and brought with it new ideas, new perspectives. Freire, Alinsky, Gramsci and Fanon are now read and appreciated in "established" NGOs, in a way that was not true 10 years ago' (Elliott 1987b: 64). It is no accident that the proportion of anthropology, development studies, geography, political science and sociology graduates working in northern and southern NGOs is much greater than in official development agencies. The concerns of this group with poverty, disadvantaged people, social differentiation, social mobilization, and issues of access and distribution, may be rooted in

personal values but also reflect the influence of their initial disciplines.

2 The discourse, concepts and (sometimes) techniques that have shaped the third sector have often been developed by researchers and academics – indigenous technical knowledge, dependency, elites, powerlessness, patron–client ties, conscientization, rapid rural appraisal, appropriate technology and gender roles, to name but a few. Love them or hate them, Frank (1969), Boserup (1970), Freire (1974) and Chambers (1983) have left their mark on the voluntary sector. In particular, the rapid international diffusion of Freire's ideas (in which Edwards places great faith) was highly dependent on transmission by researchers and academics.

So, Edwards exaggerates the 'irrelevance' of development research and studies. A more accurate image will recognize that this field of endeavour has a mix of components some of which have direct relevance to development practitioners, some of which have partial or potential relevance and some of which are irrelevant. However, of more concern than this exaggeration is the argument that relevance can be achieved only by village-based participatory research. Such an approach has merit in terms of its explicit recognition that development is something that villagers are actively involved in, not something that is done to them; the identification of problems and priorities in terms of the experience, knowledge and values of those who suffer poverty; and, the creation of intellectual frameworks that assist outsiders (NGO staff, government personnel, political activists) to begin to appreciate the world through 'villagers' eyes'. However, it has the considerable disadvantage of having a very limited capacity to relate micro-level findings to wider social, political and economic structures and forces. It can, on occasion, generate courses of action that may appear relevant to the alleviation of poverty at a local level, but which may work against the interests of other poor people (e.g. production of a good in an already saturated market, which wins additional income for new entrants but produces a fall in average and aggregate earnings of the poor because of its depressing prices). In addition, an exclusive focus on locally generated solutions to problems denies the considerable evidence that social and economic opportunities can derive from innovations that have occurred outside of the locality. By their very nature, the analysis of these wider forces, the appreciation of the linkages between micro-level and macro-level variables and the scanning of external innovations that may have utility, require the resources and often the technical abilities of outsiders of whom social development researchers are one possible form. The contribution that such outsiders can make – in terms of linking local knowledge to external knowledge – can be made more or less relevant to intended beneficiaries and development practitioners depending on the degree to which they explicitly analyse the implications of research findings for action and, by finding forms of presentation that make them accessible to different sets of actors.

When the operations of the third sector are considered then the relationships between micro- and macro-level processes are of fundamental importance. If one accepts the case that NGOs can alleviate poverty and empower poorer people (these propositions are widely accepted but by no means proven) then it must be recognized that even on their present, greatly expanded scale they are a drop in the ocean. As Korten (1990: 91) puts it, 'the problem is that too many of these efforts are inconsequential in their scope or substance'. In 1985 it was estimated that there were 1,110 million 'poor' people (less than 1985 PPP US$ 370 per capita) of whom 630 million were 'extremely poor' (World Bank 1990: 29). To make any significant contribution to the alleviation of poverty on this scale then the third sector must successfully pursue one, or a mix, of the following strategies (for a detailed discussion see Edwards and Hulme 1992).

1 Small becomes big – replicate successful approaches and programmes on a vast scale.
2 Small transfers to big – create mechanisms that permit successful NGO interventions to be transferred to the state apparatus without loss of quality.
3 Small impacts on big – develop the ability to successfully lobby for poverty-alleviating changes in public policy.
4 Small catalyses big socio-political changes – stimulate structural change that redistributes political power to the powerless.[8]

At present there is a confused mumbling from different elements of the third sector, with very few of its constituents (even highly 'successful' NGOs) having a clear strategy on how their micro-level interventions will effect macro-level changes that can impact on poverty on such a scale. Indeed, as is discussed later, the recent popularity of NGOs is creating an environment in which some of these strategies for macro-level impact are being foreclosed. The third sector is being encouraged to restructure itself from a source of innovation, organizational pluralism, alternative knowledge creation and 'new' political force into a contractor for national governments and international aid agencies.

Conventional social development research has a role to play in assisting the third sector to appreciate contemporary changes in its environment and to appraise the strategic responses that are available. In the absence of such research, it is likely that knowledge generated by other disciplines, that are making a concerted effort to examine the sector, will shape the agenda and dominate debate. In particular the economist's concepts of 'comparative advantage' and 'cost-effectiveness' are being brought to bear on NGO operations (Fowler 1988; R Riddell 1990). These have their uses, but they focus analysis on short-term economic performance, adopt a narrow definition of development and ignore social change. They need to be complemented by a consideration of socio-political variables and processes with a longer term frame of reference (both to the past and the future). These variables include the effects of the third sector on the distribution of power and social stratification at local and other levels; the relationships of SNGOs to members of local and national elites; socio-economic backgrounds and roles of NGO leaders; the significance of charismatic authority (virtually all 'success-ful' Asian NGOs are headed by charismatic leaders, but economic analy-sis treats this variable as anecdote or non-analysable);[9] and, the impacts of recently formed third sector agencies on pre-existing institutions.[10]

The nature of the third sector

The third sector is comprised of a wide variety of organizational types. They differ in terms of scale, philosophy, objectives, location, activities, management systems and style, memberships, external relationships, resources and other features. While there are many potential typolo-gies[11] it is particularly useful to distinguish between geographical locations and the differing roles, or mixes or roles, that organizations pursue. Thus we can identify northern NGOs (NNGOs) based in donor countries and almost always directed by 'northerners'; intermediate southern NGOs (SNGOs) that operate at the national level or across several regions within a developing country and commonly work with local-level organizations; and membership organizations (MOs) com-posed of members from a localized area and led by representatives selected by the membership (Table 10.1). A complex web of vertical and horizontal relationships link these organizations. Many NNGOs and SNGOs are heavily dependent on each other; the former for a recipient country base for operations and the latter for finance and technical assistance. Although some spontaneous MOs have a high degree of independence, many spontaneous MOs and all induced MOs have links with SNGOs and, through them, NNGOs.

At each level there are different roles, or combinations of roles, that NGOs can pursue (Table 10.1). They may be operational and directly manage relief or development programmes; they may be catalytic or promotional and seek to conscientize and mobilize people so that 'the poor' themselves can tackle the problems that assail them; they may be advocates or educators seeking to change policies or attitudes; or, they may pursue a mix of these roles. Depending on the role or mix of roles pursued by an organization, components of the third sector can be seen as emphasizing one of the following strategic orientations:

1 Alleviating poverty by economic activity and creating material gains within a short period of time (the modernization approach).
2 Alleviating poverty through an initial focus on non-material achieve-ments that seek to empower through 'dialogical' processes and sees material gains as accruing at some future stage (the empowerment approach).

Intermediary SNGOs are at the heart of voluntary sector development activities. They are the channel through which the bulk of NNGO funds and activities are steered to the 'grassroots'; they play a central role in inducing new MOs and increasing their capacities; 'successful' MOs usually become SNGOs as they scale up their activities and cover wider areas. Ultimately, it is their performance (or non-performance) that will

Table 10.1 A typology of the third sector

Type/location	Role(s)[1]	Activities
(NNGOs)[2] Northern NGOs (based in donor nations)	Operational	Implement projects
	Catalytic	Promote and support SNGOs
	Policy advocacy	Lobby government and multilaterals
	Development education	Education and teaching materials
(SNGOs)[2] Intermediate Southern NGOs (operating at national or regional level)[3]	Operational unit of NNGO	Implement projects
	Catalytic unit of NNGO	Promote and support MOs
	Indigenous operational	Implement projects
	Indigenous catalytic	Promote and support MOs
	Indigenous policy advocacy	Lobby national government
(MOs) Membership organizations	Induced operational	Implement projects
	Induced catalytic	Mobilize, conscientize and press for member interests
	Spontaneous operational	Implement projects
	Spontaneous catalytic	Mobilize, conscientize and press for member interests

Notes: 1 Many NGOs have mixed roles
  2 At both 'northern' and 'southern' levels regional councils have been formed; these are not included
  3 I have not included government created non-government organizations (GONGOs) as these are instruments of government policy and are accountable to the state; for further details see Korten (1990: 104–5)

be the most significant determinant of whether the third sector remains a minor contributor to poverty-alleviation and development or has a more significant impact.

While it is evident that SNGOs are increasing in terms of both scale and numbers, and that their activities are very diverse, present knowledge about the composition of SNGOs in specific countries is patchy. Much research has been on the basis of individual case studies, commonly recycling data derived from the organization's own records. Not surprisingly, such research has focused on 'success stories' and has often concluded that organizations are successful without making serious efforts to validate internal data.

In regional terms, one can speculate that Latin America, South East Asia and South Asia (especially India, Bangladesh and Sri Lanka) have experienced rapid growth of SNGOs (and MOs), while the rate of SNGO formation and expansion in Africa appears much slower (Fernandez 1987; Landim 1987; Bratton 1989). In terms of activities, the third sector in Latin America (and Latin Asia, the Philippines) has shown a greater inclination to get directly involved in political action, pushing for socio-political change and policy reform, than its counterparts in Asia and Africa (Landim 1987). In Latin America the structure of the third sector has favoured networks of small, structurally flat and often female-led organizations, contrasting with the more hierarchical, 'scaled up' and male-led organizations of other regions (see Lehmann 1991). The response to recent crises in Sub-Saharan Africa (and the large numbers of refugees in that region) has meant that relief and welfare activities remain the dominant activity.

Although most SNGOs adopt a single strategic orientation at the time of their formation there is increasing empirical evidence, at least in Africa and Asia, of a trend to espouse both modernizing and empowering orientations at the same time. That is a rapid improvement in the economic and social standards of intended beneficiaries is sought while pursuing longer-term exercises to empower memberships. There are usually substantial pragmatic grounds for attempting, or claiming to attempt, a 'double-headed' strategy. Although many (if not most) who work for SNGOs believe that political change is a prerequisite for an assault on poverty and thus that an empowering strategy is necessary, their day-to-day work provides evidence that the poor, and particularly poor women, have considerable pressures on their time and are unwilling to invest time in dialogical processes that only promise to yield benefits in the medium or longer term.[12] To maintain membership levels and members' interest the managements of many Freirian-oriented SNGOs have found it necessary to establish programmes that offer some short-term payoff. These programmes can take many forms but throughout the 1980s, there was an increasing emphasis on activities that produce divisible rather than indivisible benefits through individualized income-generating projects. The provision of small loans at 'reasonable' rates for micro-enterprise has been a programme format adopted by large numbers of SNGOs.[13] Whether for landless labourers, small peasants, disadvantaged women or the urban underemployed, credit is seen as meeting a widespread and immediate 'felt need' around which groups can be mobilized and subsequently organized.

Combining individualized income-generating projects with consciousness-raising initiatives permits SNGOs to respond to the preferences of a variety of agenda-setters and adds to the sector's popularity. However, there is an inherent contradiction within the double-headed approach, which few SNGOs have been willing or able to analyse. This is that the income-generating activities operated by SNGOs commonly integrate members more deeply into the processes that their consciousness-raising and dialogical activities identify as causes of poverty – profit maximization, competition among the poor reducing group solidarity and the acquisition of the assets of the poor by entrepreneurs. Korten (1990: 92) warns that 'some VOs (voluntary organizations) may slip into reinforcing unjust structures, even creating their own version of the enclave economy' and provides examples of this from the Philippines. Hashemi (1993) has found that in Bangladesh low-income 'foxes' (to use Chambers's terminology) have used SNGO credits to pursue activities that offer high financial returns – moneylending, mortgaging, hoarding and distress sales of land. This permits a small number of individuals to improve their economic positions, but reinforces the processes, as identified by the SNGOs themselves, that immiserize the poor majority.

In such cases successful SNGO members soon find that their own interests are in conflict with those of other members and with non-members. A fundamental tenet of Freirian doctrine – *'consistency be-tween words and actions'* (Freire 1974: 177) – is negated.

Rather than analysing or attempting to resolve this contradiction, many SNGOs have pursued a strategy of ambiguity that permits the presentation of different images to different audiences. The operational-economic development stance wins support from donors, is non-threatening to the political status quo and provides a means of rapidly expanding the membership base. The conscientization-empowerment stance provides an ideological baggage that fosters identification with NNGOs and MOs, creates an identity that is independent of the state and appeals to staff and volunteers (many of whom are 'former Left-ists'). A key dimension of this ambiguity – at least in Asia and Africa – is political; combining the claim of being a non-political development organization with the claim of promoting empowerment, that is being a political force. The claim to being non-political is usually based on the notion that the interaction between SNGOs, their memberships and wider society is 'popular participation' and not 'political participation' (Korten 1980). In such formulations political participation is defined purely in terms of involvement with formal political parties and insti-tutions. By this means the non-political image that is required by the state for approval and registration can be constructed. To memberships a different image is presented. It talks of mobilization, empowerment and social transformation but rarely is direct political action sponsored, as this could involve suspension or dissolution by the state. Ambiguity creates political space within which this 'non-political' force can manoeuvre, but it also has consequences for the membership as 'by kindling the spirit of unrest and then retreating [it] is indirectly creating confusion in the minds of the population it wants to help' (Chowdhury 1989).

The implications of this ambiguity can be interpreted in very different ways depending on the manner in which power is believed to be distrib-uted in a specific national context. Two very contrasting interpretations are of particular significance.

1 Within pluralist frameworks the SNGOs can be viewed as making a positive contribution to the political position of disadvantaged groups as they raise awareness, foster notions of participation (rather than apathy) within the evolving political culture, develop the organ-izational and, later, lobbying capacities of a new set of political actors and expand the ranks of experienced leaders who can exercise future options to compete for political office. As these alternative leadership cadres gain confidence they can chart a more directly political strat-egy for SNGOs, or move into the formal political arena as representa-tives of the poor and disadvantaged.

2 Within contexts where a political elite or a dominant class is believed to monopolize power, then SNGOs can be interpreted as creating the illusion of political pluralism, participation in decision-making and

the acceptance, by those who hold power, of the existence of agencies promoting social and political change. This is of utility for the dominant elite or class as it promotes a favourable image of the incumbent regime domestically and internationally, facilitates greater inflows of foreign aid, creates job opportunities for the educated unemployed, provides a non-threatening channel for the energies of individuals and groups who want 'change' and makes the task of political mobilization by other political parties and genuine opposition groups more difficult.

At present assessing the validity of these very different interpretations is largely a speculative task as detailed knowledge of the composition of the third sector, its strategic orientation, its political impacts and its relationships to power-holders and oppositions is very limited, particularly for Asia and Africa. In much of Africa it would appear possible to gather evidence pointing to the strength of the second interpretation. In Kenya and Zimbabwe SNGOs that have pressed the case for change have been suspended or threatened by those who hold political power (Bratton 1989). In Malawi the role of the third sector is clearly defined as operational and those within the sector are either closely linked to the political elite, or are fully aware of the consequences of any genuine mobilization activities. Across Asia there has been considerable optimism about the ability of SNGOs and MOs to strengthen the position of the poor, particularly the rural poor, within the political system (Black 1989; Korten 1990). However, the limited empirical findings available on this would suggest that the pluralist case is grossly overstated.[14] For some Latin American countries, the situation would appear to be very different from Africa and Asia with SNGOs and MOs often directly involved in political action and commonly opposing the state, and those who hold power.[15] There are many possible explanations for this, but clearly the close association of the third sector in that region with the church and liberation theology has vested in the sector a greater degree of political authority, from a societal perspective, than appears the case in other regions.

The ambiguity and diversity of SNGOs and MOs are factors that contribute to their potential to be a source for change. Ambiguity can permit them to exploit a political niche in which new constituencies and alternative leaderships can be developed without succumbing to the abuses that have discredited most political parties or appearing to threaten the status quo. Diversity permits experimentation, the formulation and testing of alternative strategies, and discourages inertia. However, as I shall argue in the following section, the forces that are shaping SNGOs and MOs are discouraging diversity and, under the cover of the sector's ambiguity, are redefining its role.

The reshaping of the third sector

A number of actors can be seen to influence the third sector. Of particular interest here are those that hold sway over the form and behaviour of

SNGOs. These actors are linked by a network of exchanges that can be conceptualized in a simple model (Figure 10.2). The significance of these exchanges varies from agency to agency, between locations and over time. In some situations certain relationships may be weak or non-existent, while in other situations one actor may almost totally condition the structure and operations of others.

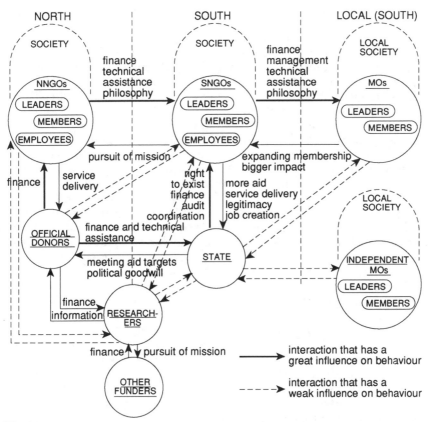

Figure 10.2 Forces for change in the third sector: actors and interactions.

MOs and SNGOs are elements of civil society and have an intimate relationship with that society. They are dependent for their existence and continuation on a group of citizens finding a common cause to devote their energies to and, at least in the initial stages, on voluntary contributions of labour, funds and resources. Some MOs have long histories and have been shaped by social forces within their immediate localities (e.g. irrigation societies). Others are recent transplants inspired by external forces (e.g. Grameen Bank replicas – see Hulme 1990). By their very nature, MOs maintain a close relationship with local society, or cease to exist. SNGOs may have an intense relationship with their memberships, and thus with society more widely. However, this relationship often weakens as they expand and professionalize, as management and direction is internalized and as external sources of finance substitute for voluntary contributions.

The state 'is the largest and most assertive actor' (Bratton 1990: 581) in the SNGO and MO environment. It exerts a major influence over the scale and form of the third sector but this relationship has only been seriously examined in very recent studies[16] (e.g. Bratton 1989; 1990). Its actions can range from permitting the third sector considerable operational freedom at one extreme (e.g. Sri Lanka), to viewing the sector as a threat to national security and actively discouraging it at the other extreme (e.g. Somalia). The state can seek to control SNGOs through a variety of mechanisms – registration, monitoring, co-ordination, co-optation, suspension and ultimately dissolution. SNGOs can attempt to maintain their autonomy by keeping a low profile, selective collaboration or policy advocacy (Bratton 1989; 1990). Very little is known about the relationship between SNGOs and the state,[17] although this is a crucial issue in explaining the role, performance and potential contributions of SNGOs. It is a complex relationship as there are pressures for both co-operation and conflict. SNGOs require state approval to be able to operate and can gain access to technical assistance, and sometimes funds, by maintaining an amicable relationship. However, close involvement with the state creates a dependence that threatens to reduce the range of strategic options available to an SNGO, most obviously in terms of objecting to state activities, and makes co-optation more likely. State polices towards SNGOs, and NNGOs, are increasingly conditioned by aid donors (see pp. 264–9).

The relationships between NNGOs, SNGOs and MOs vary, depending to a significant degree on their origins and philosophy. Some NNGOs, such as OXFAM, pursue their developmental activities by assisting SNGOs and MOs to mount their own programmes. Others, such as Action Aid, directly manage development projects through field units. In the opposite direction, there are SNGOs which actively seek out NNGO partners (e.g. the Thrift and Credit Movement in Sri Lanka), while others, as a matter of principle, adopt a more cautious stance and are wary of interaction with NNGOs (e.g. the Organization of Rural Associations for Progress in Zimbabwe).

The relationship between official donor agencies (both bilateral and multilateral) and the third sector has changed dramatically since the early 1980s. Arguably it is now the major force that shapes the third sector in terms of scale and composition. Up until the 1970s official donors saw little need to work with NNGOs, SNGOs or MOs. Early experiences with the aid-financed inducement of MOs proved disastrous with co-operatives and community development groups (Hulme and Turner 1990). SNGOs and NNGOs were seen as inconsequential. During the 1970s, a role was recognized for NNGOs in responding to crisis in Africa and Bangladesh. The 1980s have seen an enormous expansion in direct and indirect links between official donors, NNGOs and SNGOs. The intensification of these links has been fuelled by the Sahelian famines of 1984/5, by donor dissatisfaction with programme implementation by the governments and bureaucracies of developing countries (especially in the fields of poverty-alleviation and rural development), by a growing belief in the managerial capacity of the third sector and by the increasing popular support that NNGOs receive from their domestic constituencies. An emphasis on the use of the third sector has been consistent with both the 'new right' aid policies of governments in the USA and UK and the 'alternative' aid policies of the consciences of the donor community in Scandinavia and Holland. Aid administrators have welcomed this emphasis as it extends their options, provides an additional channel for meeting disbursement targets in countries where state 'absorptive capacity' is low and partially shifts accountability for performance from the aid agency to NNGOs and SNGOs.

A few examples serve to illustrate the 'rise' of the third sector (for a detailed discussion see Clark 1991). In 1985 more than 13 per cent of total development disbursements (official aid plus voluntary grants), amounting to US$4 billion, was channelled through the third sector by OECD nations (van der Heijden 1987: 104). Since 1981, the US Congress has laid down a disbursement range that USAID should achieve through NGOs. During the early 1980s this was a minimum of 12 per cent of total development and disaster assistance funding and a maximum of 16 per cent (USAID 1982). The UK's Overseas Development Administration (ODA) disburses aid through the third sector by a variety of mechanisms but under recent ministers has become very 'bullish'. The Joint Funding Scheme (between ODA and UKNGOs) is the fastest growing part of the aid programme. It disbursed only £11 million in 1988, increased this to £25 million in 1990 and is targeted to reach £64 million in 1994/5.[18] This popularity is already having profound effects in recipient countries that are perceived as having poor governments but effective NGOs.[19] In Bangladesh, perhaps in excess of 15 per cent of official aid goes through the third sector, most major donors have country-based officers, or desks, to liaise with NGOs, and the government has found it necessary to establish a 'cabinet cell' to oversee the third sector. The senior management of government agencies, such as the Bangladesh Rural Development Board, talk of being 'in direct competition' with NGOs for aid projects and funds.

The rapid inflow of aid into the third sector has had two distinct impacts. First, it has fostered a rapid expansion in the number of SNGOs,[20] and has permitted some to extend their coverage.[21] Second, it is dramatically modifying the nature of the sector. It is the second of these impacts that is of particular interest for social researchers as the qualitative modifications to SNGOs are shaped by social and political forces and have implications for the future role that SNGOs may play in promoting social change. These qualitative changes take several forms.

1 *Increased dependence on external resources* The availability of aid resources (through NNGOs, the domestic government or directly) encourages dependences on external financing and discourages local resource mobilization. For example, SNGOs in Africa are usually 90

per cent dependent on foreign aid (van der Heijden 1987: 111) and this may be as high as 95 per cent for Zimbabwean NGOs).

2 *Structure of SNGO activities*   Virtually all donor[22] funding to SNGOs is 'projectized' so that NGOs utilizing aid tend to expand in project activities, particularly those favoured by donors (such as small loans and income-generating projects) while in proportional terms mobiliz-ation, conscientization, the development of local leaders and advo-cacy become less significant. The control that donors have over the activities they finance is illustrated by a recent World Bank report (Salmen and Eaves 1989) finding that only 11 per cent of NGOs with whom the Bank co-operated in 1989/90 had an involvement in the design of the projects they are implementing.

A Sri Lankan example can illustrate the consequences. The Thrift and Credit Movement fundamentally reoriented its activities in the mid-1980s by involvement with the USAID-financed 'Million Houses' project. It was able to rapidly expand its operations but its traditional savings and loans focus became a 'loans only' focus, and the activities it financed changed from agriculture, trading and con-sumption to house construction.[13]

3 *Accountability*   Accepting aid funds requires that SNGOs account for them to donors or NNGOs or the domestic government, sometimes all three. This tends to substitute for accountability towards member-ship and supporters as external financiers have considerable 'lever-age'. Accounting to external agencies fosters an 'upwards' rather than a 'downwards' orientation among SNGO staff and commonly absorbs a large amount of leadership time.[23]

4 *Staff composition*   The need to negotiate with and account to donors favours a professionalization of SNGO personnel. This leads increas-ingly to the creation of a cadre of senior personnel within the organ-ization whose prime motivation is employment, rather than mis-sion.[24] Indeed, the claim has been made that NGOs in Bangladesh are increasingly perceived as an alternative source of employment for the middle classes now that the public sector has stopped expanding (Hashemi 1993), while in Mali a plethora of NGOs were created by government staff laid off in a structural adjustment programme (Clark 1991: 91). It is also associated with significant increases in headquarters staffing levels and administrative costs. For example, between 1986 and 1990 the Finance Department of Sarvodaya Shra-madana in Sri Lanka expanded from twenty-one to fifty-four staff, at donor insistence, and there are donor demands for further expan-sion.

5 *Composition of membership*   As the structure of an SNGO's activities changes then there becomes a strong likelihood that the membership base will change. Although aid donors seek to use the third sector to reach 'the poorest', pressures on aid projects to perform (in terms of absorbing target disbursements, sticking to timetables, producing short-term impacts that can be quantitatively measured by a visiting evaluation team etc.) can encourage recipient SNGOs to redefine their memberships or target groups.

For example, the decision of the Thrift and Credit Movement in Sri Lanka to work with the 'Million Houses' programme led to a rapid expansion of the number of lower-middle-income and middle-income households in its membership. The groups formed by such members actively excluded 'the poor' from their co-operatives as they were perceived to have too low an income to service a housing loan.

6 *Membership perceptions* As external resources become more significant, and staff become professionalized, HQ-based and donor-accountable, the perceptions of memberships shift. The SNGO, and associated MOs, are increasingly seen as an outside agency that 'deliver' external resources, not as part of an institution to which members 'belong'. The responsibility of members to participate in activities and honour obligations to the SNGO or MO increasingly become a matter for individual discretion, rather than an issue with implications for wider social relationships. Hashemi (1993) has reported on this tendency in Bangladesh, where villagers increasingly perceive SNGOs and MOs as a resource transfer mechanism rather than 'their' organization. Recent personal research in northern Bangladesh revealed that many members of NGO groups believed that the NGO assisting them was a government agency!

The types of changes that donor interest in the third sector is promoting can be interpreted in different ways. Van der Heijden (1987: 109) gleefully records that 'we are now in the midst of a process that may eventually lead to more effective collaboration between the official sector and NGOs, and may permit a further expansion of development services provided by NGOs, capitalising on their comparative advantages and recognising the need for governments to fully account for the effective use of public funds'. The 'important problem' of the 'advocacy role' of SNGOs may be overcome as 'probably newer forms of institutional advocacy will emerge' (van der Heijden 1987: 112).

By contrast, the International Council of Voluntary Agencies has been far more circumspect about the prospects of mutually beneficial co-operation. It has drawn up a list of problems that NGOs should anticipate if they accept official aid funding (ICVA 1985). Bratton (1990: 114) has argued that the dependence of African NGOs on foreign assistance correlates negatively with policy influence. Casting diplomacy aside, Jan Pronk (quoted in Hellinger 1987: 137), the former head of the Dutch bilateral aid programme, observed that 'the corruption of NGOs will be the political game in the years ahead. ... NGOs have created a huge bureaucracy, employment is at stake and contacts in developing countries'. Closer collaboration is seen as a step towards ultimate co-optation.

One approach to understanding the impacts of aid availability on the third sector is to analyse them in terms of whether they operate as voluntary organizations (VOs) that pursue a social mission based on a shared set of members' values, or as public service contractors (PSCs) (Korten 1990). The latter are non-government and non-profit but meet the demands of the market as a contractor. VOs and PSCs often have identical forms but they can be distinguished when they face a choice between social missions or market share – 'the true VO will opt for the former, while the PSC will opt for the latter' (Korten 1990: 102). Korten proposes VOs and PSCs as specific types of organizations, but it is more useful to think of these as the poles on a continuum on which third sector organizations are dynamically positioned. The position and direction of a specific NGO could be determined by the study of changes in its key characteristics (Table 10.2). The present context for NNGOs, SNGOs and MOs is one in which a move towards the PSC pole has considerable attractions. It can solve the problems of financial viability, gives relief from challenging entrenched interests, provides staff with job security and promotion prospects and permits the organization to expand and 'do more'. The ambiguous nature of NGOs allows a gradual drift from VO to PSC without any need to explicitly redefine the role of the organization. Although knowledge is limited, the examples cited in this chapter, allied to an environment that favours the elimination of 'alternatives' that challenge the status quo, indicate that such a move takes the third sector away from the confrontation of the social and political issues that surround poverty, make acquiescence with southern and northern government policies more likely and diminish opportunities for policy advocacy, political lobbying or the creation of alternative political forces and leaderships. As Korten (1990: 124) warns 'the surest way to kill a movement is to smother it with money'.

Table 10.2 Key characteristics of voluntary organizations (VOs) and public service contractors (PSCs)

| Characteristic | Continuum | |
	VO	PSC
Resources	Voluntary	Contracts
Goals	Change	New contracts
Accountability	Downward	Upward
Staff orientation	Mission	Job
Staff status	Volunteer/member	Employee
Definition of targets	By members	By donor
HQ costs	Low	High
Planning	Incrementalist	Blueprint
Capacity building	For members	For agency itself
Activity timescale	Indefinite	Two to five years

The conversion of the third sector into a PSC role is particularly attractive to state agencies and existing power-holders in developing countries who can thus neutralize a potential source of alternative ideas and opposition, supplement aid in-flows and enhance the domestic and international image of pluralism. The likelihood of drifting into a PSC role depends on many factors but of particular significance in Asia, and perhaps in Africa, is the relationship between SNGO leaders and their memberships. In Asia NGO leaders are commonly charismatic founders whose members usually exert very limited control over their directors. The analysis that these individuals bring to the strategic options facing their organizations is the major determinant of the SNGOs future course. Each leader is her or his 'own man' but, wearied by a decade or two of frenetic activity managing their organizations and fending off insolvency, the acceptance of aid funds (and membership of the international circuit to which this gives access) has considerable appeal.

Social development research can serve as a counterbalance to the pressures that aid financing has brought to the third sector. It can broaden the agenda so that SNGOs and MOs are analysed as social and political actors, rather than purely as service delivery mechanisms; can encourage NGOs to review their strategic options; can provide concepts for the understanding of the likely consequences of different actions; and can document comparative experiences. Such research had a profound impact on the voluntary sector in the 1960s and 1970s in steering parts of it towards the adoption of a mandate that transcended relief and welfare approaches. At a time when NGOs are popular with donors it is more necessary than ever.

The emerging research agenda

While acknowledging the heterogeneity of the third sector, and the variety of its contexts, the previous section has argued that the forces that now shape this sector are fostering its expansion but fundamentally changing its nature. These changes are commonly to the advantage of certain groups (those who hold political power, SNGO employees, middle-class professionals, aid agencies and aid administrators) but their implications for the intended beneficiaries of SNGO activities, the poor, are open to question. This is not a conspiracy, but equally, it is not an accident.

The directions that the third sector is now taking may permit improvements in the effectiveness of service delivery to some poor people. However, at the same time it increases the likelihood of the co-optation of SNGOs, MOs (and NNGOs with weak membership bases) by the state and the elimination of a channel by which the poor can gain involvement in decision-making, acquire 'voice' and develop a cadre of alternative leaders. This has significance for both the understanding of social change and the practice of development. What emerges is the need for a systematic effort to study the processes fuelling change within the voluntary sector, particularly for SNGOs, and analyse the implications for the actors involved in these processes.

The elaboration of a comprehensive methodology is beyond the confines of this chapter, but an outline can be sketched. It would take the form of a number of country studies covering a range of combinations of society, state (especially the degree to which opposition is tolerated) and donor influence. For each country the history of the third sector would be charted at the macro-level, its recent and present scale and composition would be described, and the forces that have shaped and are shaping it would be delimited. Subsequently, detailed meso-level case studies would be conducted of specific SNGOs to examine their internal dynamics, the external forces influencing their behaviour and any changes in their orientation on a VO–PSC continuum. Similar studies would be conducted at the micro-level of SNGO-affiliated MOs and independent MOs. The studies would follow a common framework, perhaps using a refined version of the model in Figure 10.2. This would focus upon the resources available to different actors (e.g. financial, technical, physical, informational, moral, legal); the exchanges between actors (material and non-material, scales, directions, formal and informal) and the dependencies associated with these exchanges; and the strategies that actors can adopt (e.g. bargaining, confrontation, avoidance, inducement, persuasion, control, co-optation, penetration). Political science models of inter-organizational processes might be adapted as a conceptual framework (e.g. Rhodes 1989), but these would require careful testing because of their corporatist underpinnings.

Macro-level research would involve interviews with key informants from SNGOs, NNGOs, government, political parties, bureaucracy and aid donors along with considerable documentary analysis. At the meso-level interviews would be required to explore in detail the relationships between the major actors. Of particular importance is the study of the roles, social positions and backgrounds of leaders; the significance of SNGO professionals in decision-making; SNGO strategies; and relationships with government and political parties. At the micro-level participant-observation would be utilized, alongside other techniques, to unravel the linkages between SNGOs and MOs, between MOs, MO leaderships and members, and between members and non-members. Of particular interest at this level is the analysis of the socio-political impacts of socially inclusive modes of organization (such as that pursued by the Aga Khan Rural Support Programme in Pakistan) and socially exclusive modes of organization (such as those pursued by BRAC and Proshika in Bangladesh). Who wins, who loses, when such strategic choices are made?

Such an enterprise has academic utility in providing empirical evidence about the processes by which the role of the third sector as a force for social change can be promoted or contained. At present there is only a patchy base upon which to judge the claims that SNGOs and MOs are a major force for democratization and pluralism, and the counterclaims that SNGOs depoliticize their target groups and weaken political oppositions.

In some cases research might have direct relevance to action if the implications of its findings are clearly and succinctly presented to individual case study MOs, SNGOs and the sector in general. This would cover the nature of environmental changes, the range of strategic options, the likely consequences of different courses of action and reviews of comparative experiences. An example of such direct linking of research by academics to NGO action, and a commentary on the results achieved, has been produced by Wood and Palmer-Jones (1991).

Such a direct approach would entail the creation of 'non-traditional' products and modes of work for academics. Given the contingent nature of SNGO and MO operations the paradigm for such intervention must be one of experimentation and social learning rather than 'thinking and knowing' (Johnston and Clark 1982).

A 'social engineering' approach is not the only route to relevance, however, and in many cases relevance could be achieved by a planned 'enlightenment' approach. This entails the dissemination of findings through orthodox channels (journals and monographs) alongside channels that are less regularly pursued by academics but which are more likely to have impact – newspapers, NGO magazines, involvement in NGO training programmes, briefings to NGO managers and leaders, production of teaching materials for NGO trainers and submissions to aid donors.

An additional means of enhancing the likelihood of research having relevance to action is to make serious efforts to mount it in collaboration with host-country researchers. This is a difficult and often time-consuming task for 'northern' researchers but it creates opportunities for strengthening the research capacity of local universities and research institutions (many of which are weak and isolated), means that a local presence and source of knowledge remains 'after the project', and con-tributes to the quality of the stock of latent scholar-activists who can question policies and actions and, if they wish, participate directly in the third sector or other social and political interventions.

Such a programme demands considerable sensibility on the part of researchers. They need to gain the confidence of SNGOs, MOs and individual members without becoming so involved that their capacity to state what they believe is happening is compromised. They must honour an obligation to selectively non-report key events and pieces of information, such as covert SNGO links with opposition parties or antigovernment forces. Also, they must be careful not to divert SNGO resources, such as transport and staff time, from SNGO action to their own research.

The starting-point for such an enterprise is winning research funding. This, as always, is a hassle, but fortunately it is also the first point at which research and action can coincide for, in approaching aid donors and international NGOs (the Ford Foundation and the like), a step is taken in promoting an agenda that treats the third sector as a social and political force, rather than a convenient mechanism for delivering aid.

Notes

1. This chapter attempts to generalize across low-income and middle-income countries but it has been heavily influenced by personal research in Sri Lanka and Malawi, by the work of my colleague Syed Hashemi in Bangla-desh, and by Bratton's (1989; 1990) writing on Africa. In consequence, it probably emphasizes experiences in Asia and Africa and neglects Latin America.

2. By the third sector I refer to private organizations that are non-profit-making but which are not political parties. For a typology see pp. 258–62.
3. The recent rise and restructuring of the third sector is a feature of developed as well as developing countries. It merits meta-theoretical analysis in relation to the demise of socialism as an ideological force and the ascendancy of liberalism.
4. For examples see BRAC (1987) and Singh (1988).
5. *Mea culpa.*
6. My personal highlight was an anthropologist (now chaired) who spent a couple of hours explaining the centrality of the concept of 'otherness' to a group of post-graduate development studies students. He was hurt when an articulate Indian student pointed out the implications of the concept: that expatriate anthropologists had no relevance to development, and that Indian anthropologists would need to complete PhDs on Inner London and Chicago before they could appreciate agrarian change in Bihar.
7. The development prospects for many countries, especially in Sub-Saharan Africa, are bleak. But one should not totally ignore, as Edwards does, the significant improvements in infant mortality, life expectancy, literacy, food availability, and female access to education in many countries in recent decades.
8. Such a strategy could involve linking with opposition political groups, converting into a political party (see Garilao 1987: 199 for an example of an NGO leader mooting this), or SNGO leaders moving into formal politics, as is happening in Sri Lanka. It can be framed in pluralist vernacular (competition, new parties, new pressures, alternative leaderships) or radical vernaculars (confrontation, militancy, insurrection).
9. For example Fazle Hasan Abed of BRAC, Jaya Arunachalam of the Working Women's Forum India, Dr A T Ariyaratane of Sarvodaya Shramadana and P A Kiriwandeniya of the Thrift and Credit Movement in Sri Lanka.
10. Some researchers, such as Blair (1989), make the erroneous assumption that voluntary organizations fill an institutional vacuum.
11. One of the most widely utilized typologies is Korten's (1987) 'three generations of NGO', which has since matured to 'four generations' (Korten 1990). This has value as a polemic, arguing for NGOs to change their orientation, but it has analytical problems because of NGOs being able to reverse the trend (i.e. retrogress) and because some NGOs straddle several generations.
12. Johnston and Clark (1982) present an interesting analysis of the costs of participation in MOs for poor rural people. Many populists treat involvement in MOs as having no costs. Research adopting an actor-oriented approach (see Long and van der Ploeg, Chapter 3) could shed light on the factors that condition poor people to prefer individual or collective strategies for self-advancement.
13. For examples see Egger (1986), Panos Institute (1989) and Remenyi (1981).
14. For examples see Moore (1985) and Hashemi (1990).
15. Whether this should be seen as a cause or a consequence of redemocratization is a moot point.
16. Even less is known about relationships with the 'anti-state'. Personal research into Sri Lankan NGOs in 1987 and 1988 illustrated the need for NGOs to maintain a relationship with the anti-state, in the form of the JVP. The JVP exerted unofficial control over much of the southern part of the country and NGO activities required JVP sanction.
17. Esman and Uphoff (1984) have postulated that NGO performance and

relationship with government follow an inverted-U curve, that is 'low' and 'high' involvement with government is associated with poor performance.

18. A recent UK Overseas Development Administration review has proposed that ODA intensify its linkages with SNGOs.

19. Some years ago a UK NGO director described to me 'the new scramble for Africa of the 1980s'. This was Northern NGOs desperately scouring the continent for indigenous NGOs to work with, and trying to reach a deal before a competitor NNGO staked out a territorial claim!

20. In Bangladesh from a few hundred in the mid-1970s to around 6,000 in 1989 (Westergaard 1990).

21. The most obvious example is the Grameen Bank, prior to 1984, with the assistance of an IFAD credit.

22. The Netherlands is the only exception with which I am acquainted.

23. For example, by 1989 the Federation of Thrift and Credit Co-operative Societies in Sri Lanka was accounting to fourteen different external sources of aid. This was an enormous burden for a small management team.

24. It has become common in many countries to peg NGO pay rates at a percentage above government rates.

References

Blair H W (ed) (1989) *Can rural development be financed from below?* Dhaka, University Press Ltd

Boserup E (1970) *Woman's role in economic development*. London, Allen & Unwin

BRAC (1987) Networks of Power. In: Korten D (ed) *Community management: Asian experience and perspectives*. West Hartford, CT, Kumarian Press

Bratton M (1989) The politics of government–NGO relations in Africa. *World Development* 17 (4)

Bratton M (1990) Non-governmental organisations in Africa: can they influence public policy? *Development and Change* 21

Chambers R (1983) *Rural development: putting the last first*. Harlow, Longman

Chowdhury A N (1989) *Let grassroots speak: people's participation, self-help groups and NGOs in Bangladesh*. Dhaka, University Press Ltd

Clark J (1991) *Democratizing development: the role of voluntary organizations*. London, Earthscan

Edwards M (1989) The irrelevance of development studies. *Third World Quarterly* 11 (1)

Edwards M and **Hulme D** (eds) (1992) *Making a difference: NGOs and development in a changing world*. London, Earthscan

Egger P (1986) Banking for the rural poor: lessons from some innovative savings and credit schemes. *International Labour Review* 125 (4)

Elliott C (1987a) *Comfortable compassion? Poverty, power and the church*. London, Hodder & Stoughton

Elliott C (1987b) Some aspects of relations between the North and South the NGO sector. *World Development* 15 (supplement)

Esman M J and **Uphoff N T** (1984) *Local organisations: intermediaries in rural development*. Ithaca, NY, Cornell University Press

Fernandez A P (1987) NGOs in South Asia: people's participation and partnership. *World Development* 15 (supplement)

Fowler A (1988) Non-governmental organisations in Africa: achieving comparative advantage in relief and micro-development. IDS Discussion Paper 249, Brighton, Institute of Development Studies

Frank A G (1969) *Capitalism and underdevelopment in Latin America*. New York, Monthly Review Press

Freire P (1974) *Pedagogy of the oppressed*. Harmondsworth, Penguin

Fuentes M and **Frank A G** (1989) Ten theses on social movements. *World Development* 17(2)

Garilao E D (1987) Indigenous NGOs as strategic institutions: managing the relationship with government and resource agencies. *World Development* 15 (supplement)

Gorman R F (ed) (1984) *Private voluntary organisations as agents of development*. Boulder, CO, Westview Press

Gran G (1983) *Development by people*. New York, Praeger

Hashemi S M (1990) *NGOs in Bangladesh: development alternative or alternative rhetoric*. Manchester Discussion Paper in Development Studies 9006, University of Manchester

Heijden H van der (1987) The reconciliation of NGO autonomy, program integrity and operational effectiveness with accountability to donors. *World Development* 15 (supplement)

Hellinger D (1987) NGOs and the large aid donors: changing the terms of engagement. *World Development* 15 (supplement)

Hirschman A O (1984) *Getting ahead collectively: grassroots experiences in Latin America*. New York, Pergamon Press

Hulme D (1990) Can the Grameen Bank be replicated? Recent experiments in Malawi, Malaysia and Sri Lanka. *Development Policy Review* 8 (3)

Hulme D and **Turner M** (1990) *Sociology and development: theories, policies and practices*. Hemel Hempstead, Harvester-Wheatsheaf

ICVA (International Council of Voluntary Agencies) (1985) Suggested guidelines on the acceptance of government funds for NGO programmes, mimeo. Geneva, ICVA

Johnston B F and **Clark W C** (1982) *Redesigning rural development: a strategic perspective*. Baltimore, MD, Johns Hopkins University Press

Korten, D C (1980) Community organisation and rural development: a learning process approach. *Public Administration Review* 40 (5)

Korten D C (ed) (1987) *Community management: Asian experience and perspectives*. West Hartford, CT, Kumarian Press

Korten D C (1990) *Getting to the 21st century: voluntary action and the global agenda*. West Hartford, CT, Kumarian Press

Landim L (1987) Non-governmental organisations in Latin America. *World Development* 15 (supplement)

Lehmann D (1991) The return of the subjective dimension. Paper presented to the workshop on Relevance, Realism and Choice in Social Development Research, Centre of Developing Area Studies, University of Hull, 10–12 January

Moore M P (1985) *The state and peasant politics in Sri Lanka*. Cambridge, Cambridge University Press

OECD (1988) *Voluntary aid for development: the role of non-governmental organisations*. Paris, OECD

Panos Institute (1989) *Banking the unbankable*. London, Panos Institute

Poulton R (1988) On theories and strategies. In: Poulton R and Harris M (eds) *Putting people first: voluntary organisations and Third World Organisations*. London, Macmillan

Remenyi J (1991) *Credit where credit is due*. London, Intermediate Technology Publications

Rhodes R A W (1989) *Beyond Westminster and Whitehall*. London, Unwin Hyman

Riddell R (1990) *Judging success: evaluating NGO approaches to alleviating poverty.* Working Paper 37. London Overseas Development Institute

Salmen L and **Eaves A** (1989) World Bank work with NGOs. Policy, Planning and Research Working Paper no. WPS 305. Washington, DC, World Bank

Schneider B (1988) *The barefoot revolution: a report to the Club of Rome.* London, Intermediate Technology Publications

Singh R K (1988) How can we help the poorest of the poor? In: Poulton R and Harris M (eds) *Putting people first: voluntary organisations and Third World organisations.* London, Macmillan

Tendler J (1982) Turning private voluntary organisations into development agencies: questions for evaluation. Program Evaluation Discussion Paper no. 12. Washington DC, USAID

Uphoff N T (1986) *Local institutional development.* West Hartford, CT, Kumarian Press

USAID (1982) *Policy paper: AID partnership in international development with private and voluntary organisations.* Washington, DC, USAID

Westergaard K (1990) Grassroots groups and politics in Bangladesh, mimeo. Copenhagen, Centre for Development Research

Wood G and **Palmer-Jones R** (1991) *The watersellers.* London, Intermediate Technology Publications

World Bank (1990) *World development report 1990.* Washington, DC, World Bank

Afterword

CHAPTER 11

Rethinking social development:
the search for 'relevance'[1]

Michael Edwards

'Why is so much that is said, written and spent on development having so little effect on the problems it seeks to address?' This was the question I posed in an article written a few years ago entitled 'The irrelevance of development studies' (Edwards 1989). This article was unashamedly polemical, born out of years of frustration at the way in which many academics had taken information and ideas from those whom they were 'researching', without contributing to the lives of these people either directly (by enabling them to improve their situation 'on the ground'), or indirectly (by changing attitudes and policies at the national and international levels). As a fieldworker for a number of development agencies, I also knew that much of this research was inaccurate because it failed to incorporate the views, aspirations, wisdom and imperfections of real, living people. Research and practice were 'two parallel lines that never met', and both suffered accordingly. 'Practitioners do not write, and theoreticians remain in the abstraction of their theories' (Edgar Stoesz, quoted in Bunch 1982). This amply summarized the prevailing situation.

The debate on 'relevance' in social development research has gathered pace over the last few years, and a number of critical questions (many of which are contained in other chapters in this volume) have been raised about my original article. Rightly, I have been pressed to explain parts of my argument which are seen as unclear, and taken to task for over-generalization. In this chapter, therefore, I attempt to answer these criticisms, update my arguments, and explore in more depth some of the issues touched on only briefly in the original.

The chapter begins by summarizing the major points raised in that article in order to provide enough context for the discussion that follows. The third section attempts to answer four major questions posed about my arguments by David Booth at the 1991 conference at the University of Hull, and repeated in part in his introduction to this volume. This is followed by a brief survey of recent attempts to bring research and practice closer together. The final section contains a preliminary (and personal) agenda for future collaboration between researchers and practitioners working in development.

'The irrelevance of development studies'

My original article began by juxtaposing the continued existence (and in many cases, the worsening) of poverty and exploitation in the 'Third World' with the ever-increasing amount of development research, advice and funding being undertaken, supposedly to counteract these trends. 'The fact that this immense outpouring of information and advice is having little demonstrable effect on the problems it seeks to address should at least give us cause for concern' (Edwards 1989: 116). I sought to explain this apparent contradiction through a critique of conventional approaches to the creation and use of knowledge, which are based on the separation of theory from practice, understanding from action, subject from object, and researcher from 'researched'. As Nigel Maxwell has written, 'Insofar as academic enquiry does try to promote human welfare, it does so ... by seeking to improve knowledge of various aspects of the world'. In contrast, 'for the philosophy of wisdom, the fundamental kind of rational learning is learning how to live, how to see, to experience, to participate in and create what is of value in existence' (Maxwell 1984: 2, 6).

Conventional approaches to development research and practice value the technical knowledge of the 'outside expert' over the indigenous knowledge of the people being 'studied' or 'helped'. In consequence, 'general solutions manufactured from the outside are offered to problems which are highly-localised. The practice of development work teaches us that problems are usually specific in their complexity to a particular time and place' (Edwards 1989: 120). In addition, 'it is impossible to understand real-life problems unless we grasp the multitude of constraints, imperfections and emotions which shape the actions of real people. Conventional research cannot do this because it divorces itself from the everyday context within which an understanding of these emotions can develop' (1989: 121). Researchers believe that they can understand the reality of what is going on, but do so through a series of biases and misperceptions which they carry with them from their training and cultural experiences.

'Being for the satisfaction of the researcher rather than the researched' (Edwards 1989: 122), such an approach is also selfish: it relies on the extraction of information from people who do not benefit from the uses to which this information is put. These centralizing and extractive tendencies are directly 'anti-developmental' because they prevent poor people from thinking and acting for themselves.

This is not to say that the *process* of research – of understanding the forces which affect the development of people – is irrelevant. 'We cannot change the world successfully unless we understand the way it works; neither can we understand it fully unless we are involved in some way in the processes that change it' (Edwards 1989: 125). To this extent, 'development cannot be studied at all: we can participate in the processes that underlie development and observe, record and analyse what we see, but we can never be relevant to problems in the abstract' (1989:

125). The key to being relevant lies in the participation of poor people in constructing our understanding of how their world operates. 'We cannot be relevant to people unless we understand their problems, but we cannot understand these problems unless people tell us about them' (1989: 126).

Reversing traditional attitudes to development research therefore means uniting research and practice, understanding and action, researcher and researched, into a single, unitary process. And this in turn implies that researchers must accept to be changed by the results of their research; must be accountable to the subjects of their work; and must be prepared to see the value of their work judged according to its relevance in improving the lives of the people concerned. This does *not* mean that all research that is relevant also has to be 'directly participatory'. Research which analyses similarities and differences over time and space can be extremely 'relevant', but the usefulness of such 'secondary' research will be a function of its effectiveness in changing attitudes among the powerful in a direction which will ultimately enable the less powerful to think and act for themselves.

In conclusion,

> we need consciously to adopt a position of humility with respect to our own limitations and the limitations of our kind of education and training. We must learn to appreciate the value of indigenous knowledge and the importance of popular participation in showing us what is relevant and what is not. In this way, we will begin to move from practice based on the philosophy of knowledge, to practice based on the philosophy of wisdom, to a form of enquiry on which what we do and what we are matter more than what we know. (Edwards 1989: 134).

Although the arguments for such changes are complex in their details, it is important to remember that they are based on only two fundamental assertions, one concerning ethics, and the other concerning methods.

First, the purpose of research is to promote the development of poor and powerless people around the world. Second, in order to be relevant and useful in this task, research must involve its subjects in some way and at some stage in constructing both process and output. These two underlying questions – the purpose of intellectual inquiry and the ways of knowing reality – need to be kept in mind throughout the discussion that follows. In this way, we shall be able to explore both questions in more depth without becoming lost in detail.

Critique

In his introductory paper for the workshop on 'Relevance, Realism and Choice in Social Development Research' held at the University of Hull early in 1991, David Booth posed a series of questions relating to my article on 'Irrelevance' which provide a useful structure for exploring these arguments in more depth (Booth 1991: 11). The most important of these questions are as follows.

1   To what is relevant research supposed to be relevant?
2   Does this apply only to local participatory projects, or to other forms of research also?
3   Should local studies of this kind be privileged, especially given the capacity of the macro-context to dissipate gains from purely local efforts?
4   Is it possible to determine in advance the sorts of knowledge that will be useful to the causes of which we approve but not those of which we disapprove?

I shall try to address each of these questions in turn.

To what is relevant research supposed to be relevant?

Ethics are ever-present in debates about development, because development is about things which *ought* to take place. As Kant stressed 'ought implies can', so that the development debate is as much about practice (or how to bring about what 'ought to be') as about principle (or what 'ought to be' in the abstract) (Crocker 1991: 457–83). Relevant research must help us to develop both good practice and good principle. However, this does not free us from defining what 'ought to be' in the first place; in other words, from defining what we mean by 'development'.

In my original article, I defined development in terms of 'empowerment' – increasing the control which poor and powerless people (and specifically the poorest and most powerless) are able to exert over aspects of their lives which they consider to be important to them. Not unnaturally, therefore, research which was not 'participatory' – which did not increase people's control in this way – was taken to be 'anti-developmental'. In his workshop paper, Booth pointed out that development and participation are neither synonymous nor necessarily associated with each other, citing as an example the case of rapid economic development in East Asia since the early 1970s, which has taken place with minimal participation by the poor in decision-making and the political process in these countries.

It is difficult not to fall into tautologies here – since if development is defined as empowerment, cases which are not empowerment cannot be defined as development. More seriously, economic growth may bring material benefits to people, but development is about much more than this, being a process of enrichment in every aspect of life. No one would deny that material benefits are an essential part of development, but the underlying principle of control is much more important. Rising incomes are one result of this process, as well as being a contributory factor in increasing control in other areas of life (such as health and education). But if incomes rise for only some people, or if people value other changes as much as or more than rising incomes, then clearly 'development' in its fullest sense is not occurring. There are clear moral and intellectual choices here which have to be made before one can progress to the next stage of the argument. Different people will make different choices about what is and is not 'developmental'.

Whatever one's choice of definitions, it seems axiomatic to me that the purpose of intellectual inquiry *in this field* is to promote 'development'. In contrast to 'pure' science or art history (for example), development studies concern real, living people and cannot therefore be conducted in the abstract. This is particularly true for non-governmental organizations (NGOs) such as my own, for which there is no role in a world without moral discourse. At the very least, we need to be clear about the implications of our work for people's lives, and to declare openly our beliefs and allegiances instead of sheltering behind a spurious 'objectivity'. While there is always a danger that well-meaning outsiders will determine local agendas by imposing their own moral choices, this danger is reduced if these outsiders are open and honest about their values right from the word go. At least in theory, moral stances can then be negotiated and, if appropriate, rejected. This is the only legitimate answer to a question which worries many academics, namely 'who decides' what is 'relevant' and what is not? As John Harriss once put it to me, 'should outsiders' respect for indigenous knowledge and values lead to the acceptance of indigenous injustice because the powerful in another society have a different system of ethics?'[2]

The answer to this question, at least for an NGO, must be 'no', because NGOs should articulate and declare their own underlying values – what, in other words, is *not* negotiable – before offering any assistance at all. This means that in some situations indigenous values will indeed be overridden, female circumcision in some Arabic societies being a case in point for my own agency, Save the Children. It goes without saying that this is a dangerous path to walk which carries with it an ever-present threat of 'cultural imperialism'. These dangers can be reduced if alliances are formed with local groups which themselves oppose the 'indigenous values' of other local groups. More importantly, honesty and clarity about ethics *prior to* any development intervention or research is crucial. At least these activities can then take place 'in the open'. Although most of the contributors to this volume concentrate almost exclusively on the *methodological* questions raised in my original article (and particularly the role of 'participatory research'), at least one (Stuart Corbridge) tries to tackle the question of ethics head-on. This is a brave thing to do, and much more important in my view than the debating whether or not all research has to be 'directly participatory' in order to be relevant.

Research about the forces which can impoverish, exploit or liberate people can never be neutral, but it can play a crucial role in helping to bring about progressive change. Good research (relevant research) helps us to make informed choices about alternative ways of doing things, enabling a selection to be made between more and less effective strategies to reach our goals. Whether it is possible to conduct good, relevant research without the active participation of the subjects of study is a question which is taken up in the next two sections of this chapter.

It is important to clarify here, however, that 'relevant' research does not simply mean 'research to be used by development agencies'. NGOs and other agencies have their own agendas which also need to be openly declared. They are often protective, defensive and resistant to criticism, and because of these characteristics there must, within the broad range of development research being undertaken, remain a large area which is independent of institutional practitioners.

In summary, 'relevant' development research should be 'relevant' to those whose lives it embraces. It should contribute to their self-development by opening up new and better ways of doing things and clarifying the lessons of experience. It should, in my own conception of 'development', contribute to the ability of poor and powerless people to increase the control they can exert over their own lives. It should also make explicit *how* it intends to accomplish these goals (a key point); this brings us to David Booth's second question, which concerns the structure and methodology which makes research more, or less, relevant.

Does this apply only to local participatory projects?

A good deal of confusion seems to have been caused by references in my original article to the primacy of 'participatory research' in development studies. As the above question implies, this has been taken to mean that the only research which is relevant is research which takes place directly in the context of development practice at micro- (or project) level. What I was trying to say here was that, to be relevant, research must *in some way* be linked to the real experience and concerns of people at grassroots level. Quite rightly, I have been taken to task for failing to specify precisely what this might mean in practice.

The key sentences here in my original article read as follows: 'The important distinction to be made is that such "higher-level" work must grow out of and be based upon participatory research at lower levels. . . . If the link with people's real concerns and experiences is sufficiently strong, then even "higher-level" research can be genuinely-developmental' (1989: 130–1). In other words, it is the link with people's experience that is crucial and not the link to a particular development 'project'. This link can be made in a variety of ways, some of which do not (and cannot) involve the direct participation of the subjects of the research.

For example, much of the most useful research work carried out over the last few years in areas such as gender relations, environmental concerns ('sustainable development'), empowerment and participation, and the impact and efficacy of 'structural and macro-economic adjustment', has been developed through comparison and synthesis over a long timescale and a broad geographical area. These comparative experiences have yielded powerful evidence of both positive and negative trends at grassroots level, and have stimulated important policy changes among development practitioners (including the most powerful institutions of all, such as the World Bank). But equally important is the fact that all this work was built upon careful research at micro-level which, while not necessarily 'participatory' in methodology, did highlight what was actually happening to people in their daily lives. Because of this, it was 'relevant' both in the sense of accuracy (demolishing some of the myths created by those who were ignorant of grassroots realities) and in terms of people's development (changing policy and practice in ways which ultimately enabled people to gain more control over their incomes, resources and relationships with each other).

Hence, both the 'micro' and the 'macro' levels are crucial to relevance in development research: the important thing is to ensure that they are explicitly related to one-another, a theme which is taken up on pp. 285–8. Major problems inevitably arise whenever one or the other level is considered in isolation. Then, higher-level research quickly becomes inaccurate or irrelevant, while lower-level research and practice may become ineffective in the face of more powerful forces which can crush or distort it. There are many ways of linking the two together: the crucial thing is always to build from the 'bottom upwards'. In other words, always to ensure that people's real experiences and concerns provide the raw material for higher-level analysis and synthesis. Any higher-level research which fails to do this may misinterpret what is actually happening and will therefore fail to inform development policy and practice at higher levels in a responsible way. However, in admitting that 'relevant' research may not be 'participatory' research, we are not released from the task of making explicit how research which is not participatory may still be relevant. This seems to have escaped some of those who have produced 'counter-critiques' to my original article though David Hulme does begin to address this crucial question in Chapter 10 of this volume.

Should local studies of this kind be privileged?

Naturally, the answer to this question is on much the same lines. If what matters in research is the *linkage* between micro- and macro-levels, then it follows that neither local nor global studies 'should be privileged'. Both have an important role to play. The impact of wider economic, political and environmental forces on development at community level is increasingly being recognized by practitioners, particularly by NGOs whose traditional focus has been more-or-less exclusively on small-scale projects. Village co-operatives are often undermined by deficiencies in the wider agricultural extension and marketing systems in which they have to operate, while social action groups can be frustrated by more powerful political forces at higher levels of the system. No development project can be successful in the longer term unless it takes account of these wider forces. This is why structural change at national level is a vital precondition for the successful development of people. For this reason, both academics (who call this the 'micro–macro interface') and NGOs (who call it 'scaling-up' their impact) are taking an increasing interest in finding better ways of linking different levels of research and practice together (see the discussion on pp. 292–3).

This is especially helpful because it encourages both researchers and practitioners to move away from an unhealthy concentration on one level to the exclusion of others. As I have already made clear, micro- and macro-levels exist in symbiosis and have no meaning in isolation from each-other, so adopting a 'people-centred' view of the world does not mean abandoning the analysis of global structures. We might also dispense with similarly simplistic dichotomies such as 'indigenous and modern knowledge', 'individual and structural explanations', and 'projects and processes'. In reality, it is impossible to dichotomize any of these things. Relevant research is research which understands this and illuminates the complex and ever-changing relationships between people and the environment which they live and work.

It is perhaps true that practitioners have in the past focused too much on site-specific detail and have ignored the importance of wider economic and political frameworks. Equally, there is truth in the charge that academics have focused too much on wider forces in their search for grand theory, while neglecting the infinite variation of the real world. One of the achievements of bringing research and practice closer together (analysed in detail in the next section) is that each can enrich the other, leaving behind the notion that they are somehow exclusive categories or occupations. At the same time, I would argue (as throughout this chapter) that we should always examine wider forces and trends through the eyes of those who experience and act in them, for it is their perceptions and actions which give meaning to these forces. This is the same as 'building from the bottom upwards' in development research, or, to put it simply, generalizing from the particular. For, if we are not learning by comparison from one real-life situation to another, how *are* we learning?

This brings me to one of the most difficult questions in this whole debate, which concerns the nature of theory in 'relevant' development research. Perhaps this is something which a practitioner with little expertise in theory should steer well clear of! Nevertheless, theory is important as a tool for understanding and explaining the world (and, therefore, as a necessary precondition for changing it). The relevance of theory to practice cannot therefore be avoided, but if every situation is unique and every person different, how is theory to be constructed?

It seems to me that it is perfectly possible to 'take diversity seriously' without falling into 'glorified empiricism', to use David Booth's terminology (Chapter 1). Micro-level studies do suggest that there are wider trends in development which affect people in similar ways across time and space. For example, the commercialization of markets in urban and rural areas has enriched some groups at the expense of others: given inter-household differences in the distribution of land, labour and other resources, inequality will increase over time. We know this to be true from empirical observation, and we can therefore predict what will happen in similar circumstances elsewhere (though never with complete accuracy or reliability). When the universe under study is circumscribed in some way (either contextually or in terms of the issues under scrutiny), these patterns become clearer. This is what I try to do in the final section of this chapter when mapping out a preliminary agenda for future research and action. Indeed, when used in this more limited way, many concepts from past 'metatheories' remain very useful. For example, landless labourers in South Asia would have no difficulty in understanding the relevance to their situation of concepts from classical Marxism such as 'ownership of the means of production'. A similar case could be made for aspects of 'dependency theory', despite its abandonment as an overarching, deterministic explanatory framework. Poorer countries remain very much in the grip of international trade, aid, debt, technology and financial structures over which they have little control. This more eclectic use of theory is as useful to development practice as it is essential to development studies, since it helps those involved to understand what is happening to them, and to choose between alternative options for the future.

Of course, it is not the case that there are no general theories in use today in our 'post-modernist' world. The problem is that those theories that *are* used – deriving in the main from neo-classical economics – are inadequate, at least in support the type of 'development' I am arguing for in this chapter. The ruling institutions of our world – states, multilateral agencies such as the World Bank and IMF, business and finance, and major sectors of the intelligentsia – continue to act according to an economistic, and generally a neo-classical economistic, paradigm. This paradigm has not been significantly dented by the combined efforts of social and political scientists, NGOs, and new political movements such as the emerging 'Rainbow Coalition' of environment, development and 'New Economics' groups. Although there are elements of neo-classical and other economic theories which *do* need to be taken seriously by social development researchers and activists, our vision of development as a process of empowerment and enrichment for all and in every aspect of life will not be realized so long as we rely on concepts such as economic growth, gross national product, comparative advantage, market imperfections and so on.

However, if neo-classical economics is deficient, what alternative theories can we use? My own conclusion from all this is that there is no alternative to an eclectic approach which examines everyday experience from a number of different points-of-view and then synthesizes the results into higher-level explanation. This combination of economics, sociology, anthropology, political science, psychology and other disciplines, theories and paradigms is precisely what follows from the 'bottom-up' approach that I have been recommending. To practitioners this approach is second nature because this is how we live our lives anyway. So long as theory is constructed from real experience it will have explanatory power. But it will never be 'grand theory' or 'metatheory' in the sense implied in the classical tradition. This may be a disappointment to academics, but is scarcely relevant to practitioners, whose search for conceptual clarity is inevitably circumscribed by the real-life variation of a world in which simplistic dichotomies and generalizations have little meaning or utility.

Can one predetermine knowledge which will be of value only to the causes of which we approve?

The answer to this 'old chestnut', as David Booth calls it, is obviously 'no'. In the nature of things, knowledge can be used for good or ill, because it is created and used by human beings. Progress in nuclear physics can be used to develop alternative energy sources or weapons of mass destruction; research in microbiology to create new vaccines or germ warfare, and so on. While development research is rarely involved in such stark alternatives, its findings remain open to abuse in much the same way. Imperfect human beings will use knowledge to advance themselves in relation to their neighbours, as is demonstrated countless times in communities across the world. Technological advances in agriculture, for example, are never 'neutral', because different people are more or less able to use them according to circumstance. The consequences of the 'green revolution' for rural inequality show this to be true. Anyone involved in the creation and dissemination of knowledge must therefore be conscious of the potential abuses, as well as uses, of this knowledge, and act accordingly.

Where, then, does this leave the 'participatory' approach to development studies? Although certain social, economic and environmental goals are implicit in participatory development (such as equality, sustainability and respect for human rights), none of these ideals is or should be enforced over and above participation in decision-making – the individuals' ability to share in decisions which affect them, and hence increase the control they can exert over aspects of their lives which concern them. Indeed, the real goal of participatory development is to equip people with the skills, confidence, information and opportunities they need to make their own choices. Once so equipped, the rest is up to them. By its very nature, the process of empowerment is uncertain: although it is possible to initiate the journey in a structured way (using particular techniques and methods, for example), the ultimate destination is always unknown.

The way in which individuals use their increasing confidence, knowledge, skills and resources (their power, in other words) is absolutely crucial, but it cannot be predetermined, however much outsiders might want to do so. However, evidence from many communities around the world shows that (except in situations of acute inequality and competition for scarce resources) people do co-operate and help each other, if they are given the resources and opportunities to do so. I would claim, therefore, that participation *does* increase the likelihood that people will act responsibly, and that they will use their own knowledge and the knowledge that others can bring for mutual benefit. Likewise, if people are involved in the creation and use of their own knowledge, there is more of a chance that this knowledge will be used for causes of which *they* approve, to paraphrase Booth's words. Whether they use it to advance causes of which 'we' approve is, in a sense, irrelevant.

In this respect, the role of research should be to maximize the range of ideas and information to which people have access, so that they can make their own decisions on the strongest possible foundation. By reducing complex situations to a series of answerable questions, good research can help people to find a way through the daunting constraints imposed on them by poverty, inadequate resources, lousy infrastructure and an unresponsive government. It is in this sense that participatory research (or more accurately, bearing in mind the conclusions of earlier sections, research which builds on people's real experience) can generate knowledge which is likely to be used progressively. However, to imagine that this can ever be guaranteed is clearly unrealistic.

Knowledge and action: hope for the future

A constant refrain in both my earlier article on 'Irrelevance' and the present chapter is that knowledge and action, theory and practice, understanding and change, must always go together. In this synthesis and symbiosis lies the key to relevance in both research and practice. When people are fully involved in development programmes or in research which affects them, there is a much greater chance that these programmes will be relevant to their real concerns, accurate, usable and empowering. In the same way, higher level research or action which attempts to be developmental (in the sense in which I defined this word in the second section) must also grow out of grassroots experience.

This is not, of course, an uncontroversial view of things. Indeed, in Chapter 2, Frederick Buttel and Philip McMichael state categorically that 'development sociology and development practice should be (formally) separated' (p. 44). They go on to qualify this statement by saying that these two activities should be seen as 'related, but distinct areas of work, mainly on account of their different levels of analysis and different problematics' (p. 44). Despite this qualification, I feel that this view is fundamentally wrong. Such a separation can lead only to research which is irrelevant and practice which is deficient. It imposes a divide between those who 'do' development work, and those who 'think' about development. It encourages competition within development academia on terms which have nothing to do with the usefulness of research to its subjects (and everything to do with the quantity of papers published). And it perpetuates the historical dependence of those without access to knowledge and power on those who have monopolized these things for hundreds of years. For all these reasons, such a separation is therefore 'directly anti-developmental', as I put it in my earlier article.

Thankfully, there is increasing evidence that academics and practitioners are realizing this, and are making strenuous efforts to work more closely together. They have seen that in the integration of research and practice lies one of the most fruitful directions for the future. At a recent annual conference of the UK Development Studies Association in Swansea, for example, papers on various aspects of NGO work occupied an unprecedented one-and-a-half out of the three days on offer. The conference established an 'NGO Study Group' to bring academics and practitioners together on a regular basis in order to explore issues of common concern. Indeed, it is difficult to keep up with the number of links currently being forged between NGOs and academics in the UK. University departments seem to be falling over themselves to initiate research and training programmes on and for NGOs and other develop-ment practitioners.[3] The Institute for Development Policy and Manage-ment at Manchester University co-sponsored with Save the Children a workshop on 'Scaling-Up NGO Impact: Learning from Experience' in January 1992, while Britain's Overseas Development Institute in London has recently completed a huge study of NGO effectiveness in the allevia-tion of poverty in Africa and Asia.[4]

NGOs around the world are becoming much more serious about evaluating the impact of their work and feeding the lessons of their experience back into policy and practice. Indeed, INTRAC (the Inter-national NGO Training and Research Centre, recently established with a base in Oxford) is one of four or five initiatives from among the NGO community itself which aim to encourage NGOs to reflect critically on their experience and to improve training for NGO staff in the techniques of project appraisal, monitoring and evaluation, planning and manage-ment.[5] All these initiatives have in common the desire to bring under-standing and action together so that development practitioners are better equipped to play their role effectively, and development aca-demics are better able to appreciate the reality they are studying. In the process, we are at last beginning to produce the kind of 'organic intellec-tual' beloved of Gramsci and others, the combination of theory and praxis in the same individual which enables them to 'interpret' and to 'change' the world simultaneously.

One of the most interesting of these new areas of joint work is what Norman Long has called 'demythologizing' or 'deconstructing planned intervention' – the critical analysis of development practice which takes into account the different and sometimes conflicting perceptions of the same issue or action among practitioners and the subjects of the project in question (Long and van der Ploeg 1989). For, as Long has written elsewhere, practice is 'an ongoing, socially-constructed and negotiated process, not simply the execution of an already-specified plan of action with expected outcomes' (1990: 16). This is the local corollary of the participatory approach to development *studies*. NGOs and other prac-titioners can hardly recommend the virtues of popular participation and then deny a role for those they serve in evaluating and contributing to the policy and practice of the agency in question. If, as an earlier section made clear, we must start to consider the 'ethics of ends' in develop-ment research and practice (that is the justification of what we are trying to achieve), must we not also consider the 'ethics of means' – which methods of development practice are ethically superior to others (see Crocker 1991)? This is an extremely challenging question for develop-ment practitioners, and one which, in my view, will provide fruitful territory for collaboration with researchers in the future.

Despite these encouraging developments, there is sometimes a tendency for people to use these new relationships between research and practice for what are essentially selfish ends. There is a danger that NGOs and development projects will become an *object* for academic study, in much the same way as poor people themselves were treated as objects in the conventional approach to development studies. It was this approach which I criticized so strongly in my original article on 'Irrelevance', both on the grounds that it was exploitative, and on the grounds that it was bound to produce results which were inaccurate. The point is to work together in a joint search for better practice and better theory, and this requires an acceptance of each other as equals.

Another encouraging set of initiatives are the new methodologies of 'participatory' research, appraisal and evaluation which have undergone rapid development since the late 1980s. I would also include in this category the 'actor-oriented approach' of the Wageningen School, though members of this group (such as Normal Long) might disagree! As Long has pointed out many times, 'actor-orientation' is not a tool for improving development intervention, but it shares with these other methodologies an explicit attempt to involve the subjects of development in understanding and changing their own lives. Indeed, it makes clear that there can be no successful understanding *without* an appreciation of what is happening through the eyes of those concerned.

Similarly, what was initially 'Rapid Rural Appraisal' has metamorphosed into 'Participatory Rapid Appraisal' and now into 'Participatory Relaxed Appraisal'! A wide range of new techniques have been developed to facilitate joint action among agencies and the people with whom they are working, to enable them to understand social structure and development issues within a given location. These techniques include 'well-being ranking', 'profiles', maps of various kinds, and semi-structured discussions such as 'focus groups'. Participatory monitoring and evaluation are also developing quickly, particularly in the area of social development and the evaluation of development *processes* (Marsden and Oakley 1990). Participatory research itself (a term which covers a very wide range of research methods) is now almost taken for granted in development work.

Even here, however, there is a temptation to use such techniques and methods to extract more information for outside use, rather than using it to facilitate the development of the community concerned. It is the ends to which such methods are used that are important, not the methods themselves. The acid test is whether the subjects of the research, evaluation, programme or whatever become more able to develop themselves as a result of participating in the exercise. At the same time, of course, the lessons learned can quite legitimately be fed 'upwards' into development theory, as discussed above. However, as I put it in my original article, we have to guard against using participatory techniques in a way which becomes 'merely another form of exploitation, serving the purposes of outsiders who have their own agenda but who know they cannot gain a complete picture of the problems that interest them through conventional methods alone' (Edwards 1989: 129).

In summary, there are signs that academics and practitioners are developing a fruitful collaboration in an increasing number of areas. In addition, techniques of combining research and practice, or understanding and action, into the same process are gaining ground all the time, and are being used to improve both development practice and development theory in ways which directly empower the subjects of this work. What is clear is that there is no one, single or universally agreed way of doing this successfully. The evaluation of these different methods and techniques will be another fruitful area of collaboration among researchers and practitioners over the next few years. Our priority must be to bring more people together around common themes and issues in a joint search for progress, undertaken as equal partners. In the next section of this chapter I draw up a personal and preliminary list of themes which seem to me to provide ideal ground for such a dialogue.

A possible agenda for future research and action

On the basis of my own experience, there seem to me to be at least four major issues which will be of critical importance to both development practice and development research in the 1990s. These are

1 scaling-up impact: the micro–macro interface
2 the measurement of social development
3 sustainable development in practice
4 state and civil society in a changing world.

Scaling-up impact: the micro–macro interface

Earlier in this chapter I cited the example of social action groups and agricultural co-operatives to illustrate the way in which development projects can be undermined or overwhelmed by more powerful forces or structures at higher levels of society. NGOs are increasingly aware of the limitations of micro-projects and are asking themselves some hard questions about how to increase, or 'scale-up', the impact of their work. Inevitably, this means interacting in one way or another with the systems and structures which determine the distribution of power and resources at national and international levels. If development practice is to be more effective in promoting widespread and lasting change, there must be a more explicit linkage between the 'micro' and the 'macro'. David Hulme's Chapter 1 in this volume is a useful contribution to this debate, though he fails to turn a similarly critical spotlight on parallel attempts by development academics to understand more clearly the complex ways in which local processes interact with structural factors. For, although this is an issue of critical significance to practitioners (and in particularly to NGOs with their limited resources), it is no less important for accurate research and theorising. It is precisely in this area that many previous social development theories were weakest, since they failed to incorporate the sheer variation and unpredictability of local actors within a broader structuralist perspective. One hopes, therefore, that researchers will not neglect the study of micro–macro linkages in a

general sense in their enthusiasm to 'study' efforts by the NGO community to scale-up their impact.

NGOs themselves face a range of options if they wish to increase the
impact of their work. All of these options have different advantages and
disadvantages which need to be analysed from a critical perspective.
This is what the workshop on Scaling Up referred to on p. 290 attempted
to do (Edwards and Hulme 1992). Some NGOs (such as the Bangladesh
Rural Advancement Committee) see scaling-up in terms of ever-larger
projects of their own. This can certainly bring benefits to larger numbers
of poor people, but can also turn the NGOs concerned into bureaucratic
'Public Service Contractors' (Korten 1990) which abandon any attempt to
address more fundamental issues such as land distribution and political
organization. Alternatively, NGOs may choose to work within or alongside government in an effort to improve official policy in health, education and other fields. This is more sustainable than the NGO project
approach, but is slow and difficult, and runs the risk of bolstering the
interests of the state at the expense of popular organization. A third
approach is to lobby governments and multilateral agencies from the
outside in the hope of changing fundamental attitudes and approaches
on the international stage. Thus far, little has been achieved in the way
of fundamental change at this level, and such activities (because they
may be seen as 'political') are often difficult for NGOs to undertake.
Finally, NGOs can concentrate on strengthening organizations of the
poor, encouraging networks and federations of grassroots movements
which may be able to exert pressure for change 'from below'. This is an
attractive option, but may actually dilute the impact of more genuine
political movements and can rarely be sustained unless the people
involved also receive some material benefits in their lives in the medium
term. Of course, NGOs may try all of these approaches at different times
and in different circumstances. The important thing is to subject them all
to critical scrutiny so that their real impact can be assessed. In so doing,
we will be able to understand more clearly how the 'micro' and the
'macro' fit together in different contexts in both practical and conceptual/
theoretical terms, and therefore how best to address these linkages in
order to promote people's development. This is a task which concerns
both research and practice, and around which co-operation will therefore be essential.

The measurement of social development

Traditionally, NGOs have not been very enthusiastic about, or competent in, evaluating the real impact of their work. This is partly because
evaluation can be a painful and threatening exercise, and partly because
there are severe methodological problems involved in measuring 'development in its fullest sense', including processes such as empowerment
and participation, enrichment and satisfaction. Although some progress
has been made over the last few years in the evaluation of social development, it remains difficult to establish what is actually happening as a
result of development practice, to whom and in what ways (Marsden

and Oakley 1990). Yet this is clearly a crucial task if the whole enterprise of development intervention is to be legitimized.

It is in this respect that Norman Long's intention to 'deconstruct planned intervention' takes on particular significance. The critical analysis of alternative strategies to promote development (which must include the perspectives of those who are participating in these strategies) is clearly critical to the success of NGOs and other agencies, yet it is debatable whether the NGOs themselves have the skills, time or objectivity to do this alone. It seems to me that this too is an excellent example of an issue which requires collaboration between practitioners and researchers if it is to be addressed successfully.

Sustainable development in practice

Much has been written in recent years about 'sustainable development', but what does this actually mean in practice, and how is it to be achieved? A fairly uncontroversial view of things would be that people's development should take place in ways which do not damage the ability of the natural environment which surrounds them to support the development of future generations of people. More specifically, environmental conservation has to be combined with the resolution of poverty if it is to be socially and politically sustainable. This is certainly not uncontroversial, since it involves choices of production, technology, access to resources and social and political arrangements in order to secure better livelihoods for the poor at minimum cost to their environment. This has rarely been achieved in practice in either 'Northern' or 'Southern' societies. It is a profoundly difficult and complex area which certainly cannot be addressed by practitioners alone. Research on alternative strategies for sustainable development, and their longer-term effects, needs to go hand in hand with practical attempts to solve these thorny problems at grassroots level.

State and civil society in a changing world

The roles of different actors in the development process are currently being re-defined under the influence of 'neo-liberal' thinking emanating from Northern governments and the institutions they control (such as the World Bank). Responsibilities traditionally assigned to government (such as the provision of basic services) are being taken up by the private sector, including by some NGOs. There is a new emphasis on private initiative and voluntary organization as the basis for successful 'development'. This new thinking has caught many development practitioners unawares, and they are now struggling to define what position they should adopt in the face of an increasingly powerful ideology. While many recoil from the underlying philosophy they are being offered, they also see (for example) that markets *do* play a role in allocating resources and in boosting production, that poor people probably *do* have to contribute to basic services in resource-poor economies if these services are to be sustainable, and that an overly centralized state *is* anti-developmental in the sense that it usually undermines popular organiz-ational and grassroots democracy. In other words, are all the elements of the neo-liberal approach damaging to the development of poor and powerless people in the sense that 'development' is understood by most NGOs?

At present, NGOs have no answers to these questions. They do, however, need to find some answers fairly quickly if they are not to be co-opted into the role that has been assigned to them under the neo-liberal banner – that of implementers of projects and providers of ser-vices. They need, in other words, to come up with a credible alternative model of development which will generate significant advances in pro-duction and incomes *without* sacrificing progress towards goals such as equality, conservation and empowerment. Likewise, social develop-ment research is going to have to be much more vigorous in finding credible theories to act as a counterweight to the neo-liberal paradigm. This is something that researchers have conspicuously failed to do in the recent past. Once again, research and practice face a common agenda.

Clearly, these four sets of issues reflect my own personal experience and many more could be added to the list. By way of conclusion, it is worth stressing *why* this list requires, in my view, active co-operation between researchers and practitioners if real progress is to be made. There seems to me to be two reasons:

First, researchers and practitioners have different but complementary skills, all of which are needed to unlock the kinds of issues raised above. Practitioners need to work with those who have more time, a broader viewpoint, and the analytical skills necessary to unravel complex pro-cesses and build up accurate generalizations. On the other hand, re-searchers need to work with those who are closer to the reality of what is being studied, to improve the quality of information inputs to research and ensure that research outputs are used properly in practice.

Second, all the issues I have listed turn to one extent or another on the linkages between micro- and macro-level processes. By definition, there-fore, they cannot be addressed by concentrating on one level to the exclusion of the other. Practitioners (whose focus traditionally has been at micro-level) and researchers (whose focus traditionally has been at macro-level) therefore need to co-operate in order to achieve a more accurate perspective on the issues that concern them.

For me, therefore, there is no escape from the need to forge closer links between research and practice. What remains is to explore the nature of these links and to experiment with differing ways of rendering them as effective and creative as possible.

Conclusion

As I hope to have shown in this chapter, there are encouraging signs that development research and development practice are moving closer together in ways which do empower poor people to control their own development. However, there is still, in my own view, a tendency for academics (including some of those represented in this volume) to play down some of the more fundamental questions that I raised in my original article. There are at least three ways in which this shows itself.

First, these counter-critiques tend to focus on methodological rather than ethical questions, particularly the supposed primacy of 'participatory research'. This is a relatively minor issue compared to the purpose of intellectual inquiry and the role of the development academic in relation to those whose lives are being 'studied'. Second, there is a tendency to assume rather than demonstrate that there is a distinctive role for academic researchers in improving development practice – a role, in other words, which could not be played by researchers within the practitioner community. As I mentioned on p. 290, NGOs are developing their own research capacity very quickly, and are prepared to devote more resources to building up new institutions (such as INTRAC, the International NGO Training and Research Centre) which can offer them research and training facilities more in line with their requirements. In this scenario (and particularly as university research funding continues to decline) it is possible to envisage more and more research being undertaken outside of the formal education sector, perhaps with academics providing some assistance to ensure a greater degree of objectivity in key areas. Will new development theories therefore emerge from the NGOs rather than from development academia?

Third, there is a tendency in some counter-critiques to over-estimate the real impact of development academics on development practice. David Hulme falls into this trap when citing social activists like Freire, Gramsci, Alinsky and Chambers as examples of 'academics' who have had a profound influence on practitioners (see pp. 255–6). There is, of course, a major difference between activists who write, and academics. The influence of Freire and others was spread through social action groups, base communities, NGOs and churches as much as through academic channels.

Underlying these questions is a deeper anxiety about the role of academic research itself. Do we really need more research, or just more action to implement what we already know? 'Good economic policy depends only a little on an improved understanding of economics and far more on the political processes that determine which theoretical assertions will be given credence at any moment' (Bienefeld 1991: 4). This is surely a call to action rather than to research, or if it is a call to both, then it cannot be to the primacy of academic research over development practice. 'Southern NGOs' do not 'require study', as Hulme claims (p. 252): they require encouragement and support to understand their environment, clarify their roles, and carry them out effectively. The central message of my original paper on 'Irrelevance' was that neither poor people, nor the organizations established to work with them, nor the situations in which they struggle to survive and prosper, should be treated as objects for examination by outsiders. Unless and until this point is accepted, academics and practitioners will not be able to develop an equal and supportive partnership. And if this enterprise continues to be frustrated we shall all, in the end, be the losers.

Notes

1. An earlier version of this chapter was presented to the seminar on 'Development Theories in the Nineties: Crisis and New Approaches Out of the Impasse', NICCOS, Catholic University of Nijmegen, November 1991, and subsequently published in Schuurman (1993). I am grateful to John Harriss, Peter Oakley and David Booth for their comments on the original draft. Responsibility for the content of the chapter remains mine alone. It should be particularly noted that the views expressed in it are my own views and not necessarily those of Save the Children Fund.
2. Personal communication, John Harriss, London School of Economics.
3. For instance, the London School of Economics, the Institute of Development Studies at Sussex University and the Development Administration Group at Birmingham.
4. Contact Roger Riddell at the Overseas Development Institute, Regent's College, London, for details.
5. For example, the 'El Taller Centre' in Tunis.

References

Bienefeld M (1991) Rescuing the dream of development in the nineties. Paper presented to the 25th Anniversary of the Institute of Development Studies, Brighton

Booth D (1991) Relevance, realism and choice: an introduction to the workshop. Paper presented to the Workshop on Relevance, Realism and Choice in Social Development Research. Centre of Developing Area Studies, University of Hull

Bunch R (1982) *Two ears of corn: a guide to people-centred agricultural improvement*. Oklahoma City, OK, World Neighbours

Crocker D (1991) Toward development ethics. *World Development* 19(5)

Edwards M (1989) The irrelevance of development studies. *Third World Quarterly* 11(1)

Edwards M and **Hulme D** (eds) (1992) *Making a difference: NGOs and development in a changing world*. London, Earthscan

Korten D (1990) *Getting to the 21st century: voluntary action and the global agenda*. West Hartford, CT, Kumarian Press

Long N (1990) From paradigm lost to paradigm regained? The case for an actor-oriented sociology of development. *European Review of Latin American and Caribbean Studies* 49

Long N and **van der Ploeg J D** (1989) Demythologizing planned intervention: an actor perspective. *Sociologia Ruralis* XXIX(314)

Marsden D and **Oakley P** (eds) (1990) *Evaluating social development projects*. Oxford, OXFAM

Maxwell N (1984) *From knowledge to wisdom*. Oxford, Basil Blackwell

Schuurman F J (ed) (1993) *Beyond the impasse: new directions in development theory*. London, Zed Press

CHAPTER 12

How far beyond the impasse?
A provisional summing-up

David Booth

This book opened on a cautiously optimistic note. Social development researchers are in a better position to carry out effectively the important tasks that fall to them than they were in the early 1980s. The sense of lost direction, and of theoretical 'impasse', that was widespread at that time is largely behind us. New or recently revived theoretical influences have combined with changes in the world to generate a fresh intellectual climate, typified by an enhanced interest in the diversity of development experience across different national, regional and local settings.

As Chapter 1 argued at length, this has created new opportunities for productive research with a cumulative impact on a wide range of macro, meso and micro topics. It has also raised a number of methodological and practical issues, a good many of them social science perennials in new guises, that call for co-ordinated and forward-looking discussion. The three main parts of the book have explored these issues from different points of view, providing in the process further evidence of the vitality and range of recent work on the social, political and spatial dimensions of development.

The coverage has not been comprehensive in terms of the range of substantive fields that interest social development researchers. In these terms, there is much that has been neglected and more that has been touched on only lightly. On the other hand, the different contributions between them do capture a good deal of the intellectual movement that has taken place in the field since the early 1980s or so, reflecting some of the main differences of perspective as well as the elements of convergence. In this sense, the book provides a more-or-less complete interim report on the reorientation that has taken place in social development thinking and of some of the major issues still to be resolved.

Since we are dealing very much with a subject in movement, a formal conclusion is hardly appropriate. I wish, nevertheless, to take the opportunity of this short final chapter to undertake two remaining tasks. The first is to try to address some possible objections to the orientation and content of the book which have been anticipated insufficiently or not at all in the preceding pages. The second is to say a little more about 'where this gets us' – on what remains to be done and what social development research may reasonably be expected to achieve during the remainder of the millennium and beyond.

Rethinking social development: some objections

Books can be taken to task both for what they do and for what they fail to do. Wide-ranging 'agenda' books are especially liable to objections along the lines that what they deliver falls short of the promise in their title. The likelihood of such judgements depends closely on whether the reader accepts the book's starting assumptions about what the main issues are. This book, no doubt, will please those who share the main elements of its outlook. It will with equal certainty irritate others who see the main problems and tasks of the day in altogether different terms. There may also be many who, while seeing some value in our enterprise, remain puzzled about aspects of the coverage and approach. For the sake of this last group especially, it seems worth underlining a number of points about what we were *not* seeking to do with this book, and why.

In initiating the discussions from which the book arose, I made a number of choices about its scope and fairly deliberately avoided certain options, some of which would certainly have given it a simpler and wider appeal. The book is what it is because of these decisions, and making them more explicit may help to dispel the puzzlement that some readers still feel, as well as to answer some obvious criticisms.

Choices of this sort were important in three areas. First, it was decided to treat the issue of the 'agenda' as a broad methodological problem and not as a matter of identifying important substantive topics for research and theorizing. Second, the option was taken to focus on 'social development research', and not on development studies as a whole, and to avoid using the expression 'development theory'. Lastly there was an implicit decision that 'development' still has some integrity as a field for social science, as well as for policy and practice. To each of these options corresponds a possible line of criticism of what the book has succeeded in doing. To each I should like therefore to devote a few lines of explanation or defence.

Defining the agenda: method and substance

Some readers will no doubt miss in this book a comprehensive review of some of the main substantive problem-areas or themes which have helped to invigorate social research concerned with developing countries since the early 1980s. For example, the book is an easy target for the criticism that it has relatively little to say about gender and development, and almost nothing about the other major growth area for research in recent years, the environment and ecological sustainability. What else – one might ask – has done more to transform the agenda of social development studies than the ferment of ideas around the women's movement and feminist research? How can a contemporary book about development afford to ignore the growth of interest in environmental issues?

To an extent the complaints are valid; it was more by accident than by choice that our basic team contained few, if any, who consider themselves specialists in these areas, and more examples from gender research and other rapidly expanding fields would have been helpful.[1] But to concede too much to this style of criticism would be to miss an important point not only about the purposes of this volume, but also about the kind of rethinking that has been and continues to be required in our field. Reviews of substantive areas have their place, an important one, in the journals, in textbooks and in specialist works. Maybe there is still scope for substantive reviews that range across the whole of development studies or of social research for development, although increasingly this represents quite a bold undertaking. More surely, there is also a role for studies that concentrate on the broad issues of methodological principle that cut across the main substantive areas; and this is the ground on which this book has chosen to stand.

What is meant here can be illustrated with reference to the topic of gender. Those who wave the banner of innovations in feminist research in the present context have an obligation to spell out what it is about the methodologies of gender researchers that deserves our attention. To my mind, the suggestion that there is a special magic associated with social research that concentrates on gender issues is naïve. As I suggested in my original 'impasse' article and indicated all too briefly in Chapter 1, gender-and-development research has experienced broadly the same sorts of troubles and transformations, for the same sorts of reasons, as other areas of social development research.

Socialist feminist work in particular was at one point confronted with a theoretical impasse similar in every important respect to that faced by neo-Marxist analysis of other topics. Like everyone else, those researchers have since experienced a progressive coming to terms both with some old and established intellectual currents (the fieldwork tradition in anthropology, interactionisms of various ilks) and with new critiques of mainstream social science of the post-structuralist and post-modernist sort. This applies quite broadly to feminist social research, not just to the development studies variety. Indeed, it is most striking that the best recent survey of theoretical problems and approaches in feminist research (Barrett and Phillips 1992) grapples with broadly the same challenges and reaches not dissimilar conclusions from the present work. More consideration of gender research would have enriched this book, but it would not, I think, have led us to different conclusions. In sum, the decision to focus on methodological dimensions of the agenda rather than on substantive themes seems more valid, not less, in the light of trends in feminist research.

Why social development?

A parallel decision was to concern ourselves relatively narrowly with social (a shorthand for social, spatial and political) development rather than with the whole of the interdisciplinary field of development studies. This was a deliberate option, but to some readers it may seem a retrograde one, implying reversal of the gains made toward a viable interdisciplinarity in development studies since the 1960s. As a result of its disciplinary scope, the book also tends to dwell on the shortcomings of the dominant paradigm of 1970s sociology – Marxism – while largely neglecting what are perhaps the no less striking limitations of the dominant paradigm in the wider field – neo-classical economics. To some, it may seem that this has the effect of skewing the debate ideologically to an undesirable degree, so that the relative narrowness of our approach appears doubly objectionable.

My starting-point on this issue is a distinction between genuine interdisciplinarity, on which development studies rests and which represents one of the main achievements of the subject in those countries where it is established, and the specious non-disciplinarity with which it has often been confused. In my account of the impasse, one of its main distinguishing features was a spurious attempt to produce a 'theory' of development without regard to the specificities of the economic, social, political and spatial dimensions of development processes. Among the effects of this trend were a vogue in bad amateur development economics (*mea culpa*, to some degree) and a neglect of important issues to do with social and political institutions (often addressed more lucidly by economists than by the supposed specialists in these matters). As reported in this book, one of the gains of more recent work in the 'soft' social sciences has been a renewed recognition of the autonomy and specificity of the non-economic dimensions of development, permitting a more genuine and productive dialogue with economists and technical specialists than was possible in the heyday of 'radical political economy.'

The concept of political economy has its merits, and not only in the rather narrow current usage referring to work at the interface between economics and political science. It refers more broadly to a venerable tradition, of which Marxism was one tributary among others, which predates the emergence of the rigid disciplinary boundaries of modern social science. As such, it provides a useful rallying point for all those in development and other social science fields who find it impossible to answer important questions without venturing outside their respective turfs. 'Political economy' needs to be scorned, however, when it becomes a cover for facile and irresponsible treatment of complex and technical issues – not, unfortunately, altogether a thing of the past – or (as has also happened) for tearing down barriers between some subject areas in a way that raises new barriers between others.[2]

The related expression 'development theory' needs an even firmer and less qualified rebuttal, in my view. The term came into vogue – at about the same time and for broadly similar reasons as the still fashionable term 'social theory'[3] – as a vehicle for a package of neo-Marxist and other radical ideas. It implied the absurdly arrogant claim that within the package there were answers to *all* of the important questions to be asked about development. More than 'political economy' and other such terms, it has the effect of denying the need for *inter*-disciplinary work drawing on specific traditions of generalizing and theorizing within disciplines. *Inter alia*, it implies a somewhat low priority for dialogues with economists of more or less neo-classical persuasion. The term lives on, partly on account of its relative brevity and 'sexiness' as a way of adorning and selling books, but it scarcely deserves this longevity.

For my part, then, I would stand by the decisions taken regarding the disciplinary scope of the book. Rather than a retrogression to narrow mono-disciplinary concerns, the focus on 'social development' indicates recognition of the specifity of the methodological and theoretical issues that have arisen in a cluster of related 'soft' subjects – sociology, anthropology, social geography, political science – and their distinctiveness with respect to the main debates in economics (as reviewed by e.g. Toye 1987; Killick 1989). More controversially, it implies rejection of the more absurd pretensions of pre-impasse thinking in these fields.

The integrity of 'development'

The final area in which our approach might seem a trifle conservative as well as, perhaps, inconsistent, is in respect of the concept of development itself (whence development studies, social development, etc.). In its normal usage, the concept both sets apart a set of national societies (the developing or less-developed countries) as sufficiently distinctive to require specialized treatment, and signals the existence of a shared process, experience or set of social aspirations. Yet within the pages of this book repeated references have been made to the 'end of the Third World', to the large and growing differences between the different sub-sets of LDCs, to which may be added the increasingly apparent similarities between some countries of the former Third World and some members of the former Soviet bloc. The need to break with Third Worldism – the exclusive focus on poor countries, and the treatment of less-developed nation-states as analytical units – has been one of the clearer points of consensus among our contributors. At the same time, from post-modernist quarters, the concept of 'development' has been condemned as conveying indefensibly teleological, universalist and even ethnocentric assumptions, while some environmentalists regard it as intrinsically bound up with naïve assumptions about the possibilities of the planet. Why then specify the field as social *development* research?[4]

This is less easy to answer than the other objections considered, but I do think our position is defensible. I am not convinced by the suggestions that the concept of development is intrinsically objectionable in the ways suggested (it is certainly a different case from words like 'modernization'); but the breakup of the 'developing world' is a palpable fact, and the growth of interesting inter-regional comparative and global research possibilities is real and important. The rationale for encouraging researchers concerned with poor countries to cluster together with others interested in poor countries, rather than with those with whom they share other interests – e.g. market liberalization, ethnicity – has certainly been weakened. But there are in my opinion at least two reasons for continuing to defend the 'space' and institutional expressions of development studies.

One arises from the issue of interdisciplinarity discussed above. As was argued during the opening shots of the battle to establish development studies as a distinct subject during the 1950s and 1960s, the study of very poor societies implies closer interdisciplinary collaboration than the study of even moderately rich societies, because of differences in the degree of institutional differentiation. Even though an amazing amount has happened in terms of how particular societies fit into the different categories, nothing has happened to weaken the principles of this argument. This is one reason why it is worth continuing to regard development as a special area, with its own institutions and publications and links with recognized specialisms within subjects such as sociology and geography. The other is that (*pace* Buttel and McMichael, Chapter 2) the study of poor societies has generally benefited from the special relationship between the worlds of academic research and those of policy and practice that is the other constitutive feature of the field in the UK and elsewhere. Whether or not one chooses to regard this as a moral issue (cf. Corbridge, Chapter 4), academic research does seem to gain from this connection with more practical concerns, which is not at all so apparent in other fields. This should at least give us pause for hesitation before dissolving development into general social science.

Where now? What next?

The aim of this book has not been to establish a new 'paradigm' for social development research. The authors set themselves the modest objective of thinking through some of the implications of recent tendencies in research and theoretical reflection, aiming to consolidate some of the sense of collective direction they felt had been achieved. The choice of words was deliberate. Although the book does not embrace the post-modernist spirit of 'a plague on all paradigms', it has retained a measure of scepticism not only with regard to the overarching neo-Marxist conceptual frameworks of recent notoriety, but also towards all or most of the bolder or more imperialistic claims made on behalf of currently fashionable alternative approaches – post-modernism, state-centred analysis, rational choice, actor orientation, etc. This is not because these more programmatic claims do not deserve to be taken seriously. On the contrary, it reflects the view that they are in fact far too serious to be treated with a summary judgement at this early stage of the debate and deserve to remain 'on the table' for some time yet.

It is for these reasons that we have limited ourselves to a minimal characterization of what is 'new' in the research trends that have emerged or re-emerged over the years since the discussion about the impasse in social development began. On the same basis, we have tried to conduct a selective review of some of the main methodological and practical issues that arise from the confrontation of the different theoretical perspectives now in play. 'What is the new paradigm?' is not, therefore, a question that should arise. However, we should at this point be able to answer a more limited form of question. We should be able to say something about which of the programmatic claims deserve to be taken most seriously, and which, if any, can be safely set aside. It is also fair to ask how far the discussion in the book gets us towards distilling some general principles for the design of future research projects. Can we, that is, extract from all that has been said a basic 'template' for successful social development research in the coming years?

The following represents a personal answer to these questions, drawing on and bringing together points already expressed in the editorial introductions and adding some further and hopefully more mature reflections. What seems worth saying falls under three broad heads, to do with respectively research design, avenues for theory and implications for practice.

'Diversity' and the design of research

What incontrovertibly distinguishes current research practice from that which took place under the influence of pre-impasse thinking is the interest in the diversity of development experience. From the point of view of taking this as a template, the trouble is that there are significant differences in the meaning attached to 'diversity' in different quarters. At one extreme, what is involved is an indiscriminate addiction to the culturally rooted specifics of individual and group experiences, accompanied by an unwillingness to countenance even moderate levels of generalization about the patterning of such experiences. This point of view is scarcely represented, if at all, in the pages of this book, and enough has probably been said to establish that what interests us is the discovery of *systematic* differences or regularities, an approach that contains a potential both for the building of better theories and for better-informed action.

At the other extreme is the approach to 'diversity' which concentrates more or less exclusively on the appearance of significant differentiation across space and time within the international socio-economic system, retaining a strong attachment to the study of differences that can be regarded as not merely systematic but 'systemic' – reflecting the 'central tendencies' of change in our time. While explicitly distancing themselves from functionalist and teleological formulations, those taking this view wish to retain from Marxian political economy an interest in inequality, as a special form of difference, and hence in the positions and relations of superordination and subordination that persist within the national and international orders of the world.[5] While many of the contributors, including this writer, share in whole or in part these concerns, they are articulated most clearly in Chapter 2 by Buttel and McMichael and are represented well in a more general way by the trend in rural sociology reported there concerned with the comparative study of 'food regimes' and changes in the dominant food system.

The most obviously challenging confrontation that has emerged in the pages of this book is the one, already discussed at some length in

Chapter 1, between this neo-structuralist political-economy line of work and the position of the 'actor-oriented' researchers (Long and van der Ploeg, Chapter 3, and Arce, Villarreal and de Vries, Chapter 6), who would perhaps claim to represent some sort of intermediate position on the continuum just described. For the neo-structuralists, actor-orientation is a red herring and the notion of actor-orientation as the paradigm for post-impasse research (e.g. Long and Long 1992) a dangerous diversion from the tasks of comparative analysis. For the actor-oriented researchers, the focus on regimes of accumulation and regulation shows too marked a continuity with pre-impasse research trends, the distinguishing feature of which was precisely over-concern with 'central tendencies' at the expense of the exploration of heterogeneity, understood as significant variability of social response to and real outcomes from such allegedly primary shifts at the global or national level.

Is this an unresolvable conflict or an unnecessary polarization? My suggestion throughout has been that it is mostly the second. Both positions identify potential points of weakness in the other as a general template for social development research, and hence from both we have important things to learn.

The strongest thing going for actor-oriented research is part of the case for fieldwork-based research in general: the critical importance for many purposes of getting 'inside' the sort of cultural and social milieu with which one is concerned, and the impossibility of deducing conclusions about what is happening generally 'on the ground' from perspectives, however derived, about central (global or systemic) processes of change. At the risk of platitude, there is much to be said for investigating and refining analysis of core processes which, because of the uneven distribution of economic and political power, form crucial points of reference for the world as a whole. But there is no substitute for research designed specifically to explore the nature of the processes actually occurring on the ground, and in view of the enormous variety of the societies that are of interest to development policy and practice, the bias in this field at least ought to be strongly in the direction of such studies.[6]

In other words, the strictures of the actor-oriented researchers on the neo-structuralists have some validity. This is so not because comparative analysis 'treating structures as given' is necessarily illegitimate (as I suggested in Chapter 1, this seems to be a mistake); it is rather that in practice the design of food design work and other research like it, often does not do enough to avoid falling foul of 'the twin errors of deducing changes on the ground from immanent laws and of reifying analytical concepts such that they acquire an internal rationality that appears to orchestrate the pattern and experience of change in all places' (Whatmore 1994, citing Lipietz 1986: 17). In the particular case of agro-food complexes and the refashioning of rural society in Europe, there seems a good case for Whatmore's strategy of 'reversing the lense of regulation theory' so as to give adequate attention to the 'cold spots' as well as the 'hot spots' of late-capitalist development, thereby doing justice to the striking heterogeneity of patterns of production, consumption and social life outside the heartlands of corporate capital (Whatmore 1994).

In the field of social development research, there is a parallel need to make the case for empirical work – wherever possible comparative – on the processes 'on the ground' which correspond to the 'global' issues or core processes of developing country debt, economic liberalization, structural adjustment and so forth. Again, the fallacy to be avoided is the conflation of global or otherwise central processes with *general* processes (Whatmore 1994: 3). The corresponding challenge, of course, is to design research projects and programmes that are capable of moving beyond mere recognition of diversity of response towards identification of significant regularities or *patterns* of difference.

A good deal, though not all, of this work needs to be fieldwork-based, and quite a lot can usefully follow the model of actor-oriented research focusing on the cultural and interactional origins of significant variations in structural outcomes, at what Long calls the 'rural development inter-face' as well as at other levels of analysis. To repeat what I wrote in Chapter 1, the promise that actor-oriented work of an anthropological or modified rational-choice (Bates) type will continue to be a source of powerful reinterpretations of otherwise mystifying development prob-lems (e.g. the so-called 'urban bias' of so much of the institutional set-up in many poor countries) still holds good, and is worthy of a big invest-ment of research effort. In addition, even where such spectacular forms of payoff are unlikely in the immediate future, anthropological styles of empirical work are particularly appropriate where, for policy or other reasons, there is special interest in the circumstances of the poor and the oppressed – of rural women, children, ethnic minorities, and so on. There are some issues that are simply incapable of being investigated seriously in a top-down structuralist mode.

The biggest danger here, and the accurate perception that may lie behind the assertion that actor-orientation is a red herring, is that means and ends become confused. What some comparative structuralists detect correctly, in my view, is that in practice actor-oriented analysis can easily cease to be a means of identifying significant patterns of difference or structural heterogeneity and become a self-justifying end in itself.

Again the problem has to do with the design of research, not just recognition of principles. Leaving apart the post-modernist fringe, anthropologists in general agree on the need for elements of both emic and etic discourse in their analytical work, and actor-oriented re-searchers are in principle committed to the notion that the purpose of research is the detection and/or explanation of observed patterns of continuity or change. But practice is something else. What comes nat-urally to the comparative structuralist – the design of research that effectively isolates particular variables or relationships for empirical inquiry – may be more difficult not only logistically and financially, but perhaps temperamentally as well, for those who work mainly at the level of localized 'case studies'.

In other words, the risk is that 'actor-orientation' will provide an apparent rationale for the multiplication of local studies from which generalizations of any kind, and especially those about patterns of difference, are impossible to infer, because the possibility of such inference has not been built into their design. Meeting this challenge, by insisting that actor-oriented research must address structural issues, is every bit as important for the future of social development research as ensuring that structural analysis begins to take heterogeneity seriously.

An achievable level of theory

The argument just sketched confirms, I believe, that there is much more to post-impasse theoretical discussion than a sheer mish-mash of contending critiques of previous orthodoxy. But where does it, and the rest of the discussion in this book, get us in terms of the prospect of substantial theoretical developments in the social development field? As was argued in Chapter 1, (re)building a capacity for theory in social development is important not only as a means of avoiding dissipation of scholarly effort, but also as the key to the 'relevance' of that effort in the broadest sense. It is only by generalizing and abstracting from the particular that we, researchers, can make ourselves heard by policy-makers and practitioners as well as by scholars outside our immediate areas of specialization. What, then, is it reasonable to hope for on these lines during the coming decade or so? In particular, from what sources are new theoretical statements likely to come?

It is easier to approach this question negatively, by means of two propositions about where new theories are *not* going to come from. First, they are not going to arise in a purely deductive fashion from critiques of the reified constructs or premature generalizations that have been the stuff of previous theories. While such critiques continue to be necessary and represent an unavoidable stage in the production of new theories, the latter will materialize only on the basis of fresh empirically rooted analytical comparisons, such as those reported or indicated in these pages for food systems (Buttel and McMichael), styles of farming (Long and van der Ploeg), class relations (Harriss), institutional of civil society (Bebbington) and forms of state (Mouzelis). The comparative work in question may be more or less 'incorporated' in the Buttel/McMichael sense – that is sensitive to the structural positions in which units of analysis are situated – and more or less deeply embedded in the sort of cultural specifics explored by Harriss. It will be more or less concerned with the dominant socio-economic institutions of the planet, with 'systemic' issues in the sense discussed earlier, and more or less focused on diversity 'on the ground'. It will, nevertheless, involve a major element of inductive generalization from new research.

No doubt predictably, my other negative concerns the impossibility of operating wholly or mainly by induction. The main point here, however, is not the standard logical objection to pure induction or to 'grounded theory' but, once again, an observation about research design. Even if purely inductive theory were conceivable – that is if it were possible to infer theoretical conclusions from a piece of empirical work without the latter being coloured in any way by previous theoretical ideas – there would still remain the problem of designing empirical work in such a way as to facilitate the drawing of general conclusions, and it is on this aspect that discussion needs to centre.

I believe that one of the conclusions that must arise from the problems considered in this book is that there is now a strong case for the organization of social development research in the form of co-ordinated collaborative projects. I refer to projects which while they entail empirical work of a variety of sorts in different locations, are designed explicitly with a view to the illumination of some significant middle-range analytical issue. Recent instances which seem (to a complete outsider, let it be said) to bring together some if not all of the required features would be the project on 'real markets' co-ordinated by Cynthia Hewitt de Alcántara at UNRISD in Geneva (see e.g. Hewitt 1992), and the series of studies on NGOs, the state and sustainable development organised at the Overseas Development Institute, London (see e.g. Farrington et al. 1993; and Anthony Bebbington's Chapter 8 in this volume). An earlier example would be the collaborative programme at the Institute of Development Studies (IDS-Sussex) that resulted in the trend-setting volume on *Developmental States in East Asia* (White 1988).

It is typical of such more or less ambitious collaborations that their results seem more impressive to their eventual readership than to those who have seen the monster from the inside. I nevertheless think that the chances of extending analysis of social development issues to the point of new theoretical statements drawing only on uncoordinated research by individuals and small teams are so poor that the risks and costs normally associated with more ambitious collaborations are more than justified.

There will no doubt always remain some scope for the individual researcher to produce an excellent case study that becomes material for a later synthesis. For some purposes, the problem of generalizing from case studies may be overcome by the substitution of 'rapid' or shortcut methods for standard research procedures.[7] There may also be a case, both practical and intellectual, for concentrating the work of a relatively large team of researchers in a single region of one country, as in the Long-Roberts study in Peru referred to on several occasions in this book. But even taking for granted a clear analytical focus (as distinct from clarity about the field methodology, etc.) in all of these cases large gaps are likely to remain to be bridged before the density of analysis can approach a theoretical level. The deliberate co-ordination of projects around a coherent analytical theme seems such an obvious next step that it is amazing how seldom it is attempted.

The relevance of 'relevance'

The payoff from a more empirically rooted approach to theory building is, as I have already emphasized more than once, the possibility of better policy and practice for development, or, in other terms, more freedom for social actors in development situations arising from the recognition of possible alternatives – or 'room for manoeuvre' – and the unmasking of false necessity. This, to my mind, also signals the main way the issue of relevance should come into the discussions about research. There are a number of implications.

The first is that it is important to distinguish consistently between *relevance* (to policy and practice) and the more or less *applied* character of research. This distinction has been observed by several contributors but it is worth spelling out a little more here.

First of all, it seems to make sense to regard the types of development research ranging between the more academic and the more applied in terms of a *continuum*, the distinction here having to do with the nature of the sponsorship and eventual audience of the work. Responding to externally defined terms of reference, in which there is a relatively direct relation between the research problem and the decision-making processes of a particular agency, is different in certain regular and well-understood ways from doing purely academic research, where the problem is defined through some combination of individual initiative and peer review (competitive assessment of funding proposals, etc.). Intermediate types are increasingly familiar, in which research funding bodies like the Economic and Social Committee on Overseas Research (ESCOR) of the ODA in the UK, the European Community's research programme and semi-autonomous research councils in many countries, define a set of priorities and invite bids from individual researchers and consortia.

In spite of the remaining prejudices in some disciplines (e.g. anthropology), applied research is not in general less challenging than academic research. There may well be a case for *more* applied research in the development field, or more of the intermediate sort where agencies take a firm line on what issues they wish to see addressed while leaving applicants ample leeway in interpreting the brief. There is certainly a case for including a stronger social development component in the considerable volume of applied development research that is done, and probably also for the orientation of more of this work towards the sorts of practical issues that concern the 'third sector', NGOS and voluntary organizations, as opposed to those that preoccupy governments and official agencies. On the other hand, not all development research needs to be applied; development studies is and should remain an academic subject. But this is a different issue from the matter of whether or not research in general should be *relevant*.

The issue of relevance is *not* usefully regarded in terms of a continuum, least of all if the continuum is seen as running from 'theoretical' or 'analytical' to 'relevant'. What has on occasion tended to make social development theory irrelevant to the spheres of policy and practice is not that it has been too theoretical but that theorization has taken a particular limited form: over-generalized, over-deductive, functionalist, etc. It is not even the case (and here is where there seem to be remaining differences between my approach and Michael Edwards's) that to be relevant in the sense of increasing the capacity for informed choice about alternative ways of doing things, research has to have a 'bottom-up'

character, be linked in some way or other to empowerment or be moti-
vated in a particular way – desirable as some of these things are for
reasons that have to do with understanding, not relevance. The key
thing is the illumination of alternatives, and I persist in thinking that this
is sometimes achieved by research done in quite a top-down fashion, as
well as by researchers who are either uninterested or deliberately disin-
terested (because they see it as a different sort of activity) in practical
efforts towards empowering the poor. On some issues, those who are
relatively uninvolved may well have a clearer vision than those in the
thick of the struggle, although this is no doubt not true in general.

In terms of 'where it gets us', I think that what the contents of this
book most usefully does is to document the contention that post-
impasse research is, or has the potential to be, more relevant across the
board, in the important sense just identified. This conclusion does not
provide a means of resolving all the sharp differences of opinion that the
theory–practice relation evokes in general and has called forth within
the pages of the book. Thus, for example, the issues raised by Corbridge
in Chapter 4 about post-Marxism, international poverty and ethics will
very properly exercise philosophers and philosopher-practitioners for
some time to come. The claim that there is a moral as well as intellectual
basis for regarding issues of inequality as essential to the agenda of
development studies as a whole and that of social development in particular, is certainly one that deserves to be debated further.

In other senses, too, reflection about theory and practice needs to
continue. The questions raised by John Harriss (Chapter 7) about identity, culture and 'false consciousness' among Indian peasants provides,
among other things, stuff for a fundamental discussion of the kinds of
mass politics, if any, social researchers should be helping to promote
through their academics and non-academic links in the subcontinent
and elsewhere. Barnett and Blaikie's reflections (Chapter 9) represent
the tip of the iceberg in terms of necessary discussion of what is
involved, scientifically and personally, in doing applied social research
on 'sensitive' issues such as HIV/AIDS. And the efforts by Hulme and
Edwards (Chapters 10 and 11 and in Edwards and Hulme 1992) to set
out some priorities for research to facilitate the specific practical objective of scaling-up NGO impacts, are already the basis of a continuing
dialogue between NGO staff and academically based researchers. All
these are subjects that go well beyond the scope of this book. However,
it is to be hoped that we have given some new reasons for regarding
them as central to the social development agenda.

Notes

1. See the useful contributions on gender (by Janet Townsend), the environment (by Bill Adams) and new social movements (by Frans Schuurman) in
   what readers may regard as a companion to this volume (Schuurman 1993b).
2. To some extent, I think 'radical political economy' set development sociology apart from anthropology in a way that was bad for both.

3. Cf., once again, Mouzelis's critique (1991: 1–9).
4. As Aidan Foster-Carter asked of the presidential symposium on Developments in Sociology at the 1993 conference of the British Sociological Association: has not the notion of a 'sociology of development' become an obstacle to doing good international sociology in the 1990s?
5. In his introduction to the book already cited, Frans Schuurman (1993a: 29–32) argues plausibly that the distinctive *explanandum* of development studies should be diversity *plus* inequality, though, rather confusingly for readers here, he treats Buttel and McMichael as unsympathetic towards this suggestion. The importance of asking inequality questions ('which rural people?, whose livelihoods?') is also a theme of the excellent text on *Rural Livelihoods* edited by Henry Bernstein *et al.* (1992) for the Open University.
6. See Booth *et al.* (1993) for a similar argument with particular reference to the study of structural adjustment programmes in Africa.
7. See again Booth *et al.* (1993).

References

Barrett M and **Phillips A** (eds) (1992) *Destabilizing theory: contemporary feminist debates*. Cambridge, Polity Press

Bernstein H, Crow B and **Johnson H** (eds) (1992) *Rural livelihoods: crises and responses*. Oxford, Oxford University Press/Open University

Booth D, Lugangira F, Masanja P, Mvungi A, Mwaipopo R and **Redmayne A** (1993) *Social, economic and cultural change in contemporary Tanzania: a people-oriented focus*. Stockholm, SIDA

Edwards M and **Hulme D** (eds) (1992) *Making a difference: NGOs and development in a changing world*. London, Earthscan

Farrington J and **Bebbington A** with **Wellard K** and **Lewis D** (1993) *Reluctant partners? Non-governmental organizations, the state and sustainable agricultural development*. London, Routledge

Hewitt de Alcántara C (ed) (1992) Real markets: social and political issues of food policy reform. Special issue, *European Journal of Development Research* 4(2)

Killick T (1989) *A reaction too far: economic theory and the role of the state in developing countries*. London, Overseas Development Institute

Lipietz A (1986) New tendencies in the international division of labor: regimes of accumulation and modes of regulation. In: Scott A and Storper M (eds) *Production, work and territory*. Winchester, MA, Allen & Unwin

Long N and **Long A** (1992) *Battlefields of knowledge: the interlocking of theory and practice in social research and development*. London, Routledge

Mouzelis N P (1991) *Back to sociological theory: the construction of social orders*. London, Macmillan

Schuurman F J (1993a) Introduction: development theory in the 1990s. In: Schuurman F J (ed)

Schuurman F J (ed) (1993b) *Beyond the impasse: new directions in development theory*. London, Zed Press

Toye J (1987) *Dilemmas of development: reflections on the counterrevolution in development theory and policy*. Oxford, Basil Blackwell

Whatmore S (1994) Global agro-food complexes and the refashioning of rural Europe. In: Thrift N and Amin A (eds) *Holding down the global*. Oxford, Oxford University Press

White G (ed) (1988) *Developmental states in East Asia*. London, Macmillan and the Institute of Development Studies, Brighton

Index

emergent properties 19, 39, 52, 69, 74, 80–1
emic/etic 22, 26, 28n, 192
empiricism 14, 90, 112, 286
  theoretically informed 228, 247
empowerment 11, 25, 47, 95, 97, 106, 110, 200, 253, 258, 261, 282–4, 287–8, 296, 309–10
'end of history' 93
England 147n
  see also UK
environment/sustainability 12, 110, 119, 205–14, 217, 220, 284–5, 287, 294, 299–300, 302
essentialism 6, 9–10, 12, 19–21, 36, 49–50, 58n, 92–3
ethics 40–1, 91, 103–12, 207, 231, 247
  communitarian 105–6, 108
  see also justice
ethnicity 12, 41, 84n, 94, 97, 102, 175, 181, 192–3, 213, 302, 306
ethnocentrism 40, 65, 96, 302
Europe 37, 40, 54–5, 58n, 93, 95, 109, 120, 241
  farming in 70–6, 79, 305
European Community/Union 54, 77, 81, 309
evaluation of social development 293–4
everyday resistance 186–8, 211
exceptional demographic change 231–2
exploitation 40–1, 63, 84n, 102, 146, 280
  imperialist 142–3
  Roemer on 108–9, 114n
'extractive' research 200, 252, 280, 291

Fanon, F 255
FAO (United Nations Food and Agriculture Organization) 247
farmers' movements/organizations 15, 18, 72, 80, 174, 212
  in Ecuador 203, 205, 207, 217–21
  in India 174, 180, 189
farmer first strategies 62, 82, 198, 207, 209
farming
  intensification/extensification of 70–2, 75
  styles of 70–1, 74, 85n
  systems 199, 231, 242–3, 246, 248–9n
'false consciousness' 175, 192–3, 310
feedback effects 19
female circumcision 114n, 283
feminism 9, 91, 110–12, 114n, 299–300
  post-modernist 123
Finland 120, 128
food regimes 36–7, 54–6, 304–5
  see also regulation theory
Ford Foundation 86n, 271
Fordism/post-Fordism 37, 48
  see also regulation theory
Foster-Carter, A 311n
Foucault, M 12, 158

foundationalism 14, 96–8, 103
  see also post-modernism
Frank, A G 36, 145
Freire, P 94, 254, 296
functionalism 6, 9–10, 17–19, 21, 36, 43, 45–6, 49, 52, 70, 93, 173, 182, 304, 309

Gambia 211
GATT (General Agreement on Tariffs and Trade) 54, 108
gender 9, 12, 21, 41, 102, 123, 125, 159–61, 222n, 246–7, 256, 284, 299–300
  and identity 167–9
Germany 147n
Giddens, A 113n
globalization/global processes 7, 10, 36–7, 40, 44, 51–6, 59n, 91–2, 99–103, 105, 110–11, 285, 305–6
Gonzalez, H 86n
Gospel Missionary Union (Ecuador) 216
Grameen Bank (Bangladesh) 263, 273n
Gramsci, A 174, 255, 290, 296
grassroots 7, 25–6, 258, 284, 289, 293–5
Greece 129–49 *passim*, 191
green revolution 22, 55, 124, 172, 176–80, 182, 187, 189, 205–6, 208, 220, 288
guided democracy 141
Guzman, E 86n

habitus 65
Harriss, J 113n
Hawthorn, G 113n
heterogeneity, structural 3, 305, 307
  in farming 10–11, 38–9, 70–6, 80–2, 211, 306
  of the Third Sector 252, 258–62, 269
  of the Third World 59n
Hindess, B 6, 15, 93
Hirschman, A O 119
Hirst, P Q 6, 15, 93
HIV/AIDS *see* AIDS/HIV
Hobsbawm, E 182, 188
Hoefsloot, L 86n
Hong Kong 8
household
  AIDS status 230, 236–7
  concept of 237, 246
  coping capability 229, 231, 233–40, 245–6
  developmental stage 237–8, 246
  producer-consumer ratio 229–30, 237, 239–40, 246
Hull, University of 279, 281–2

ideal-types 78
identity, socio-cultural 97, 125, 181, 198, 204, 215–19
IDS-Sussex (Institute of Development Studies, at the University of Sussex) 308

modernity 40–1, 90–2, 97–103, 105, 110, 113n, 216
modernization 203, 216
  agricultural 128–32, 137, 142, 198, 218
  approach (NGOs) 258–61
  economic 141
  and globalization 92, 105
  political 136
  theory 38, 42–9, 50, 52, 56, 58n, 62–4, 96, 98–102, 120, 126
modes of domination 8, 12, 20–2, 58n, 120, 126–49, 175, 179–81, 191–2
modes of objectification 160
modes of production 5, 8, 12, 20, 45, 58n, 63, 124, 127, 172–4, 244
moral economy 22, 176, 181–2, 185–6, 190
mutuality (among labourers) 187–8

nation-state 48–9, 51–7, 119–21, 246
  settler states 54–5
necessitism/necessitarianism 5, 9, 43, 45, 49, 92
  false necessity 9, 309
neo-classical economics 20, 126, 287, 301–2
neo-liberalism 6, 82, 144, 294–5
Netherlands 71–6, 81–2, 265, 273n
New Economics 287
newly-industrializing countries (NICs) 8, 50, 53
new professionalism 207
New Right 105–6, 110, 265
New Zealand 120, 128, 139, 143
Nietzsche, F 98–100
nihilism 15, 92
Nijmegen, Catholic University of 297n
non-government organizations (NGOs) 11, 23–6, 121, 197–8, 200–1, 218–19, 227, 247, 251–73, 283–5, 290, 292–3, 296
  accountability 200, 219, 265–8
  advocacy 253, 259, 267–8
  and agrarian change 202–5, 214–19
  co-optation 264, 269–70
  membership organizations (MOs) 258–73 *passim*
  professionalization 266
  scaling-up their impact 200, 257, 286, 290, 292–3, 310
  strategy of ambiguity 261
  and sustainable development 308
  as users and subjects of social inquiry 251–73
  voluntary organizations (VOs) versus public service contractors (PSCs) 267–9, 270, 293–4
North America 197
  see also USA
Norway 120, 128, 133–4
Nutritious Noon Meals Scheme (Tamil Nadu) 179

Oakley, P 297n
OECD (Organization for Economic Co-operation and Development) 253, 265
oppression 40, 102, 125, 161
Organization of Rural Associations for Progress (Zimbabwe) 264
Orientalism 95, 103, 193
Overseas Development Administration (ODA, UK) 23, 197, 227, 231, 247, 248n, 253, 265, 273n, 309
Overseas Development Institute (ODI, London) 290, 308
OXFAM 253, 264

Pakistan 270
Panama 101
paradigms 16, 62–5, 232, 244, 271, 287, 295, 301, 303–5
  'paradigm filling' 199, 227, 244–5
parliamentary government 120, 129, 131, 136, 138–40
  'parliamentary semi-periphery' 129
Parsons, T 140, 244
participation
  social 24, 26, 68, 214, 261, 281, 284, 290
  political 131, 136, 138–40, 261
participatory research 18, 24–5, 39, 62, 82–4, 95, 208, 252, 256, 281–2, 284, 288–91, 296
participatory rapid appraisal 291
particularism/universalism
  ecological 208
  moral 15, 41, 105–6
  social 132–49 *passim*
patrimonial systems 120, 128, 134–5, 139, 142, 149n
Payer, C 113n
peasant economy 10
peasant organizations *see* farmers' movements/organizations
people-centred approaches 286
Peru 175, 308
phenomenology 12, 64, 153
Philippines 259
pluralism (political) 261–2, 268, 270, 272n
Polanyi M 37
Popkin, S 181
populism
  new agrarian 40, 62, 83, 91, 94–6, 110, 198, 205–10, 221
  in Balkan politics 138
  in Indian politics 124, 180, 191
  in Latin American politics 131
policy and practice 3–4, 6, 8–9, 11, 15, 23–7, 35–6, 92, 94–5, 109–12, 197–201, 227, 251–2, 254–8, 279–97, 303
  need to delink development sociology from 42, 44, 46–9, 57, 58n, 103
  see also 'relevance'